An Illustrated History of
SOUTHERN COACHES

Frontispiece: Unclassed General Saloon No 4448, completed at Eastleigh in June 1933, for Continental boat traffic. These were provided with seating of almost First-class standards and could be labelled First, Second or Third class, as occasion demanded. The Southern was obliged to provide accommodation for all three classes on boat trains, to match the arrangements on the other side of the Channel, and these 'Nondescript Saloons' were its answer to the problem of predicting the volume of each class of travel. Another view of this coach appears on the rear of the dust jacket. *Southern Railway*

An Illustrated History of SOUTHERN COACHES

Mike King

An imprint of
Ian Allan Publishing

Author's Notes and Acknowledgements

My interest in carriage stock goes back to the early 1960s: indeed the present publisher can take some responsibility for this interest. In those days all spotters carried their Ian Allan 'ABC' booklets, and I was no exception. Each of the four main Regions had a book to itself, but that devoted to Southern locomotives was getting a little thin, due to the large number of electrified lines. I would guess that someone in the organisation came upon a Southern Region Carriage Working Appendix (listing all SR sets and their formations) and had the idea of bulking out the booklet with an abridged version of this information. For the author, this gave a whole new range of numbers to collect — numbers that appeared in large yellow figures on each end of a permanently formed set of coaches — and this added to the interest. Soon the discovery that individual coaches also carried yet another series of numbers was made, and the germ of this book was started.

It took many years to piece the whole story together — indeed, much that happened was never (and never will be) recorded, but introduction to other like-minded souls who took an interest years before the present author was born has helped immensely to fill the gaps and has enabled a complete register of Southern carriages to be compiled.

In particular I should like to thank (in alphabetical order) James Aston, Terence Barry, Richard Casserley, Phil Coutanche, Denis Cullum, the late Frank Foote, David Gould, John Harvey, Laurie Mack, the late Tony Sedgwick, the late John Smith (of Lens of Sutton), Peter H. Swift, the late John Tatchell, the late Ray Tustin, Gordon Weddell, the late Ted (A. E.) West, Glen Woods and also the staff of the Southern Railway/Region, who took such meticulous care to record the carriages, both in written and photographic form; for most of them it was, after all, just a job. Any errors will, of course, be mine. Finally, I should like to thank my wife, Rosalind, for help with typing and computer work. She now feels confident that she can identify a Maunsell coach from a Bulleid one — whether she wants to or not!

Select Bibliography

Many books have now been published on carriage stock. However, the reader may find the following works to be particularly useful.

Author	Title	Publisher
Gould, D.	*Maunsell's SR Steam Carriage Stock*	Oakwood Press 2000
Gould, D.	*Bulleid's SR Steam Passenger Stock*	Oakwood Press 1994
Gould, D.	*Southern Railway Passenger Vans*	Oakwood Press 1992
Gould, D.	*Bogie Carriages of the LBSCR*	Oakwood Press 1995
Gould, D.	*Bogie Carriages of the SE&CR*	Oakwood Press 1993
Kidner, R.	*Service Stock of the Southern Railway*	Oakwood Press 1993
Maycock, R., and Reed, M.	*Isle of Wight Steam Passenger Rolling Stock*	Oakwood Press 1997
Kidner, R.	*Pullman Cars on the Southern 1875-1972*	Oakwood Press 1987
Chacksfield, J.	*Richard Maunsell — An Engineering Biography*	Oakwood Press 1998
Weddell, G.	*LSWR Carriages in the 20th Century*	OPC 2001
Tavender, L.	*HMRS Livery Register No 3: LSWR & Southern*	HMRS 1970 and 1990
Haresnape, B.	*Railway Liveries: Southern Railway*	Ian Allan 1982
Jenkinson, D.	*British Railway Carriages of the 20th Century Volumes 1 and 2*	PSL 1988/90 and Pendragon Books 1996
Lloyd, J., and Brown, M.	*Preserved Railway Carriages*	Silver Link Publishing 1992
Johnson, P.	*The British Travelling Post Office*	Ian Allan 1985
Parkin, K.	*British Railways Mark 1 Coaches*	Pendragon Books / HMRS 1991
Bulleid, H.	*Bulleid of the Southern*	Ian Allan 1977
Klapper, C.	*Sir Herbert Walker's Southern Railway*	Ian Allan 1973
Dendy Marshall, C. (revised Kidner, R.)	*A History of the Southern Railway*	Ian Allan 1968
Lynes, L.	*Railway Carriages and Wagons*	Locomotive Publishing Co 1959

Also of interest are the former British Transport Historical Records — now housed at the Public Record Office, Kew — and listed under various references, but all grouped under the main SOU category.

First published 2003
Revised edition 2006
Second revised edition 2008

ISBN 978 0 86093 570 4

All rights reserved. No part of this book may be reproduced or transmitted in any form or by any means, electronic or mechanical, including photocopying, recording or by any information storage and retrieval system, without permission from the Publisher in writing.

© M. King 2003

Published by Oxford Publishing Co

an imprint of Ian Allan Publishing Ltd, Hersham, Surrey KT12 4RG.
Printed by Ian Allan Printing Ltd, Hersham, Surrey KT12 4RG.

Code: 0804/3

Visit the Ian Allan Publishing web site at:
WWW.ianallanpublishing.co.uk

Contents

Author's Notes and Acknowledgements		**4**
Select Bibliography		**4**
1.	**An Overview of the Southern Railway**	**7**
2.	**Liveries**	**21**
3.	**The Last Pre-Grouping Designs**	**29**
4.	**The 'Thanet' Stock**	**49**
5.	**Maunsell Stock 1926-1934**	**55**
6.	**Maunsell Stock 1935-1937**	**103**
7.	**Non-corridor Stock**	**117**
8.	**Bulleid Stock 1938-1945**	**123**
9.	**Bulleid Eastleigh-built Stock 1946-1951**	**133**
10.	**Bulleid BRCW-built Stock 1947-1949**	**169**
11.	**Passenger Brake Vans**	**175**
12.	**Luggage Vans and 'Covcars'**	**183**
13.	**Livestock Vans, Milk Tanks, Carriage Trucks, Scenery Vans and Post Office Vans**	**195**
14.	**Inspection Saloons and Ambulance Cars**	**215**
Appendices		**218**

Title Page: 'Schools' class 4-4-0 No 917 *Ardingly* at Ashford in 1936 with a Cannon Street–Folkestone express. Three-coach set No 961 is leading, with a Pullman car cut into the rake. This was Maunsell's last steam-hauled set, outshopped from Eastleigh in July 1936 and described in Chapter 6. *Southern Railway*

This revised edition adds further details of the rolling stock proposed for construction between March 1935 and February 1942 and subsequently cancelled, amending details of the corridor-side windows of Hastings-line Thirds 1115/6 and revision of Figures 34, 36 concerning corridor-side windows, and 18. 39 regarding window details of the 1930/3 open saloons thirds.

Plate 1 The first Bulleid six-coach Bournemouth-line set, No 290, posed in the up loop at Wallers Ash, between Winchester and Basingstoke, in July 1947. These 11 sets (Nos 290-300), including a Restaurant and a Dining car as the third and fourth vehicles, were probably Bulleid's finest contribution to Southern Railway rolling stock, and remained the mainstay of Bournemouth-line services until 1964/5. *Southern Railway*

Chapter 1.
An Overview of the Southern Railway

In several ways the Southern Railway was unique amongst the 'Big Four' Grouping companies and it was also by a considerable margin the smallest. Alone of the four, it accrued by far its greatest revenue not from goods traffic but from passenger travel, and enjoyed widespread levels of passenger traffic density almost unknown in many other parts of the country. With the possible exceptions of the former Great Eastern and the Lancashire & Yorkshire railways, no other pre-Grouping companies could boast levels of suburban passenger traffic to match those of the London & South Western, the London, Brighton & South Coast or the South Eastern & Chatham. The bringing-together of these three passenger-orientated companies would ensure that the Southern's inherited carriage-stock fleet of well over 7,000 vehicles would place it in a very respectable third position in the league table, with 1,000 more carriages than the Great Western, whose route mileage exceeded that of the Southern by the same number of miles. The LMS and LNER, whilst both owning more carriages than the Southern, had route mileages in excess of treble the Southern's figure, but this was most certainly not reflected in the number of carriages owned.

The preponderance of suburban and short-distance passenger traffic would considerably influence the carriage policies of the newly formed Southern Railway. Firstly, the SR never built any new steam-hauled non-corridor coaches and, secondly, it remained (until 1945) firmly wedded to the tradition of building corridor coaches with a door to each compartment — for rapid ingress/egress of passengers — long after other Grouping companies had ceased to do so. Such was the density of the suburban traffic that, prior to the Grouping, two of the SR's three constituents had already invested in electrification, whilst the third was already formulating plans to do the same. It came as no surprise that the Southern should continue this policy, which would have the effect of considerably reducing the requirement for new steam-hauled passenger vehicles. Indeed, from mid-1936 until 1945, production of such vehicles ceased altogether. Had it not been for World War 2, most of the system east of Basingstoke and Bournemouth might have seen the third rail by 1950, some 17 years before electrification finally arrived. This electrification policy removed any need for steam-hauled non-corridor vehicles; by 1939 the lines on which they might have been employed had simply been removed from the steam-hauled network. Those steam-hauled routes that remained could be adequately served using the inherited non-corridors until such time as the older corridor vehicles could be 'cascaded' down to them. This became the standard procedure — new coaches being built for the best express services, allowing those previously employed to drop back to secondary services, with a consequent 'knock-on' effect until the oldest vehicles on the branch lines could be withdrawn from traffic. Typically, new vehicles might enjoy 8-10 years on principal services before replacement. By the late 1950s, following the introduction of British Railways' standard Mk 1 stock, the earliest Southern Railway corridors had reached even the remotest branch line, so few non-corridors were to survive beyond 1958.

For the electrified suburban lines a very different policy would be adopted. Many of these lines had been served, prior to electrification, by relatively new steam-hauled non-corridors, and these had many more years of service left in them. Consequently, most of these timber-bodied coaches were re-framed and rebuilt, serving as electric stock for as long as (if not longer than) their remaining steam-hauled counterparts. Only for longer-distance electrification schemes, starting in 1932, were new vehicles

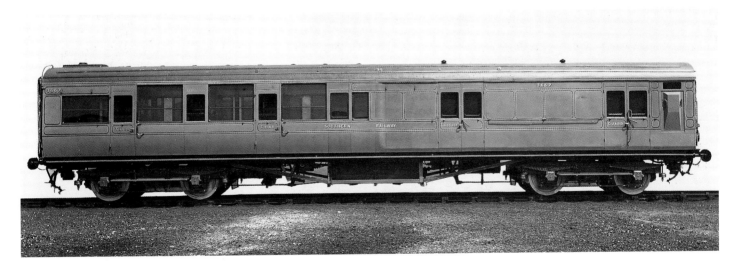

Plate 2 Maunsell four-compartment Brake Third No 3667, in photographic grey livery, seen in July 1929. The style of painting, complete with fully lined finish, shows up well. Less obvious is the fact that the brake end is equipped with British standard (CA) gangways — the adaptor clips to allow them to couple with Pullman (CP) gangways just being visible at the right-hand end.
Southern Railway

Plate 3 The Southern's publicity machine could never claim to be as imaginative as that of the rival Great Western. However, under its then Public Relations Officer, John Elliot, it was quick to advertise new rolling stock. LSWR 'X6' class 4-4-0 No 665 was photographed at Barnstaple Junction in July 1925 with three brand-new Maunsell 'Thanet' coaches in tow — probably the first sighting that West Country staff and public alike had of the latest Southern carriages. *Southern Railway*

constructed, and these mirrored the construction of contemporary steam-hauled stock. However, the history of all these electrification schemes and their rolling-stock provision are outside the scope of this present survey. Some limited rebuilding and re-framing of existing steam-hauled non-corridors did take place (amounting to approximately 150 ex-LSWR, eight ex-LBSCR and just one ex-SECR vehicle) and these will be briefly referred to in Chapter 7.

Non-passenger coaching stock — guards' brake vans, luggage vans, special cattle vans — would also be required and here again the Southern chose construction methods at variance with those of the other three Grouping companies. Elsewhere the passenger 'vans' would mirror the appearance and construction of the passenger coaches, but on the Southern the various classes of 'utility' van would employ a goods-wagon form of construction, which contrasted sharply with the outline of the passenger stock. Re-use of redundant underframes left over after conversion of existing bodywork to electric stock was to be another feature of 'new' luggage vans. The history of the non-passenger coaching stock is considered in full in Chapters 11, 12 and 13.

The lack of long-distance travel, particularly on the lines in Kent, Surrey and Sussex, resulted in neither the LBSCR nor the SECR building many corridor vehicles — indeed, on the Brighton it would be difficult to find a true corridor carriage at all — and only on the LSWR were corridor vehicles to be found in any quantity. This line was the only one of the three to boast any form of long-distance services, and it also found itself in competition with the Great Western for some of its traffic. By 1923 there was a recognised need for corridor stock on shorter-distance trains, so the newly formed Southern Railway, under its Chief Mechanical Engineer R. E. L. Maunsell, had some catching-up to do, compared to the other 'Big Four' companies, all of which inherited a rather greater proportion of corridor vehicles. For the reasons outlined above they had relatively little previous experience to draw upon, and there was one further problem to consider. Whilst the LSWR and LBSCR had a generous loading gauge, the SECR, for historical reasons, did not. Any vehicle constructed to run on South Eastern lines would, perforce, be restricted in length and, more especially, width, but this was not the case on the other two lines. How best to address this problem, with either a composite design or disparate designs, would continue to exercise the minds of Maunsell and his design team until the arrival of O. V. S. Bulleid some 15 years later. The solution adopted was to produce designs capable of being built to three different body widths, to suit the various route restrictions then in force.

At this point, it is worth briefly examining the carriage-stock position of each of the pre-Grouping companies as at 1 January 1923.

The London & South Western Railway
The largest of the pre-Grouping constituents and probably the only true main-line company of the three, the LSWR served the commuter lands of South West London and the main lines to Portsmouth, Bournemouth (and, to some extent, Weymouth), plus the West of England. In the latter areas it was in competition with the Great Western but otherwise held a virtual monopoly. Some of the more distant lines generated sparse passenger traffic, but otherwise passenger service levels were high.

Electrification of the inner-suburban network had commenced in 1915, using the 600V DC third-rail system, and it was this company, under Carriage & Wagon Superintendent Surrey Warner, which initiated the large-scale rebuilding of steam-hauled suburban vehicles as electric stock — a process at which the Southern would later become past master. Four-wheeled passenger coaches had already been withdrawn before 1923, whilst some six-wheelers remained on suburban and workman's trains. Otherwise the company was well served by a fairly modern fleet of timber-bodied non-corridor stock, plus some very similar corridor vehicles dating from 1903-21. Alone of the three pre-Grouping companies, the South Western ran its own fleet of dining cars, with only the staff and catering equipment being supplied by a contractor, Messrs Spiers & Pond Ltd.

Plate 4 The Southern Railway inherited about 300 wooden-panelled LSWR corridor vehicles, of which this five-coach set, dating from March 1904, is typical. Notice that the corridor alternates from side to side down the train, this being a typical South Western feature, often requiring left- and right-handed brake coaches. The distinctive livery of salmon pink and brown was replaced from March 1921 by dark green. No gangways were provided at the brake ends when the coaches were built, this omission being rectified from 1906 onwards. *LSWR*

Plate 5 An up Portsmouth express, hauled by 'S11' class 4-4-0 No 396, near New Malden *c*1925. The leading five-coach set is one of the original 1921 'Ironclads', the Pantry Third being the second vehicle in the train. Despite this provision of modern corridor stock, the rear three 'swingers' are most definitely ancient, being arc-roofed Non-corridors of 1890s vintage. *Ian Allan Library*

Nevertheless, by no means all principal services were provided with corridor vehicles, lavatory-equipped non-corridors being much in evidence, even on long-distance trains.

More modern corridor coaches made their appearance in 1921 with the 'Ironclad' stock, so named because, for the first time in the company's existence, the vehicles were obviously steel-clad (over timber body framing), without the addition of a panelled exterior finish. They were also finished in a lined green livery, replacing the previous (and unusual) colour scheme of salmon pink and brown. This was to be significant for the Southern

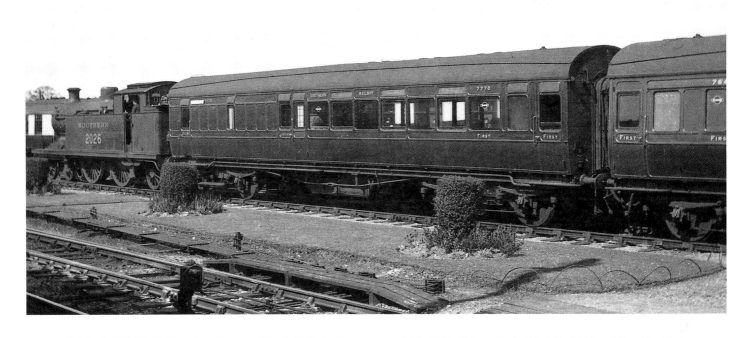

Plate 6 LBSCR 'Balloon' set 933 on a Lingfield First-class race special in 1938. Saloon Brake First No 7770 and Corridor First No 7641, just visible at the right, represent the high-point of Brighton carriage-stock development in 1906/7, being used on the 'City Limited', an almost exclusively First-class commuter service between Brighton and London Bridge. *E. R. Lacey*

Plate 7 Far more typical of LBSCR carriage stock is 1912-vintage Driving Brake Third No 3824, seen at Brighton in the 1950s, running in push-pull set 727. Although a corridor coach (the British standard gangway is just visible between the coaches), this is not immediately apparent. Note the scenery van — for scenery and props being delivered to Brighton's Theatre Royal — in the bay road behind. *Author's collection*

Railway, as will be noted in Chapter 2. By the Grouping there were only four sets of 'Ironclads' for the Bournemouth line and two further sets of First-class vehicles for Southampton boat traffic, with another six sets on order for Bournemouth and Portsmouth services. These represented really the only modern general-purpose carriage stock contributed to the Southern in 1923 and would form the basis of the earliest post-Grouping designs, which will be described further in Chapter 3.

All the vehicles were built at Eastleigh Carriage & Wagon Works, this establishment having replaced the cramped workshops at Nine Elms in 1891. Eastleigh continued to serve the Southern as a carriage works, taking on responsibility for most new construction right through to British Railways days. Surrey Warner continued in post at Eastleigh until he retired in May 1929, in the capacity of Assistant Mechanical Engineer, with particular responsibility for carriages, wagons and road vehicles.

The London, Brighton & South Coast Railway

The smallest of the three major constituents of the Southern Railway, the LBSCR was basically an extended suburban network, with main lines to Brighton, Eastbourne and Worthing, with somewhat circuitous routes to Hastings in the east and Portsmouth in the west. At each extremity it was in competition with, respectively, the South Eastern and the South Western, but otherwise held the monopoly of traffic throughout most of South London, Surrey and Sussex. Few journeys exceeded 1½ hours'

Plate 8 SECR 'Birdcage' Corridor Brake Composite No 6634, seen at Ashford in June 1951. One of 15 such corridor coaches completed in 1907 for through services to other companies, it was later paired with 'Thanet' Third No 989 as two-set 331, for Ashford—Hastings services. Note that the Third is in crimson lake and cream, the Brake in SR malachite green. *A. E. West*

duration, and few ran for many miles without a stop, and corridor vehicles were thus practically unknown. Most services were provided by arc-roofed compartment stock of four-wheel, six-wheel or bogie designs, but, with the possible exception of the relatively few high-roofed 'Balloon' coaches of 1905-7 vintage, none could be considered modern. Many bogie coaches were themselves rebuilds of 1908-10, when existing six-wheelers were re-mounted on new 54ft-long underframes. Whilst this may have been an economical way of improving the stock during the first decade of the 20th century, by 1923 it had the effect of keeping the company's rolling-stock profile firmly within the Victorian era. Despite this, new vehicles of identical appearance continued to be built at Lancing Works until 1924.

Electrification of the South London line was completed in 1909, using the 6.7kV AC overhead system — technically far superior to the South Western's DC third-rail electrification. This was extended to Crystal Palace in 1911/12, whilst plans for further expansion were halted by World War 1, the electrical equipment being German. The Southern Railway finally completed this scheme in 1925. However, despite the technical advantages of the overhead system itself, the rolling-stock provision was largely traditional. By the mid-1920s the extent of DC electrification far exceeded the LBSCR's 'Elevated Electric', and the system was replaced by the third rail in 1929.

The LBSCR had also forged a close association with the Pullman Car Co — a partnership that would survive for many years beyond the Grouping (witness the 'Brighton Belle' and the 6-PUL electric units) — and all catering was provided by Pullman, using its own vehicles and staff. This company probably managed to capture the best of the Brighton's First-class patronage as well. Consequently, no catering vehicles were ever owned by the LBSCR, this fact further reducing the company's need to build corridor stock.

Hardly surprisingly, the retarded development of LBSCR carriage stock meant the company had no influence on later Southern Railway construction; the Brighton's lasting contribution was to be the organisation at Lancing Carriage Works, which had opened in 1909. This was a modern, well-laid-out establishment capable of further expansion. Some new SR vehicles were constructed there soon after the Grouping, but the works were then reorganised to carry out overhauls rather than new construction. Under the control of G. H. Gardener, and employing additional staff drafted in from Ashford, Eastleigh and elsewhere, carriage-stock overhauls would eventually exceed 2,500 per year, using the 'progressive' method of working, whereby coaches moved through the works in stages, each task being completed at a given point in the cycle.

LBSCR carriage design was in the hands of Albert Panter (son of William Panter, who had been the LSWR's Carriage & Wagon Superintendent until 1905), but Panter the son was not an innovator and continued to build vehicles following the style set by Robert Billinton many years before. He retired shortly after the Grouping, leaving the way relatively clear for Maunsell and his team from Ashford Works to take over.

The South Eastern & Chatham Railway

The SECR company was formed in 1899 by a working union between the South Eastern Railway and the London, Chatham & Dover Railway. These two companies had previously engaged in bitter rivalry over traffic in Kent in general and the Continental traffic from Dover and Folkestone in particular. Whilst this might have been bad news for the shareholders, it resulted in many locations' being served by both companies, which would later materially assist the growth of commuter traffic in South East London and into Kent. However, it bequeathed to its successors a difficult and complicated system to operate, with no fewer than six London termini. Apart from the jewel of the Continental traffic, the company also served the whole of Kent, plus parts of East Sussex and Surrey, as well as having an extremely circuitous route to the GWR at Reading, crossing both LBSCR and LSWR territories into the bargain. Some rationalisation of duplicate lines had started prior to 1923, and this process would continue under the Southern Railway.

From a relatively disadvantaged start in 1899, the new company had made good progress and this was also reflected in its rolling stock. Many LCDR and SER carriages were fairly elderly, and a fair proportion of four- and six-wheeled vehicles remained in traffic in 1923 — certainly far more than on the other two companies' lines. William Wainwright had taken charge of SER carriage matters in 1882, succeeded by his son, Harry, in 1896. The younger Wainwright became Locomotive, Carriage & Wagon Superintendent to the SECR in 1899. Between 1892 and 1897 the SER had taken delivery of 15 'American-style' vestibule cars (not all of which were actually built in America), and these were mainly employed on 'Car' or prestige trains between London and Hastings or London and Folkestone, providing a level of luxury previously unheard of on the South Eastern. However, they were hardly typical, and the SECR used World War 1 as a good excuse to withdraw them from traffic and then to sell them to the Pullman Car Co in 1919.

Harry Wainwright's SECR bogie carriages were well designed and pleasing in appearance, as well as being comfortable to ride in, the First-class compartments especially so. Accommodation for First, Second and Third class was still being provided in 1923, in contrast to the LBSCR and LSWR, which had phased out Second class in 1912 and 1918 respectively. Three classes of travel would be retained on Continental services until 1956, but otherwise the Southern removed Second class from SECR vehicles during 1924. Because of the short-distance nature of most services, corridor stock had been regarded as unnecessary, although generous lavatory provision was made, particularly for First- and Second-class passengers. Apart from the 'American' cars, Wainwright's only other corridor coaches were the 15 Brake Composites of 1907, used on through workings to other companies' lines, which reached the SECR either via Reading or over the West London line.

From 1910 the Pullman Car Co held a similar position on the SECR to that which it had done for many years on the LBSCR, providing catering and much of the best boat-train facilities — another arrangement which would be largely unaffected by the Grouping. Thus by 1923 the South Eastern did not own any catering vehicles of its own, nor had there been a need to provide corridor access to such facilities.

Harry Wainwright remained Locomotive, Carriage & Wagon Superintendent until 1913, there being no separate Carriage & Wagon department on the SECR — a situation which differed from that on both the LSWR and LBSCR. Just whether this was too great a remit for one man — or whether Wainwright neglected his responsibilities — is open to debate, but by late 1913 his retirement had been requested by the Board. Matters within Ashford Works were then causing concern: many overhauls were protracted, costs were rising, and much new construction had been entrusted to outside contractors. The former LCDR works at Longhedge had been run down with seemingly undue haste, yet Ashford clearly did not have the capacity to take on additional work.

The SECR appointed Richard Edward Lloyd Maunsell to the new post of Chief Mechanical Engineer, at a considerable increase in salary over that of Wainwright, with effect from December 1913. Maunsell came from the Inchicore Works of the Great Southern & Western Railway of Ireland. There he had held the posts of Works Manager and, later, Locomotive

Plate 9 The Maunsell/Lynes late-SECR and SR standard bogie. This was used under almost all subsequent Southern bogie vehicles, proving easy and economical to maintain. In service it gave an adequate if not exceptional ride, and Bulleid made only one attempt to better it, for his Inspection Saloon of 1946. The photograph dates from March 1935. *Southern Railway*

Plate 10 Bulleid 'West Country' Pacific No 21C140, yet to be christened *Crewkerne*, heads a Victoria—Dover (via Maidstone East) boat train at Sydenham Hill on 24 May 1947. The leading coach is a Diagram 164 'Continental' Brake Third of 1924, the next seven vehicles all being Maunsell Nondescript Saloons — a remarkably tidy boat-train formation. A Pullman car is just visible as the ninth vehicle. *E. R. Wethersett / Ian Allan Library*

Superintendent and had proven himself to be an excellent administrator. He rapidly set about the reorganisation of Ashford Works, recruiting a first-class team of staff to assist him. From Swindon came George Pearson, to become Assistant CME and Works Manager, Harold Holcroft, to assist with workshop organisation, and Lionel Lynes, the latter being given responsibility for carriage and wagon design, now effectively split away from locomotive matters. Charge of the Locomotive Drawing Office was placed in the hands of James Clayton, recruited from the Midland Railway at Derby.

Within a year the country was plunged into World War 1, and the works soon became fully occupied keeping on top of SECR maintenance matters, as well as undertaking much additional war work. The design and construction of new rolling stock had to wait, so the last Wainwright-designed carriages were turned out slightly modernised by the replacement of the timber bodyside panelling by steel-sheeting, omission of the raised 'birdcage' lookouts and, in the last sets, inclusion of a new type of coach bogie — one which would subsequently become the Southern Railway standard. In 1918 Lynes produced drawings for a new luggage van, the prototype (or 'pattern' van) being completed the following year. This is described in Chapter 11 and, like the carriage bogie, was to have far-reaching consequences.

One batch of six steel-panelled Corridor Thirds was completed in 1920, to run with the Corridor Brake Composites of 1907, but it was the rapid return of Continental travel (once hostilities had ceased) that prompted construction of a new train of corridor vehicles. Designed by Lynes and completed at Ashford in 1921, this comprised eight vehicles of most distinctive appearance. Pullman gangways and buck-eye couplings were provided within the train (it being anticipated that Pullman cars would still be included), but not at the brake ends. With their match-boarded panels below the waistline and inward-opening doors, the coaches looked rather un-English in appearance, and this, together with their intended duties, ensured the nickname of 'Continentals' throughout their working lives. Prior to 1939 they were seldom seen elsewhere, and only a few vehicles gravitated to excursion and other less important services by the late 1950s. Two more trains of these vehicles were on order in 1923, and we shall look further at this stock in Chapter 3.

Plans for suburban electrification, using various different third- and fourth-rail 1,500V DC systems, were being considered at the Grouping, but no physical work had yet been undertaken. Several batches of rather austere 60ft 10-compartment Thirds were completed in 1921-3 with a view to possible conversion to electric stock in the near future, and these were the last new vehicles built at Ashford before the Grouping. In terms of seating capacity these coaches represented the highest passenger density in a bogie vehicle on offer to the Southern Railway in 1923. In the event they were to remain as steam-hauled stock, eventually being amongst the last pre-Grouping non-corridors in revenue-earning service outside the Isle of Wight, a few examples running until 1962.

The minor companies

These comprised the three Isle of Wight concerns, the Plymouth, Devonport & South Western Junction Railway and the narrow-gauge Lynton & Barnstaple Railway. All contributed their own (often second-hand) stock to the Southern Railway in 1923, but none was to have any influence whatsoever on future carriage-stock development. Indeed, only the Isle of Wight lines merit another mention, simply for the fact that just seven 'utility' vans were transferred there in 1950, becoming (by a considerable margin) the most modern SR carriage stock to serve the Island network during the steam era (the Southern continuing the time-honoured procedure of sending second-hand or much-rebuilt pre-Grouping vehicles to the Island).

In 1930 some non-corridor stock was acquired from the Somerset & Dorset Joint Railway, but none of this was modern, and it thus had no influence on Southern Railway construction either. Almost all were withdrawn from service within eight years of acquisition.

The Maunsell era, 1923-37

The upheavals at Ashford Works following Wainwright's departure in 1913 gave the SECR, under Maunsell, what was probably the youngest and most vigorous design and construction team presented to the Southern Railway in 1923. Maunsell had also been involved with the Railway Executive Committee during World War 1, and this would have brought him into contact with Sir Herbert Walker, the LSWR and, later, SR General Manager. Walker too could spot a talented man when he met one. Not surprisingly, therefore, Maunsell and many of his team took senior positions in the Southern's new CME's office, now relocated at Waterloo, somewhat to the chagrin of several of the senior Eastleigh staff. Lionel Lynes continued in his position as Chief Draughtsman in charge of carriage and wagon design, and in 1929, following the retirement of Surrey Warner at Eastleigh, his title became Technical Assistant (Carriages & Wagons).

For a short period following the Grouping, each workshop functioned as before, Lancing completing some new carriage stock in 1924-6, and Ashford doing likewise until 1927, despite the fact that many areas of Ashford Works could not accommodate bogie vehicles. All new carriage building was then concentrated at Eastleigh, leaving Ashford to deal with almost all aspects of wagon construction and repairs; Lancing Works took on responsibility for carriage-stock overhauls. There were a few other locations where repairs, repainting and renumbering work was carried out, including Ryde (Isle of Wight), New Cross Gate, Longhedge and Exmouth Junction, but some of these dealt only with wagons or departmental conversions. From the mid-1930s Lancing would construct underframes, which were then sent to Eastleigh or Ashford for bodying and finishing. This was particularly true for utility vans, many of which continued to be completed at Ashford, as their construction was more akin to that of goods wagons. Recourse was made to external contractors on occasions when workshop capacity was unavailable or if the vehicles were required rapidly.

Rolling stock was ordered using a series of Head Office Order (HOO) numbers, commencing at 1 and usually being allocated an appropriate prefix letter (A, E or L) to indicate which workshop would be responsible for construction. The series could include orders for anything required — locomotives, carriages, wagons, conversions, workshop equipment etc. Carriages were, at first, ordered by type, each class of vehicle to make up a set constituting an order number, but later the order might read: '10 three-coach sets for Waterloo-Bournemouth services'. Later still (especially during Bulleid's term of office) the allocated use of the vehicles became less specific, but until 1937 this was quite clearly defined, at least for ordering purposes. However, the time lapse between authorisation and construction might result in the vehicles' being deployed elsewhere than originally intended. Generally the Rolling Stock Committee would meet around March or April each year to discuss the following financial year's construction programme, based upon the requirements of the General Manager and the various traffic committees. This would subsequently be approved by the Board (or occasionally cancelled, deferred or modified) and construction put in hand. The stock requirements for each scheme or route were carefully planned, resulting in some rather odd numbers of coaches being ordered. Economy was always practised, and 'rounding up' to give a tidy number of vehicles was seldom permitted — certainly not during the 1923-37 period. During World War 2 much work was carried out on behalf of outside organisations working towards the war effort, and these also had HOO numbers issued.

Carriage-stock numbering

An important yet easily overlooked clerical matter was the renumbering of the pre-Grouping carriage stock and the subsequent allocation of new numbers for new vehicles. Pre-Grouping numbering procedures varied, but even at its simplest, the Southern might inherit at least three vehicles carrying, for example, the number 1, and quite possibly there could be Third No 1, Composite No 1 etc from each pre-Grouping company into the bargain. This matter was addressed by the Chief Rolling Stock Clerk, C. W. Pepper, and his staff. The decision was taken to renumber all pre-Grouping stock into a logical series, separated by class and origin, and, as far as possible, in ascending order of capacity within each block of numbers. Gaps were left between each block to allow for new stock to take its appropriate place. The original intention was for new vehicles for the South Western section to follow on from LSWR stock and so on, but this proved unworkable in practice and was soon abandoned, any available gaps within the relevant class's number block then being used. As pre-Grouping vehicles were scrapped their numbers were reallocated to new stock, so in time the system lost its initial logic, but at least each class of vehicle remained largely within its allotted block of numbers. Steam-hauled vehicles were allocated the range 1-8000, with electric stock from 8001 upwards. As vehicles were re-classified, or sent to the Isle of Wight, they would be renumbered as necessary. A separate list of non-passenger coaching stock was also maintained, and this is detailed at the start of Chapter 11.

The following table gives the position as in early 1924, once some duplicate coaches and others with short life-expectancy had been included in the list. The vehicles acquired from the Somerset & Dorset Joint Railway were added in 1930, and these are shown in a separate column, see Table 1 below.

Southern Railway diagram numbering was organised along similar lines to the carriage numbering, both inherited and later conversions of pre-Grouping passenger coaches and vans being allocated the number range from 1-1300, again being sub-divided by class or type, origin and capacity. New Southern passenger coaches were allocated numbers from 2001 upwards, again sub-divided by class, although no distinction was made between steam-hauled and electric stock. Diagrams of new Southern-built passenger-van stock began at 3091. The number blocks were very fragmented, and there were always many more numbers vacant than occupied.

Set formations

This subject could well form a study in itself, but it is not intended here to detail the many alterations which inevitably took place as traffic requirements changed. David Gould has already most ably covered the subject in his series of Oakwood Press books (see Bibliography, page 4), and this volume will confine itself mainly to original formations and a few other selected examples.

All three pre-Grouping companies made extensive use of fixed set formations, with the set number painted prominently on each end of the set. Anything between two and 10 bogie coaches (more if four- or six-wheeled) might constitute a set, and vehicles of different types could be permanently coupled together to provide a service. To the operating department, the correct number and balance of First- and Third-class seats, plus appropriate luggage accommodation, was paramount, the homogenous appearance of the train being less important. **Plate 11** may be taken as typical. Not surprisingly, the Southern continued this process and extended it as far as possible, thereby simplifying the provision of carriage stock for its extremely complicated stock workings and reducing the number of spare or loose vehicles. The vagaries of traffic demand ensured that loose coaches (mostly Third-class) would always be needed, but, from its inception in 1923, the Southern was, by an enormous margin, the greatest user of fixed set formations. The system was perpetuated by the Southern Region until early 1966, by which time stock was being scrapped faster than the sets could be reformed.

The original allocation of set numbers was as shown in Table 2 opposite (many changes taking place later). Between 1923 and 1966 every set number from 1 to 999 was used at least once, and very often twice or three times over. Electric stock occupied the

Table 1
Renumbering of Southern Railway carriage stock

Class of Vehicle	Number range	LSWR stock	SECR stock	LBSCR stock	S&DJR stock	Minor companies' stock
Thirds	1-2600 (later 1-2500)	1-744, 763/4 *	845-976, 995-1112, 1429-1775 #	1776-2340/2-5	1402-28	2421-72
Brake Thirds	2601-4150 (later 2501-4390)	2601-3202	3234-3561, 3580-3663 #	3664-4042	2782-92 3759-66	4098-4108
Seconds and Brake Seconds	4151-4500 (later 4391-4500)	(none)	4151-67	4487-94	(none)	(none)
Composites	4501-6400	4501-5132, 5547-81 *	5178-5504, 5741-94 #	5795-6286	5717-40	6329-65
Brake Composites	6401-7000	6401-6559	6605-41, 6909-22 #	6923-38	(none)	6987-94
Firsts	7001-7700	7001-7191, 7677-7700 *	7233-7375, 7406-85 #	7486-7651	(none)	(none)
Brake Firsts	7701-7800 (later 7701-80)	7701-14, 7717-20 *	7735-47, 7764/5 #	7766-75	(none)	(none)
Saloons	7801-8000 (later 7781-8000)	7801-51, 7933-8 *	7872-7932	7952-73	7997-8000	7995

Notes

* These blocks were ex-LSWR duplicate stock, which had originally been allocated numbers 01-071 (Nos 070/1 only being renumbered, as 763/4), 0501-35, 0701-24, 0801-4, 0901-6.

Ex-SER/LCDR four- and six-wheelers, not originally included in renumbering scheme. In addition, a further 350 ex-SER/LCDR four- and six-wheelers were retained until 1926/7 but were not allocated Southern Railway numbers. Most were scrapped on completion of the first South Eastern section electrification scheme. Vehicles could still be seen carrying pre-Grouping livery and numbering until c1930.

Plate 11 When this photograph was taken in the mid-1920s a complete corridor train was a rare sight on the Southern. Ex-LBSCR 'B1' class 0-4-2 No B619 approaches Brighton with a through service from the north, possibly *en route* to Eastbourne. The leading ex-SECR three-corridor set is formed of two 1907 Brake Composites and a steel-panelled Third of 1920 (one of sets 389, 400 or 430, often used on the Hastings line), followed by an ex-LSWR three-corridor set plus a Dining car. All three pre-Grouping SR companies are thus represented in the picture. *R. S. Carpenter collection*

Table 2
Summary of Southern Railway set formations c1924

Set numbers	Stock
1-55	Ex-LSWR two-coach sets
56-99	Ex-LSWR three-coach sets
100-270	Ex-LSWR four-coach sets (Nos 181-244 were suburban 'block' sets)
271-308	Ex-LSWR 4½-coach sets (four bogies + six-wheeled van)
309-50	Ex-LSWR long sets (six to 10 coaches, including some six-wheeled stock)
351-75	Ex-LSWR push-pull sets (including 'gate' stock)
401-22/31-8	Ex-LSWR three-, four- and five-coach corridor sets (Nos 431-8 'Ironclads')
481-509	Ex-Isle of Wight sets
510-2	Ex-SECR 'Continental' boat sets (1921 and 1923 stock)
513/4	Ex-SECR railmotor articulated sets for Sheppey Light Railway
515-639	Ex-SECR three-coach 'Birdcage' sets
640-8	Ex-LCDR three-coach sets (including six-wheeled vans)
649-54/77	Ex-LCDR six-wheeled push-pull sets
655-76	Ex-SECR four/five-coach sets (including some six-wheeled stock)
678-83	Ex-SER/LCDR/SECR long sets (very mixed, including four- and six-wheeled stock)
684-99	Ex-SECR long sets (five to eight coaches, including some SER/LCDR stock)
700-29	Ex-SER/LCDR six-wheeled long sets (up to 14 vehicles)
730-3	Ex-LCDR two/three-coach sets (Nos 732/3 bogie push-pull sets)
734-60	Ex-LBSCR push-pull sets
761-829	Ex-LBSCR three-coach sets
830-8	Ex-LCDR six-wheeled sets (up to 14 vehicles)
839-59	Ex-LBSCR four-coach sets (including some 'Balloon' stock)
860-940	Ex-LBSCR long sets (five to 10 coaches, very mixed, including 'Balloon' and six-wheeled stock)
941-957	Ex-LBSCR seven-coach suburban 'block' sets
958-973	Ex-LBSCR four- and six-wheeled sets (up to 10 vehicles)
974-99	Ex-LBSCR two-coach sets (Nos 979-99 push-pull)

Notes
1. There was also a duplicate series of set numbers from 01 to 036, used for four- and six-wheeled LSWR, LCDR and SER stock between 1923 and 1930.
2. Ex-S&DJR sets, acquired in 1930, were slotted into gaps at Nos 87-94 (two-coach bogie) and 704-6 (six-wheeled stock).
3. Ex-LBSCR push-pull sets numbered in the range 979-99 were renumbered 503/4, 714-30/3 c1937 to clear this series for additional electric-stock trailer units.

numbers from 1000 upwards and eventually also numbers 987-99 formerly used for steam stock.

The above is a much-summarised list, many individual details having been omitted, but one fact which does emerge is the well-ordered state of LSWR set formations compared to that of the other two companies. New Southern Railway construction was at first slotted into gaps, making use of 381-400/23-30/9-80 up to 1929, after which sufficient pre-Grouping stock had been withdrawn to allow the re-use of most numbers between 168 and 250, thence from 939 to 961, and this re-use continued into the Bulleid era. Some sets, especially the shorter ones (two, three and four vehicles) remained in the same formations for many years, but the longer sets were much more prone to annual and seasonal variation. With few exceptions, restaurant and Pullman cars were not permanently allocated to sets, these being cut into the formations as required. Sets were not supposed to be split up; if one coach were defective then the whole set would be taken out of traffic. However, if no suitable substitute were available, then this instruction might conveniently be ignored by the staff on the ground. Reuniting the missing coach with the rest of the set might take some ingenuity — but it was usually achieved!

Stock working

Each type of set would be allocated to a particular group of carriage workings, non-corridor and corridor stock generally being segregated in the Carriage Working Notices — published internally within the company at least twice a year (June — summer, September/October — winter). In later years each type of set was given an operational code letter (two-set: R; three-set: O, etc), and any one of these sets could be used on any of the group of duties, so the likelihood of the same set appearing on the same service on two consecutive days was not great. It could happen, of course, especially if the set had a unique or specific make-up, but otherwise was by accident rather than design. A four-coach corridor set might, for example, start its duty at Clapham Yard, ending up in Plymouth and returning to Clapham the following day, whilst another might start at Southampton Terminus and finish up at Waterloo, having visited Weymouth in the meantime. For a good example, read 'Stock Jigsaw' on pages 106-8 of *SR150* by David St John Thomas and Patrick Whitehouse (David & Charles, 1988).

Prior to the electrification of the Brighton main line in 1933, most coaches remained on the duties for which they had been built, while most pre-Grouping vehicles had also remained on their respective sections. However, in time, South Western stock began to appear on Central-section workings, and there was also some interworking between LBSCR and SECR stock. The Central and South Western sections had few physical restrictions on stock workings, but several South Eastern lines, particularly between Tonbridge and Hastings, as well as those in North Kent, could only accept vehicles of, respectively, 8ft and 8ft 6in width, so, as more intensive working of stock was introduced, so too was some visible form of marking on the vehicles themselves.

Route restrictions

From May 1924 all carriages were provided with a rectangular cast-iron dimension plate (giving overall length and width), plus a round tare-weight plate, these being mounted on each end of the vehicle, in the lower left-hand corner. Also painted on the coach end was the works code letter — A, B or E — to indicate the vehicle's origin, or, in the case of new stock, which workshop was responsible for maintenance (a somewhat arbitrary decision, in view of the reorganised nature of the works after 1927). From 1934 a further circular plate was added, giving the Route Restriction number (0-6). For SR-built stock, this was usually 0, 1 or 4. Restriction 0 vehicles were all utility vans, plus those coaches built specifically for the Hastings line, which were 8ft 0¾in wide. Restriction 1 vehicles were for North Kent and Eastbourne line services and were 8ft 6in wide. Restriction 4 vehicles were 9ft 0in wide and were originally intended for all other Central-section lines except Eastbourne (but see the Newhaven Continental boat-train stock, page **xx**) and for the South Western-section lines. By 1939 almost all the Kent lines, plus Eastbourne, could accept Restriction 4 stock (so Bulleid did not need to consider this problem), but the restrictions on the Tonbridge-Hastings line would remain in force until the 1980s.

A full list of the route restrictions, taken from page 147 of the General Appendix to the Working Timetables dated 26 March 1934, may be found in Appendix 2 on page 224.

The Bulleid era, 1937-49

By 1934 Maunsell's health was beginning to fail him (he was then 66 years of age), and he was incapacitated for much of late 1934 and early 1935, Pearson and Clayton having to deputise in his absence. It was clear that the time for retirement was approaching and that the Southern Railway would soon be in need of a new Chief Mechanical Engineer. Sir Herbert Walker was asked to consider a suitable successor before he too retired in October 1937, and his choice fell upon Oliver Vaughan Snell Bulleid, at that time personal assistant to Sir Nigel Gresley on the LNER. Bulleid was known to be a highly inventive man who might be relied upon to inject some new thinking into what had become, by then, a somewhat jaded department. The interview took place in Walker's office on 11 May 1937, and the Board approved his appointment, together with both Walker's and Maunsell's retirements, at its May meeting. Bulleid joined the Southern Railway on 20 September 1937, with a six-week handover period until Maunsell formally retired at the end of October. Walker's replacement was Gilbert Szlumper, previously Assistant General Manager, so within the space of a month the Southern gained both a new GM and a new CME.

Bulleid had joined the Great Northern Railway in 1901 and, apart from two interruptions (Westinghouse and the Board of Trade in Europe, 1908-11, and war service, 1914-19), had risen from engineering apprentice to become Gresley's assistant, firstly at Doncaster and later at King's Cross. Much of his time was spent dealing with carriage-stock design and maintenance, and he was also involved in the development of the LNER Pacifics and 'P1' and 'P2' class 2-8-2s. He was thus at the forefront of British steam-locomotive development in what was probably its most exciting period, including the streamlined era of the 1930s. Two other areas that interested him were welding techniques and carriage interior design.

Bulleid could clearly see that there was much on the Southern that needed modernising. He was not alone in this view, as the Southern's Chairman, Robert Holland-Martin, was also aware of the need to improve the Company's public image — in particular the steam-hauled services, which by 1937 were falling behind the best offerings from the other three main-line companies. Bulleid, with his highly individualistic and mercurial temperament, was likely to be the man to meet this challenge.

On arrival at Waterloo, Bulleid found that there were no outstanding orders for steam-hauled carriages; indeed, none had been built for over a year, and proposed orders dated March 1935 for 109 coaches had been held in abeyance, although several batches of utility vans were under construction. Electrification of the mid-Sussex route to Portsmouth was in progress, with rolling-stock provision in traditional Maunsell form, using 2-BIL, 4-COR and 4-BUF electric units. Bulleid restyled the buffet cars internally with a somewhat 'art deco' finish (see **Plate 12**) and externally in malachite green, contrasting with the rest of the unit, which retained Maunsell dark green. The subject of liveries and their changes under Bulleid is recounted in Chapter 2. The Doncaster experience was put to good use, as buffet cars and modern-style interiors had been part of the LNER coaching scene for several years. However, the 'Bognor Buffets' (as they became known) were perhaps just too comfortable, and passengers lingered over a cup of coffee or a light snack. This led to complaints from the Pullman Car Co — still in charge of catering on the Central section — as its turnover suffered, as well as from passengers who failed to get a seat. Bulleid remembered this episode and, although making no comment at the time, resolved to do differently when the opportunity arose — some 10 years later, with his 'Tavern' cars.

Plate 12 The restyled interior of the 'Bognor' electric-stock Buffet cars, completed by Bulleid in June 1938. The pale-coloured interior was in complete contrast to the royal-blue Wilton carpet, with gold diagonal lines. The restyling was said to have been prompted by Mrs Bulleid's reaction to the previous extremely conservative Maunsell interiors. *Southern Railway*

Plate 13 Maunsell interior of 1930 open-saloon Third No 1335 — somewhat dark and traditional, despite the optimistic caption on the reverse of the photograph: 'Interior of new Third-class Dining Pullman cars'. *Southern Railway Magazine*

Plate 14 Bulleid interior of 1936 open-saloon Third (one of Nos 1410/2/3/9) as refurbished in July 1938 for the 'Bournemouth Limited' service. The reverse is endorsed: 'Beige/lake upholstery, dark beige carpet; light stone/lake rexine panelling'. Quite a contrast to **Plate 13**. *Modern Transport*

Improvements to steam stock were at first confined to further internal restyling and external repainting in either 'Dover green' (for the 'improved' Dover boat stock) or malachite (for the 'Bournemouth Limited') in 1938/9. The publicity department made much of these improvements, claiming that the stock was new rather than refurbished. **Plates 13 and 14** illustrate how improvements could be made at relatively little expense. Undoubtedly this was the first stage in brightening up the image of the steam-hauled stock, but history was about to repeat itself, as World War 2 would impede Bulleid in much the same way as World War 1 had hindered Maunsell a quarter of a century earlier. In the event, no new steam-hauled passenger vehicles were completed before 1945, and Bulleid turned his attention to locomotive matters, with startling and controversial results.

The last new vehicles ordered in 1939/40 were for very different electrified lines, comprising 2-HAL stock for the Maidstone electrification and replacement tube stock for the 1898 Waterloo & City line. In both instances Bulleid made good use of welding, but, whereas the interiors of the Waterloo & City vehicles were well received, the 2-HAL interiors were decidedly (and perhaps unnecessarily) spartan. Fortunately this was not repeated in any of the postwar main-line stock, although some suburban vehicles got similar treatment. The 2-HALs would also run over some lines for which Maunsell had been obliged by the Chief Civil Engineer to provide stock of restricted width (8ft 6in maximum), although by 1939 most 'tight spots' had been eased sufficiently to enable the passage of Maunsell 9ft-wide vehicles. The 2-HALs were 9ft wide but were also longer than the steam-hauled stock they replaced; however, in recent years close scrutiny of correspondence relating to stock clearances within the CCE's department (in preparation for the introduction of 'Networker' stock) failed to reveal any permission to allow the 9ft-wide vehicles to pass, nor for the 2-HALs or the later Bulleid steam-hauled stock — and these were 5ft 6in longer than the Maunsells! Relations between the CME and CCE had been strained ever since the Sevenoaks derailment of August 1927, and 'side-swipes' with Bulleid stock were not unknown at London termini, so readers are left to draw their own conclusions.

By late 1939 Bulleid and Lynes had investigated further the possibilities of all-welded construction, plus the formation of complete bodysides using jigs, to speed up and ensure uniform construction; if side sheeting were to be butt-welded, such accuracy would be essential. The Bulleid coach profile of a shallow curve from floor to cantrail was the logical result and also called for curved glass, to achieve a true flush-sided appearance. It also gave maximum width where it was most needed, allowing six-a-side seating in new suburban stock built from 1941 onwards. Although all-steel construction became the rule for new suburban vehicles in 1945, a composite timber-and-steel body framing was used for main-line stock, with a timber-and-canvas roof. It was not considered justifiable to 'jig up' for each type of corridor coach, in view of the relatively small number of each type required, but the suburban vehicles were built in much greater numbers and with a far more repetitive window/door configuration. Bulleid would also have preferred to redesign the coach bogie, having experimented in this area on the LNER, but, other than on his 1946 Inspection Saloon, he chose to retain the existing Maunsell/Lynes SECR bogie, which gave an adequate ride and was economical to maintain.

Plate 15 Ten lightweight luggage vans were completed in 1943/4, this being the first example. Livery was black, using pre-coloured reinforced plastic sheeting with Bulleid's new 'sunshine' lettering. These vans are described and illustrated further in Chapter 12.
Southern Railway

Plate 16 The first Bulleid steam-hauled carriages appeared in 1945, at first following the Maunsell design concept of individual doors to each compartment. Coach No 5726 from set 980 entered service in April 1946, by which time Bulleid had far more radical plans for future carriage stock. *Southern Railway*

Bulleid's only major contribution to the non-passenger coaching stock was the single batch of 10 lightweight luggage vans of 1943/4, upon which a 20% saving in weight was effected by the use of welding, lightweight plastic body panels and a rather unusual underframe. The first van was displayed at Victoria in March 1944, as seen in **Plate 15**.

Construction of new steam-hauled vehicles recommenced in 1945, by which time they were urgently needed. The first batch retained Maunsell dimensions and layout (the underframes having, in some instances, been completed five years previously) but used the Bulleid construction technique and profile. For the last time, side doors were provided for each compartment, whilst the final four sets were increased to 64ft 6in over body, having one additional compartment per vehicle. **Plate 16** illustrates the shorter version, in postwar malachite green.

A new composite coach was exhibited at several London stations in October 1945, the public being asked to fill in a questionnaire giving their views on this vehicle. The results were used to formulate the design of future main-line stock, production of which commenced in late 1946. There is little doubt that the new coaches were highly satisfactory, the image of the Southern Railway being considerably enhanced by these and the new Pacifics which hauled them. All this was achieved against the postwar backdrop of austerity, perpetual shortages and other problems of the period. It is fair to state that Bulleid's contribution to the Southern's carriage stock at this time caught up with and probably exceeded the products of the other three companies. Almost at a stroke, the essentially conservative (but highly practical) Maunsell image was replaced by a modern-looking, clean-lined Bulleid style — just what Sir Herbert Walker was looking for back in 1937. True, there were some failures — the 'Tavern' cars of 1949 being perhaps the most widely publicised carriage-stock *faux pas* — but in terms of general rolling stock, Bulleid had certainly succeeded. Whether he achieved the same level of success in other areas will continue to be debated.

For Bulleid himself, with his highly individualistic approach, Nationalisation of the railways in 1948 would prove a disappointment. He wished to do things his own way (sometimes good, sometimes not), and the consensus mood which pervaded the nationalised industry was seen by him as stifling. In April 1949 he was appointed Consulting Engineer to Coras Iompair Éireann, the new Irish Transport organisation, and in September finally departed to join it full-time at Inchicore Works; the wheel thus turned full circle, Maunsell having come to Ashford from Inchicore in 1913. Bulleid would serve the Irish railway system until May 1958, eventually taking a well-earned retirement at the age of 76.

Plate 17 Captioned by the photographer as a 'flying pub', 'Tavern' car No 7894 is seen at Clapham Junction in May 1950, exhibiting the brickwork-and-half-timbered variation in livery to which the crimson lake and cream colours lent themselves. To the right is the almost-windowless Composite Dining car, No 7835 — the source of so many passenger complaints. *D. Cullum*

Plate 18 The Bulleid image. 'Battle of Britain' Pacific No 34089 (later *602 Squadron*) heads a down Folkestone train near Hildenborough in 1949. Bulleid/BRCW three-set No 797 is leading and matches the profile of the Bulleid tender to perfection. Not so perfect, however, is the fourth coach of the train — a 'Thanet' Restriction 1 Composite. Next comes a Maunsell Restaurant car, plus two more Maunsells, with another Bulleid three-set at the rear. *E. R. Wethersett / Ian Allan Library*

Chapter 2.
Liveries

Following the Grouping, each of the 'Big Four' companies was anxious to establish a new corporate identity. One of the most obvious aspects of this was the question of livery — of everything from locomotives, carriages and wagons to stations and structures etc. On the other three railways, one or two dominant companies, usually the largest pre-Grouping constituents, tended to govern the subsequent choice, but on the Southern the outcome was rather less certain. For carriage stock the Great Western had announced in 1922 that it would be returning to chocolate and cream, replacing the crimson lake used since 1912. The LMS was expected to perpetuate the former Midland Railway colour of crimson lake, while the LNER, with Great Northern bias, chose varnished teak.

Maunsell and his team took their time to consider the matter, and by July 1923 one ex-SECR carriage had been outshopped at Ashford in dark blue, similar to the Somerset & Dorset Joint Railway colour, lined out in white, yellow and red. This vehicle, which carried Maunsell's own preferred livery, was later compared alongside carriages in SECR pre-1916 lined crimson, SECR post-1916 lined brown, LBSCR lined umber and LSWR lined dark green. The directors selected the LSWR green — perhaps wisely, for it proved to be a hard-wearing colour (the same could not be said of 1920s blue pigments) and, moreover, was different from the colours chosen by the other companies. It was also a good choice diplomatically, since, although the colour had been used previously by the LSWR (and was perhaps viewed by some as a victory for the South Western), it was not as widely recognised as the earlier livery of salmon pink and brown. Electric stock had carried the green colour since 1915, but it was not widely adopted until March 1921, and by 1923 perhaps less than 20% of the company's carriages had been repainted in the new colour. However, the actual shade of green used by the Southern would vary considerably over the years.

The whole matter of colour is almost impossible to describe in words, but two previous publications have attempted to deal with the subject in great detail and are recommended reading. These are *HMRS Livery Register No 3: LSWR and Southern* by L. Tavender (published by the Historical Model Railway Society in 1970 and updated with an addendum in 1990) and *Railway Liveries: Southern Railway* by B. Haresnape (published by Ian Allan in 1982).

The 1923-5 period

For a time, probably until late 1923 or even early 1924, each works continued to outshop vehicles in pre-Grouping liveries, while some coaches may have carried their new numbers, with possibly just the wording 'SOUTHERN RAILWAY' on an otherwise old paint finish. Eastleigh, of course, would already be using the correct colour, described by some (rather inaccurately) as sage green, to distinguish it from the later, slightly lighter, true Maunsell green. It is almost certain that existing LSWR paint stocks were used up during this period. Lining was yellow and black, with either rounded or square-cornered panels, to suit the stock. Former LCDR vehicles, for example, would have square-cornered lining to match their timber mouldings. Ex-LSWR 'Ironclads' (practically the only steel-panelled vehicles) at first also had square-cornered panels, which matched the square corners of the external window frames but not the rounded corners of the windows themselves. From about July 1925 this was altered to rounded corners, and it is likely that, for steel-panelled stock at least, the square-cornered style was applied only to the LSWR green livery. Lettering was gold, shaded black. Roofs were at first white, later grey; ends and underframes were black. **Figure 1A** and **Plate 19** show this livery. When new, the Maunsell 'Thanet' stock also utilised this style, confirmed by **Figure 1B**.

Plate 19 A close-up of LSWR 'Ironclad' Corridor Third No 747 at Clapham Junction c1924, showing the original square-cornered lining. Photographs of this short-lived style are uncommon. Also visible is the 1923 'VS'-type 9ft-wheelbase bogie fitted to the second batch of 'Ironclads'. *J. Tatchell collection*

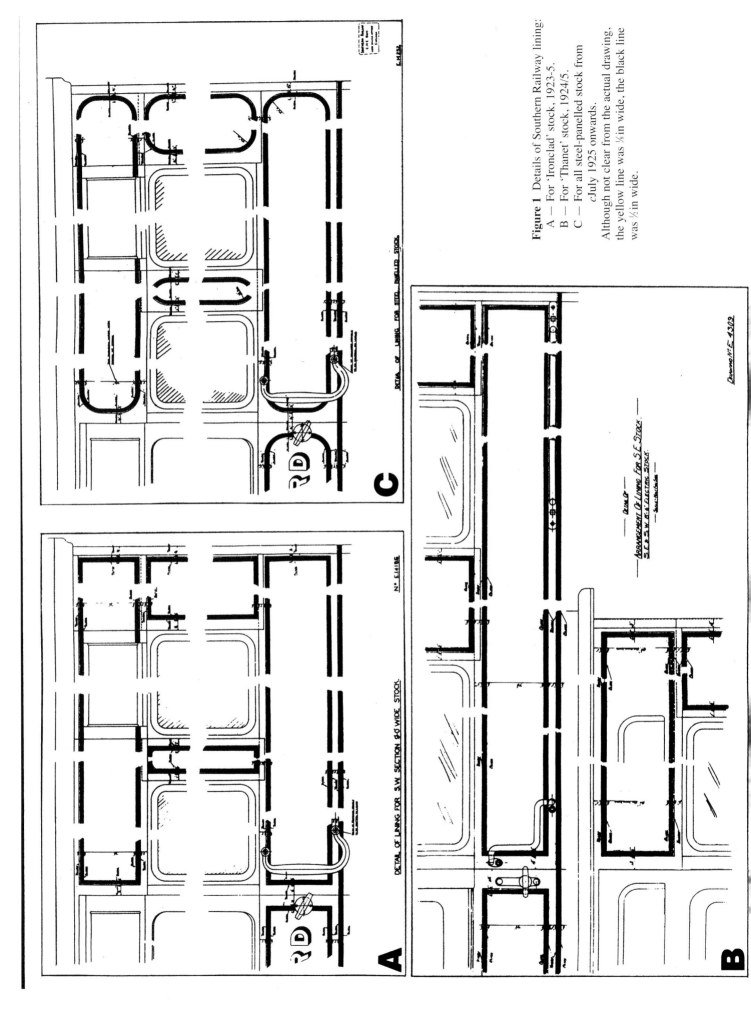

Figure 1 Details of Southern Railway lining:
  A — For 'Ironclad' stock, 1923-5.
  B — For 'Thanet' stock, 1924/5.
  C — For all steel-panelled stock from c.July 1925 onwards.

Although not clear from the actual drawing, the yellow line was ⅛in wide, the black line was ½in wide.

Ex-SECR 'Continental' vehicles, with their match-boarded construction below waistline, did not lend themselves to the panelled style and had a single horizontal band of lining at waist level, which turned downwards through 90° at either side of each door opening. The window frames and two lines of horizontal half-round beading on the upper bodyside were also originally lined out. Some coaches were outshopped late in 1923 carrying SECR lined brown with SECR numbers and insignia, but these were repainted early in 1924 in LSWR green. Later repaints may have omitted the lining above waistline, while from the late 1930s some were completely unlined. Those built by contractors in 1924 also appear to have been unlined from the start (see **Plates 30 and 31**).

The 1925-38 period

This substituted the true Maunsell green colour (described by all as olive green — again, perhaps inaccurately!), together with rounded corners for the lining panels, at least for steel-panelled stock. This is illustrated in **Figure 1C**. Note, however, that the lower continuous horizontal line, below the commode (grab) handle, was omitted after mid-1929. The lining colour is described as yellow on this drawing (No E14252) but is sometimes later referred to as chrome yellow or chrome orange, and it is uncertain whether this was a change merely of description or of actual colour (or possibly the effect of many coats of varnish on the original). **Plate 20** illustrates the style in use in 1928. Droplights and timber window frames were varnished teak, but these were later painted green to match the remainder of the coach side, possibly at first overhaul or maybe as an economy measure towards the late 1930s. Just how different the Maunsell green was, compared with the original LSWR colour, is uncertain. Some contemporary observers have recorded a change in colour, while others maintain there was little or no difference (at least, not c1925), simply stating that a lighter colour scheme became evident later, possibly as a result of changes in the chemical composition of the paint itself. Nearly 80 years later, it is somewhat difficult to be precise.

The full company title, using 3⁵⁄₁₆in-high gold letters (the black blocking adding ⁷⁄₁₆in, to give a maximum depth of 3¾in) was placed as symmetrically as possible about the centre line within the eaves panels, or in the waistline panelling on the corridor side of high-windowed vehicles built from 1929 onwards. The coach number appeared towards each end, again in the eaves panels using 3in-high gold figures (the black blocking again adding ⁷⁄₁₆in) as shown in **Figure 2A**. Great standardisation was achieved with this livery, including luggage vans, and it is doubtful if such consistency was ever achieved post-1938. Class designations appeared in full on all doors, the first letter of the word being 3⅛in high, the rest 2⅜in high (again with black blocking adding a further ½in). The words 'GUARD', 'LUGGAGE', 'PANTRY' etc were applied similarly. Seat numbers for reservation purposes also appeared alongside each door (usually to the right) in the eaves

Plate 20 Maunsell Pantry Brake First No 7716 when new in June 1928. This is actually in photographic grey and shows the style of lining extremely well. By 1930 the lower continuous horizontal line had been deleted. *Southern Railway*

Figure 2 Examples of carriage stock lettering:
A — Maunsell standard lettering.
B — Bulleid lettering with either black or green 'in-line', 1938.
C — Bulleid 'sunshine' lettering, used from 1941 onwards.

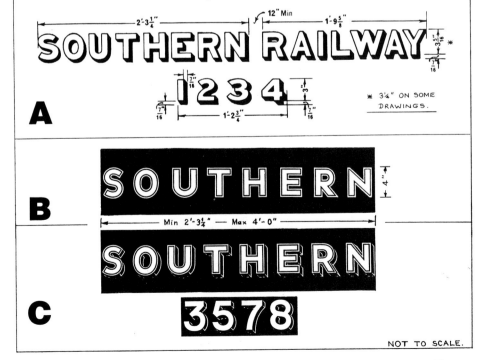

Plate 21 A useful detail photograph of a Maunsell Brake Composite at Barnstaple Junction in 1935. The seat reservation letter board (in this case 'H') was 2ft 6in long, green with pale yellow letters. The roof destination boards were each 11ft x 6¾in x ⅝in thick, green with yellow/gold letters, shaded black. The seat reservation numbers appear in very small lettering to the right of each door. 'NO SMOKING' signs were green with white lettering; 'SMOKING' signs were similar but had a red background. Note that the coach is fully lined, but this is almost invisible in the picture. *D. E. H. Box*

Plate 22 Special cattle van No 3700, still retaining Maunsell green livery at Stewarts Lane in May 1949. The company initials are 12in-high plain yellow letters while the 'XP' and wheelbase brandings are white. *A. E. West*

panel, using very small letters/numerals. These may be seen in **Plate 21**, together with 'SMOKING' and 'NO SMOKING' window labels and letter-boards indicating destination and seat reservations. Later, some class designations (in particular on Open Thirds) employed 8½in- or 9in-high figures at eye level alongside the appropriate door. Catering vehicles were at first labelled 'DINING SALOON', altered by 1934 to 'RESTAURANT CAR' in the waist panelling in letters varying from 4½in to 6½in high, as seen in **Plate 46**. Set numbers were painted on brake ends, centrally or either side of the gangway at high level, using 9in yellow figures. Details on the dimension, tare and route restriction plates were also picked out using yellow paint.

By 1935 certain economies were being made. Flush-sided vehicles completed in that year received only the waistline panelling, while the Open Thirds simply had the panels between the windows lined out, with a single continuous horizontal line just below them. Evidently this was not judged to be very satisfactory, as the 1936 Open Thirds were given window and full

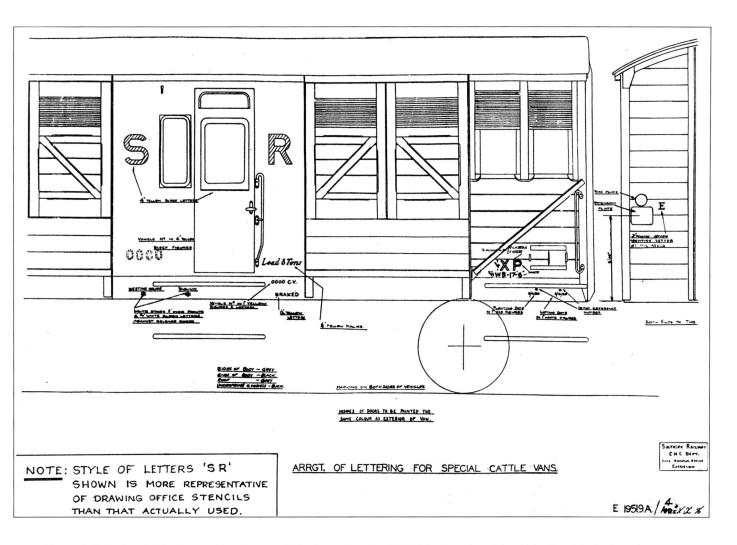

Figure 3 Lettering details for special cattle vans. This shows Drawing E19519A, Amendment 4, which altered the bodywork colour from Maunsell green to grey and repositioned the company initials on the door, using 4in yellow letters. These changes date from 1942.

waistline panels but no eaves panels. The 1936 corridor vehicles (sets 952-61) were, however, fully lined out. Utility vans followed the same general rules but, of course, were unlined. Their class designations (Luggage, 'Covcar' etc) were picked out in 3¼in primrose-yellow letters at the bottom right-hand corner of each side. Several other bodyside markings (XP branding, wheelbase etc) appeared in the mid-1930s, usually in white. **Figure 3** and **Plate 22** illustrate a special cattle van of the period, including some of the less obvious solebar brandings.

The 1938-49 period
By the mid-1930s many older vehicles and luggage vans were being outshopped without lining, and in due course some of the corridor stock appeared similarly unadorned. It was, perhaps, this lack of lining which dulled the Maunsell green sufficiently for a shareholder to complain at the 1935 Annual General Meeting that the colour of the stock was too dowdy. Soon afterwards, 6-PUL unit 3015 was repainted in a vivid green, described as emerald green, in order to test opinion; however (initially, at least), this did not appear to achieve the desired result. The unit nevertheless ran for a very considerable period (perhaps even until 1950) in this or a similar light green, so Lancing's painters must have done an excellent job. The Southern's workshops were, incidentally, experts at re-varnishing, and thus some carriages retained obsolete paint finishes for many years, although this constant re-varnishing could darken quite considerably the original paint colour.

The next development appears to have been the well-documented discussion between Maunsell, Bushrod and Cox on a trip to Portsmouth and the Isle of Wight in 1936 concerning the effect of train colour on passenger bookings. Sir Herbert Walker, who listened to the arguments, reputedly then purchased a reel of green spectacle cord in a local shop, giving a portion to each of the above officers, keeping the remainder as a reference and stating that this should henceforth be the livery of Southern locomotives and passenger rolling stock — an executive decision, if ever there was one! The origin of Bulleid's malachite green has been ascribed to this episode, but this may be incorrect. During 1938/9 a true olive green — lighter than the Maunsell green — was tried, and it is probably this colour which has its origins in the 1936 discussion. Known as 'Dover green', perhaps because the 'improved boat stock' was so painted, this colour wore badly in ordinary service.

Bulleid is reputed to have disliked the choice and, when it became apparent that the colour was somewhat unstable, grasped the opportunity: perhaps with the emerald-green 6-PUL unit in mind, he selected a brighter, bluer colour known as malachite green and managed, with a little persuasion, to convince the directors of its merits. Locomotives and carriages for certain specific services, including the 'Bognor Buffets' and the 'Bournemouth Limited' stock, began to appear in this colour from June 1938. At first it was intended to add two horizontal lines at waist level (the 1938 Portsmouth electrics did receive this treatment), but otherwise the coaches would be unlined. Bulleid introduced new lettering and numerals to go with the colour. The company title, abbreviated to 'SOUTHERN', appeared at the waistline using 4in unshaded gilt letters, complete with a black or green 'in-line' as shown in **Figure 2B**. Possibly some early

Plate 23 Maunsell Composite No 5664 as refurbished for the 'Bournemouth Limited' service in July 1938. Malachite green livery with Bulleid unshaded company title and 8in door numerals in place of full wording. The seat reservation letter board ('J') is clearly darker — Maunsell green or possibly red. *Southern Railway*

Plate 24 Maunsell Diagram 2001 Corridor Third No 1147, photographed in a rather sorry state in April 1950. Unlined Maunsell green is still carried, together with a variety of different lettering styles. The white triangular window stickers are revised 'NO SMOKING' notices, first introduced in 1939. The lettering and surround was red and these continued to be used by British Railways. *K. G. Carr*

transfers omitted the 'in-line' — the coach illustrated in **Plate 23** appears to have neither this nor any shading to the company title. Door designations were shown using 8in numerals on the doors, in gold shaded black. Carriage numbers remained as before. This style was not widely applied before war intervened, with the result that a mix-and-match policy soon prevailed, vehicles often being outshopped with new transfers on an old paint finish, as typified by the coach illustrated in **Plate 24**. Towards the end of the war even grey-painted vehicles (especially utility vans) were seen in service, lettered as if on a green base colour.

In the depths of war, with most locomotives now painted plain black, Bulleid tried to brighten up the stock a little by the introduction of his 'sunshine' lettering (**Figure 2C**). This took the previous style of lettering and added either green blocking (for black locomotives) or black blocking (for all other applications), 'shot' with yellow highlights. The base colour was no longer gilt but a more economical golden yellow or 'old gold'. This was used on locomotives from 1941 onwards, but its first definite application on rolling stock was 'plastic' luggage van No 1401 in December 1943 (**Plate 15**). Numerals to go with this lettering

Plate 25 Bulleid Diagram 2123 semi-open Brake Third No 4369 from Bournemouth-line six-coach set 300, ex works in March 1948 but still fully lettered with the company title on the waistline. With the exception of set 290 (see **Plate 1**), these six-coach sets were unique in having green coach ends. Malachite green livery with 'sunshine' lettering and seat reservation numbers over the relevant windows. *Southern Railway*

were also produced but did not feature the black 'in-line'. **Plate 25** shows a Bulleid semi-open Brake Third in malachite carrying this lettering. This became standard until Nationalisation, but many older vehicles and non-passenger coaching stock continued to be finished in Maunsell green, with several variations in lettering style. It has been estimated that in excess of 10% of the carriage stock and most luggage vans still carried Maunsell livery in 1948. Livestock vehicles had received grey livery since 1942 but featured standard lettering of the period.

British Railways

For a full account of the post-1948 changes, the reader is referred to *British Railways Mark I Coaches* by Keith Parkin (published by HMRS/Atlantic Publications 1991), but an outline of practice is given here.

The use of malachite continued until early 1949, with omission of the company title and Third-class door designations (Firsts continuing to be identified), plus the addition of an 'S' prefix to the running number. At least one drawing shows these numbers

Plate 26 Maunsell Third No S1200 in 'plum and spilt milk' livery, as carried from June 1948 until c1954. Third No 1254 and First No 7224, together with Bulleid sets 299 and 788, also carried this livery. The style followed was the same as that eventually chosen for the crimson lake and cream, but note the rather unusual placing of the carriage number — a feature of all these experimentally-liveried coaches. *P. Coutanche*

Plate 27 Throughout most of this book, the author has used the term 'steam-hauled' to describe the stock, but from 1947 onwards 'locomotive-hauled' would be more appropriate. Electric locomotive No 20003 hauls the down 'Newhaven Continental' express away from Lewes in the summer of 1949. The Newhaven boat set was the first to be repainted in crimson lake and cream (in April 1949) as seen here. Note the deep, crimson-coloured band at cantrail level, characteristic of all early repaints, although how best to deal with the corridor side of high-window Maunsell vehicles posed a problem and led eventually to the abolition of the deep band; thereafter just the roof rain strip was painted crimson lake. Pullman car *Grosvenor* or *Myrtle* may be seen towards the rear of the formation. *Author's collection*

dropped to the waistline at each end, but no photographic evidence of this has come to light.

In May 1948 the Railway Executive had eight sets of coaches painted in various experimental liveries in an attempt to interest the public in new colours. On the South Eastern section one set of Maunsells appeared in GWR chocolate and cream, while on the South Western two Bulleid sets, plus some loose Maunsells, were painted 'plum and spilt milk', rather akin to the old LNWR carriage livery. Although much interest was generated, few viewed the trials favourably, and none of the experimental liveries was eventually chosen. The writer's father recalls seeing the 'plum and spilt milk' set, which after a time showed considerable over-ripening of the fruit and souring of the milk! **Plate 26** illustrates one of these coaches, before the livery deteriorated.

The eventual choice was crimson lake and cream ('blood and custard' to many), using the same styles as the 1948 experiments, with a gold/black line separating each colour, the gold always being adjacent to the crimson lake. This proved to be a bright livery for postwar austerity Britain, but in normal service the cream was difficult to keep clean. Non-corridor vehicles and vans were crimson lake. Numerals were at first placed below the waistline, near the left-hand end, using Gill Sans lettering in a pale-straw colour with a black surround, but this was away from the tare, restriction and dimension plates on the coach end and from 1951 was repositioned towards the right-hand end. Various alterations to the depth of the crimson-lake cantrail panel were made, as seen in **Plate 27**. From 1951 the carriage numbers were both prefixed and suffixed 'S', to distinguish them from new British Railways Mk 1 coaches, which might carry the same running number, these having a regional prefix letter only. Some Bulleid vehicles carried the 'blood and custard' livery from new.

By 1956 about 60-70% of the Southern Region's stock had been repainted in the new colours, the rest remaining in Southern Railway green (of both Bulleid and, occasionally, Maunsell shades). In 1956 the Regions were given greater autonomy, including the freedom to choose different liveries. Predictably the Southern returned to green (a slightly darker malachite than used pre-1949) from June 1956, and by 1960 few passenger coaches remained in crimson lake and cream or unlined crimson lake. However, some utility vans continued to run in crimson — often unseen beneath the grime. BR green would be the final livery for most SR locomotive-hauled corridor coaches; a few received lined maroon if transferred away to other Regions, while a handful survived long enough to carry British Rail blue and grey (or plain blue in departmental service). The non-passenger coaching stock fared much better, and quite a few of these vehicles acquired Rail blue before the last was withdrawn in 1986. Examples of all liveries may be found within the illustrations, any specific variations being noted individually.

Chapter 3.
The Last Pre-Grouping Designs

While the make-up of the new CME's department was being decided, several outstanding pre-Grouping orders were being completed at Ashford, Eastleigh and Lancing. The last LBSCR Non-corridors had been authorised as late as December 1922 and were completed in 1923/4. No more carriages of LBSCR design were built, but Lancing soon made a start on converting these from Westinghouse to vacuum brakes — a task not completed until October 1934. At Eastleigh, six sets of 'Ironclads' were under construction, and, in due course, more would be ordered to Surrey Warner's designs. Ashford was completing some 10-compartment Non-corridor Thirds and had a further outstanding order for two boat-train sets, similar to that completed in 1921.

The 'Continentals'
The origins of the 1921 boat-train set go back to 1913, when Wainwright was still in charge at Ashford. He had prepared drawings for a traditional set of 'Birdcage' vehicles, but the low headroom of this style of carriage was causing a problem, due to the large quantities of hand luggage regularly taken by Continental passengers. By dispensing with the 'birdcage' lookouts altogether, the entire roof profile could be raised, giving considerably more headroom above the luggage racks. The drawings were duly amended, but there matters rested — Wainwright departed, and World War 1 curtailed all Continental services. It was not until 1918, with Maunsell and Lynes now in charge of carriage construction, that the subject was pursued anew. In July 1919 the SECR Board was asked to approve the construction of a new train of eight vehicles, providing First- and Second-class accommodation only, at a cost of £32,000. Consent was forthcoming, and the vehicles (of four types) were completed at Ashford Works in August 1921.

At 62ft 0in long over body, 8ft 0¾in wide and with a height of 12ft 2in to roof, the new vehicles were the largest yet built by the SECR. They were also the first to be equipped with Pullman gangways, buck-eye couplings and retractable buffers, as inclusion of Pullman cars within the boat trains was almost certain to continue. However, no gangways were provided at the brake ends, these alone being equipped with Spencer's patent non-retractable buffers and standard screw couplings. In appearance they resembled no other South Eastern carriage, having inward-opening doors at each end of the vehicle only, instead of the more usual door to every compartment. For boat-train services this did not pose a problem, as rapid ingress/egress at stations was not an important consideration. The lower bodysides were vertically match-boarded, and this, plus their almost exclusively boat-train duties, ensured the nickname of 'Continentals'. To a very slight extent, their appearance was reminiscent of the SER 'American' cars of 1892-7, which may have been Lynes' starting point for the design. The 'Continentals' were finished in SECR brown, lined in gold, with the company's coat of arms in the centre of the bodyside. The new standard bogies were fitted, in place of the Fox pressed-steel pattern previously used under most SECR bogie vehicles. The train comprised a Brake Second, three Corridor Seconds, three Corridor Firsts and a saloon Brake First, the latter including a small four-seat saloon adjacent to the guard's van, and was to be formed as follows:

Vehicle Type	SECR Nos	SR Nos
Six-compartment Brake Second	2504	4156
Seven-compartment Seconds	2501-3	4159-61
Six-compartment Firsts	2505-7	7367-69
Five-compartment Saloon Brake First	2508	7745 (later 6642, as Brake Composite)

The stock was illustrated and described in *The Locomotive* magazine in June 1923. The usual arrangement was to have the

Plate 28 1921 'Continental' Brake First No 7745, now running as Brake Composite No 6642, at Faversham in May 1950. By this time it was a loose coach with a regular daily working to Sheerness and back. Unlike the LSWR corridor stock, the lack of a gangway at the brake end was never regarded as an operational failing — probably due to the somewhat restricted nature of their boat train duties. *D. Cullum*

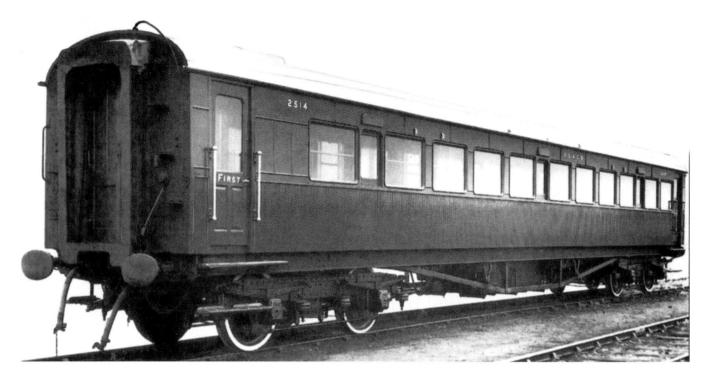

Plate 29 1923 'Continental' First No 2514, as completed in December of that year and lettered 'SE&CR', possibly in lined brown livery. It was renumbered as SR 7375 and presumably repainted green as early as February 1924. *Southern Railway*

First-class accommodation at the London end of the train. First-class compartments were finished in walnut with sycamore panels, upholstered in green cord cloth, while the Seconds received mahogany panelling with red, black and orange velvet seating.

In practice the train was seldom formed as above, since the requirements of boat-train accommodation varied considerably according to season; vehicles 2504/3/5-8, plus two Pullman cars in the centre, constituted SECR boat-train set No 2, the other vehicles standing spare or running with older stock in other boat-train sets. The regular duty for set No 2 was the 11am Victoria-Dover Marine and 5.55pm return service. Coupling to other stock was possible by withdrawing a cast-iron pin in the buck-eye coupling, which allowed it to be swung downwards, revealing a standard coupling hook behind. The buffers would then be pulled out fully, being retained in the extended position by placing a cast-iron saddle over the buffer-rod.

For a while in the mid-1920s the above nominal formation became SR set 510 but again seldom ran as the full eight vehicles, being noted on several occasions minus vehicles 4159 and 7368. The coaches acquired their Southern Railway numbers (and, presumably, LSWR green livery as well) in November 1923. Brake First No 7745 was altered to a Brake Composite and renumbered 6642 in March 1925, the saloon (now with eight seats) and the adjacent compartment being reclassified Second class. In its later form it appears in **Plate 28**.

Two more eight-coach boat trains were ordered in 1922 and completed at Ashford in October and December 1923, both appearing in SECR lined brown, or at least with SECR lettering and numbers, but possibly in green livery, as seen in **Plate 29**. All received their Southern Railway numbers in February 1924, just prior to the delivery of some contractor-built 'Continentals', so perhaps the Southern was attempting to ensure that all these prestige vehicles carried the new livery as soon as possible. Most details were as per the 1921 vehicles, but, instead of a lavatory at each end of the Corridor Firsts and Seconds, only one was provided. In place of the other lavatory was a coupé (half) compartment, seating either two additional First- or three additional Second-class passengers. The saloon in the Brake First was also enlarged, at the expense of the guard's van; this reduced luggage space somewhat, and there was often a need to include a luggage van in the train — hopefully one of the new utility vans, but sometimes one of the older ex-SECR six-wheelers — which somewhat marred the appearance of the complete formation. Brake coaches originally had just a single guard's door each side; later this was modified, and double doors were provided. Details of these vehicles are as follows:

Vehicle Type	SECR Nos	SR Nos
Six-compartment Brake Second	2523/4	4157/8
7½-compartment Second	2517-22	4162-7
6½-compartment First	2509-14	7370-5
Five-compartment Saloon Brake First	2515/6	7746/7

Coaches 4157/62-4, 7370-2 and 7746 were completed in October 1923 and nominally constituted SR set 511. Coaches 4158/65-7, 7373-5 and 7747 were completed in December 1923 and nominally constituted SR set 512. Again, as with set 510, these allocations proved academic, and coaches could soon be seen running in any combination, plus Pullmans, while from 1928 onwards the new Maunsell unclassed Open Saloons started to appear in the formations as well. Most boat trains ran between Victoria and either Folkestone Harbour or Dover Marine, but there was also a service to Gravesend West Street, connecting there with a London-Rotterdam boat service. This train could sometimes be formed of just two or three vehicles, perhaps hauled by an 'H' class tank or a rather grubby 'C' class goods engine — hardly the desired image for a boat train!

The demand for more boat-train stock was so urgent that the Southern ordered the next four batches of vehicles from outside contractors in October 1923, delivery being far sooner than Ashford, Eastleigh or Lancing could manage. Both the Metropolitan Carriage, Wagon & Finance Co and the Birmingham Railway Carriage & Wagon Co were involved, 41 vehicles of four types being placed in service by August 1924. Individual details may be found in the vehicle summary on page 34. One important change was made to these, the width being increased to 8ft 6½in over body. The height to roof was also increased, by 1in, owing to

Plate 30 Photographs of the 'Continentals' carrying Second-class lettering and numbers are difficult to find. This is a builder's photograph of Diagram 235 Second No 4171, in what appears to be unlined green livery when new in 1924. In June 1934 the coach was re-graded to Third class and renumbered 999, then being allocated to Diagram 2002. *BRCW / HMRS collection*

Plate 31 Similarly-finished First No 7383, photographed in June 1924. This was eventually downgraded to Third-class No 649, in June 1954. Diagram numbers were 496 and finally 54. *BRCW / HMRS collection*

their greater width. The increased width effectively barred these coaches from the Tonbridge-Hastings line, Route Restriction 1 eventually being allocated to these vehicles, whereas the 1921 and 1923 stock were to Route Restriction 0. However, in 1924 this was not seen as an important issue, due to the exclusive nature of their duties. For the first time a Third-class design was added to the range, and the 12 Brake Thirds completed in 1924 would be much in demand. The builder's photographs (**Plates 30 and 31**) appear to show the vehicles in unlined green but with a very high standard of finish. None of these later 'Continentals' was allocated to a permanent set until BR days.

A final 10 coaches were ordered in November 1926, and it was presumably intended that construction would take place at Eastleigh, as Order No E162 was issued (sub-divided into E162A for six Corridor Firsts and E162B for four Corridor Thirds). There is some doubt about this, and it seems likely that the underframes for the First-class coaches (at least) were built by the Metropolitan Carriage, Wagon & Finance Co, although another source states that the Thirds were built by BRCW (the underframes carried manufacturer's plates, so this may also be correct). All 10 coaches entered service in October 1927, bringing the total number of 'Continentals' to 75. One interesting fact about the Thirds (Nos 779-82) is that their diagram number (2002) was in the range allocated to new Southern construction — all other 'Continentals' were allocated diagram numbers in the ex-SECR series.

By the early 1930s Third-class patronage on boat trains was increasing, and in 1934/5 all permanent Second-class compartments were downgraded to Third class, resulting in the 21 Corridor Seconds and three Brake Seconds being renumbered into the appropriate Third-class ranges. Their place was taken by Maunsell Nondescript Saloons which had been built between 1928 and 1933 — these being capable of being labelled First, Second or Third class as occasion demanded, thereby taking care of the vagaries of traffic. Coaches 779 and 7372 had their bodies burnt out at Dover Marine in July 1935, their underframes then being reused under electric-stock conversions, while Third No 1014 (ex-Second 4163) and Firsts 7369/82 were destroyed by enemy action during World War 2.

The suspension of boat-train services in 1940 saw the coaches redeployed elsewhere for the next six years. Vehicles were noted as far west as Bournemouth, Plymouth, the Somerset & Dorset Joint line and (on one occasion) standing in the bay platform at Seaton! An amusing story recounted to the author concerns a passenger who attempted to board one of these vehicles at Netley during the war. Having turned the door handle and pulled like mad, he gave up and instead gave the door a hefty kick. Imagine his surprise when it opened inwards, quite possibly resulting in a rather undignified entry to the coach! However, on a more serious note, this same feature caused a child to fall from a moving train soon after the war, and an immediate start was made to re-hang the doors to open outwards. The removal of the left-hand grab-rail and the reshaping of the right-hand rail to clear passengers' knuckles as they grasped the door handle identified this modification. Most coaches were dealt with before withdrawal, the change being indicated by an 'A' suffix to the diagram number.

From 1938 the vehicles could also be seen on the Newhaven boat trains, while after 1950 some were cascaded onto

Plate 32 Twelve Brake Thirds were completed by the Metropolitan Carriage, Wagon & Finance Co in 1924, to SR Diagram 164. This is No 3558, in malachite green with original inward-opening passenger doors, at Ashford in May 1949. *J. H. Aston*

Plate 33 Diagram 164A Brake No 3550, in typically grimy crimson lake and cream at Eardley Road (Streatham) carriage sidings *c*1953, now with outward-opening doors. The underframes of the Brake vehicles were extended at the brake end only to be flush with the coach end, resulting in the non-Brake underframes' being 61ft long, the Brake vehicles being 61ft 5½in over headstocks. *The Lens of Sutton Collection*

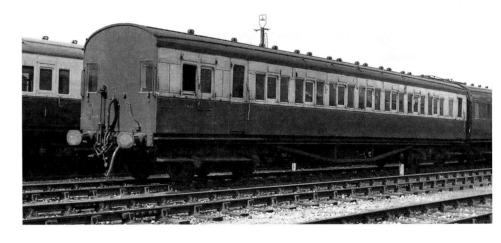

Plate 34 Former Brake Second No 4157, by now running as Brake Third No 3588, in malachite green at New Cross Gate *c*1949. This coach was completed in October 1923. *The Lens of Sutton Collection*

Plate 35 Brake First No 7750, with broad crimson cantrail band and left-hand numerals identifying it as one of the early BR repaints. This was one of several coaches, described as 'Improved Boat Stock', to receive refurbished interiors and 'Dover green' livery in 1938/9. *The Lens of Sutton Collection*

Plate 36 The interior of First-class compartment 'E' of Brake No 7750, as refurbished in 1939. The upholstery colours are not recorded but, if the same as the 'Bournemouth Limited' stock, would have been pale green for First class, pale pink for Third class. *Southern Railway*

Plate 37 Diagram 2002 Restriction 1 Corridor Third No 782 at Victoria *c*1951. This was one of the last 'Continentals' to be completed, in October 1927. *P. Coutanche*

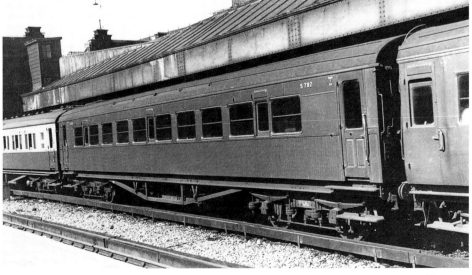

Plate 38 Diagram 56A Restriction 0 Corridor Third No 1015 (ex-Second No 4164) at Hastings c1957, in Southern Region green livery. Several of the Restriction 0 vehicles ended their days on the Hastings line in 1958/9.
The Lens of Sutton Collection

excursion and other services, including, for the Restriction 0 vehicles, the Tonbridge-Hastings line. Thirteen Firsts were downgraded to Third class in 1954, but others remained on Continental boat trains to the end. By 1959 British Railways was being criticised for charging premium fares on Folkestone and Dover boat trains — in reality for the privilege of travelling in rather old (albeit still comfortable) coaches. Stage 1 of the Kent Coast electrification rendered most 'Continentals' redundant, and all except Brake Thirds 3550/4 and Thirds 780-2 (designated since June 1956 as Brake Seconds or Seconds) were condemned 1957-9. The last five ran until 1961, the Seconds in 'special traffic' set 212 allocated to the London Central section, while Brake vehicle 3550 migrated westward to Okehampton for the Meldon Quarry workmen's service. Brake Second 3554 was subsequently preserved (and is now on the Keighley & Worth Valley Railway), while similar vehicle 3557 entered departmental service at Woking and was eventually sold to the Kent & East Sussex Railway in the 1990s.

Plates 29-38 and **Figures 4-7** illustrate these vehicles.

Table 3
Summary of SECR 'Continental' stock

Diagram No	Vehicle Type	Route Restriction	Seats 1st	Seats 2nd	Seats 3rd	Running Nos	Built by	Remarks
54	6½-compartment Third	1			39	643-55	(Renumbered 5-6/54)	Ex-Firsts 7376-81/3-9
55	Seven-compartment Third	0			42	1010-2	(Renumbered 1934/5)	Ex-Seconds 4159-61
56	7½-compartment Third	0			45	1013-8	(Renumbered 1934/5)	Ex-Seconds 4162-7
164	Seven-compartment Brake Third	1			42	3548-59	Metro 6-8/24	No 3554 preserved
169	Six-compartment Brake Third	0			36	3587	(Renumbered 1934)	Ex-Brake Second 4156
170	Six-compartment Brake Third	0			36	3588/9	(Renumbered 1934)	Ex-Brake Seconds 4157/8
233	Seven-compartment Second	0		42		4159-61	Ashford 8/21	To Thirds 1010-2 in 1934/5
234	7½-compartment Second	0		45		4162-7	Ashford 10-12/23	To Thirds 1013-8 in 1934/5
235	7½-compartment Second	1		45		4168-79	BRCW 4-5/24	To Thirds 996-1007 in 1934
245	Six-compartment Brake Second	0		36		4156	Ashford 8/21	To Brake Third 3587 in 1934
246	Six-compartment Brake Second	0		36		4157/8	Ashford 10-12/23	To Brake Thirds 3588/9 in 1934
427	Five-compartment Saloon Brake Composite	0	12	14		6642	(Renumbered 3/25)	Ex-Brake First 7745; to First/Third class in 1934
494	Six-compartment First	0	24			7367-9	Ashford 8/21	
495	6½-compartment First	0	26			7370-5	Ashford 10-12/23	No 7372 destroyed by fire 7/35
496	6½-compartment First	1	26			7376-83	BRCW 6/24	Nos 7376-81/3 to Thirds 643-9 5/54
496	6½-compartment First	1	26			7384-9	Metro/Eastleigh 10/27	To Thirds 650-5 in 6/54
550	Five-compartment Saloon Brake First	0	20			7745	(Renumbered 8/21)	To Brake Composite 6642 3/25
551	Five-compartment Saloon Brake First	0	22			7746/7	Ashford 10-12/23	
552	Five-compartment Saloon Brake First	1	22			7748-56	Metro 7-8/24	Nos 7750/6 internally refurbished in 1939
2002	7½-compartment Third	1			45	779-82	Metro/Eastleigh 10/27	No 779 destroyed by fire 7/35
2002	7½-compartment Third	1			45	996-1007	(Renumbered 1934)	Ex-Seconds 4168-79

Notes
1. Coaches 1014, 7369/82 destroyed by enemy action 1940/1.
2. Diagram numbers suffixed 'A' after 1945 to indicate outward-opening passenger doors.

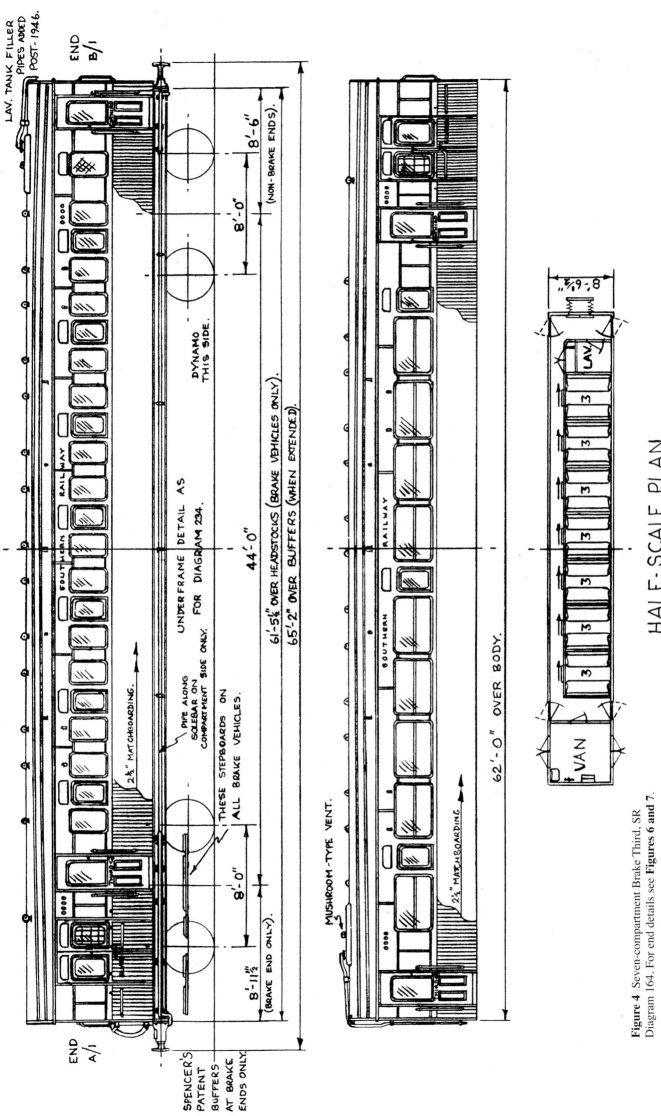

Figure 4 Seven-compartment Brake Third, SR Diagram 164. For end details see **Figures 6 and 7**.

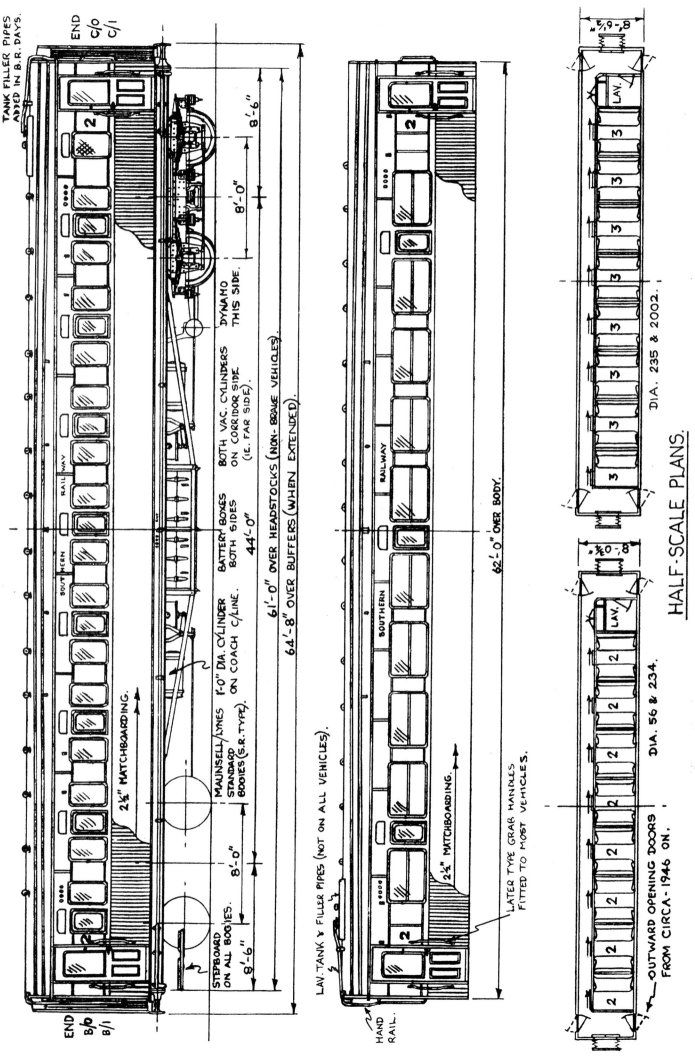

Figure 5 7½-compartment Corridor Second/Third, SR Diagrams 234, 235, 2002 and 56.

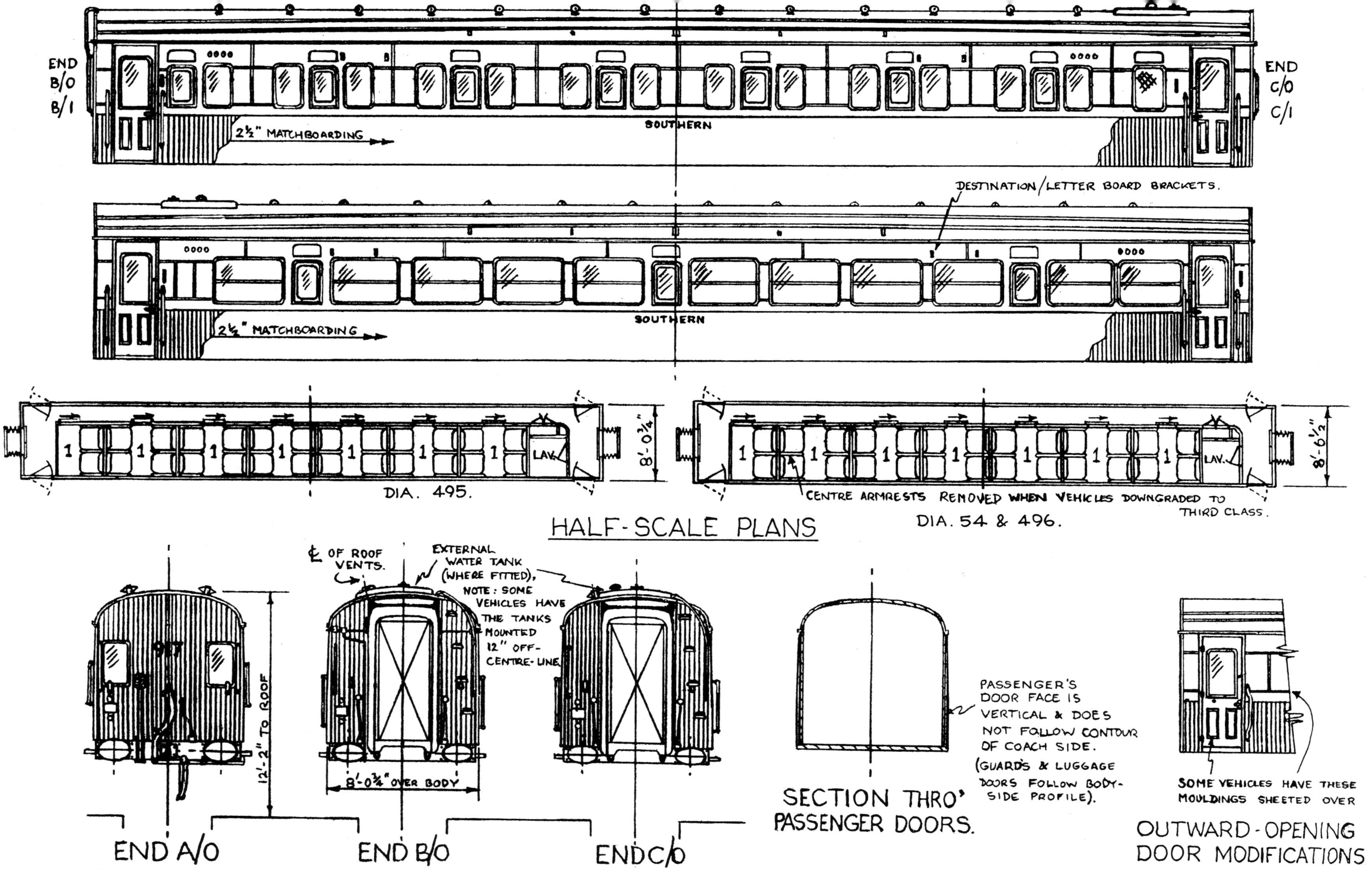

Figure 6 6½-compartment Corridor First/Third, SR Diagrams 495, 496 and 54.

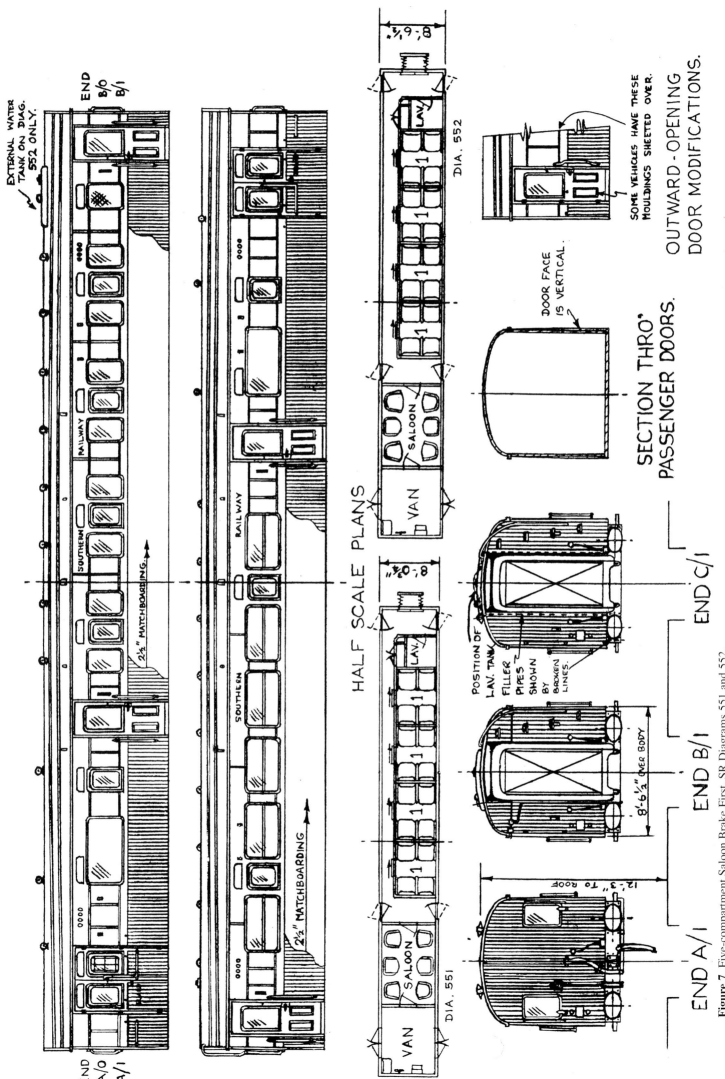

Figure 7 Five-compartment Saloon Brake First, SR Diagrams 551 and 552.

The 'Ironclads'

By 1921 the South Western owned a fleet of some 300 wooden-panelled corridor coaches, varying in length from 46ft 6in to 57ft. All resembled the non-corridor coaches of the period but were either 3in or 6in wider over body. Most carried the same semi-elliptical roof profile, but a dozen vehicles completed in 1913 and 1918 received a much higher full elliptical roof, and this feature was perpetuated with the new stock completed from July 1921. These were originally authorised in 1915, but, owing to wartime restrictions, construction had been deferred. Surrey Warner also increased the body width to 9ft 0in and adopted steel panelling over timber body framing, finishing them in the new dark-green livery. British standard gangways and screw couplings were provided throughout. Body length remained at 57ft 0in — identical to the last of the wooden-panelled vehicles (which were, in fact, steel-clad but over-panelled in traditional style). The flush-sided steel panels, so different from all previous LSWR stock, earned the new coaches the nickname of 'Ironclads', while Warner, mindful of possible unsteady riding, mounted them on heavy double-framed 9ft-wheelbase bogies, giving rise to another naval nickname — 'Dreadnoughts'. Either name was appropriate, as they were heavy vehicles (most exceeding 33 or 34 tons tare) and were extremely well constructed; consequently some enjoyed almost 40 years in passenger service, followed by almost another 40 in departmental use.

The 1921 vehicles were ordered as four five-coach sets for Waterloo-Bournemouth services, becoming LSWR sets 1^c-4^c (the suffix indicating a corridor set), later SR sets 431-4, in the same order and formation. All comprised a Brake Third at each end, two Corridor Thirds and a Corridor First at the centre. One of the Thirds was provided with a small pantry, occupying the equivalent space of one compartment and the lavatory at one end of the coach, being equipped to serve tea, coffee and light snacks rather than full meals; some observers of the period referred to them as 'Tea-car sets'. All four were in service by November 1921. The Brake Thirds had half of their accommodation given over to the guard and luggage van, while the brake end tapered inwards to a width of 8ft 3in, to give clearance for side lookouts, which were 9ft 1in wide (reduced to 9ft 0in on later vehicles). The LSWR wished to form the sets in its customary manner, such that the corridor alternated from side to side down the train, and the Brake Thirds were built in left- and right-handed versions, in order to preserve this arrangement. Had the sets been formed of an even number of coaches, this provision would not have been necessary. The original formations, together with their SR renumberings, are as below.

Vehicle Type	Set 1^c (Set 431)		Set 2^c (Set 432)		Set 3^c (Set 433)		Set 4^c (Set 434)	
Four-compartment Brake Third	1276	(3181)	1278	(3183)	1280	(3185)	1281	(3186)
Seven-compartment Pantry Third	930	(713)	931	(714)	932	(715)	933	(716)
Seven-compartment First	3867	(7170)	3864	(7168)	3922	(7171)	3923	(7172)
Eight-compartment Third	773	(717)	774	(718)	778	(719)	929	(720)
Four-compartment Brake Third	1277	(3182)	1275	(3180)	1279	(3184)	1282	(3187)

Note: Some sources give position of Brake vehicles transposed

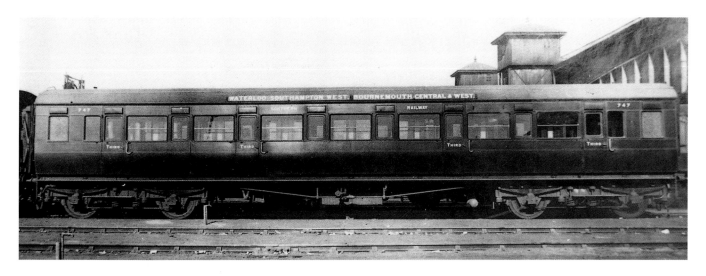

Plate 39 'Ironclad' Third No 747, completed in April 1924, is seen at Clapham Junction with the original square-cornered lining panels. Note the roof destination boards — 'WATERLOO SOUTHAMPTON WEST / BOURNEMOUTH CENTRAL & WEST'.
J. Tatchell collection

Plate 40 Pantry Third No 713 at Southampton Docks in 1935, during the period when these were running as six-compartment vehicles, with an enlarged pantry. On the original print the round-cornered lining panels are just visible. *F. Foote*

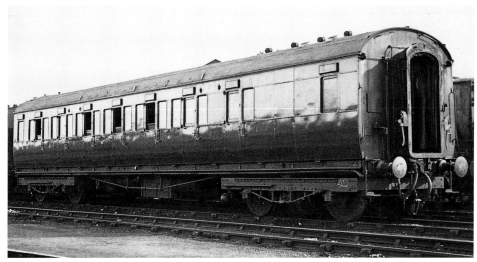

Plate 41 Former Pantry Third No 714 in 'blood and custard' livery at Templecombe in June 1956, now running in eight-coach set 441. These rebuilds could be identified by the asymmetrical positions of the doors on the corridor side; on a standard Corridor Third these were opposite the first, third, sixth and eighth compartments. *A. E. West*

All received their Southern Railway numbers between February 1924 and April 1927. Theoretically, SR even-numbered Brake Thirds were right-handed-corridor and odd-numbered ones left-handed-corridor, but this was not quite achieved in practice (see **Table 4** for full details).

In 1917 two sets of First/Second-class vehicles were authorised for Southampton boat traffic. These were originally proposed as 10-coach sets plus a luggage van, but when built in 1922 each appeared with eight Corridor Firsts running between two Kitchen Pantry Brake Firsts. The Corridor Firsts were identical to those in the five-coach sets, but the Pantry Brakes included three compartments, a pantry and a kitchen, the latter being equipped to provide rather more extensive meals than the earlier Pantry Thirds. However, only demountable tables were provided within the ordinary compartments, so one wonders how effective this arrangement might have been, especially bearing in mind that a Waterloo- Southampton run would not have given much time to cater for a full trainload of passengers. The corridors again alternated from side to side, but, as the trains were formed of 10 coaches, left- and right-handed Brakes were not needed, and all four Pantry Brakes had right-handed corridors (when viewed from the guard's van, which is the convention used here). No permanent set numbers were allocated to these two boat sets, as the trains would not always run with the full 10 vehicles. They were seldom seen anywhere other than on Southampton boat trains. Details of the vehicles are:

Corridor Firsts: LSWR Nos 3854/8/66, 3924-36
(later SR Nos 7166/7/9/73-85)
Pantry Brake Firsts: LSWR Nos 4061-4
(later SR Nos 7711-4)

Perhaps because they saw less intensive use than the five-coach sets, renumbering did not take place until 1927/8. The nominal SR formations of the two sets were:

7711+7166+7167+7169+7173+7174+7175+7176+7177+7712
7713+7178+7179+7180+7181+7182+7183+7184+7185+7714

Four more Bournemouth-line five-coach sets were ordered in May 1921, together with 24 loose Thirds, Firsts and Composites, followed shortly after by two six-coach sets for the Portsmouth line, the latter including a Dining Saloon in each set. However, all six appeared in late 1923 as five-coach formations, similar to the earlier sets but having two Corridor Thirds instead of one Pantry Third and one Corridor Third. The Bournemouth sets received LSWR livery and numbers (sets 5^c-8^c, later SR sets 435-8), while the Portsmouth pair entered service in October 1923 in SR livery as sets 439/40, despite having LSWR coach numbers allocated. On this evidence at least, the Southern Railway renumbering scheme seems to have been finalised by September/October 1923. The original formations, together with their SR renumberings, are shown in the table below,

The two Dining Saloons were completed as LSWR Nos 4150/1 in October 1923, later renumbered as SR 7850/1, while loose Thirds 745-54, Firsts 7192-7201 and Composites 5133-6 appeared early in 1924, these completing the orders outstanding at the Grouping. Some Ashford influence was felt, as all vehicles built after June 1923 received 9ft-wheelbase single-framed bogies of a style rather similar to the Maunsell/Lynes standard SR bogie. Sets 437 onwards and the loose coaches all had these bogies, described as 'vertical suspension' or 'VS' type. The stock was described in an article in *The Locomotive* magazine for June 1925, which stated that the First-class compartments featured figured blue moquette upholstery and polished walnut woodwork. The Thirds used figured brown plush and polished mahogany. Ceilings were white, with gold decoration in First-class compartments only.

All the 'Ironclad' stock has been most ably drawn by Gordon Weddell in his book *LSWR Carriages in the 20th Century* (published by OPC, 2001) and are therefore not fully repeated here, **Figures 8-10** only being included to illustrate these five-coach sets, plus the two-coach sets described next.

With Surrey Warner continuing in charge at Eastleigh and likely to remain so for a number of years, together with the pressing need for yet more corridor stock on the South Western section, it was hardly surprising that further 'Ironclads' were ordered in April 1924. These comprised four more five-coach

Vehicle Type	Set 5^c (Set 435)		Set 6^c (Set 436)		Set 7^c (Set 437)		Set 8^c (Set 438)	
Four-compartment Brake Third	1353	(3190)	1310	(3188)	1356	(3192)	1365	(3195)
Eight-compartment Third	67	(724)	64	(722)	70	(726)	74	(728)
Seven-compartment First	3938	(7187)	3937	(7186)	3939	(7188)	3940	(7189)
Eight-compartment Third	66	(723)	62	(721)	69	(725)	73	(727)
Four-compartment Brake Third	1354	(3191)	1325	(3189)	1357	(3193)	1366	(3196)

The two Portsmouth sets were identical in formation, as follows:

SR Set No	Vehicles
439	3194+730+7190+729+3197
440	3198+732+7191+731+3199

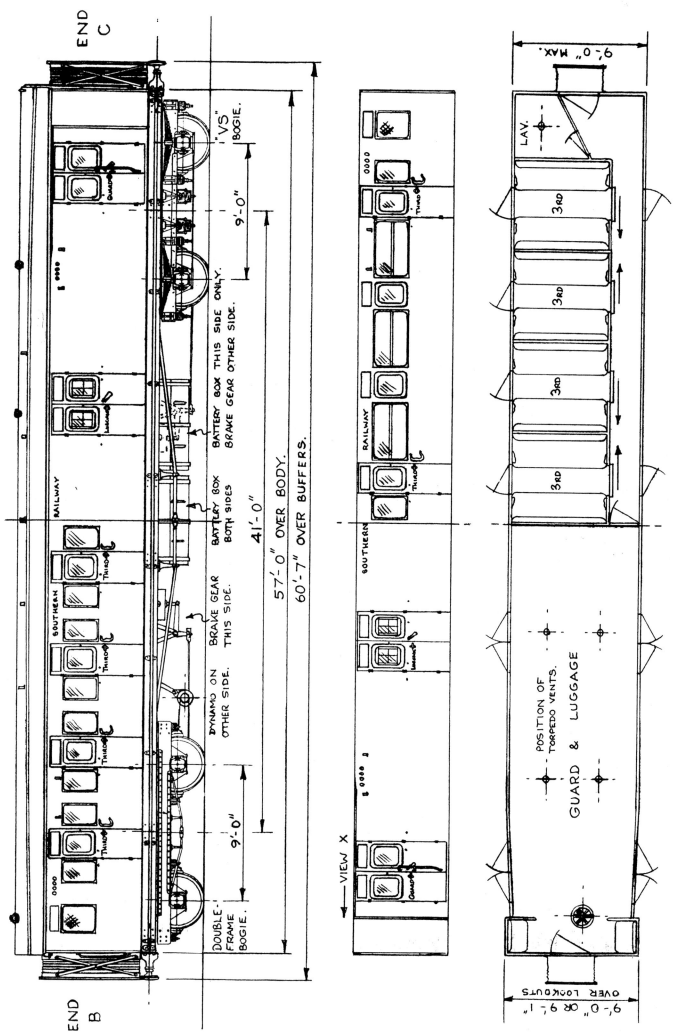

Figure 8 'Ironclad' four-compartment Brake Third with right-handed corridor, SR Diagram 135. For end details see **Figure 9**.

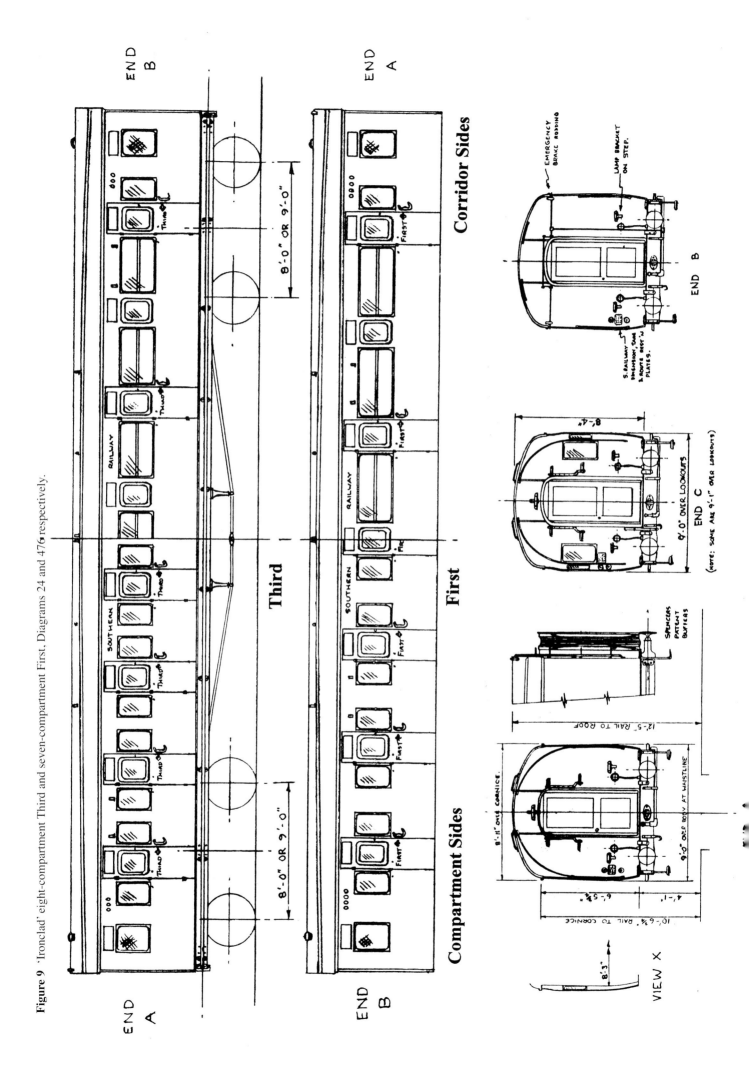

Figure 9 'Ironclad' eight-compartment Third and seven-compartment First. Diagrams 24 and 476 respectively.

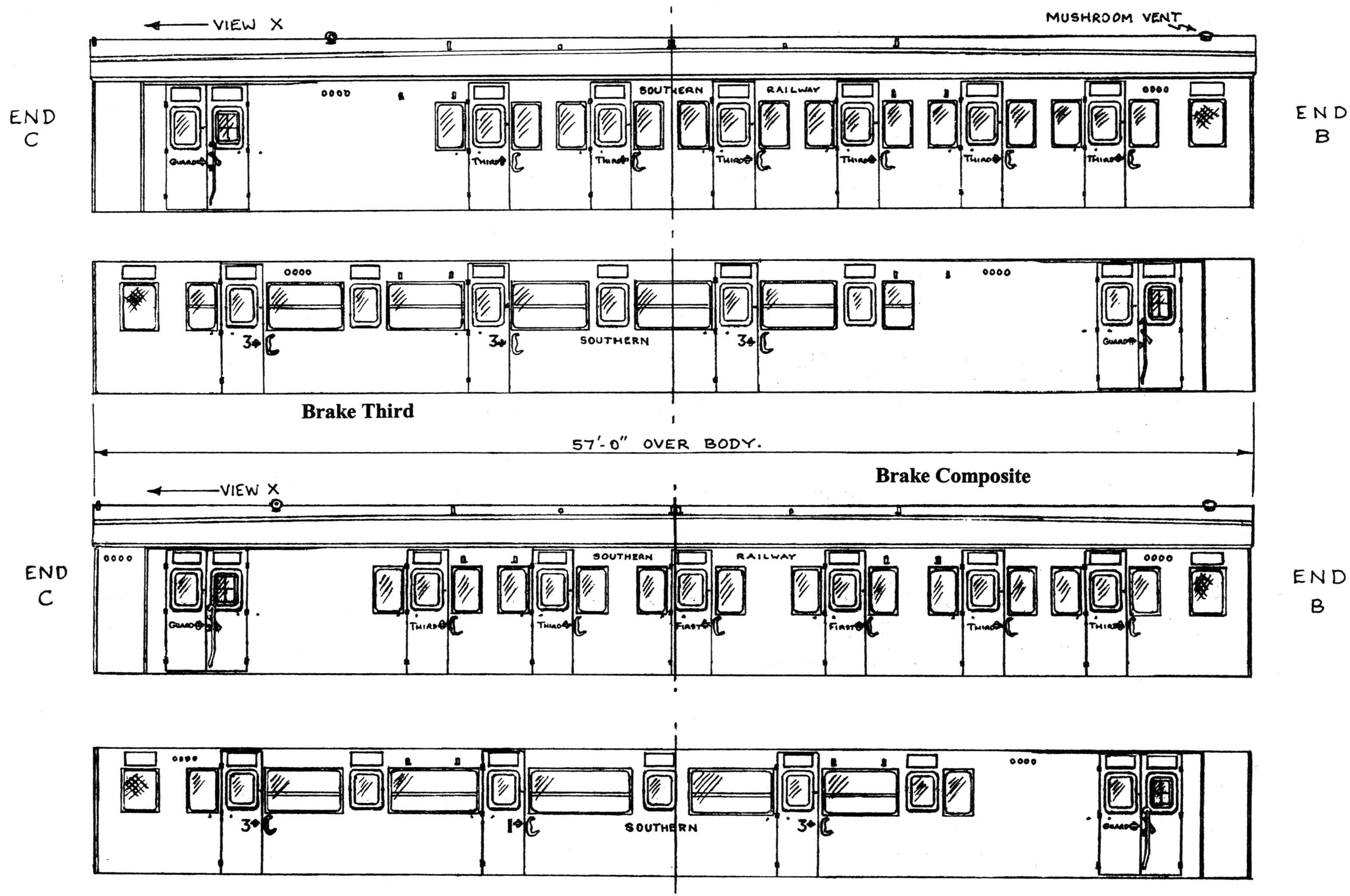

Figure 10 The two-coach 'Ironclad' sets 'E'-type, Nos 381-5.

Plate 42 Diagram 135 Brake Third No 3182 at Walton-on-Thames carriage sidings in April 1938. This was an important stabling point for South Western-section carriage stock not in everyday use. *F. Foote*

Plate 43 Diagram 284 Composite No 5135 in malachite green at Fratton in June 1950. Unlike most Maunsell coaches, these Composites only had three First- and four Third-class compartments — the reverse of the usual SR arrangement. *D. Cullum*

sets for Waterloo-Bournemouth services (sets 441-4), five two-coach sets for Waterloo-Lymington/Swanage through services (sets 381-5) and six Dining Saloons for Waterloo-Bournemouth services (coaches 7852-7).

The Dining cars were identical to the original pair and were intended to run within the existing five-coach formations, but were seldom permanently allocated to any particular set, an arrangement which would be followed for most subsequent Maunsell vehicles. The additional five-coach sets were identical in formation to the last batch and comprised Brake Thirds 3203-10, Corridor Thirds 755-62 and Corridor Firsts 7202-5, these last four vehicles alone receiving SR standard 8ft-wheelbase bogies; but this time all were correctly formed in exact numerical order. They were completed at Eastleigh in August/September 1925, under Orders E17, E21 and E23. Dining Saloons 7852-7 entered service in July/August 1925, being completed against Order E16. Note that each type of coach constituted a separate order number at this time.

The two-coach sets were formed of a six-compartment Brake Third and a six-compartment Brake Composite, both having rather smaller guard's/luggage vans than previously. Both had left-handed corridors — indeed, the Brake Thirds of five-coach sets 441-4 were the last vehicles built with opposite-handed corridors — and sets 381-5 entered service in late 1925/ early 1926, formed as below:

Set No	Brake Third	Brake Composite
381	4052	6560
382	4053	6561
383	3211	6562
384	3212	6563
385	3213	6564

Referred to in Carriage Working Notices as two-sets 'E'-type

Order numbers were E20 for Brake Composites and E24 for Brake Thirds. All were originally scheduled for construction at Lancing, which may explain why the first two Brake Thirds received Central-section carriage numbers, but all 10 were eventually completed at Eastleigh in October 1925. Although specifically for Lymington and Swanage through services, they also appeared on West of England trains, in contrast to the other five-coach sets, which were normally seen only on Bournemouth and Portsmouth workings.

Lancing did finally get the opportunity to build one set of 'Ironclads' for the Central section, in December 1925, these being the last new stock completed there before reorganisation of

Date Authorised	Vehicles	Set No
4/24	One 11-coach set for London-Brighton ('City Limited') services	471
4/25	One 11-coach set for London-Worthing & Bognor services	472

the workshops removed all new construction to Eastleigh. This was followed by a final set for the Central section, completed at Eastleigh early in 1926, as above:

Both included a high level of First-class accommodation as they were intended for business travel to and from the City. Formations were as below:

Vehicle Type	Set 471
Six-compartment Brake Third	4043
Seven-compartment Composite	6287
Seven-compartment Firsts	7652-8
Eight-compartment Third	2341
Six-compartment Brake Third	4044

Orders E18, E19, L22 and L24 were placed separately for set 471, while E85 was for set 472, sub-divided into E85A, B and C for the three types of coach. As far as can be ascertained, all vehicles of set 471 were completed at Lancing, despite the HOO prefix letters.

The coaches were similar to those ordered previously, vehicles in set 471 having 9ft-wheelbase 'VS' bogies, while set 472 ran on the SR standard 8ft pattern. Completion of these brought the total stock of 'Ironclads' to 154 vehicles, all except the last 22 being allocated to the South Western section. These allocations seldom (if ever) changed, although the individual vehicles within each set

Vehicle Type	Set 472
Six-compartment Brake Third	4046
Seven-compartment Firsts	7659-64
Eight-compartment Thirds	2346-8
Six-compartment Brake Third	4047

were to vary considerably over the next 35 years.

Soon after completion, sets 471/2 were reduced somewhat in formation, and both then ran between Brighton and London until electrification in 1933, formed as below.

Set 471: 4043+6287+7652+7653+7654+Pullman First+7656+7657+7658+2341+4044
Set 472: 4046+2346+7661+7662+Pullman Third+7663+7664+2348+4047

Plate 44 'Ironclad' two-coach set 385, with Brake Third 3213 nearer the camera, leaving Swanage at the rear of the branch push-pull train c1937. The roof boards read: 'WATERLOO WAREHAM SWANAGE'. *F. Foote*

Plate 45 Corridor First No 7199 at Clapham Yard in May 1949, still running as a loose coach. The destination board reads 'SALISBURY' in red letters on a white ground. The First-class window stickers used white letters on a blue background. *J. H. Aston*

Some of the vehicles removed from these two sets were then formed into Corridor set 455, between two wooden-panelled LSWR Brakes, also allocated to the Central section. On electrification, sets 471/2 were reduced to four coaches and then ran on London-Bognor/Portsmouth services until electrification caught up with them again. They then moved to the Oxted line, set 471 later running as a six-coach set and 472 running as a five-coach set. However, both ended their days in 1959 made up to eight vehicles, including Maunsell stock.

On the South Western section, sets 431-44 were soon equipped with Pullman gangway adaptors, enabling them to couple with the new Maunsell vehicles introduced from 1926. Sets 431-5 and 444 gave up one of their Corridor Thirds (sets 431-4 losing the Pantry Third) in 1927, the new Maunsell Kitchen/Dining pairs of vehicles taking their place. In this form they were designated Six-Dining sets 'A'-type, although it was also possible to find them running as a basic four-coach set — a formation to which most of the 'Ironclad' sets from time to time reverted. The other eight sets (Nos 436-43) remained as five-coach basic formations but could have an 'Ironclad' or LSWR wooden-panelled Dining Saloon added, making them Six-Dining sets 'B'-type. Both formations became the mainstay of Waterloo-Bournemouth West services, with only occasional rostered trips to Weymouth or Salisbury.

For Portsmouth-line trains, one or two of the five-coach sets would be made up to seven vehicles by the addition of a Dining Saloon and a Composite (both of LSWR and/or 'Ironclad' origin) and these became Seven-Dining sets 'C'-type. The Pantry Thirds were modified in 1927 under Order E208, enlarging the pantry to include the adjacent Third-class compartment and reducing the passenger accommodation to six compartments. This undoubtedly gave them greater catering capacity, and they were regularly inserted into a basic four-coach 'Ironclad' formation, to make Five-Pantry sets 'D'-type, although they could also be seen running as loose vehicles within or between other sets. In this form they ran to Weymouth, Swanage or Southampton Docks, as seen in **Plate 40**. However, the construction of more Maunsell catering vehicles made them surplus to requirements, and in July 1936 they were rebuilt again into eight-compartment Corridor Thirds, under Order E904. In this final form they were considered identical to all other Corridor Thirds, only the different position of the corridor side doors betraying their original status, seen in **Plate 41**.

Plate 46 'Ironclad' Dining Saloon No 7854 (now re-lettered 'Restaurant Car') at Walton-on-Thames sidings in July 1938. It is coupled next to a Maunsell open-saloon Third (right) to provide additional dining capacity but is otherwise running in a set of ex-LSWR wooden-panelled coaches. *F. Foote*

Plate 47 Pantry Brake First No 7711 at Clapham Junction in November 1946. At this time these coaches were running with kitchen and pantry out of use but were still on Southampton Docks boat trains. Note the position of the door numerals, adjacent to the door handles. *D. Cullum*

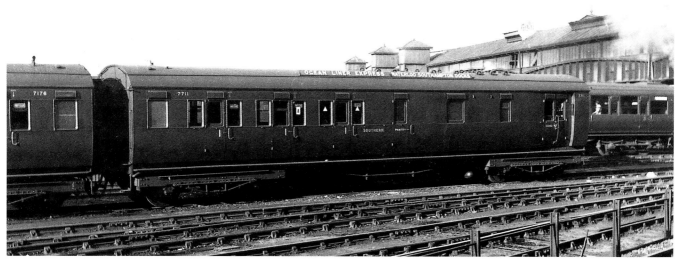

West of England trains were, at this time, more usually formed of LSWR three-coach wooden-panelled Corridor sets, the new Maunsell 3-P Corridor sets, a Dining Saloon and several loose Brake Composites, the latter providing the through portions to the numerous branch lines served.

The 'Ironclad' workings varied only a little until electrification of the Portsmouth Direct line in 1937, the introduction of new Maunsell stock releasing only a couple of sets for Brighton-Cardiff services during this period. Firsts 7169/80 were badly damaged by fire on 15 August 1936 at Micheldever while in an up Jersey boat express. The cause was not exactly confirmed — it may have been an electrical short-circuit or sparks from the locomotive lodging under the canvas covers to the gangways. Maunsell First 7227 and Pullman car *Rainbow* were also destroyed, but the three SR underframes were later reused under push-pull conversions 6406-8, mentioned briefly in Chapter 7.

Once the Portsmouth Direct line was electrified, all regular Bournemouth trains could be formed using Maunsell stock, and 'Ironclad' sets 431-44 were all reduced to basic four-coach formations and cascaded onto secondary services. Perhaps surprisingly, these formations still included the original Brake Thirds and Corridor First, but both 'Ironclad' Thirds were removed and their place was taken by a single Maunsell Third in each set, some of which were almost-new flush-panelled coaches and failed to match the 'Ironclads' in style. Sets 431-44 now included Maunsell Thirds 1194/85, 1854/43, 1184, 1204, 1902/3, 842, 1831/26/14, 1230 and 1901 respectively. The sets could still be made up to at least six vehicles at busy times and could also now be seen more often on the West of England line, Brighton-Plymouth workings, through services to the Midlands and Portsmouth-Salisbury-Bristol-Cardiff trains. Sets 440-4 remained on the last-named until 1948; however, from 1946 most sets were increased to eight vehicles (all being so formed by 1954), using additional loose 'Ironclad' and Maunsell Thirds. They could then be seen on excursion and special traffic duties until withdrawn between 1957 and 1959. During this period many of the sets ran in mixed liveries — the original four coaches might have been 'blood and custard', but the additions were green. Those marshalling the stock appeared to delight in alternating the colours down the set.

By 1941, under wartime restrictions, most catering facilities were being withdrawn, and all eight 'Ironclad' restaurant cars entered departmental service during the war, providing Civil Engineer's Department staff catering at various strategic locations. Only coach 7853 returned to passenger use after the war, being rebuilt *circa* April 1950 as a cafeteria car, to SR Diagram 600. This work may have been carried out at Swindon, as the coach was then allocated to the Western Region, numbered W7853S. It remained there until withdrawn in January 1963, managing to outlive the last Southern Region 'Ironclads' by just one month. The four Pantry Brake Firsts were also withdrawn from catering service in the 1940s and ran for most of the time as ordinary Brake Firsts, the kitchen and pantry being out of use. They also did a stint on ambulance duty towards the end of the war and were finally rebuilt in 1948/9 as six-compartment Brake Firsts, the former catering facilities being replaced by three additional compartments. They were then returned to Southampton boat-train services, on which they remained until withdrawn in 1958/9.

An excess of First-class accommodation became apparent in the 1950s, leading to 21 Firsts' being downgraded to Thirds 2320-40 during the second half of 1954, these being formed with Maunsell vehicles into 10-coach 'special traffic' sets 274-6, allocated to the South Western section. All were withdrawn in 1958/9.

Order 3434 was issued in June 1947 to convert two-coach sets 'E'-type 381-4 into push-pull sets — a task completed at Lancing between October 1948 and September 1949. Similar set 385 was at that time employed on a Bournemouth West-Chester service, augmented by two Corridor Thirds, and was not converted until March 1952, under Order L3735. The modifications were quite extensive — all corridor connections were removed and the former lavatories converted into coupé compartments, while a standard push-pull end was provided in the Driving Brake Third; one additional Third-class compartment was created in the former van space of this vehicle as well. Sets 381-4 were initially allocated to the Seaton, Gosport, Yeovil Town and Bordon branches, while in later years they also ran on the Swanage and Lymington branches — lines they had previously served as through coaches from Waterloo. Carriage and set numbers remained unaltered. Set 382 suffered fire damage at Bournemouth West in August 1959 and was subsequently condemned, but the other four remained in service until late 1962, being the last 'Ironclads' in ordinary service on the Southern Region. Five other coaches (Nos 725/9/58 and 7660/4) were allocated in 1961/2 to the Bertram Mills Circus train, based at Ascot West, and were also amongst the last survivors.

The rugged nature of their construction meant that, despite being surplus to requirements, many 'Ironclads' were still in good condition at the time of withdrawal. Consequently, between 1958 and 1962, no fewer than 48 were converted for further departmental service, and some of these lasted long enough to be sold on to various preservation societies during the 1970s, '80s and '90s. At the time of writing, apart from one Third (which has become hotel accommodation at the former LSWR Horsebridge station, on the Andover-Romsey line), none is scheduled to return to passenger traffic, most continuing to serve their present owners as departmental support vehicles. The 'Ironclads' were undoubtedly a very successful design, very wisely adopted by the Southern Railway as a temporary standard between 1923 and 1926.

Plate 48 Between 1948 and 1952 all five two-coach sets 'E'-type were converted to push-pull operation, retaining the same coach and set numbers. Set 383 is seen at Yeovil Junction c1960, providing the shuttle service to Yeovil Town. *Author's collection*

Table 4
Summary of LSWR 'Ironclad' stock

Diagram No	Vehicle Type	Seats 1st	Seats 3rd	Running Nos	Bogies	Built by	Remarks
23	Seven/six-compartment Pantry Third		56/48	713-6	D	Eastleigh 7-11/21	Rebuilt 3/27
23	Eight-compartment Third		64	713-6	D	Rebuilt 7/36	Ex-Pantry Thirds
24	Eight-compartment Third		64	717-32	D	Eastleigh 7/21-10/23	
24	Eight-compartment Third		64	745-62, 2341	VS	Eastleigh 4/24-12/25	No 2341 built Lancing
24	Eight-compartment Third		64	2346-8	SR	Eastleigh 1/26	
25	Seven-compartment Third		56	2320-40	Various	(Renumbered 6-10/54)	Ex-Diagram 476
135	Four-compartment Brake Third		32	3180/2/4/7/8/90	D	Eastleigh 7/21-3/23	RH corridor
135	Four-compartment Brake Third		32	3192/4/5/8, 3203/6/7/9	VS	Eastleigh 6/23-9/25	RH corridor
213*	Four-compartment Brake Third		32	3181/3/5/6/9/91	D	Eastleigh 7/21-3/23	LH corridor
213*	Four-compartment Brake Third		32	3193/6/7/9, 3204/5/8/10	VS	Eastleigh 6/23-9/25	LH corridor
137	Six-compartment Brake Third		48	3211-3, 4052/3	VS	Eastleigh 10/25	Later to Diagram 136
136	7½-compartment Brake Third		62	3211-3, 4052/3	VS	Rebuilt Lancing 1948-52	Push-pull fitted
137	Six-compartment Brake Third		48	4043/4/6/7	VS/SR	Lancing/Eastleigh 12/25-1/26	Nos 4046/7 built Eastleigh
284	Seven-compartment Composite	18	32	5133-6, 6287	VS	Eastleigh 5/24, Lancing 12/25	No 6287 built Lancing
416	Six-compartment Brake Composite	12	32	6560-4	VS	Eastleigh 10/25	Later to Diagram 414
414	6½-compartment Brake Composite	12	38	6560-4	VS	Rebuilt Lancing 1948-52	Push-pull fitted
476	Seven-compartment First	42		7166-87	D	Eastleigh 7/21-3/23	Some later Diagram 25
476	Seven-compartment First	42		7188-7201	VS	Eastleigh 6/23-4/24	Some later Diagram 25
476	Seven-compartment First	42		7202-5	SR	Eastleigh 7-9/25	Some later Diagram 25
476	Seven-compartment First	42		7652-8	VS	Lancing 12/25	Some later Diagram 25
476	Seven-compartment First	42		7659-64	SR	Eastleigh 1/26	Some later Diagram 25
542	Three-compartment Pantry Brake First	18		7711-4	D	Eastleigh 6-8/22	Later Diagram 542A
542A	Six-compartment Brake First	36		7711-4	D	Rebuilt 1948/9	Ex-Diagram 542
592	Dining Saloon		29	7850-7	VS	Eastleigh 10/23-8/25	No 7853 later Diagram 600
600	Cafeteria car		40	W7853S	VS	Rebuilt 4/50	Ex-Diagram 592

* SR records originally listed all as Diagram 135, later corrected to 213.
Thirds 2320-40 were ex-Firsts 7166/7/89/73-8/83/7/95/8, 7202/3, 7654/6/9/61-3 respectively.
Coaches 7169/80 destroyed by fire 8/36.

Plate 49 'Thanet' Brake Third No 3569 from set 461, seen at Eardley Road carriage sidings in July 1951, still retaining malachite green. *D. Cullum*

Chapter 4.
The 'Thanet' Stock

The almost complete lack of ordinary corridor vehicles on the South Eastern section in 1923 was of considerable concern to the new Southern management. In June 1923 Orders E4, E5 and E6 were authorised for nine eight-coach sets of corridor vehicles, plus five loose Composites, of an unspecified design for London–Ramsgate/Dover services. These were the first orders for new passenger rolling stock placed by the company. The two existing pre-Grouping designs were unsuitable for two reasons: firstly, the SECR 'Continentals' were really only satisfactory for non-stop boat services, having too few passenger doors to cater for ordinary traffic; secondly, the LSWR 'Ironclads' exceeded the permitted width for certain sections of the line. The Chief Civil Engineer refused to sanction vehicles in excess of 8ft 6in width on the lines in North Kent, so Maunsell and Lynes had to come

Plate 50 Corridor Third 980 at Bexhill West in September 1957, in Southern Region green. This was also in set 461, which at that time was used once a week for a Hastings–Walsall inter-Regional service — hardly gainful employment. *J. H. Aston*

Plate 51 Composite No 5535 in four-coach set 425 at Bromley South in April 1949. The slightly odd layout of the corridor-side windows came about through the desire to use only one size of large window frame on this stock. *D. Cullum*

up with a new design for these coaches. Known as the 'Thanet' stock, they were, in effect, an Ashford version of Warner's 'Ironclad' vehicles, having the same 57ft 0in body length but cut down to 8ft 6in wide over body. Many traditional Ashford details were incorporated, making these coaches visibly different from all subsequent SR stock. They were equipped with Maunsell/Lynes SR bogies, British standard gangways and screw couplings.

Three types of vehicle were built — a five-compartment Brake Third, a seven-compartment Composite and an eight-compartment Third. As if to emphasise their Ashford parentage, both diagrams and running numbers were in the former SECR number blocks. When new they carried the LSWR livery of dark green with square lining panels, as depicted in **Figure 1B**. On first overhaul the rounded-panel style was substituted, probably with the later Maunsell green colour. To date the author has been unable to trace any clear photographs of the vehicles carrying their original livery. Construction was shared between Eastleigh and Lancing (probably to expedite production), and they entered service between October 1924 and May 1925. Coach numbers were 3562-79 for the Brake Thirds, 977-94 for the Thirds and 5505-45 for the Composites. Rather surprisingly, no set numbers were allocated, each set originally comprising four Composites in the centre, flanked at each end by a Third and a Brake Third. Apart from the five loose Composites — Nos 5525-29 — all coaches were originally marshalled in numerical sequence, which may be inferred from the following two examples:

First set formed:
3562+977+5505+5506+5507+5508+978+3563
Last set formed:
3578+993+5542+5543+5544+5545+994+3579

Set numbers were not allocated, perhaps because it was anticipated that these initial formations would not remain constant for very long. Catering facilities were provided by insertion of a Pullman First at the centre of the train — presumably the lower orders were not expected to have refreshments!

Services commenced on 17 November 1924, with sets running between Ramsgate and Victoria via Chatham. Most sets were very soon reduced to seven vehicles by the removal of one Third (the Pullman car making a total of eight), allowing some flexibility in the make-up of the trains, with several loose Thirds now being available. At least three of the new coaches made a tour of the West Country in the summer of 1925 (probably as much for staff to view them as for the general public), and they were photographed at Barnstaple Junction (**Plate 3**). This was almost certainly the first time that modern stock had visited the area, as the 'Ironclads' were still confined primarily to the Bournemouth and Portsmouth routes.

By 24 August 1927 the initial formations had certainly changed quite a lot, evident from the formation of the 5pm Cannon Street-Folkestone/Deal service on that day. The train was hauled by 'River' class tank locomotive No A800, which left the track at speed near Sevenoaks. The train comprised a 'Thanet' set of seven coaches plus a Pullman car. Vehicles 3564, 5518/20 and Pullman car *Carmen* were damaged beyond repair, while Composites 5533/41, Third 988 and Brake Third 3575 all sustained some damage but were repaired and returned to traffic. Comparison with the original formations will show that virtually none of these coaches remained in the same sets as when first delivered. This reduced to 74 the number of 'Thanets' in service.

By 1931 there were only eight sets in traffic, set numbers 388, 423-5 and 460-3 now being allocated. Sets 388 and 425 were each formed of just four vehicles, while just 423/4/63 remained as nine coaches, the others all being reduced to seven vehicles. Sets 460-2 only included a Pullman First in addition to the 'Thanets'. By 1935 the formations were as shown at the foot of the page.

The Pullmans included were most often those of the 'J' class, which had been built on ex-LNWR underframes and were fitted with British standard gangways instead of the more usual Pullman type. The other seven Thirds, 16 Composites and Brake Third 3574 were loose stock. The Pullman cars had been reclassified as Composites in 1933, so presumably the Third-class passengers had by then demanded refreshment facilities! Sets 423/4/60-2 were usually found on Victoria-Chatham-Ramsgate services, while the rest (which often did still have a Pullman First added) ran between Charing Cross and Ramsgate via Dover. Some of the loose Composites appeared occasionally on the Central and South Western sections, sometimes running west of Exeter, while loose Brake Third 3574 eventually ran in Maunsell 59ft set 220 as a replacement for coach 3714, which had been damaged by fire at Swanley Junction on 10 March 1938. Composite No 5537 was also burnt out at Swanley and was converted into staff cinema coach 1308s in November 1939 (and is further described in Chapter 14).

No other permanent set changes were made until 1940, when these Pullman facilities were withdrawn for the duration of the war. Many of the sets became spare at this time, owing to the reduced traffic levels experienced throughout Kent. In 1941, only set 461 had a booked regular working, outward from Charing Cross to Margate and returning to Victoria from Ramsgate — and this on Sundays only. The other sets were held spare at various carriage sidings, but, with the inevitable disruption of the period, probably saw some intermittent use. Set 388 suffered damage by enemy action in November/December 1940, causing the withdrawal of Composites 5513/4, their place being taken in the set by Nos 5523/40, which had been removed from set 462. In turn, Third 992 replaced the Composites in set 462, which now ran with seven vehicles only. These vehicles were destined to be unlucky, as set 460 was involved in an accident at Catford in 1946, with the further loss of coaches 977/91 and 3563, bringing the total number of 'Thanets' down to 68. The losses to this set were made good using Thirds 978/9 and 59ft Brake Third 3677.

Two-coach sets 331-3 were formed in 1946 for the Ashford-Hastings line, each including an ex-SECR birdcage Corridor Brake Composite paired with 'Thanet' Thirds 989/8/5 respectively. One of these is illustrated in **Plate 8**. In this instance the Third ran in crimson lake and cream, but the SECR Brake was in green, while, for some sets, the reverse applied.

The other eight sets remained on Kent Coast- or occasional Oxted-line duties until the completion of Stage 1 of the Kent Coast electrification — although set 461 was kept at Bexhill West

Set No	Vehicles
388	3566+5513+5514+3573 (after 1940 formed 3566+5523+5540+3573)
423	3567+5516+5515+5543+Pullman Composite+983+3570
424	3571+5528+986+982+5542+Pullman Composite+5536+3579
425	3565+5535+5539+3575
460	3562+977+5507+991+5506+Pullman Composite+5508+3563
461	3568+980+5511+5510+Pullman Composite+5509+5512+3569
462	3576+5534+Pullman Composite+5533+993+5540+5523+3577
463	3572+994+984+5532+5526+990+3578

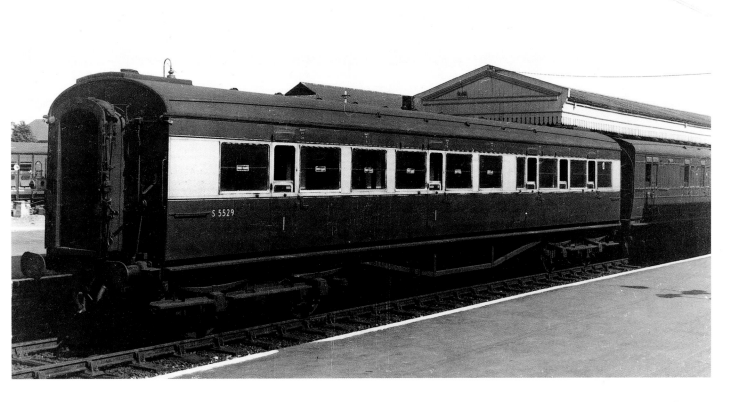

Plate 52 A few of the Composites — easily the most numerous 'Thanets' — carried crimson lake and cream, in this case with broad cantrail band and left-hand numerals. No 5529 is seen at Fareham in July 1950, at the rear of a Portsmouth-bound local otherwise composed of ex-LSWR stock. Whilst the permanently-formed 'Thanet' sets were seldom seen away from the South Eastern section, the loose Composites sometimes wandered far and wide. *D. Cullum*

in the 1950s, for a Hastings-Walsall Summer Saturday through service. To reach Bexhill West the set had to run from St Leonards and reverse at Crowhurst Junction; being Route Restriction 1, it could not negotiate Mountfield Tunnel further up the Hastings direct line.

Some vehicle changes had taken place during the 1950s, there being very few loose Thirds or Composites in service after 1955. Almost complete withdrawal came in 1958/9, when all except Brake Thirds (now Brake Seconds) 3566/73 were taken out of traffic. These two remained in use until late 1961, coach 3566 in set 465 on the Margate-Canterbury miners' train and coach 3573 in set 156 on the Clapham Junction-Kensington Olympia service.

Seven Brake vehicles entered departmental service, several being favoured by the Work Study section as mobile offices — their arrival at any particular location most definitely not being welcomed by the local staff! Five Composites were converted to staff and tool vans, while the body of Third 981 was grounded as a mess room at Horsham. Composite 5542 was put to similar use at Newhaven Harbour but remained on its bogies and could thus be moved around as required. None survived into preservation.

Figures 11-13 illustrate the three types of coach.

Table 5
Summary of Maunsell 'Thanet' stock

Diagram No	Vehicle Type	Seats 1st	Seats 3rd	Running Nos	Built by
53	Eight-compartment Third		64	977-86	Eastleigh 10/24-3/25
				987-94	Lancing 3/25-5/25
165	Five-compartment Brake Third		40	3562-71	Eastleigh 10/24-3/25
				3572-9	Lancing 3/25-5/25
317	Seven-compartment Composite	16	24	5505-29	Eastleigh 10/24-5/25
				5530-45	Lancing 3/25-5/25

Notes
1. Vehicles 977/91, 3563/4, 5513/4/8/20/37 all withdrawn as a result of accident damage or enemy action.
2. All coaches were Route Restriction 1.

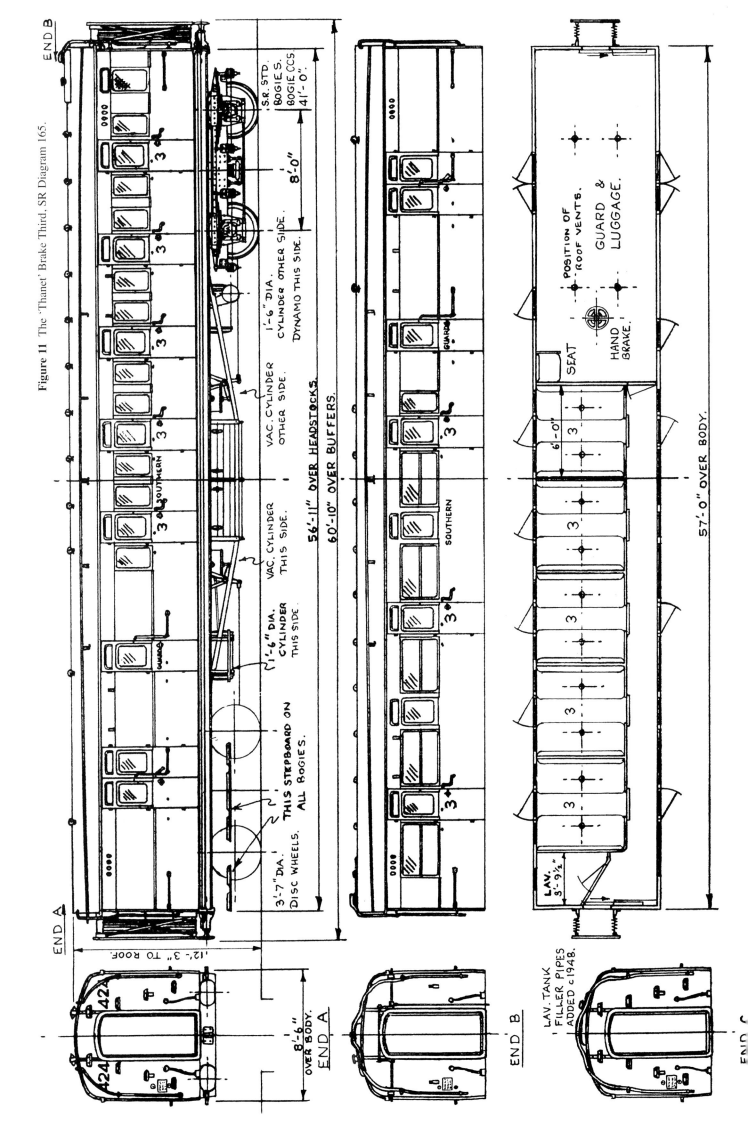

Figure 11 The 'Thanet' Brake Third. SR Diagram 165.

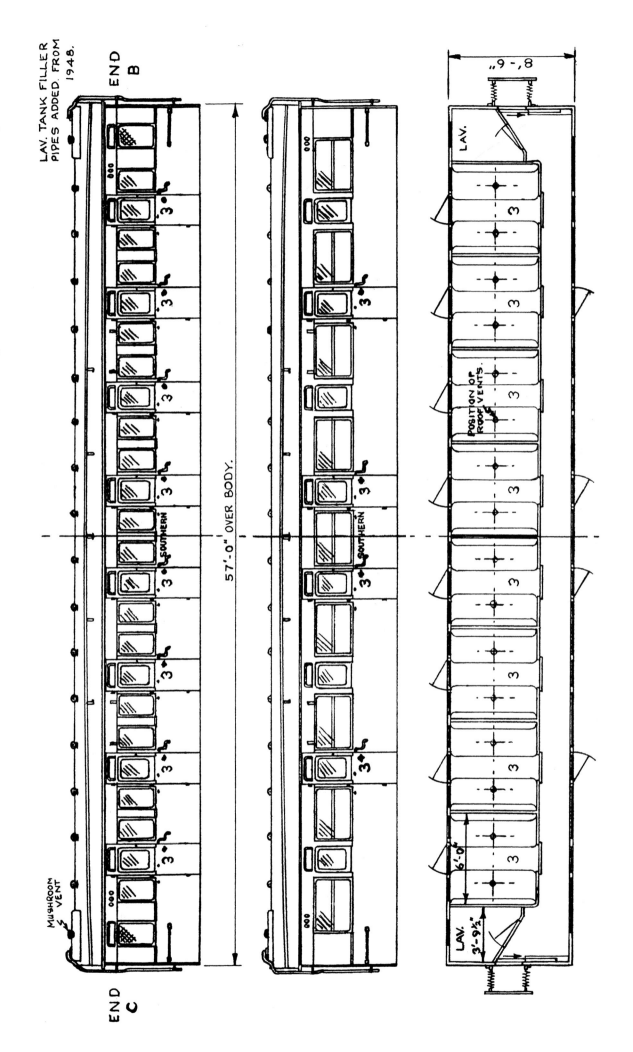

Figure 12 The 'Thanet' Corridor Third, SR Diagram 53.

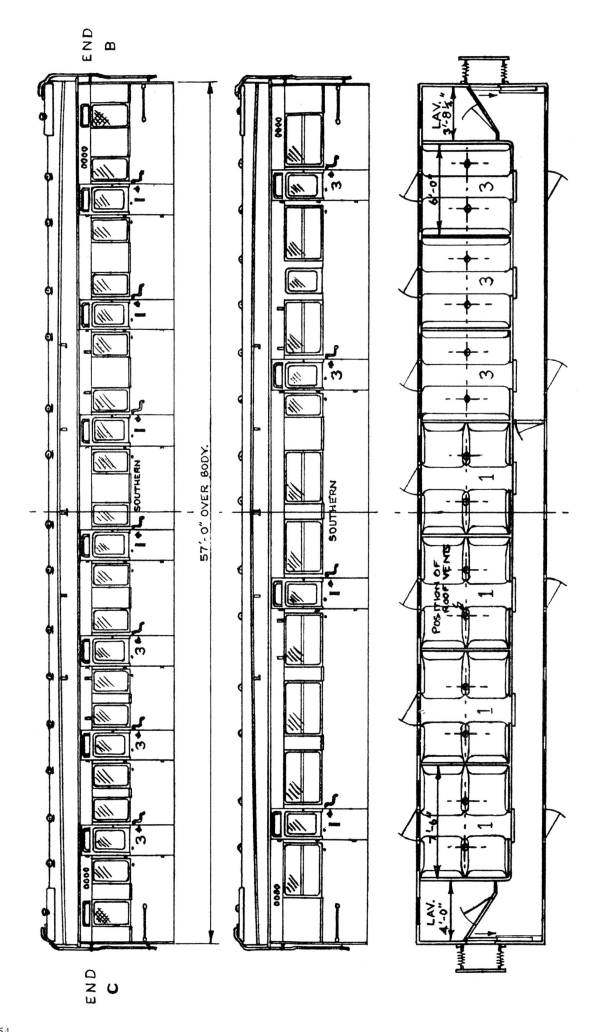

Figure 13 The 'Thanet' Corridor Composite, SR Diagram 317.

Chapter 5.
Maunsell Stock 1926-1934

We now enter the period during which most Maunsell steam-hauled carriage stock would be built. In 1926 main-line electrification was still something for the future, so a considerable number of new steam-hauled vehicles would be needed in the meantime. Further orders for pre-Grouping LSWR and SECR vehicles, plus the 'Thanets', had dealt with immediate needs, which allowed Maunsell and Lynes some time to prepare designs for the future Southern 'standard' vehicles. These would need to take account of the various width restrictions then in force — including those on the Tonbridge-Hastings line, where vehicles of not more than 8ft 1in width were required. Apart from a couple of hastily contrived ex-SECR/LSWR Corridor sets, one of which appears in **Plate 11**, all services on the line were still in the hands of SECR Non-corridors. Six new Pullman cars of restricted width were introduced in 1926, but with precious little else to run with them.

The decision to standardise on Pullman-type gangways and buck-eye couplings had been taken in January 1924 — unsurprising, in view of the reliance on Pullman cars for the provision of catering on the Central and South Eastern sections. That said, it must be added that some Pullmans were equipped with British standard gangways and screw couplings. The use of Pullman gangways and buck-eye couplings (or Gould automatic couplings, to name them after their designer) had been pioneered by Gresley on the Great Northern, so the LNER readily agreed to continue their use; the GWR also agreed but swiftly reverted to the British Standard type, while the LMS remained faithful to BS gangways and screw couplings. Thus from 1923 to 1948 the situation existed whereby two companies were using one system and two another. This meant that some Maunsell vehicles had to be equipped with BS gangways at one or both ends for through services to some destinations and also required most vehicles fitted with BS gangways to have adaptors provided, so they could match any vehicle with Pullman-type fittings. Starting in 1926, the Southern's workshops would be obliged to manufacture many sets of these adaptors, in order that they could be fitted to ex-LSWR and SECR corridor vehicles, as well as the 'Thanets' and the Corridor Luggage Vans built from 1930.

One obvious advantage of using Pullman gangways arose from their semi-rigid construction and the fact that they incorporated their own buffing gear; this, plus the buck-eye coupling, rendered the use of side buffers unnecessary but required the coach body to be slightly longer than the underframe, to give clearance for the buffing gear. Maunsell standardised an underframe length of 58ft (actually 57ft 11in over headstocks) with a body length of 58ft at the corners and 59ft at the centre. This remained the standard for all new steam-hauled stock until 1945, although contemporary electric vehicles were rather longer. Few vehicles were built without retractable side buffers, as the need to couple with other screw-coupled stock remained, but a few three-coach sets lost their intermediate side buffers experimentally from 1928 onwards. **Plate 53** shows a Maunsell 9ft-wide coach end with Pullman gangway and buck-eye coupling, the latter dropped down to reveal a standard coupling hook behind.

The 'low-window' stock 1926-9

The first new designs were ready by early 1925, and at the Rolling Stock Committee Meeting in April of that year the following programme of construction was proposed:

Plate 53 The non-brake end of Brake Composite No 6648 at Yeovil Town in September 1948. The buck-eye coupling has been dropped clear of the standard coupling hook, and the buffers have been extended fully to allow a locomotive to couple to the coach. Note the circular tare (empty) weight and Route Restriction plates, plus the rectangular dimension plate. The latter gave the overall length and width details, in this case 61ft 7in and 9ft 3in respectively. This coach has already been equipped with lavatory-tank filler pipes. *A. E. West*

HOO No	Stock	Coach/set Nos
E94	Ten three-coach trains for London-Plymouth/Torrington/Ilfracombe services	390-399
E95	One eight-coach train for London-Eastbourne services	470
E96	One eight-coach train for London-Worthing services	469
A97	One 11-coach train for London-Newhaven boat services	(See text)
E98/99	Six First-class Kitchen/Dining cars and six Third-class Dining Saloons for SW section services	7858-69
E100	One 10-coach train for Waterloo-Southampton Docks boat services	(See text)
E101	10 Corridor Brake Composites for Waterloo-West of England services	6565-74
E102	10 General Saloons for race, boat and school-party traffic	7974-83

Orders E103 and A104 were also placed for new luggage vans, described in later chapters.

Authority for construction was given in August 1925, and work started with the vehicles for West of England services at Eastleigh early in 1926. At first all were intended to be 9ft wide, including the coaches for Eastbourne services, but this had to be revised somewhat following a side-scrape in Lewes Tunnel during March 1927, of which more anon.

The 10 three-coach sets for Waterloo-West of England services entered traffic between July and October 1926, formed of two Brake Thirds, with just four compartments each, and a Composite in the centre, with three Third- and four First-class compartments. Seating capacity was thus quite low, but a considerable amount of luggage space was available within each van. The Brake Thirds were similar in one respect to the 'Ironclads' which preceded them, half of the coach being given over to the guard's van and luggage space. Pressed-steel lookouts were provided for the guard, and to accommodate these within the loading gauge the bodyside of the entire luggage van was reduced to 8ft 7in wide, giving a somewhat curious half-rounded, half-flat bodyside profile. The flat-sided luggage van would continue to be incorporated into all 9ft-wide Maunsell Brake vehicles — making this (plus the lookout) Maunsell's trademark carriage-stock feature. On the corridor side alternate compartments had direct access through a door, but at the other locations there was just a droplight, which passengers would inevitably lower to reach for a non-existent door handle (despite internal 'NO EXIT' notices above the droplights); it was not until the 1934 design changes that this annoying feature was replaced. All corridor-side windows were the same height as those on the compartment side — a characteristic of all coaches built from 1926 until mid-1929.

Coach numbers were 3214-33 for the Brake Thirds and 5137-46 for the Composites. The Composites were completed in advance of the Brakes, so when the time came to marshal the sets together only the Brakes were in strict numerical sequence, the Composites going into the sets in the random order that the works shunter provided them. In the event, sets 390-9 received Composites 5138/9/41/37/43/6/0/2/4/5 respectively. Incidentally, the Brake coaches would have been completed in the carriage shop the same way round, so one of each pair would have to be turned on the triangle behind the locomotive shed at Eastleigh before final placing in each set. There would then be a trial run to Romsey or Micheldever before the stock was released to traffic. **Plates 54 and 55**, together with **Figures 14 and 15**, illustrate these vehicles.

The 10 Brake Composites were intended for through services to the numerous West Country branch lines, the South Western already having 45 similar wooden-panelled corridor vehicles allocated to these duties. They included four Third- and two First-class compartments, together with a much shorter guard's/luggage van featuring the same narrowing of the bodyside but for only about a quarter of the length of the vehicle. **Plate 56** shows one of these coaches in BR days.

Next to be completed, in December 1926 and February 1927, were the two sets for the Central section. These also owed something to the two 'Ironclad' sets that preceded them: both included six-compartment Brake Thirds and incorporated a high level of First-class accommodation. Set formations were as follows:

Vehicles	Set 469	Set 470
Six-compartment Brake Third	4048	4051
Eight-compartment Third(s)	2350/1	2354
Seven-compartment Firsts	7665-7	7671-4
Eight-compartment Third	2349	2355
Six-compartment Brake Third	4049	4050

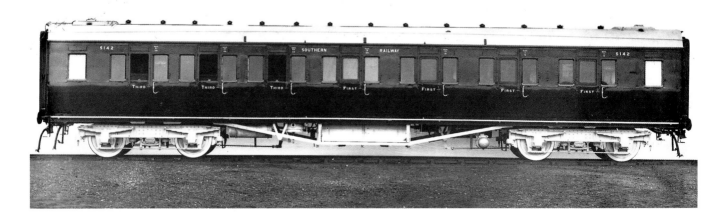

Plate 54 Diagram 2301 Composite No 5142 as completed in October 1926 and placed in set 397. The underframe (but not the bodywork) has been finished in photographic grey livery, all of which would have been repainted black before the coach entered traffic. *Southern Railway*

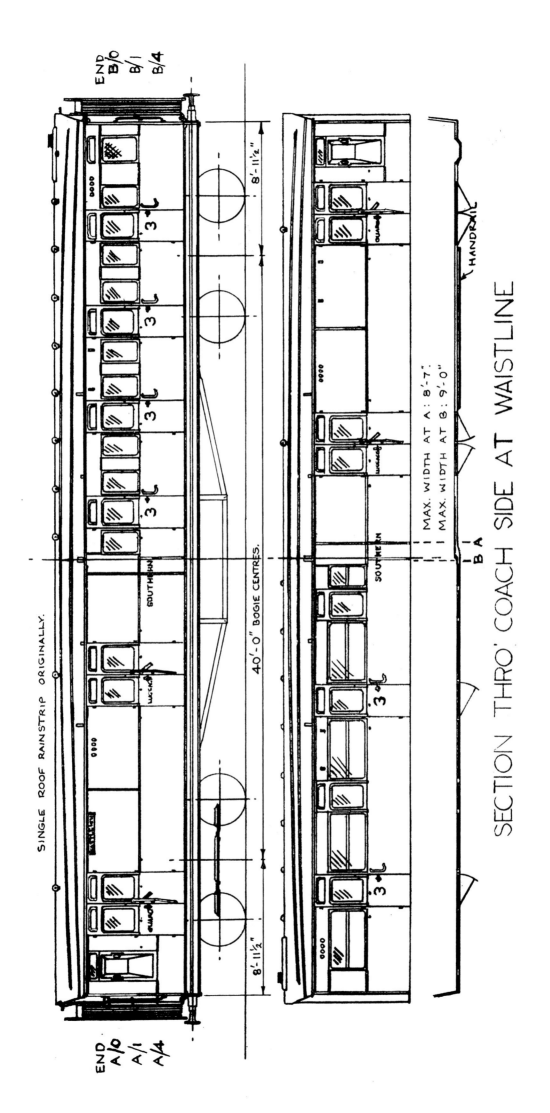

Figure 14 Diagram 2101 low-window four-compartment Brake Third. The high-window version appears as **Figure 23**. For end details see **Figure 20**

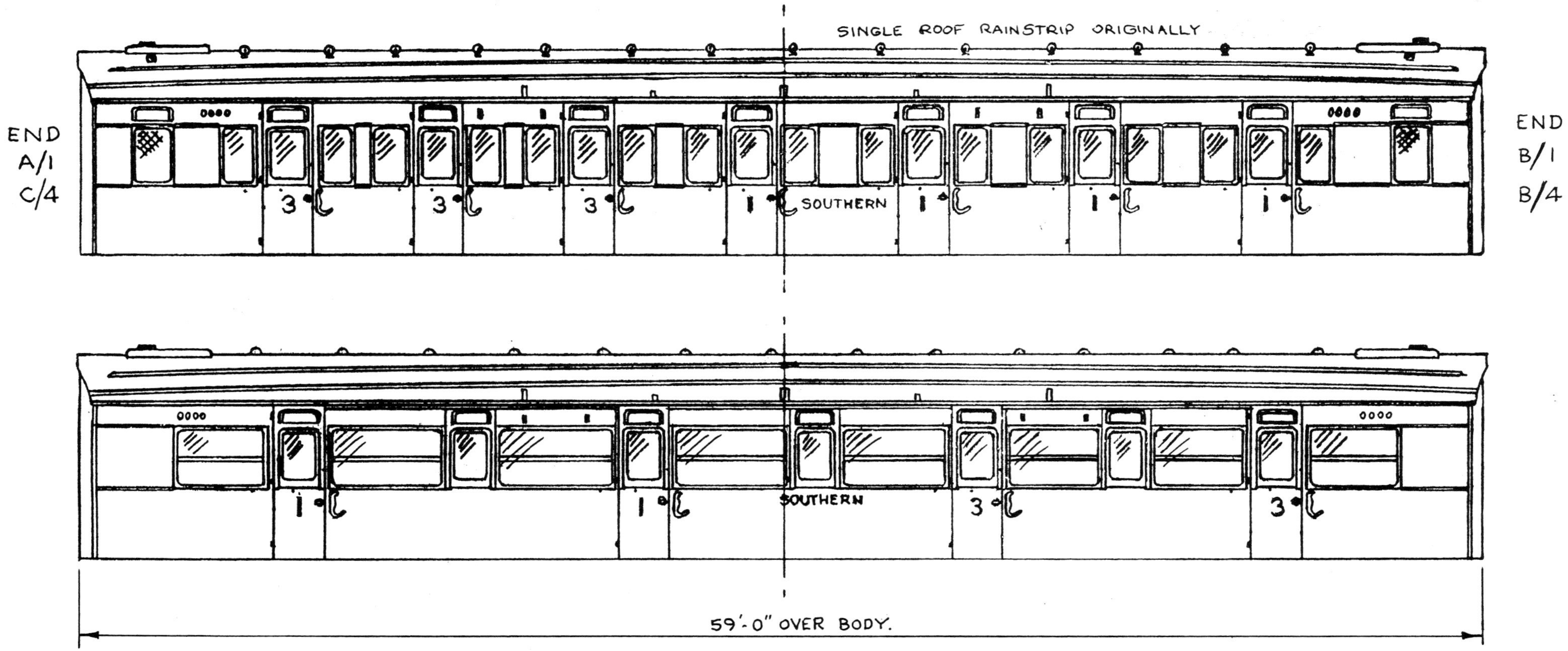

Figure 15 Diagram 2301 low-window Composite.

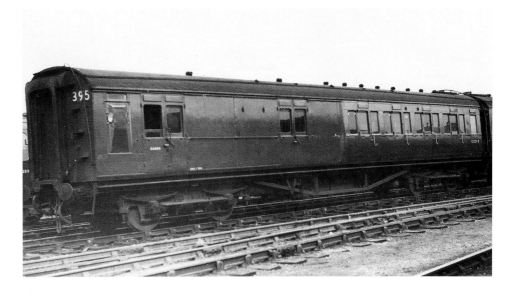

Plate 55 Brake Third No 3224, to Diagram 2101, at Eastleigh in September 1959, carrying Southern Region green. Three-coach sets 390-9 were regularly used on Somerset & Dorset-line local services during the 1950s, and all retained their original formations until withdrawn between 1958 and 1961. Close examination of the photograph will reveal that this set has lost its intermediate buffers. *A. E. West*

Set 470 had not been running for very long on London-Eastbourne services before a side-scrape occurred at the southern end of Lewes Tunnel, causing the banning of all 9ft-wide vehicles from this section of line. Set 470 was immediately transferred to the London-Worthing route, joining set 469 on these services. The problem was not caused just by the Maunsell vehicles, as, following this incident, a start was also made on removing the side lookouts from ex-LBSCR Brake vehicles. This did have one advantage, however: the LBSCR three-coach sets so modified could now join the substantial pool of SECR 'Birdcage' three-coach sets Type R (for 'Rover') on many Central- and South Eastern-section local services. The Rolling Stock Committee also decreed that the general standard for newly built trains should now be 8ft 6in wide, resulting in a greater number of these coaches being completed from 1928 to 1933 than might have originally been planned.

Construction of the next 11 9ft-wide vehicles for Newhaven boat services was already far advanced by this stage and was allowed to proceed on the strict instruction that no other train be allowed on the adjacent line between Cooksbridge and Lewes

Plate 56 Diagram 2401 low-window Brake Composite No 6567 at Clapham Junction in August 1956, at that time formed with 1935 Brake Composite 2788 (just visible at left) as 2-P set 29, for West of England local services. On Summer Saturdays these would be pressed into main-line service and could be seen on Waterloo trains, as here. Livery is Southern Region green, as repainted just one month previously. *J. H. Aston*

Plate 57 1927-vintage Corridor Third No 2350 of set 469, at Ramsgate in August 1948, in malachite green. Diagram 2001 was allocated. This set was originally built for London—Worthing services and was transferred to the Kent Coast in 1935, being reduced to six coaches by the removal of Firsts Nos 7666/7. *J. H. Aston*

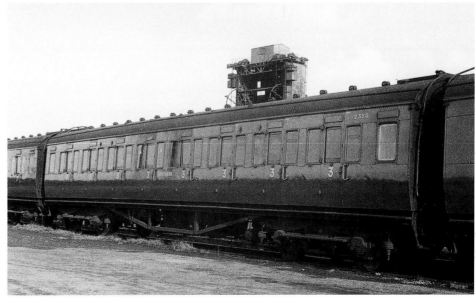

while the boat train was passing; with only one set of vehicles involved, this was not considered too great an operating restriction. Appendix 2 on page 224 gives the official operating arrangement (Clause 4e). The simple expedient of substituting other stock was not easily available, as this set uniquely included Second-class accommodation. On electrification of the line in 1935 the tunnel was opened out and the restriction lifted. The vehicles, constituting Order A97, were:

Eight-compartment Thirds	2352/3
Six-compartment Brake Seconds	4481/2 (structurally identical to Brake Thirds)
Eight-compartment Seconds	4483-6 (structurally identical to Thirds)
Seven-compartment Firsts	7668-70

The coaches were (unusually) completed at Ashford Works in June 1927. **Plate 58** shows one of the Brake Seconds as running in 1952. As with other boat trains, no permanent set number was allocated, and the train could often be formed with fewer than the full complement of vehicles. In September 1928 the basic formation was:

4481+Pullman First+7669+4484+4482 (with 2353 added for the night service only)

The other six vehicles were spare for use as required. Some remained on the service for a considerable period, as seen in **Plate 58** A rare bird indeed! Newhaven boat-train Brake Second No 4482 is seen at Eardley Road sidings in April 1952, retaining malachite green but with the door numerals in BR (rather than Southern Railway) positions (compare with **Plate 57**). The coach is coupled between a Restriction 1 Maunsell, with broad crimson cantrail panel, and a BR standard Mk 1 coach. *D. Cullum*

Plate 27. All Second-class coaches were demoted to Third class in 1954, being renumbered as Thirds 1921-4 and Brake Thirds 2772/3. It is believed that at least one coach was renumbered incorrectly, the error being spotted only when two vehicles bearing the same number turned up at the same location together!

The Southampton boat set — Order E100 — mirrored the 1922 'Ironclad' sets exactly, being formed of eight Corridor Firsts with a Pantry Brake First at each end. The nominal formation was:

7715+7208+7209+7210+7211+7212+7213+7214+7215+7716

Plate 59 Southampton Docks Corridor First 7208, seen in Southern Region green at Eastleigh in September 1958. *A. E. West*

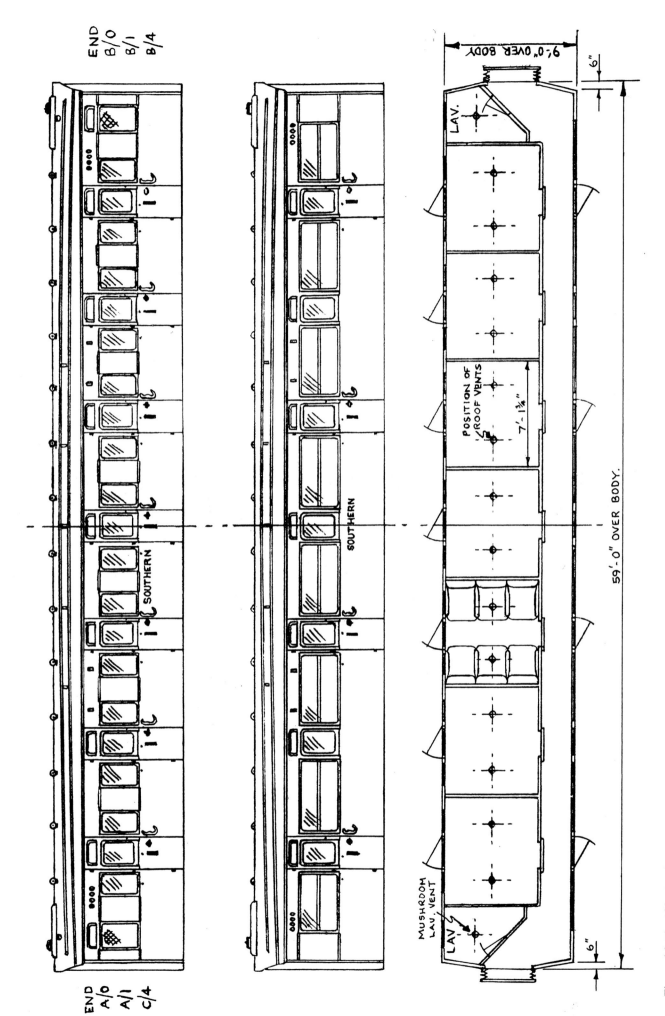

Figure 16 The 1927 Corridor First, SR Diagram 2501.

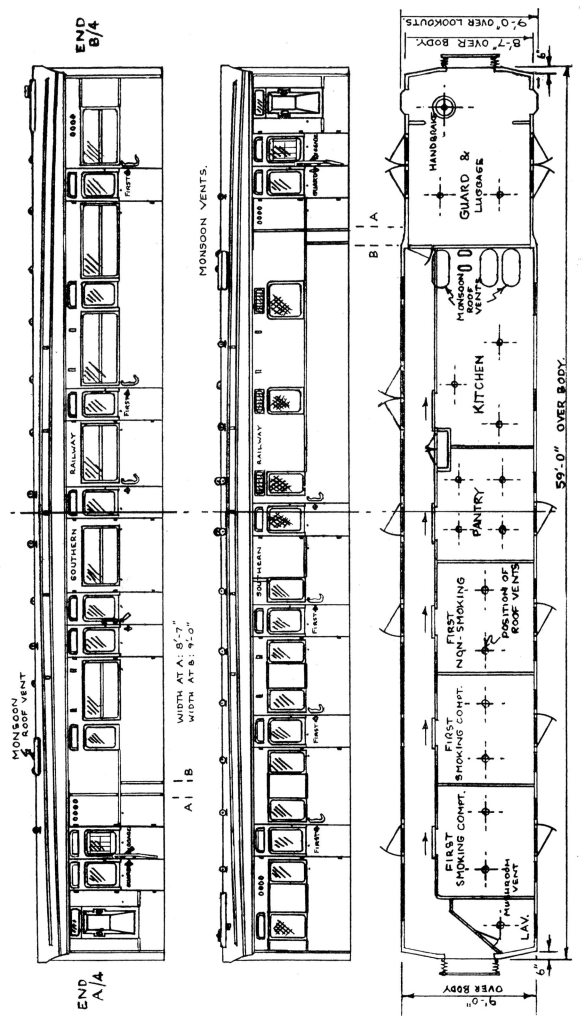

Figure 17 The 1928 Pantry Brake First, SR Diagram 2551. When rebuilt as six-compartment Brake Firsts, the kitchen/pantry section was occupied by three compartments of equal width. On the corridor side the opening doors were then opposite the first, third, fourth and sixth compartments.

Plate 60 The corridor side of Pantry Brake First No 7715 at Southampton Docks in September 1935. Compare the livery with the photographic grey finish of 7716 in **Plate 20**. *F. Foote*

Plate 61 Brake First rebuild No 7716, with broad crimson cantrail band and left-hand numerals, at Clapham Junction in September 1949. Compare with Bulleid Corridor First No 7608, just visible at the left. The shunting trucks, SR Nos 61322/3, spent most of their working lives at Clapham Yard and are described further in Volume 4 of *An Illustrated History of Southern Wagons* (OPC 2002). *D. Cullum*

Plate 62 Kitchen/Dining First No 7861 as completed in May 1927, recorded in photographic grey livery. The original six cars to Diagram 2651 did not have a transverse vestibule with doors at the right-hand end — all later Kitchen/Diners were so equipped. Compare with **Plates 100, 101 and 102**. *Southern Railway*

The Firsts were completed in July 1927, but the Pantry Brakes did not follow until June 1928, so again the full formation was not always required. **Plates 20 and 60** illustrate the Pantry Brake — the least numerous of all the Maunsell designs. Their subsequent history is almost identical to that of the 'Ironclad' Pantry Brakes, and they were similarly rebuilt in 1949 as six-compartment Brake Firsts, continuing to run on Waterloo-Southampton boat trains until withdrawn in 1961 (**Plate 61**).

The six Kitchen and Dining saloon pairs were completed May-July 1927, primarily for Waterloo-Bournemouth/Portsmouth services. Although not necessarily running together, each pair was originally placed in 'Ironclad' Six-Dining sets 'A'-type Nos 431-5/44. The First-class Kitchen vehicles, labelled 'DINING SALOON' in true South Western manner, had four bays of seating at one end with a pantry and fully equipped kitchen at the other. Vehicle numbers were 7858-63 (see **Plate 62**). The Third-class Dining Saloons seated 64 passengers in eight bays, the saloon being divided into three sections. A lavatory was provided at one end (normally that coupled farthest from the adjacent Kitchen car), with two end vestibules. To give clearance for the opening doors and grab-handles at each end, this portion of the bodyside

Plate 63 Third-class Dining Saloon No 7867, again in photographic grey livery when first built in July 1927, to Diagram 2652. This would be coupled to the kitchen end of Diagram 2651. *Southern Railway*

was recessed to 8ft 7in wide, rather like the Brake vehicles. Coach numbers were originally 7864-9 (see **Plate 63**).

Both types of vehicle were extensively described in *The Locomotive* magazine for 14 April 1928, which stated that the First-class seating was upholstered in green imitation leather, the Thirds in a similar brown material. The carpet in the First-class saloon was figured blue and old gold, while the Thirds had a brown 'cork' linoleum finish, with carpet (in similar blue and old gold) along the corridor portion only. The vehicles spent most of their lives on the South Western section, although not always running together, but, whereas the Saloon Third design was not repeated (at least not in this form), the Kitchen First design formed the basis of all subsequent Maunsell catering vehicles built until 1934. Both types will be described and drawn together at the end of this chapter, along with the subsequent history of these original 12 vehicles.

The Dining Saloon Thirds were permanently reclassified as Open Thirds in 1930, being renumbered soon after as 1363-8, and were collected together between 1938 and 1942 in SW-section 'special traffic' set 310. This also included two ex-LSWR wooden-panelled Corridor Brake Thirds and an ex-SECR 'Continental' First as the centre vehicle. From 1944 to 1946 three ran in Oxted-line eight-coach 'business' set 194, before all six were returned to dining-car duties in 1947, renumbered as Composite Diners 7841-4 and Night Ferry First-class Diners 7846/47; their subsequent history also appears at the end of this chapter. Rather confusingly, their original coach numbers (7864-9) were reallocated to new restaurant cars built in 1932.

The last 10 vehicles of the 1925 orders were General Saloons 7974-83, completed at Eastleigh in January 1928 on underframes provided by the Midland Railway Carriage & Wagon Co. These alone were 8ft 6in wide and were open-plan, with seven bays of seats of almost First-class standard. They were known as Nondescript Saloons and could be labelled First, Second or Third class, using removable side boards, as occasion demanded. In later years most were employed on Folkestone or Dover boat services, but they were originally intended for First-class race traffic, Second-class boat accommodation or very comfortable Third-class school or party traffic. It was not long, however, before some were being substituted for the Dining Saloons described above, especially if First-class patronage was expected to be high. Their restricted width ensured that they could travel over almost all sections of the Southern Railway system. They were the first batch of 62 similar vehicles completed between 1928 and 1931, illustrated in the next section.

The next three groups of authorisations, dated November 1926, February and July 1927, are listed at the foot of the page.

Also ordered at this time were the final 10 'Continental' vehicles described in Chapter 3 (Order E162). Some detail changes were made before construction commenced. Internally the traditional droplights suspended on heavy leather straps were replaced by counter-balanced droplights, with a spring-loaded closure bar at the bottom, while Third-class seating was altered from bench-type to hammock-sprung cushions. Externally a flat cornice plate replaced the heavy moulded cornice rail, and the brackets for roof destination boards were moved higher up the roof, away from the cornice plates. Earlier vehicles eventually had their brackets repositioned similarly, while from 1929 most coaches had two roof rain strips fitted on each side.

Three-coach sets 445-8 were very similar to sets 390-9 completed previously. In this instance they were formed with all coaches in correct numerical sequence, Brake Thirds being Nos 4055-62, with Composites 5147-50. Some sources state that they were built by the Metropolitan Carriage, Wagon & Finance Co.

HOO No	*Stock*	*Coach/set Nos*
E160	Two eight-coach trains for Kent Coast & Eastbourne services	467/8
E163	10 general saloons for race, boat and school party traffic	7984-93
E241	10 Corridor Thirds for Waterloo-Southampton boat services	769-78
E242	12 Corridor Firsts for Waterloo-Southampton boat services	7216-27
E250	Four three-coach trains for London-Plymouth/Torrington/Ilfracombe services	445-8
E268	50 Corridor Thirds for general use	783-832
E286	Two eight-coach trains for London-Eastbourne services	465/6
E288	Six four-coach trains for London-Folkestone/Deal/Ramsgate services	449-54

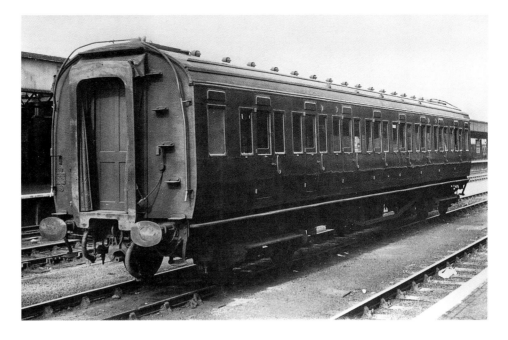

Plate 64 Typical of the Restriction 4 Corridor Thirds built between 1926 and 1928, No 808 was completed in March 1928, probably by Birmingham Railway Carriage & Wagon Co, and is seen standing on one of the centre through roads at Exeter Central in September 1958. Livery is Southern Region green. *A. E. West*

The Carriage Working Notices referred to them as 3-P Corridor sets, the 'P' indicating that Pullman gangways were fitted. They joined the earlier sets on West of England services in August/September 1928 and, owing to their low seating capacity, seldom moved away from the South Western section, being seen on Waterloo-Bournemouth-Weymouth trains as well as on the West of England main line. In their final years these and sets 390-9 were often allocated to the Somerset & Dorset Joint line, returning to main-line services only at Summer Saturday peak periods. The other 9ft-wide stock, Corridor Thirds 769-78/83-832 and Corridor Firsts 7216-27, entered traffic between July 1927 and April 1928. All were loose stock, although some would later be incorporated into sets. Some of these vehicles (or at least their underframes) were built by outside contractors — Metropolitan, Midland or BRCW — as the workshops were undergoing much reorganisation at this time, but all had HOO numbers allocated, so perhaps the original intention was for Eastleigh to construct them all. **Plate 64** shows a typical Corridor Third.

The remaining orders were all for 8ft 6in-wide vehicles. The 10 General Saloons were as before and also suffered from the 'dummy droplight' syndrome, only alternate bays having direct access to a door, as seen in **Plate 65**. Some of these were later reclassified as permanent Seconds (a few from later batches being renumbered into the Second-class series, as apparent from **Plate 96**), while in the 1950s some gravitated to excursion and other seasonal traffic — a far cry from their boat-train duties. All other vehicles were standard side-corridor coaches with side elevation similar to that of the 9ft stock (save for the lack of lookouts on the Brake Thirds); in these cases the whole of the coach side was almost flat, with just a slight tumble-home below the waistline.

Plate 65 1931-batch General or Nondescript Saloon No 7787 being exhibited at an unidentified location, together with a Restaurant car, Corridor Third and a 'Lord Nelson' class 4-6-0. The General Saloon is clearly not ex works, unlike the other stock. All 62 vehicles built to Diagram 2653 were identical, irrespective of their construction date. This shows the lavatory side — on the other side there was no vent over the two end windows. *Author's collection*

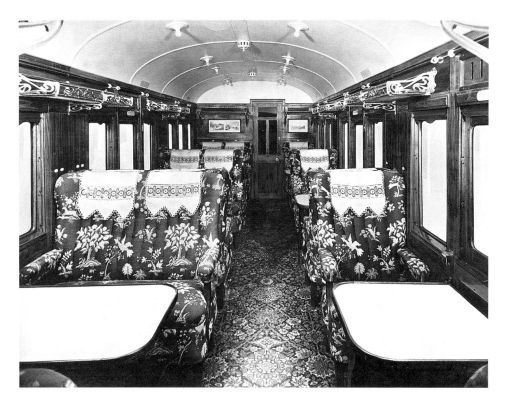

Plate 66 An interior view of one of the Nondescript Saloons, showing the comfortable seating. The photograph was taken in November 1938, so is likely to be of one of the 'Improved Boat Stock' Second-class Saloons, Nos 4391-7, for 'Golden Arrow' service. *Southern Railway*

Plate 67 The Restriction 1 four-compartment Brake Thirds were possibly the least distinctive of all the Maunsell 59ft designs. Near St Mary Cray Junction on 13 June 1959 'N1' class 2-6-0 No 31876 heads a down train formed of 10-coach set 460 with Diagram 2103 Brake No 4066 leading, followed by a pair of Nondescript Saloons and seven 'Thanets'. *P. H. Groom*

Plate 68 From the compartment side the same coach is even less obviously a Maunsell vehicle. No 4066 awaits the call to the scrapyard at Worthy Down spur in August 1962, surrounded by condemned Gangwayed Bogie Luggage Vans. The vehicle was actually withdrawn from traffic in November 1961. *P. H. Swift*

Plate 69 Six-compartment Restriction 1 Brake Third 4079 at Redhill in June 1963, still running in set 454. It lasted for a further six months after the picture was taken. *J. H. Aston*

Plate 70 Former Restriction 1 First-class coach No 7393, now running as Third No 656, at Clapham Junction in February 1960. Diagram 2502 was originally allocated, this being revised to 2022 upon reclassification in June 1954. *K. G. Carr*

Plate 71 'L1' class 4-4-0 No 784 heads a Kent Coast service comprising Restriction 1 set 449 with a Pullman car in the centre, *c*1930. Apart from the provision of the Pullman, the same train formation could still be seen in Kent until 1961. *Author's collection*

Sets 467/8 were unique in having four-compartment Brake Thirds (the only Restriction 1 vehicles of this type built) and entered service in October and November 1928 respectively. Formations are shown to the right.

Both sets normally ran with a Pullman car in the centre of the train.

Vehicle	Set 467	Set 468
Four-compartment Brake Third	4063	4065
Eight-compartment Third	765	767
Seven-compartment Composites	5151-4	5155-8
Eight-compartment Third	766	768
Four-compartment Brake Third	4064	4066

Two more eight-coach sets were provided for London-Eastbourne services in March/April 1929, these being specifically for morning and evening businessmen's trains and thus including four Corridor Firsts instead of the Composites. The Brake Thirds also contained six compartments, as the volume of luggage expected on such services was considerably less. Formations were:

Vehicle	Set 465	Set 466
Six-compartment Brake Third	4079	4081
Eight-compartment Third	833	835
Seven-compartment Firsts	7390-3	7394-7
Eight-compartment Third	834	836
Six-compartment Brake Third	4080	4082

Again, either set would operate with one or two Pullman cars at the centre of the formation. In later years the First-class accommodation was reduced, and the sets were transferred to the Kent Coast lines. In 1954 Firsts 7393/4/6 were downgraded to Thirds 656-8 (**Plate 70**).

Four-coach sets 449-54 were the first of a number of 8ft 6in-wide sets completed from 1929 to 1931 specifically for either Eastbourne or Kent Coast traffic. Formed of two Composites and two six-compartment Brake Thirds, these and the later sets became the mainstay of services between Charing Cross/Cannon Street and Folkestone/Dover/Deal/Ramsgate for the next 30 years, often running with a Pullman car added in the centre, as seen in **Plate 71**. Sets 449-54 were formed of Brake Thirds 4067-78 and Composites 5159-70 in matched pairs — formations that would endure almost until their withdrawal in the 1960s.

This brings (almost) to an end the low-window period of Maunsell 59ft vehicles. Further Dining cars, Open Thirds and the later Nondescript Saloons would also perpetuate the style, but from mid-1929 most corridor-side windows were extended almost to roof level, giving standing passengers a far better view of the passing scenery and resulting in a far brighter interior for the coaches.

Table 6 summarises the 'low-window' vehicles completed between 1926 and April 1929.

The 'high-window' stock 1929-34

A note on all diagrams for Maunsell 1926-34 side-corridor vehicles reads: 'Vehicles built since 1928 have large corridor lights, 1/10/43' — the date presumably that on which it was decided (belatedly) to upgrade the diagrams. While this was to have a profound effect on the appearance of the vehicles, it meant little to the Operating Department and did not warrant the issuing of a new diagram number. To all intents and purposes, the change was of no significance whatsoever. However, the travelling public was probably of a very different opinion. Strictly speaking, the note should have read '....since June 1929', as the first coaches to have this feature entered service at that time, having been ordered in August 1928. (**Plate 72** shows the improved appearance.) Those orders were as listed on page 69:

Table 6
Summary of Maunsell 'low-window' stock 1926-9

Diagram No	RR	Vehicle Type	Seats 1st	2nd	3rd	Running Nos	Built by	Remarks
2001	4	Eight-compartment Third			64	769-78	Eastleigh 7-8/27	
						783-832*	Eastleigh/BRCW/Metro 3-7/28	823-32 believed built Eastleigh
						2349-55	Ashford/Eastleigh 12/26-6/27	2352/3 built Ashford
						1921-4	(Renumbered 10/54-1/55)	Ex-Seconds 4483-6
2003	1	Eight-compartment Third			64	765-68	Eastleigh 10-11/28	
						833-6	Eastleigh 4/29	
2022	1	Seven-compartment Third			42	656-8	(Renumbered 5-6/54)	Ex-Firsts 7393/4/6
2101	4	Four-compartment Brake Third			32	3214-33	Eastleigh 7-10/26	
						4055-62	Metro 8-9/28	
2102	4	Six-compartment Brake Third			48	4048-51	Eastleigh 12/26-2/27	
						2772/3	(Renumbered 12/54)	Ex-Brake Seconds 4481/2
2103	1	Four-compartment Brake Third			32	4063-6	Eastleigh 10-11/28	
2104	1	Six-compartment Brake Third			48	4067-82	Eastleigh 1-4/29	
2201	4	Eight-compartment Second		48		4483-6	Ashford 6/27	To Diagram 2001 1954/5
2251	4	Six-compartment Brake Second		36		4481/2	Ashford 6/27	To Diagram 2102 1954
2301	4	Seven-compartment Composite	24		24	5137-46	Eastleigh 7-10/26	
						5147-50	Metro 8-9/28	
2302	1	Seven-compartment Composite	16		24	5151-70	Eastleigh 10/28-3/29	
2401	4	Six-compartment Brake Composite	12		32	6565-74	Eastleigh 8/26	
2501	4	Seven-compartment First	42			7208-27	Eastleigh/Midland 6-11/27	7208-15 built Eastleigh
						7665-74	Ashford/Eastleigh 12/26-3/27	7668-70 built Ashford
2502	1	Seven-compartment First	28			7390-7	Eastleigh 3-4/29	Nos 7393/4/6 later Diagram 2022
2551	4	Three-compartment Pantry Brake First	18			7715/6	Eastleigh 6/28	To Diagram 2551A 1949
2551A	4	Six-compartment Brake First	36			7715/6	Rebuilt 1949	Ex-Diagram 2551
2651	4	Kitchen & Dining First	24			7858-63	Eastleigh 5/27	
2652	4	Dining Saloon Third			64	7864-9	Eastleigh 7/27	Later Open Thirds 1363-8
2653	1	General Saloon		42 (unclassed)		7974-93	Metro/Midland 1-2/28	Some completed at Eastleigh

* Body of No 802 damaged by fire 7/35; new Diagram 2008 body provided 7/36.
Vehicles 801/7, 4049/65/77/81, 5156, 7227 and 7395 all lost through enemy action or accident damage.
Further examples of Diagrams 2651 and 2653 were completed later; these, together with the subsequent history of Diagram 2652, are detailed in the next section.

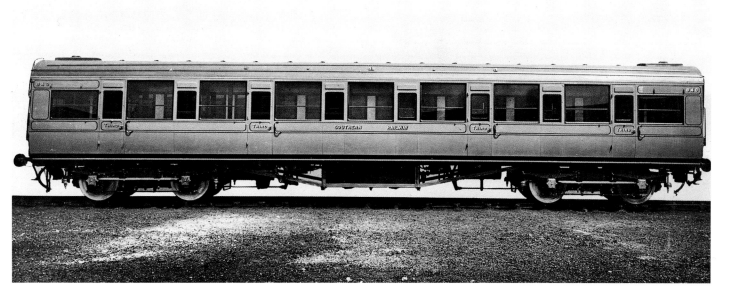

Plate 72 One of the earliest high-window Maunsell Corridor Thirds, No 840, completed in August 1929. Diagram 2001 was again allocated. The loss of the cantrail panels meant that the company title now appeared at waistline on the corridor side only; on the compartment side the usual cantrail position continued to be used. *Southern Railway*

HOO No	Stock	Coach/set Nos
E361	One six-coach train, one three-coach train for London-Bognor/Chichester services	456 and 387
E362	Four four-coach trains for London-Folkestone/Deal/Ramsgate services	181-4
E363	One nine-coach train for Bournemouth-Newcastle/Bradford/Leeds through services	458 (part)
E364	One 10-coach train for Bournemouth-Birkenhead/Manchester through services	427/59 (part)
E365	One 11-coach train for Eastbourne-Bradford/Birmingham/Manchester/Liverpool through services	(See text)
E366	One 11-coach train for Brighton-Cardiff/Ilfracombe/Plymouth through services	428 (part)
E376	Two eight-coach trains for London-Bexhill/Hastings services	475-8
E377	One eight-coach train for London-Bexhill/Hastings services	479/80

Sets 181-4 were identical in make-up to the previous 8ft 6in four-coach sets (449-54) and included Brake Thirds 4087-94 and Composites 5173-7, 5582-4 in pairs (the Composites in set 183 being 5177 and 5582 — the numbers between already being occupied by pre-Grouping Composites), but they had the benefit of full-height windows on the corridor side. The window nearest each end of the coach remained at the lower height to allow space for the destination and seat-reservation boards.

Order E361, for the Central section, was originally allocated as follows:

Vehicles	Set 387	Set 456
Six-compartment Brake Third	4085	4083
Seven-compartment Composite	5171	5172
Seven-compartment Firsts	-	7398/9
Eight-compartment Third	-	837
Six-compartment Brake Third	4086	4084

Set 456 ran regularly with a Pullman First and a Pullman Third in the centre but by 1935 had been reduced to three vehicles — identical in make-up to set 387, which always ran as just three coaches. (The latter set was one that did not have intermediate side buffers, which may explain why it never changed formation during its entire lifetime.) By 1935 both sets were in use on Kent Coast services, so some relaxation of width restrictions must have taken place by that time.

The vehicles completed against Orders E363-6 were somewhat loosely allocated, and few actually ran as complete sets. They were for through services to other companies and all Brake coaches were equipped with British Standard gangways at the brake end — some at both ends. If the former, these were annotated in Carriage Working Notices as 'CA1/CP1' (British Standard gangway with adaptors one end, Pullman gangway at the other). In most instances the stock would alternate with that of the LMS, LNER or GWR, so it was important for seat-reservation purposes that the make-up of each vehicle matched those from the other companies. For this reason all seven Composites included on these orders had three First- and four Third-class compartments — the reverse of the usual SR arrangement. This was achieved by the simple expedient of putting false partitions into the centre compartment, reducing its width to that of a Third-class compartment and trimming the seating as Third class. Structurally they were identical to all other 9ft-wide Composites of the period but received a unique diagram number — 2303 (instead of 2301 for the usual configuration). Vehicle numbers were as follows:

Order No	Thirds	Brake Thirds	Composites	Brake Composites	Dining car
363	838/9	3664/5	5585/6	6575/6	7939
364	840/1	3666-9	5587-9	-	7940
365	842-4	4095-7	-	6577-80	7941
366	1113/4	3670/1	5590/1	6581-4	7942

Plate 73 One of the Brake Composites originally built for through services and equipped with British Standard (CA) gangways, in this instance at both ends. No 6581 is seen in pristine crimson lake and cream at Clapham Junction in September 1952. *D. Cullum*

The catering vehicles will be described at the end of this chapter. The only permanent sets made up from the above were:

Set 427:	3668+5588+3669	Bournemouth-Manchester
Set 428:	3670+5590+3671	Brighton-Cardiff
Set 458:	3664+5585+5586+3665	Bournemouth-Newcastle
Set 459:	3666+5587+5589+3667	Bournemouth-Birkenhead

Sets 428/58/9 regularly had the extra Thirds and the Dining car inserted as required, making a maximum formation of seven vehicles within each set. The Brake Composites provided through single-vehicle portions to destinations such as Bradford, Leeds, Ilfracombe or Plymouth, often being coupled ahead of or behind rakes from other locations for part of their journeys. The operation of these through services was quite a feat of organisation between the various companies — one that seems difficult to manage in the 21st century! Order 365 was not formed into a numbered set and may never have run on its intended services from Eastbourne, as the 'Sunny South Express' was almost invariably provided with LMS stock. Some of these coaches were later used on a Margate-Birkenhead service, while others were noted on a Margate-Bournemouth through train which ran via Redhill, Guildford and Alton.

Plate 2 is an excellent broadside view of one of these CA-equipped carriages when new, while **Plate 73** shows one of the Brake Composites in later years — most certainly not on inter-Regional services. There soon became apparent a risk inherent with vehicles fitted with British Standard gangways: SR shunters more accustomed to Pullman gangways would forget to unclip the CA adaptors when uncoupling the coaches; inevitably, as the coaches parted company, the BS gangway would remain coupled to the Pullman one and promptly be ripped off the end of one vehicle to land on the track! A works visit would then be necessary for a new gangway to be fitted.

The last 1928 orders were for the Tonbridge-Hastings line, for which the body width was reduced to 8ft 0¼in. First-class compartments very generously sat only two-a-side, Third-class three-a-side. Most other details mirrored the 8ft 6in-wide vehicles, except that the bodyside doors stopped just short of the bottom of the coach sides, the edge of the coach floor being visible; this is a useful identification point for Restriction 0 stock. Although ordered as eight-coach trains, each was actually formed of two three-coach sets with two loose coaches in the centre. One of the 1926 Pullman cars was inserted near the middle of the train to provide catering facilities and make up the usual nine-coach Hastings-line rake. At this time most Hastings-line services included a three-coach set for Bexhill West, detached at Crowhurst; in later years the whole train ran to Hastings, the Bexhill connection being provided by a push-pull service from Crowhurst.

The original formations of sets 475-480 were Brake Thirds 3672-83 (in pairs), with Composites 5592-7 in numerical sequence. However, it was soon found that the First-class accommodation was insufficient, so Firsts 7403/2/0 replaced

Plate 74 Late in 1929 the Tonbridge—Hastings line received some much needed corridor stock. Diagram 2503 First No 7401 is seen in Tonbridge Jubilee sidings in April 1947, wearing malachite green. Note the original position of the lavatory window, compared to coach 7405 in **Plate 91**. *D. Cullum*

Plate 75 Hastings-line Composite No 5592, photographed c1958 in Southern Region green. The almost vertical sides are noticeable, as are the doors, which do not extend to the bottom of the bodyside on Restriction 0 vehicles. After withdrawal similar vehicle 5600 was rebuilt as Inspection Saloon DS70155, described in Chapter 14. *Author's collection*

Plate 76 A typical Hastings-line train of the 1950s: 'Schools' class 4-4-0 No 30934 *St Lawrence* on Southborough Bank in April 1955. By this time all the Restriction 0 coaches had been internally refurbished and repainted in crimson lake and cream. Three-coach set 479 is leading, followed by a loose Composite, with another three-set at the rear. *E. R. Wethersett /Ian Allan Library*

Composites 5595-7 in sets 478-80, the Composites then running as loose stock. Sets 475-7 did not run for very long in this form, all three being disbanded by 1934/5. All coaches on the Hastings line had high windows, although some records suggest that loose Thirds 1115/6 had low windows. Recent photographic evidence now confirms that this is incorrect and these two coaches were identical to the remainder. The other coach types are illustrated in **Plates 74-76**.

The next authorisations, in May 1929, were for the following vehicles shown in the table below.

The open-saloon Thirds were 9ft wide and were the first of a new type of vehicle. Rather similar to the six Third-class Dining Saloons completed in 1927, they seated 56 passengers in seven bays, but had a lavatory and entrance vestibule at both ends of the coach. The end-door section of the body was recessed to 8ft 7in wide as previously. Many of these coaches were semi-permanently allocated as dining cars, for which they were equipped with tables and they would run coupled to the kitchen end of a Dining First to provide Third-class dining facilities. These vehicles had large frameless, self-balancing windows, which could be opened by lowering the pane to a maximum of 7in for ventilation. **Plate 77** illustrates a similar coach from the next batch (completed in 1930), while an interior view may be found at **Plate 13**. The *Southern Railway Magazine* for October 1930 described the coaches as 'New-type Third-class Dining Pullman Cars'; it was stated that the interior seating was red, black and yellow velvet — the standard material used in all Third-class coaches.

The other 1929 coach orders were all repeats of earlier designs, while the Dining Saloons will be dealt with collectively at the end of this chapter.

HOO No	Stock	Coach/set Nos
E461	20 open-saloon Thirds for general use	1369-88
E462	50 Brake Composites for Waterloo-West of England services	6585-6604/43-72
E463	20 General Saloons for race, boat and school-party traffic	7781-7800
E464	10 Dining Saloons for general use	7943-52

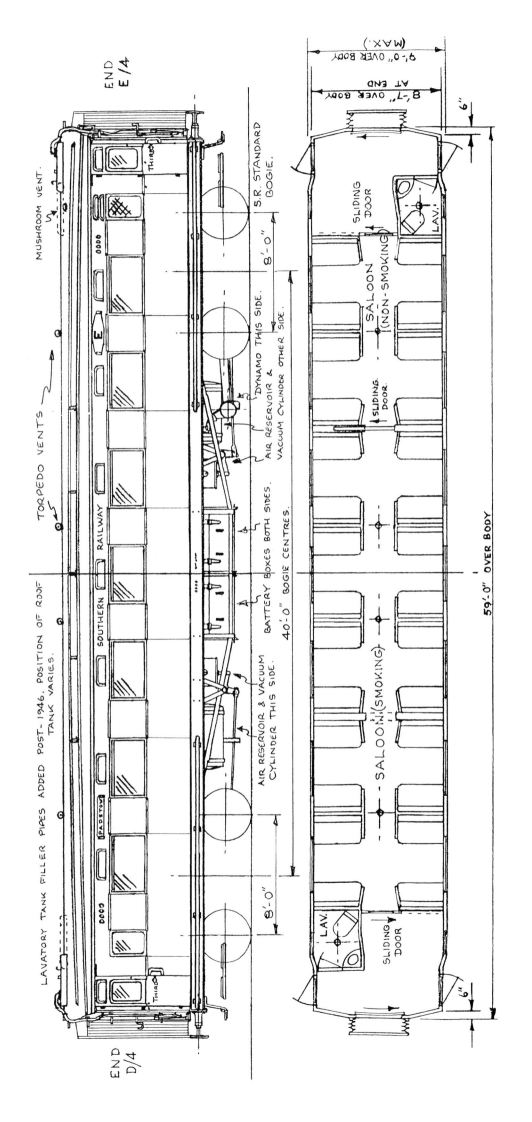

Figure 18 The 1930 Open Third design, SR Diagram 2005.

Plate 77 Open-saloon Third No 1400, one of those completed in 1930 against Order E488, in photographic grey livery.
Southern Railway Magazine

In 1929 the Government abolished Railway Passenger Duty payments, and the release of these funds allowed the ordering of no fewer than 200 new vehicles in July of that year — the largest orders yet placed for steam-hauled stock. Hardly surprisingly, not all vehicles ordered at this time ended up on the workings for which they were intended. The original orders were as follows:

HOO No	Stock	Coach/set Nos
E487	One 10-coach train for Waterloo-Bournemouth-Swanage/Weymouth services	179, 202/7
E488	One 12-coach train for Waterloo-Bournemouth-Swanage/Weymouth services	180, 201/6
E489	Two 10-coach trains for Waterloo-Portsmouth services	204/5
E490	Two 11-coach trains for Waterloo-Southampton boat services	208/9
E491	Two eight-coach trains for London-Bognor/Portsmouth services	193/4/9, 200/3
E492	Two eight-coach trains for London-Worthing/Littlehampton services	195, 426/9/64
E493	Two eight-coach trains for London-Folkestone/Deal/Ramsgate services	185-8
E494	Two eight-coach trains for London-Ramsgate services	217/8
E495	Two eight-coach trains for London-Eastbourne/Hastings services	189-92
E496	Two eight-coach trains for London-Eastbourne services	219/20
E497	22 General Saloons for race, boat and school-party traffic	7901-11/59-68/94
E498	Two nine-coach trains for London-Bexhill/Hastings services	213-6

All vehicles were built to existing designs, those on Orders 487-92 being 9ft wide, 493-7 8ft 6in wide and 498 alone 8ft 0¾in wide. They were completed between July 1930 and June 1931.

Appendix 1 gives details of the individual coach numbers against each order. Orders 487-90 for the South Western section ran as the following sets:

Vehicles	Set 179	Set 180	Set 199	Set 200
Six-compartment Brake Third	3732	3733	3736	3737
Six-compartment Brake Composite	6673	6674	6657 *	6588 *

Vehicles	Set 201	Set 202	Vehicles	Set 203
Four-compartment Brake Third	3730	3726	Six-compartment Brake Third	3734
Seven-compartment Composite/First	5635	7675 (First)	Seven-compartment Composite	5636 or 5637
Four-compartment Brake Third	3731	3727	Six-compartment Brake Third	3735

Vehicles	Set 204	Set 205	Set 206	Set 207	Set 208	Set 209
Four-compartment Brake Third	3716	3718	3728	3724	3720	3722
Seven-compartment First	7228	7229	7219 *	7218 *	7407	7411
Eight-compartment Third	1122	1123	1124	1128	1129	1127
Four-compartment Brake Third	3717	3719	3729	3725	3721	3723

* From previous orders, ex-loose stock

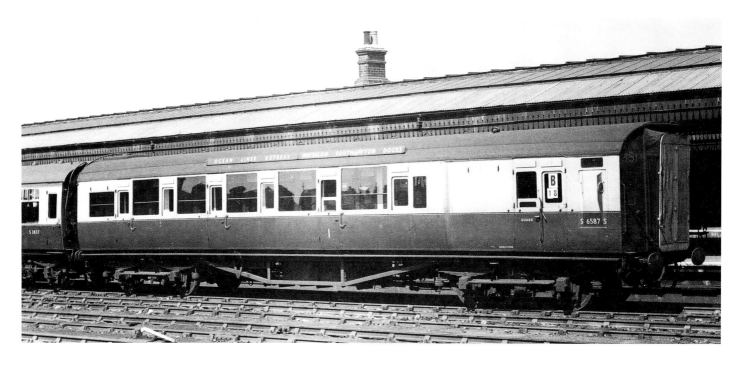

Plate 78 Corridor Brake Composite 6587, built in 1930 for Waterloo–West of England services. At off-peak times a single coach of this type would provide the through portion to numerous West Country branch lines. This vehicle was photographed at Clapham Junction in May 1954, being formed in Ocean Liner set 351, along with BR Mk 1 stock. *J. H. Aston*

Plate 79 A useful close-up of the brake compartment of Diagram 2401 Brake Composite No 6595, then running as part of two-set 'W' No 110 on the Lyme Regis branch. The date is June 1959. For details of set formations see Chapter 6. *A. E. West*

Plate 80 1930-vintage Corridor Third No 1130, part of Order E489, originally for Waterloo–Portsmouth stock. *Southern Railway*

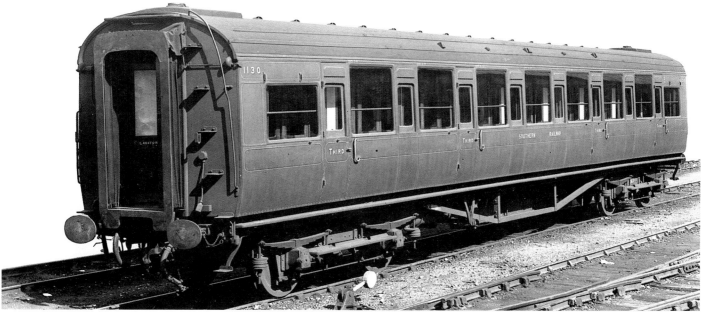

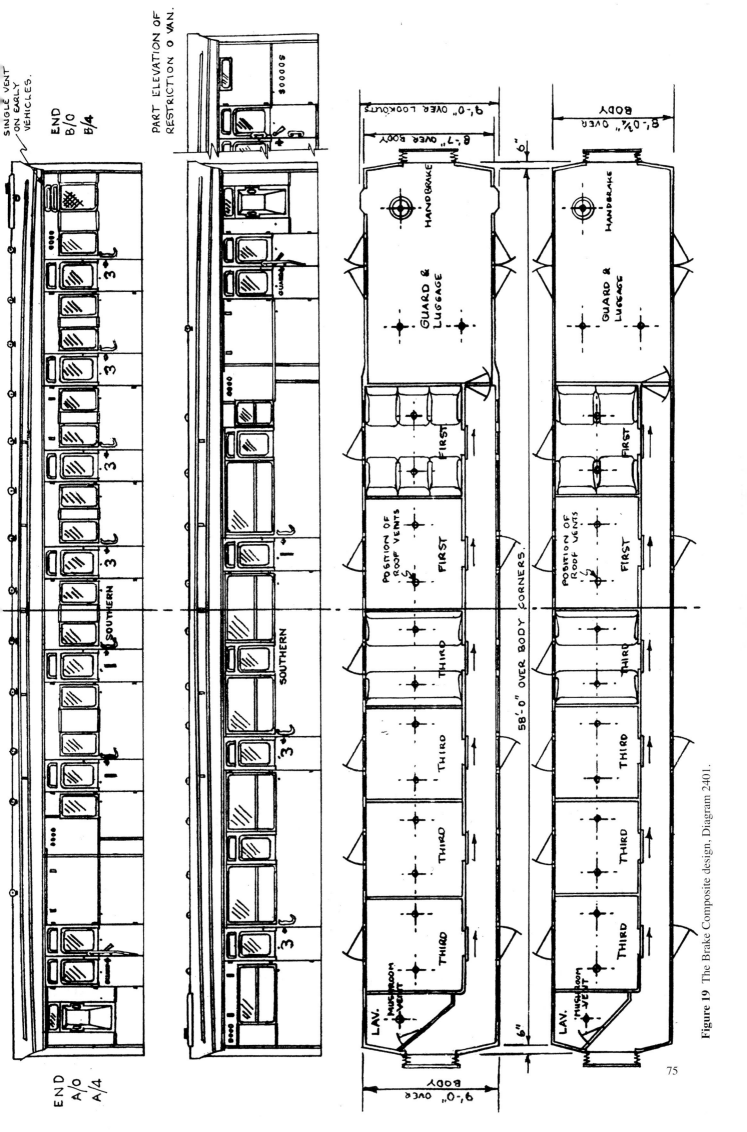

Figure 19 The Brake Composite design, Diagram 2401.

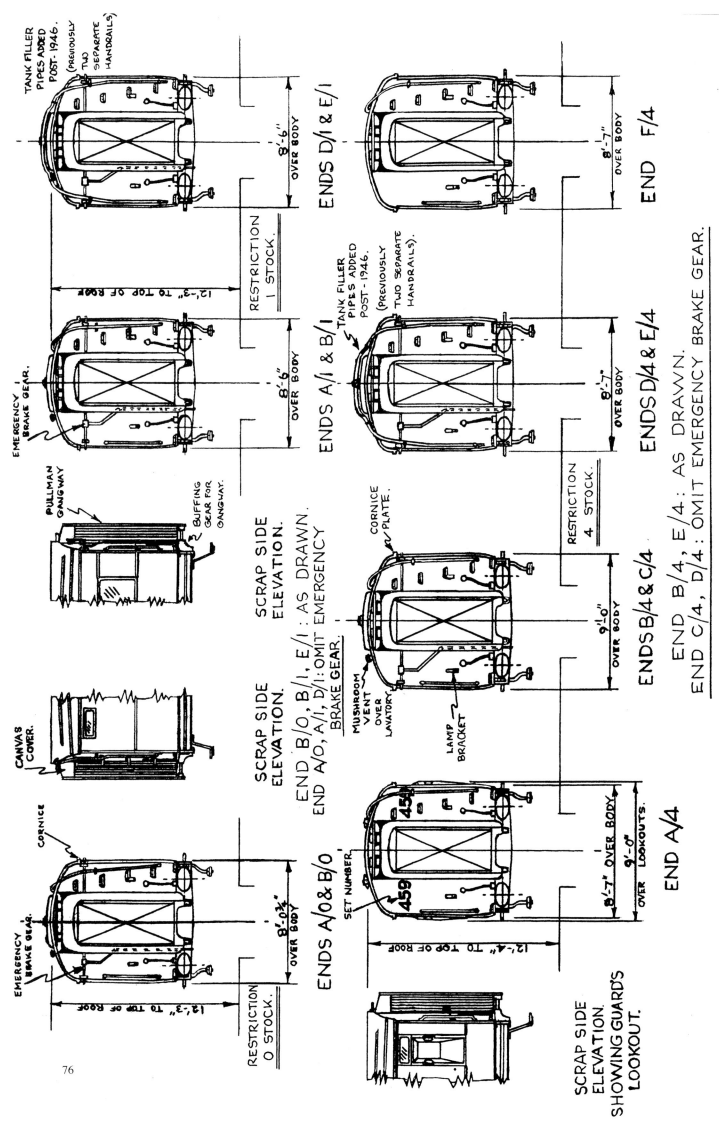

Figure 20 Typical coach end details for Maunsell 59ft stock. For Restriction 0 vehicles, use ends A/0, B/0, for Restriction 1 vehicles, use ends A/1, B/1 etc. and for Restriction 4 vehicles, use ends A/4, B/4 etc.

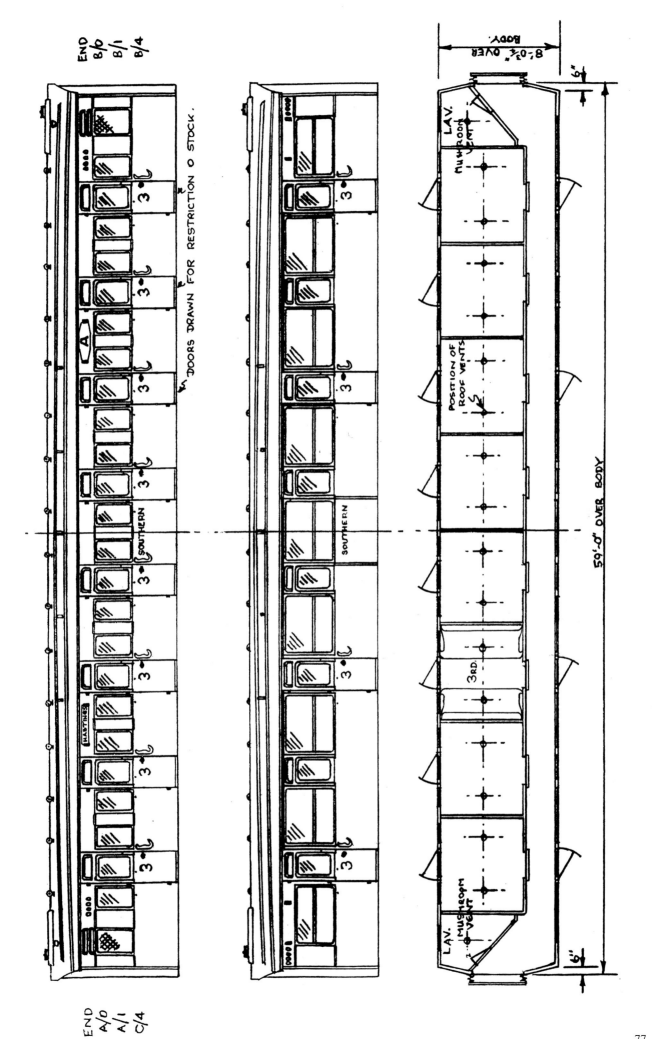

Figure 21 The Corridor Third design, Diagrams 2001, 2003 and 2004.

Plate 81 1930-vintage Corridor First No 7230, also part of Order E489. *National Railway Museum*

It will be noted that several vehicles included on Order E491 were diverted from the Central to the South Western section. The two-coach sets were primarily for Waterloo–Swanage through portions, although they were later much used on West of England trains. The three- and four-coach sets would be strengthened by the addition of a Dining First and an Open Third, usually running between Waterloo and Portsmouth, Waterloo and Bournemouth West or Waterloo and Weymouth in these formations. The remaining coaches ran as loose stock, and it seems likely that very few of the vehicles included on Order E490 were actually used on Southampton boat trains.

By comparison, the Central-section formations were somewhat simpler, being either three- or four-coach sets:

Set 193 ran on Brighton-Bournemouth services, 194/5 with a Pullman Third added in the centre on the intended Central-section duties, while 464 was made up to seven vehicles and is seen in this form in **Plate 82**, also on the intended Central-section services. Sets 426/9 were increased to four vehicles by the insertion of a Dining Saloon (usually an 'Ironclad') and worked the Brighton–Plymouth service, each set running one way daily.

Inevitably, many of these allocations and set formations did change. Central-section electrification in the mid-1930s moved many sets onto the South Eastern or South Western sections. Towards the end of World War 2, on the Oxted line, set 194 assumed a unique formation: the original four vehicles were augmented by three Thirds and a First but with the Brake coaches

Vehicles	Set 193	Set 194	Set 195	Set 426	Set 429	Set 464
Six-compartment Brake Third	3738	3740	3742	3746	3748	3744
Seven-compartment Composite(s)	5640/1	5642/3	5644/5	5649	5651	5646/7
Six-compartment Brake Third	3739	3741	3743	3747	3749	3745

Plate 82 'H1' class Atlantic No B37 *Selsey Bill* passing Honor Oak Park in 1931, hauling seven-set 464 plus a luggage van on a Sussex Coast service. *Author's collection*

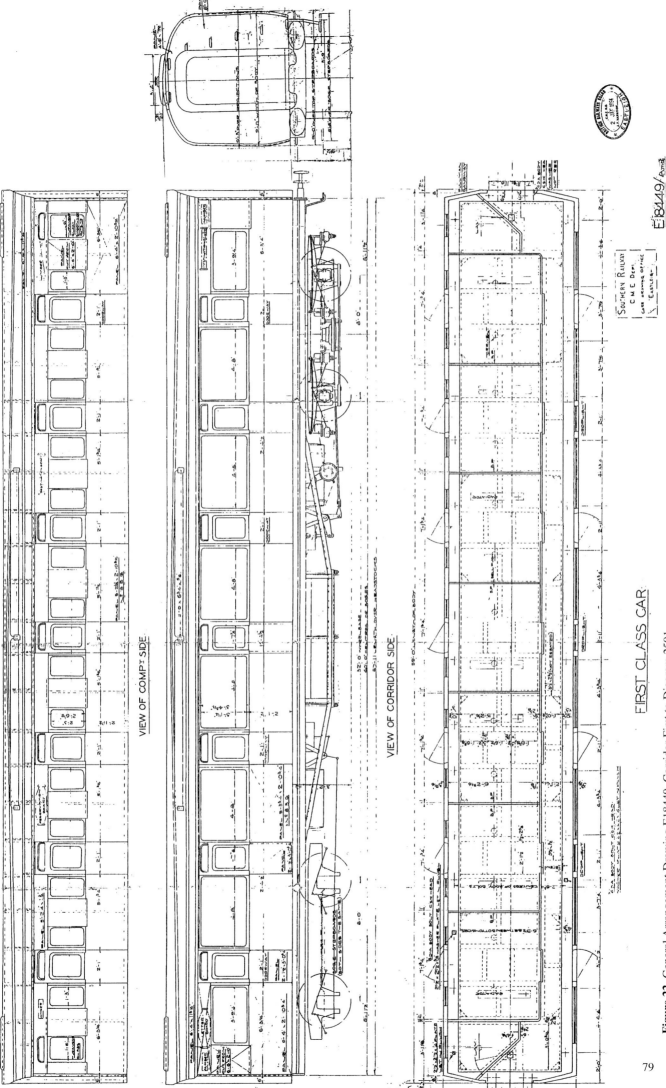

Figure 22 General Arrangement Drawing E18449, Corridor First to Diagram 2501. This drawing was prepared specifically for vehicles 7398/9 of Order E361A.

Plate 83 Diagram 2301 Composite 5645 in Southern Region green at Clapham Junction in June 1957, by which time it was running in three-coach set 962 between Brake Thirds 3734/5. *J. H. Aston*

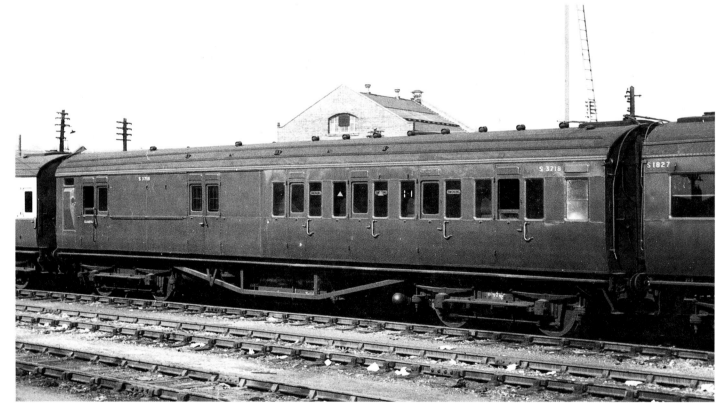

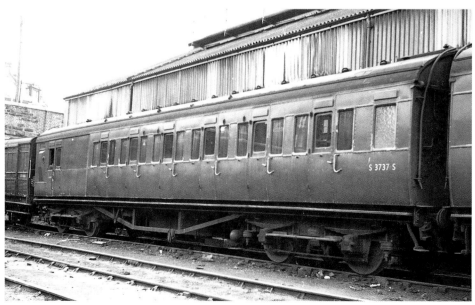

Plate 84 The later version of four-compartment Brake Third, this being No 3718 in set 205 at Eastleigh in June 1951. Livery is malachite green, with 'S' prefix to numbers in Southern Railway style. *J. H. Aston*

Plate 85 Six-compartment Restriction 4 Brake Third 3737, to Diagram 2102, at Exeter Central in September 1962, still coupled to Brake Composite No 6588 as 2-P set 200. The pair were withdrawn two months later, having spent their entire working lives in this formation. *A. E. West*

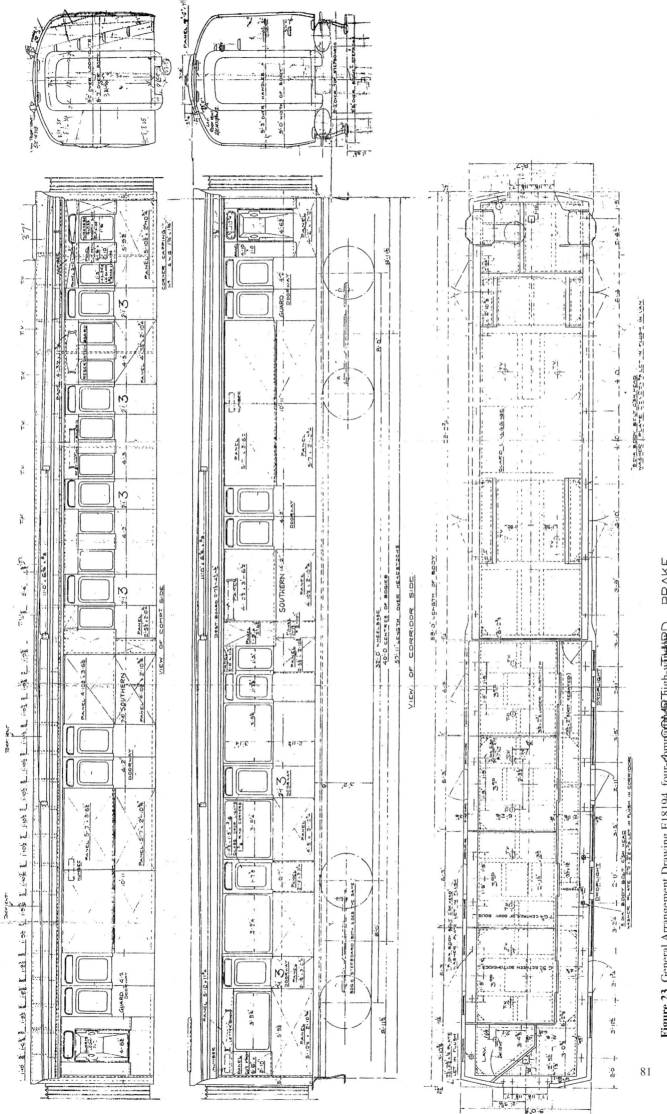

Figure 23 General Arrangement Drawing E18194, four-comp@OMR high-window D. BRAKE Brake Third to Diagram 2101.

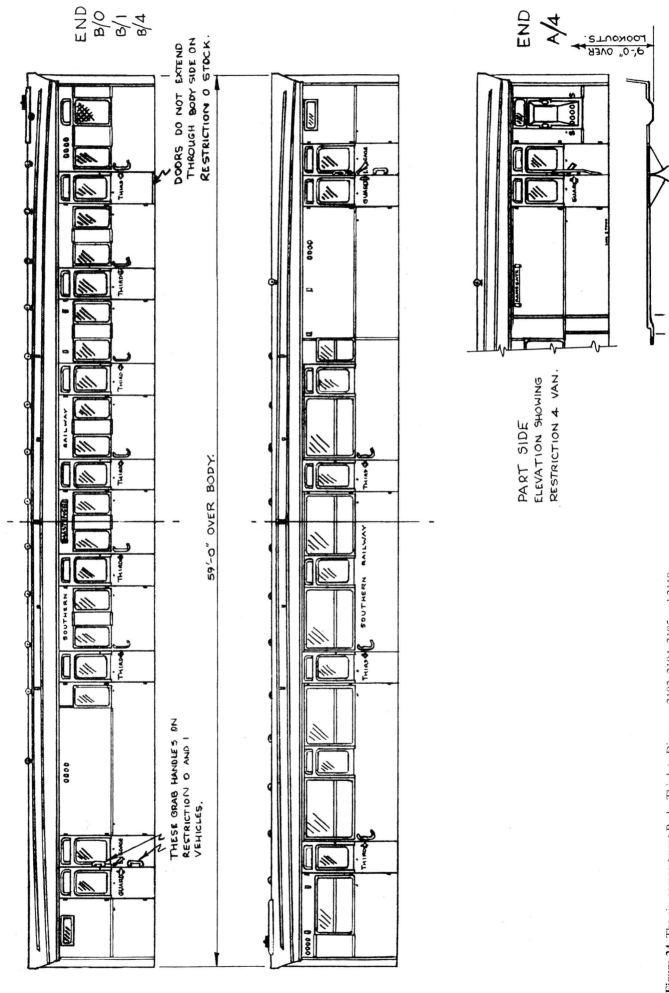

Figure 24 The six-compartment Brake Third, to Diagrams 2102, 2104, 2105 and 2110.

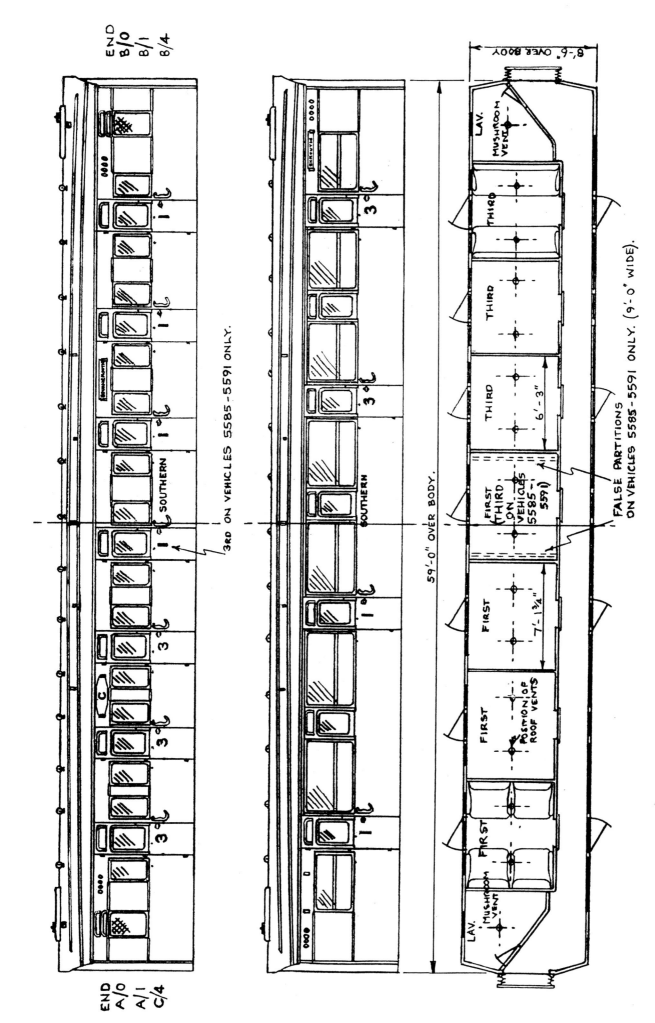

Figure 25 High-window Composite, to Diagrams 2301, 2302, 2303 and 2304.

Plate 86 The equivalent Restriction 1 vehicle, No 3693, of set 185 at Ashford in April 1949. Diagram 2104 was allocated. *J. H. Aston*

Plate 87 Restriction 1 Composite 5603, also in set 185, at Ashford on the same date. Diagram 2302 was allocated. Note that only the First-class doors now carry class designations. *J. H. Aston*

reversed so that their guard's compartments were innermost, while one Third-class coach ran at each end of the set. This ensured that the guard's van was within platform limits at many of the stations, which might not otherwise have been able to accommodate an eight-coach train. Approval to form the set in this manner had to be obtained from the Ministry of Transport — which considered that, without a brake compartment at each end of the train, any collision might result in more injuries than if the 'buffer zone' of the luggage van were present. The Ministry appeared blind to the fact that many trains ran with loose coaches coupled outside the sets regardless! Two typical formations of set 194 during this period were:

1944-6: 1366+3740+5642+7226+5643+1365+3741+1367
(1365-7 ex-Dining Saloon Thirds)
1947-51: 1231+3740+5642+7226+5643+1232+3741+1233
(ordinary Corridor Thirds included)

The same formation was held until 1954 but with changes to the Third- and First-class vehicles.

Orders for 8ft 6in stock produced eight four-coach formations (sets 185-92), comprising two Brake Thirds and two Composites each, plus four eight-coach sets (217-20), these comprising four Composites in the centre, flanked at each end by a Third and a Brake Third. Details are shown at the foot of the page and the vehicles are illustrated in **Plates 86-88**.

With the completion of the 22 General Saloons on Order E497, identical to the previous batches and 20 Saloon Brakes yet to be described, these were the last 8ft 6in-wide vehicles completed by the Southern Railway. Sets 189-92 and 219/20, allocated to Eastbourne and Hastings workings (via the Central section), were soon reduced to three coaches only, some of the Composites being reformed in unnumbered three-coach sets between two ex-LSWR wooden-panelled Brake Thirds, again for Eastbourne services. Electrification of these lines in 1935 caused the transfer of all Restriction 1 sets to the Kent Coast, where they were restored to four coaches and joined similar sets 181-8 and 449-54. Sets 217/8, by comparison, retained their longer formations until 1959, when they were also reduced to four vehicles.

Set Nos	Vehicles
185-8	Brake Thirds 3692-9 and Composites 5602-9 in pairs
185-92	Brake Thirds 3704-11 and Composites 5618-25 in pairs
217/8	Brake Thirds 3700-3 and Thirds 2356-9 in pairs, Composites 5610-17 in sequential groups of four
219/20	Brake Thirds 3712-5 and Thirds 2360-3 in pairs, Composites 5626-33 in sequential groups of four

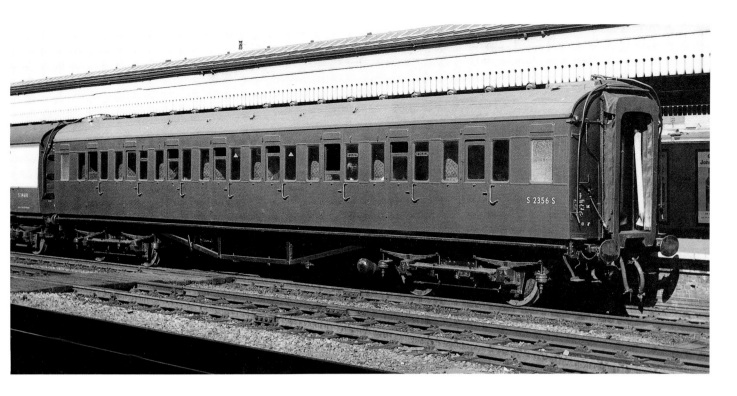

Plate 88 Restriction 1 Corridor Third No 2356 to Diagram 2003, again at Ashford but 10 years later, in September 1959. Livery is Southern Region green. *J. H. Aston*

Plates 89 and 90 Both Brake Thirds of Restriction 0 set 213, after withdrawal at Hassocks, in September 1963. This set had been reformed in 1959 with Composite No 5598 as the centre vehicle and was the last Restriction 0 set in service, withdrawn a year before the photograph was taken. *(both) J. H. Aston*

The final completion of Stage 2 of the Kent Coast electrification in 1961/2 might have reasonably justified the withdrawal of the last Restriction 1 stock, but this was still needed for Oxted-Tonbridge and other services in that area which were required to negotiate the tunnels in the vicinity of Tunbridge Wells, which were still unable to accept 9ft-wide vehicles. Some of the duties took the coaches as far afield as Brighton, Eastbourne and Reading, and they were in constant use until early 1965, surprisingly being amongst the last Maunsell coaches in regular traffic. By the end, many were in poor condition, and most sets had been split in half — a Brake Third (now Second) and a Composite constituting sets 180-92, 217-9 and 444-67. When stock availability allowed, two sets would form a service, but at other times just two coaches would have to suffice. The last two half-sets, 190/2, were finally condemned in July 1965. The Kent & East Sussex Railway then purchased two Composites for preservation.

The last 1929 orders were for the Hastings line. As before, these were ordered as complete trains but were formed as four three-coach sets together with loose Composites 5598-5601 and Thirds 1117/8. Sets 213-6 were formed of Brake Thirds 3684-91 in pairs, with Firsts 7404/5/16/5 respectively in the centres. These are illustrated in **Plates 89-91**.

After all this activity, it is perhaps not surprising that the 1930 orders were confined to non-passenger coaching stock, and it was not until April and November 1931 that the next carriage-stock orders were placed, as follows:

HOO No	Stock	Coach/Set Nos
E633	20 four-coach trains for London-Bognor-Portsmouth and Waterloo-Portsmouth/Bournemouth/West of England services	221-240
E634	One 10-coach train for London-Bexhill/Hastings services	939/40
E635	10 Dining Saloons for general service	7864-71, 7931/2
E686	25 Corridor Thirds for general use	1131-55
A687	25 Corridor Thirds for general use	1156-80

Plate 91 Restriction 0 First No 7405, seen at Stewarts Lane after withdrawal in 1959, prior to being converted into departmental coach DS70035 for the Work Study section at Basingstoke. Note the position of the lavatory windows, close to the ends of the coach. This change dates from the 1952-4 refurbishment (compare with **Plate 74**). *Author's collection*

One small external alteration was made at this point, two ventilator bonnets being provided over the lavatory windows instead of the single one previously fitted; otherwise all details were as before.

Sets 221-32 were completed as three coaches each, plus loose Composites 5652-63, while 233-40 were formed as planned with two Brake Thirds and two Composites in each set. Formations were as below:

Sets 221-32:   Brake Thirds 3750-58, 2754-68 in pairs, with Composites 5664-75 in order (set 225 having Brakes 3758, 2754)
Sets 233-40:   Brake Thirds 2769-71/93-2805 in pairs, with Composites 5676-91 in pairs (set 234 having Brakes 2771/93)

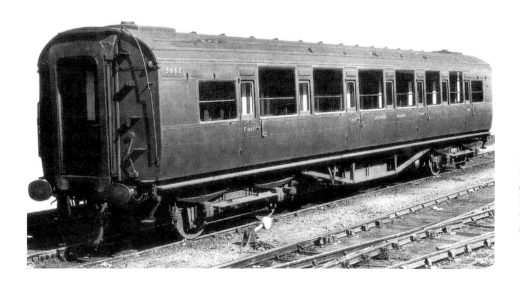

Plate 92 Diagram 2301 Restriction 4 Composite 5662, completed in 1932 as part of Order E633, running as a loose coach until 1947, when it was included in set 429. *Southern Railway*

Plate 93 Corridor Third No 1183 at Walton-on-Thames carriage sidings in April 1938. This shows the position of the company title on the corridor side of high-window Maunsell stock. Although almost invisible in the photograph, the coach carries full lining.
F. Foote

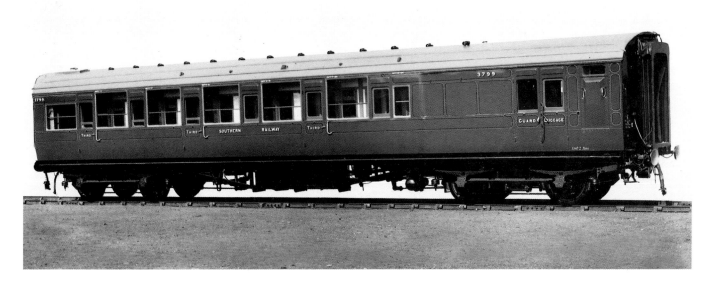

Plate 94 Diagram 2110 Brake Third No 3799 as completed in 1933. At this time the droplights and window frames were still being finished in varnished teak, at least for new stock.
Southern Railway

Sets 225-31/3-7 were allocated to the Central section; the rest were on the South Western. Those allocated to the Central eventually went to the Kent Coast lines, while some were later running as five-, six- or eight-coach formations. In this form, set 237 was experimentally repainted in chocolate and cream in May 1948, together with some loose vehicles and Dining Saloon 7934. It then ran on the 7.20am Ramsgate-Cannon Street and 1.15pm(SO) or 5.15pm(SX) return service, plus a Sunday round trip between Ramsgate and Victoria, formed:

2798+1161+1162+5684+5685+5686+7934+5637+1252+1163+2799

Several locomotives were specially repainted in apple green to work with the set, but in service the colours wore badly, the cream upper panels in particular suffering much staining. The record card for set 237 states that it was outshopped on 24 June 1948, while the 'Remarks' column includes the note 'Special renovation'. Further works visits occurred in March 1950, March 1952 and February 1954, but none mentions the date when the livery was replaced by more conventional colours.

Repainting in Southern Region green occurred in February 1957. The 50 Corridor Thirds on Orders 686 and 687 entered service during 1932, all probably being completed at Eastleigh, despite the 'A' allocation prefix for Order 687. All ran as loose vehicles and were only later incorporated into sets.

Order 634 for the Hastings line included Brake Thirds 3234-7, Thirds 1119/20, Composites 5578/9 and Firsts 7414/8, formed into seven-coach set 939 and three-coach set 940, as follows:

| Set 939: | 3236+1119+5578+7418+5579+1120+3237 | London-Hastings |
| Set 940: | 3234+7414+3235 | London-Bexhill West |

HOO No	Stock	Coach/set Nos
E705	50 Corridor Thirds for general use	1181-1230
E706	50 open-saloon Thirds for general use	1312-61
E707	30 Brake Thirds for general use	3771-3800
E708	20 General Saloons with Brake compartment for Continental boat traffic	4431-50
E709	10 (later 22) Corridor Thirds for London-Bexhill/Hastings services	476, 941-51
E710	24 Brake Thirds (later Brake Composites) for London-Bexhill/Hastings services	476, 941-51
E711	12 Corridor Composites for London-Bexhill/Hastings services	(Cancelled 12/32)
E712	Four Corridor Firsts for London-Bexhill/Hastings services	951 (part)
E713	10 Dining Saloons for general use	7878/80, 7933/4/69/95/7-8000
E760	100 (later 90) Corridor Thirds for general use	1231-80, 1801-40

Between March 1932 and April 1933 the last authorisations for the 1929 'high-window' stock were issued. For all later orders the design was modified somewhat, especially with regard to the arrangement of corridor-side windows. Details of these last orders are listed above.

The vehicles for general use were all 9ft wide and were repeats of previous designs, with one very minor alteration to the Brake Thirds, a sliding (instead of hinged) door being provided between the corridor and the luggage compartment. This seemingly trifling change resulted in the issue of a new diagram number — 2110 instead of 2102.

Most of the Brake Thirds were soon allocated to SW-section four-coach sets 241-7, five-coach sets 327/8 and six-coach sets 329/30, with one, two or three Thirds plus a First drawn from the by now extensive pool of loose stock. In addition, a new three-coach set 203 was formed using coaches 3781, 5653 and 3784, replacing the previous vehicles forming this set.

Other formations were as follows:

Vehicles	Set 241	Set 242	Set 243	Set 244	Set 245	Set 246	Set 247
Six-compartment Brake Third	3799	3790	3778	3786	3785	3771	3777
Eight-compartment Third	1219	1217	1224	1218	1197	1193	1187
Seven-compartment First	7676	7675	7412	7215	7211	7213	7212
Six-compartment Brake Third	3800	3791	3779	3787	3796	3788	3794

Vehicles	Set 327	Set 328	Set 329	Set 330
Six-compartment Brake Third	3773	3797	3793	3782
Eight-compartment Third	1208	1215	1227	1221
Seven-compartment First	7223	7406	7230	7231
Eight-compartment Third	1209	1216	1225/6	1222/3
Six-compartment Brake Third	3774	3798	3792	3783

Plate 95 Unclassed open-saloon Brake No 4439 is seen in crimson lake and cream, with Second-class door insignia, at Folkestone Harbour in September 1955. The roof boards read 'CONTINENTAL EXPRESS / SHORT SEA ROUTE' — the usual method of advertising the Folkestone and Dover routes to France. The roof boards were painted crimson with pale straw letters, edged in black. *J. H. Aston*

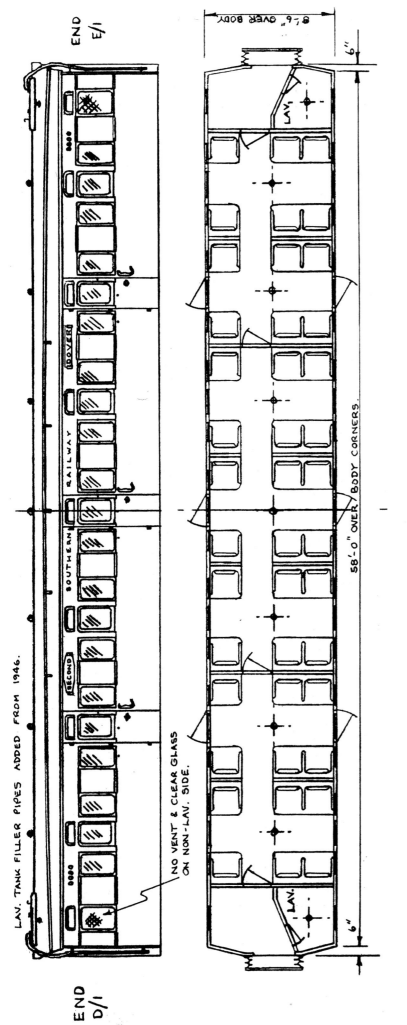

Figure 26 Unclassed General Saloon, Diagram 2653.

Plate 96 In 1938 some of the General Saloons were permanently reclassified as Second class. Coach 4396 arrives at Victoria as part of a Dover boat train in 1947. The roof boards on this occasion read 'CONTINENTAL EXPRESS / LONDON PARIS'. All coaches are in malachite green. Note Corridor Second No 4483 of the Newhaven boat train (at right). *P. Coutanche*

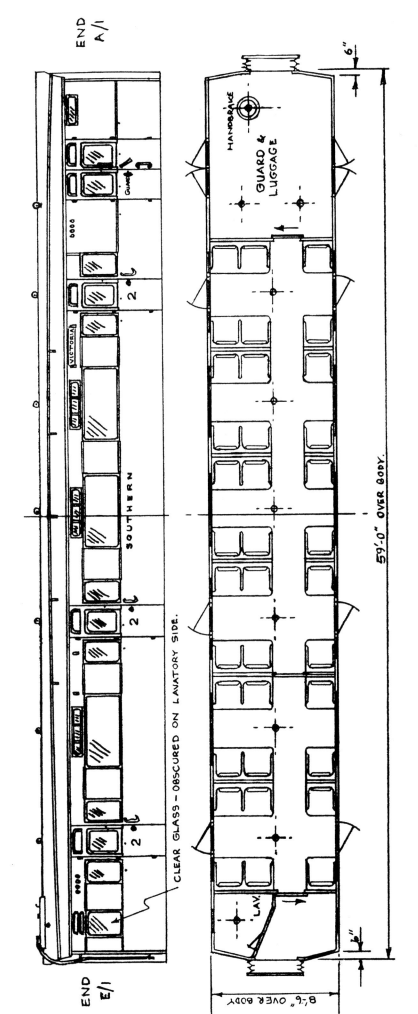

Figure 27 Unclassed General Saloon with brake compartment, Diagram 2654.

Plate 97 Hastings-line Restriction 0 Brake Composite No 6896, part of set 947, at Tonbridge in September 1949. *J. H. Aston*

Set 203 was allocated to the 'Bournemouth Limited', 241-7 could regularly be made up to six vehicles by the addition of a Dining First and an Open Third, while the others were used mainly for special traffic. In this form, sets 241/2, together with two-coach sets 180/99 and three-coach sets 221/32, were selected for repainting in malachite green in July 1938, for the 'Bournemouth Limited' service. Their livery was described in Chapter 2, and they will feature in Chapter 8 as part of Bulleid's changes to the rolling stock.

The 20 General Saloons for Continental boat traffic represented the only new design to appear during this period. A Brake version of the Nondescript Saloon, this had a slightly updated window arrangement, removing the 'dummy droplight' feature. One of these vehicles appears as the frontispiece, in ex-works condition. They could be labelled First, Second or Third class in the same way as the earlier saloons. The vehicle numbers, in the Second-class series of the list, were appropriate, as some were later permanently labelled as Second class, as seen in **Plate 95**. Some of the full saloons were also permanently labelled as Seconds in 1938, renumbered 4391-7, illustrated in **Plate 96**.

The final Hastings-line coaches complete the 1932/3 orders. Three-coach sets 941-50 and the second 476 were intended to be formed of Brake Thirds and Composites, but by 1934 the level of First-class patronage, even from Tunbridge Wells and southwards, had declined, so, by altering the formation to Brake Composites and Thirds, a slight increase in Third-class accommodation could be achieved within each three-coach set. The final set, No 951, emerged as a seven-coach formation, with a First at the centre, flanked on each side by two Thirds and a Brake Composite at each end. The remaining Thirds and Firsts ran as loose stock. Formations were as follows:

Vehicle	Set 941	Set 942	Set 943	Set 944	Set 945	Set 946	Set 947	Set 948	Set 949	Set 950
Six-compartment Brake Composite	6881	6883	6903	6889	6891	6893	6895	6897	6899	6901
Eight-compartment Third	1038	1028	1033	1037	1036	1039	1040	1032	1035	1034
Six-compartment Brake Composite	6882	6884	6904	6890	6892	6894	6896	6898	6900	6902

Set 951 was formed 6886+1027+1029+7419+1030+1031+6885
Set 476, disbanded previously, was reformed as 6887+1026+6888

Plate 98 Diagram 2402 coach No 6881 at Hastings c1957, in crimson lake and cream. *The Lens of Sutton Collection*

In Carriage Working Notices these three-coach sets were described as three-set Type O; those with two Brake Thirds and a First were Type F. From 1934 most Hastings-line trains included one of each type, plus two loose coaches and a Pullman dining car.

The Restriction 0 sets soldiered on over the Hastings Direct line until the early 1950s, by which time most other lines were receiving the benefit of newer Bulleid and BR standard stock. These, of course, were barred from the Hastings Direct line, so the decision was taken in 1952 to refurbish completely all 101 extant Restriction 0 vehicles. (One coach, Brake Composite 6884, had been lost to enemy action in 1944, its place in set 942 being taken by 6886, ex-set 951, whose place was in turn taken by Brake Third 3674, then running as a loose coach.) Order E3941 was placed for 'Special Renovations', which entailed full internal refurbishment, including BR-style lavatory fittings. Externally all coaches now ran in crimson lake and cream, while the only obvious structural change was the repositioning of the lavatory windows very close to the coach ends (compare **Plates 97 and 99**).

Even more surprisingly, as this programme drew to a close in March 1954, the Southern Region proposed building 32 new Hastings-line coaches, to run as eight-coach sets 934-7. It is not known exactly what form these vehicles might have taken, but the scheme got as far as having orders issued (E4096-8) and coach numbers allocated. Cancellation came in 1955; instead, some 'Continental' Restriction 0 vehicles and some of the loose Restriction 0 Maunsells were formed into additional sets 937/8 as an interim measure before 'dieselisation' plans were finalised two years later. Despite receiving extensive modernisation, most Restriction 0 vehicles were withdrawn in 1959, only a handful lasting until 1962. Several entered departmental service, and a few of these have since been purchased for preservation.

Many other Maunsell Restriction 1 and 4 vehicles have entered departmental service, only a handful being purchased direct from passenger traffic for preservation. Most departmental conversions received extensive modification, and those later purchased by preservation societies will require a great deal of work before they can carry fare-paying passengers. At the time of writing only the Bluebell Railway and the Kent & East Sussex Railway own vehicles in running order.

Plate 99 Diagram 2004 Corridor Third No 1119, in Southern Region green, awaiting disposal in 1959. Again, the refurbishment of 1952-4 is evident from the position of the lavatory window. *Author's collection*

Table 7
Summary of Maunsell 'high-window' stock 1929-34

Diagram No	RR	Vehicle Type	Seats 1st	2nd	3rd	Running Nos	Built by	Remarks
2001	4	Eight-compartment Third			64	837-44	Eastleigh 7-8/29	
						1113/4	Eastleigh 12/29	
						1121-1280	Eastleigh 7/30-9/34	1131 on had two lavatory vents
						1801-40 *	Eastleigh 10-11/34	Two lavatory vents
2003	1	Eight-compartment Third			64	2356-63	Eastleigh 2-4/31	
2004	0	Eight-compartment Third			48	1019-40	Eastleigh 1-3/34	Two lavatory vents
						1115/6	Eastleigh 10/29	
						1117-20	Eastleigh 1/31-5/32	Nos 1119/20 had two lavatory vents
2005	4	Seven-bay Open Saloon Third			56	1369-1400	Eastleigh 8-12/30	
						1312-61	Eastleigh 3-5/33	Two lavatory vents
2023	4	Seven-bay Open Saloon Third (push-pull)			56	(Ex-Diagram 2005)	Rebuilt 1959/60	See Chapter 6
2101	4	Four-compartment Brake Third			32	3664-71, 4095-7	Eastleigh 7-12/29	CA gangways
						3716-31	Eastleigh 7-10/30	
2102	4	Six-compartment Brake Third			48	2754-71/93-2805	Eastleigh 2-4/32	Two lavatory vents
						3732-49	Eastleigh 9-11/30	
						3750-8	Eastleigh 4/32	Two lavatory vents
						4083-6	Eastleigh 12/29	
2110	4	Six-compartment Brake Third			48	3771-3800	Eastleigh 8-9/33	Two lavatory vents
2104	1	Six-compartment Brake Third			48	3692-3715	Eastleigh 2-4/31	
						4087-94	Eastleigh 11/29	
2105	0	Six-compartment Brake Third			36	3234-7	Eastleigh 4/32	Two lavatory vents
						3672-91	Eastleigh 9/29-1/31	
2301	4	Seven-compartment Composite	24		24	5171/2	Eastleigh 12/29	
						5634-91	Eastleigh 9/30-4/32	Nos 5652 on had two lavatory vents
2302	1	Seven-compartment Composite	16		24	5173-7, 5582-4	Eastleigh 11/29	
						5602-33	Eastleigh 2-4/31	
2303	4	Seven-compartment Composite	18		32	5585-91	Eastleigh 7-12/29	Three First-class compartments
2304	0	Seven-compartment Composite	16		18	5578/9	Eastleigh 4/32	Two lavatory vents
						5592-5601	Eastleigh 9/29-1/31	
2401	4	Six-compartment Brake Composite	12		32	6575-6604/43-74	Eastleigh 6/29-10/30	Nos 6656/60 to Diagram 2404 in 1947
2404	4	Six-compartment Brake Composite First/Second (for boat trains)	12	24		6905/6 (retained until withdrawn)	(Renumbered 11/47)	Ex-Diagram 2401 Nos 6656/60; reverted to Diagram 2401 in 1949
2402	0	Six-compartment Brake Composite	8		24	6881-6904	Eastleigh 3-5/34	Two lavatory vents
2501	4	Seven-compartment First	42			7228-32, 7675/6	Eastleigh 7-9/30	
						7398/9, 7406-12	Eastleigh 12/29-9/30	
2503	0	Seven-compartment First	28			7400-3 #	Eastleigh 9/29	
						7404/5/15/6	Eastleigh 1/31	
						7414/8-22	Eastleigh 4/32-5/34	Two lavatory vents
2653	1	General Saloon		42 (unclassed)		7781-7800	Eastleigh 5-7/31	Some later reclassed as Seconds 4391-7 in 1938/9
						7901-11/59-68/94	Eastleigh 5-6/31	
2654	1	General Saloon with Brake		36 (unclassed)		4431-50	Eastleigh 6/33	Two lavatory vents
2654A	1	General Saloon with Brake		36 (unclassed)		4431-7/9-41	Modified 1956	As Diagram 2654 with roof periscopes added

* Body of No 1834 damaged by fire 7/35; new Diagram 2008 body provided 5/36.
\# Body of No 7403 destroyed by enemy action 5/41, new body with two lavatory vents provided 12/41.
Twenty earlier vehicles to Diagram 2653 are listed in Table 6.
General saloons 7793, 7800, 7902/4-6/11 were reclassified as permanent Seconds 4391-7 in 1938/9.
General Saloon Brakes 4438/44/5/9 rebuilt as Ambulance Ward cars 7920-3 in 1959.
Vehicles 1145/6, 1255/63, 1836, 3714/96, 4393 and 6884 lost through enemy action or accident damage.

Maunsell catering vehicles

The original 1927 Kitchen First/Dining Saloon Third pairs were described in the section dealing with the 'low-window' stock, but for the sake of convenience their later history, together with all subsequent Maunsell catering vehicles, will be described collectively here. This has been done for several reasons: firstly, minor details aside, all Kitchen/Dining cars shared the same body structure; secondly, none was ever permanently allocated to a set; thirdly, many were converted into buffet or cafeteria cars from 1946 onwards.

The vehicles, in their original forms, are listed against the relevant HOO numbers in the appropriate sections of this chapter. With the exception of the four vehicles ordered for through services to other companies in 1928 (Orders 363-6) and the six 1929 cars for specific South Western-section duties (Orders 487-90), all are described as being 'for general use'. Bearing in mind the existing Central- and South Eastern-section contracts with the Pullman Car Co, this effectively meant that most cars served on the South Western section, under the previously LSWR Spiers & Pond contract, superseded in 1930 by Messrs Frederick Hotels Ltd. The majority ran between Waterloo and Portsmouth, Bournemouth and Weymouth, on Southampton boat trains and over the West of England line to Exeter. With the exception of the Brighton-Plymouth service, Dining cars seldom ventured west of Exeter, apart from on summer weekend services.

It was not at all unusual to find a three-, four- or five-coach set of Maunsell or 'Ironclad' vehicles running with one of these Dining cars inserted, sometimes with an Open Third or a Nondescript General Saloon to provide additional seating capacity, sometimes without. Maunsell sets 202-9, 241-50 and 'Ironclad' sets 431-44 regularly included Dining cars on Waterloo-Bournemouth/Portsmouth services, while sets 428/58/9 included one of vehicles 7939-42 on through Cardiff, Newcastle and Birkenhead services, although as more Diners entered traffic the later vehicles might be substituted in their place. On the West of England main line, 3-P sets 390-9 and 445-8 could be augmented by a Dining car and Open Third, while even the 2-P sets numbered between 168 and 200 could also include a Dining car, especially if working beyond Exeter on a Summer Saturday. Only on such high days and holidays would all the Dining cars be required; at other times there seemed always to be an excess of spare vehicles at Clapham Junction, Bournemouth West or Exeter Central, with no booked duties.

By mid-1934 there were no fewer than 46 Maunsell Kitchen/Dining Firsts in service, plus the eight 'Ironclad' Diners, six Pantry Brake Firsts, four Pantry Thirds and at least six ex-

Plate 100 Dining First No 7869 in unlined Maunsell green and lettered 'Restaurant Car', photographed showing the corridor side in a van train near Addlestone Junction in March 1940 as it was being returned to Clapham Yard after overhaul. This coach was originally built in July 1932, to Diagram 2656. *F. Foote*

Plate 101 The kitchen side of Diagram 2656 Dining First No 7866, in malachite green at Stewarts Lane in June 1951 while working in Pullman Car Co service on the South Eastern section. The dimension plate on this vehicle gave overall length and width as 61ft 7in and 9ft 0in — 3in narrower than normal, because all doors and grab-handles were inset. *A. E. West*

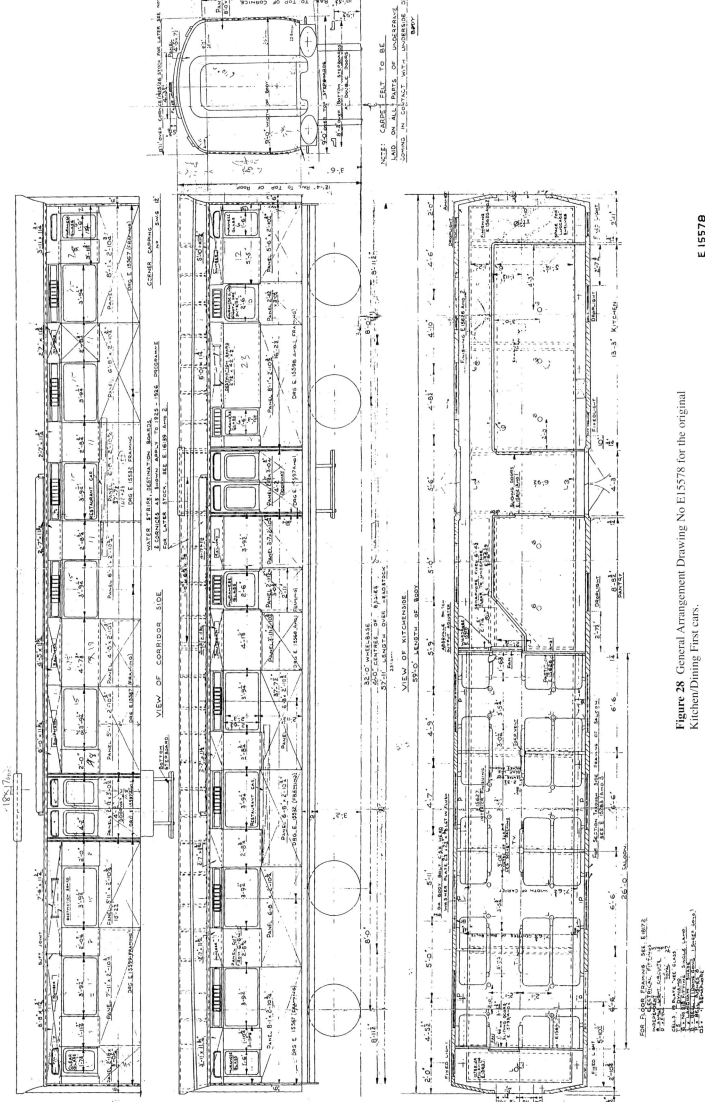

Figure 28 General Arrangement Drawing No E15578 for the original Kitchen/Dining First cars.

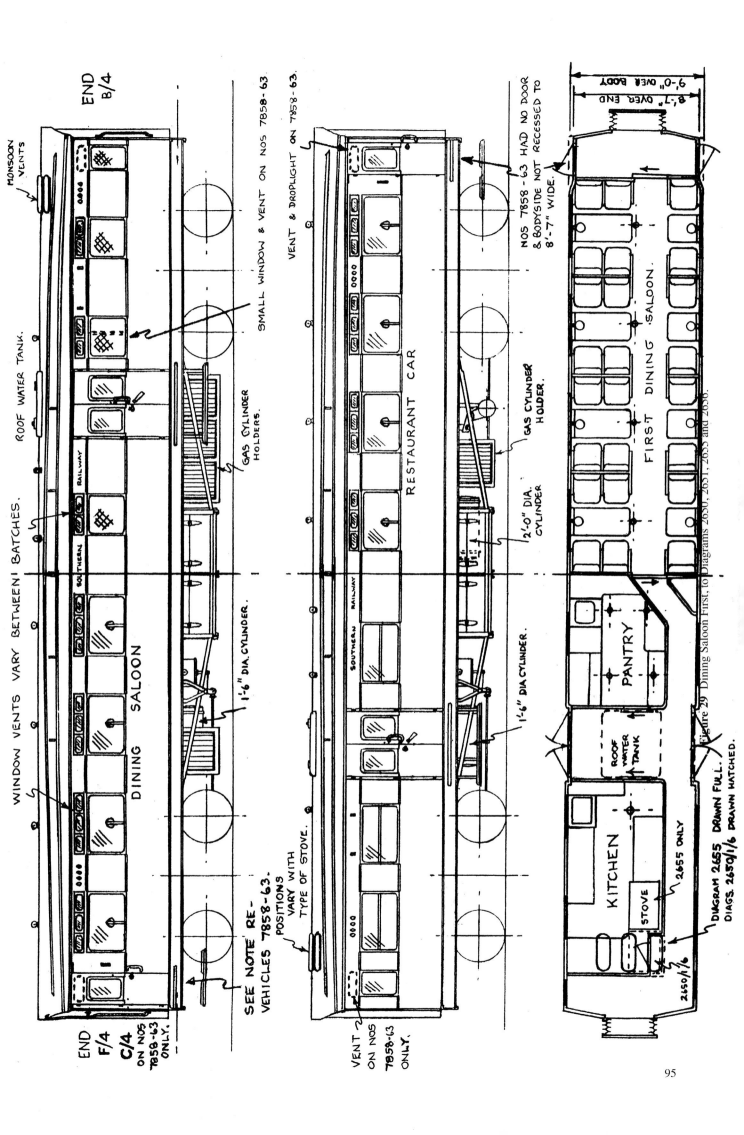

Figure 29 Dining Saloon First, to Diagrams 2650, 2651, 2655 and 2656.

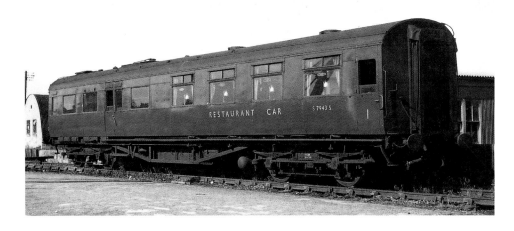

Plate 102 Diagram 2651 Restaurant car No 7943, one of those refurbished in 1938 for the 'Bournemouth Limited' service, photographed in 1960, carrying Southern Region green livery. The square 'boxes' on the solebar at the far end were lead weights, placed on the corridor side to even up the weight distribution. *R. E. Lacy*

Plate 103 56-seat open-saloon Third No 1374 at Stewarts Lane in August 1950. Built in 1930, these vehicles were much used as Dining Saloons, usually being coupled to the kitchen end of a Dining First. *A. E. West*

LSWR wooden-panelled vehicles. By this time, most of the older LSWR clerestory-roofed cars had been converted into Nondescript Saloons, and, surprisingly, authority to construct nine Maunsell replacements was sought (but not authorised) in March 1935. Subsequent Rolling Stock Committee minutes state 11 were ordered. The Maunsell Diners were allocated four different diagrams (Nos 2650/1/5/6), although these differences were concerned more with the internal cooking arrangements rather than any visible external variations, and each diagram was really only discernible by the vehicle running numbers. The six original (1927) cars differed externally from all later examples in not having any passenger-access doors at the saloon end; instead, they had merely fixed frosted windows in this position. However, this difference was not correctly reflected on Diagram 2651, as all later cars to this diagram *did* have a transverse vestibule with side doors at this point, with this portion of the bodyside recessed to 8ft 7in wide, in the same manner as the Open Thirds. The six 1927 cars were altered to match the others between 1935 and 1939, the diagram being amended to this effect in June 1939.

All cars had a pair of double doors recessed into the bodyside on each side, giving access to the kitchen and pantry areas for staff, but these were never intended for passenger access and were not labelled in any way. Minor variations in window and door ventilators could be found amongst the various batches, but again these were seldom correctly reflected on the rather basic diagrams. The title 'Dining Saloon' had given way to 'Restaurant car' by the time the last batch was completed in June 1934. **Plates 62, 100-102** and **Figure 29** illustrate the cars in their original Kitchen First configuration.

Third-class dining facilities were provided either by the six purpose-built 64-seat saloons of 1927 (Diagram 2652) or, from 1930, by ordinary 56-seat open-saloon Thirds (Diagram 2005) equipped with tables, one of which appears in **Plate 103**. If additional First-class diners were expected, one of the unclassed General Saloons would be used instead; this appears to have been a regular arrangement in the early 1930s but not in later years. After 1930 the 1927 saloons were permanently reclassified as Open Thirds 1363-8 and by 1938 were no longer being used as Dining cars. By this time the trend away from full three-course meals had begun, and four buffet cars were proposed for construction in 1935. This proposal was not acted upon (at least, not at the time), although construction of three such vehicles was again put forward in 1939 — this time to be halted by wartime restrictions, the order eventually being cancelled in May 1945.

As World War 2 progressed, fewer and fewer Restaurant cars remained in traffic; from mid-1942 just four workings remained, between Waterloo and Exeter only, and even these ceased in April 1944. Some limited restoration of facilities restarted in mid-1945, by which time only cars 7862/6/71, 7932/9/41/50/4/7/69 were still serviceable to cover the four Exeter workings and two occasional Southampton boat duties, with four spare. By 1946, therefore, most Restaurant cars had been out of use for some time, so, avoiding the need to construct new vehicles, the cheaper expedient of converting existing Maunsell vehicles was adopted. Four (Nos 7858, 7946/9/52) were refurbished internally and provided with loose chairs and special fittings, for which Diagram 2657 was issued; these were employed on Waterloo–West of England services. In 1947 four more (Nos 7864/5/7 and 7999) were converted into Kitchen & Buffet cars, to Diagram 2659, having just eight stool-type seats and a large buffet counter and display area in place of the former First-class dining area; kitchen and pantry areas remained unaltered. To run with these, four of the 1927 Third Saloons were refurbished as Composite Saloons and renumbered 7841-4.

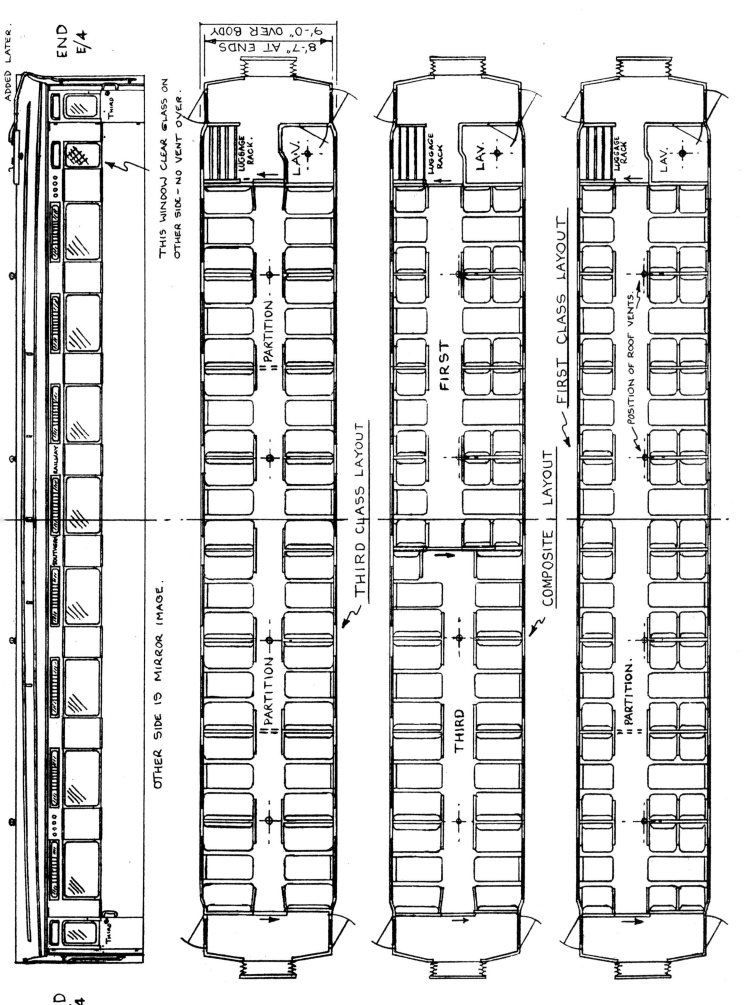

Figure 30 Dining Saloon Third/Composite, to Diagrams 2652, 2658 and 2662.

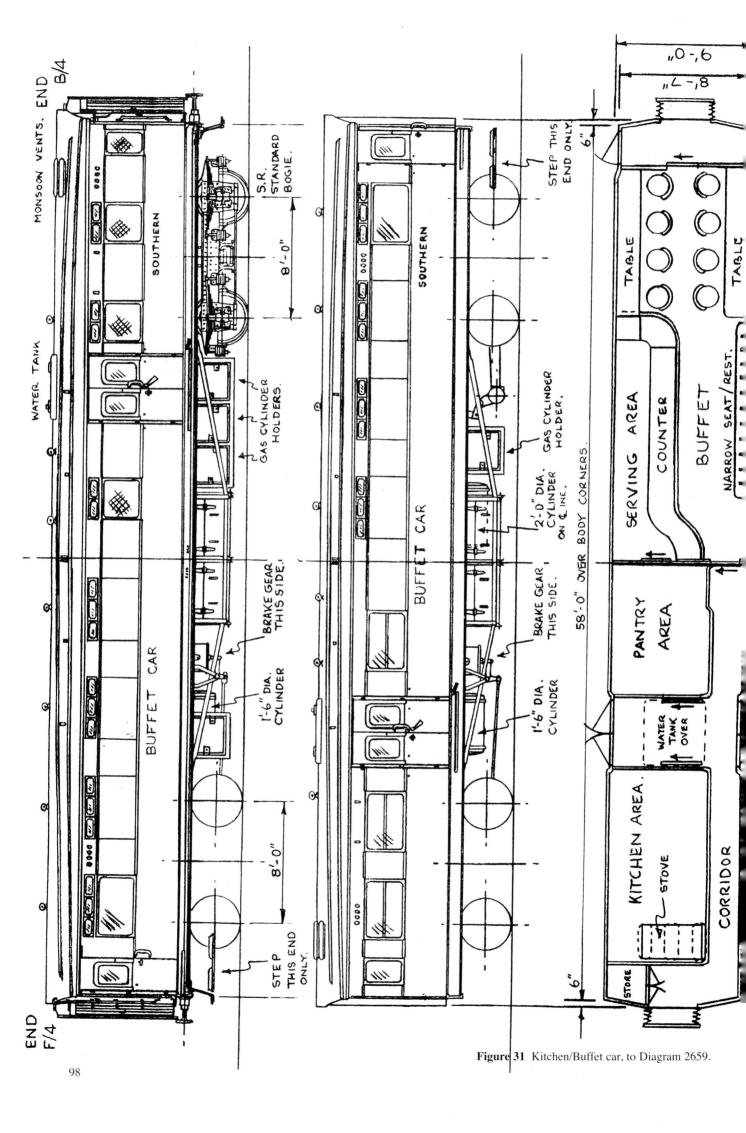

Figure 31 Kitchen/Buffet car, to Diagram 2659.

Plate 104 Diagram 2658 Composite Dining Saloon (BR carriage code RCO) 7841 at Eastleigh, c1959. This was previously Open Third No 1365 and before that Dining Third No 7866. It is now owned by the Bluebell Railway, but has not seen service for over 20 years. *R. E. Lacy*

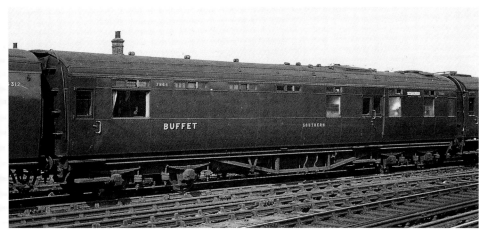

Plate 105 Diagram 2659 Buffet car 7864 — the second Maunsell carriage to carry this number — seen at Clapham Junction in March 1949 in malachite green, with one of the Diagram 2658 Composite Diners just visible to the right. *J. H. Aston*

One of these is seen in **Plate 104**. These pairs were allocated to the South Western section and could be seen on a variety of services, including inter-Regional trains, until their withdrawal in the early 1960s (apart from 7844, withdrawn as a result of accident damage in 1954 and replaced permanently by a standard 56-seat Open Third). Two vehicles (Nos 7841/64) were sold to the Bluebell Railway and for a number of years provided the original catering facilities at Sheffield Park station; both have now been out of use for over 20 years. These are the sole surviving Maunsell catering vehicles.

Also converted into Buffet cars in 1947 were vehicles 7878 and 7969, to Diagram 2661. In plan they were very similar to Diagram 2659, but the window layout was slightly different. They were employed on the reinstated 'Night Ferry' service, running between Victoria and Dover only. To run with these, the other two 1927 saloons were renumbered as First-class Diners 7846/7, having 48 loose chairs arranged 2+1 each side of the central gangway. These also had a Continental-type Wagon Lits gangway provided at the lavatory end of the coach, enabling them to couple direct to the ferry stock. All four remained on 'Night Ferry' duties until 1962, latterly being dual-heated to be compatible with electric haulage from 1959. Buffet car No 7969 was later re-deployed on the South Western section, remaining in occasional use until finally withdrawn in December 1967 — four years after all the other Maunsell catering vehicles had been withdrawn. Perhaps unfortunately for enthusiasts, it never carried blue-and-grey livery.

The two cars (7940/3) refurbished internally for the 'Bournemouth Limited' service in 1938 were transferred to departmental stock in July 1948, renumbered as 98s and 99s. These ran with Bulleid Inspection Saloon 100s (and generator van 97s) on staff tours of inspection, for which various special internal fittings were provided. One was returned to normal traffic in 1951, the other in 1953.

All Pullman catering services were finally withdrawn from South Eastern- and Central-section lines in May 1942. Central-section facilities were reinstated in 1946, but those on the South Eastern were limited to the all-Pullman trains (the 'Golden Arrow' and the 'Thanet Belle') and three Restriction 0 cars on the Hastings line (there had been six prewar). The Southern had not built any narrow-bodied catering vehicles, which compelled the retention of the Pullman cars on this route. To replace the others, 14 Maunsell Restaurant cars were reallocated to the South Eastern section, being staffed and provisioned by the Pullman Car Co. All 14 cars were rebuilt into Diagram 2666 Buffet cars in 1953/4, continuing to provide a Pullman Car Co presence on ordinary services to the Kent coast.

In addition, eight more cars were similarly rebuilt at the same time for Hotels Executive Ltd services on the South Western section. Seating was reduced to 18 diners, but in place of the kitchen/pantry area were a large buffet counter and display area. The rebuilding was much more extensive than on the earlier conversions, as illustrated by **Plate 107** and **Figure 32**. Those allocated to the SW section ran on certain selected Waterloo-Bournemouth/Exeter services, plus the Brighton-Plymouth train, often being used in sets comprising Bulleid or BR standard Mk 1 stock.

Two further reconstructions took place in 1953, when cars 7940/55 were converted into Diagram 2667 Kitchen/Buffet cars, again for Hotels Executive SW-section services. These lost all save three seats at one end but retained the kitchen/pantry areas unaltered, having a buffet counter incorporated as well. These two vehicles were often used on inter-Regional services. All the 1953/4 rebuilds were initially repainted crimson lake and cream, but all were green by 1960. Between 1953 and 1959 all vehicles were converted to propane gas cooking; previously they had been either Calor- or oil-gas fired.

In June 1952 Order E3889 was issued for the conversion of five Restaurant cars into Cafeteria cars. Only two Maunsell vehicles (Nos 7939/54) were actually rebuilt, in August 1952, before the scheme was halted. Diagram 2675 was allocated, and this states that cars 7947/50 were also to be rebuilt. (Was 'Ironclad' Cafeteria W7853S to have been the fifth vehicle?) At one point 15 conversions were to be done; whether the balance

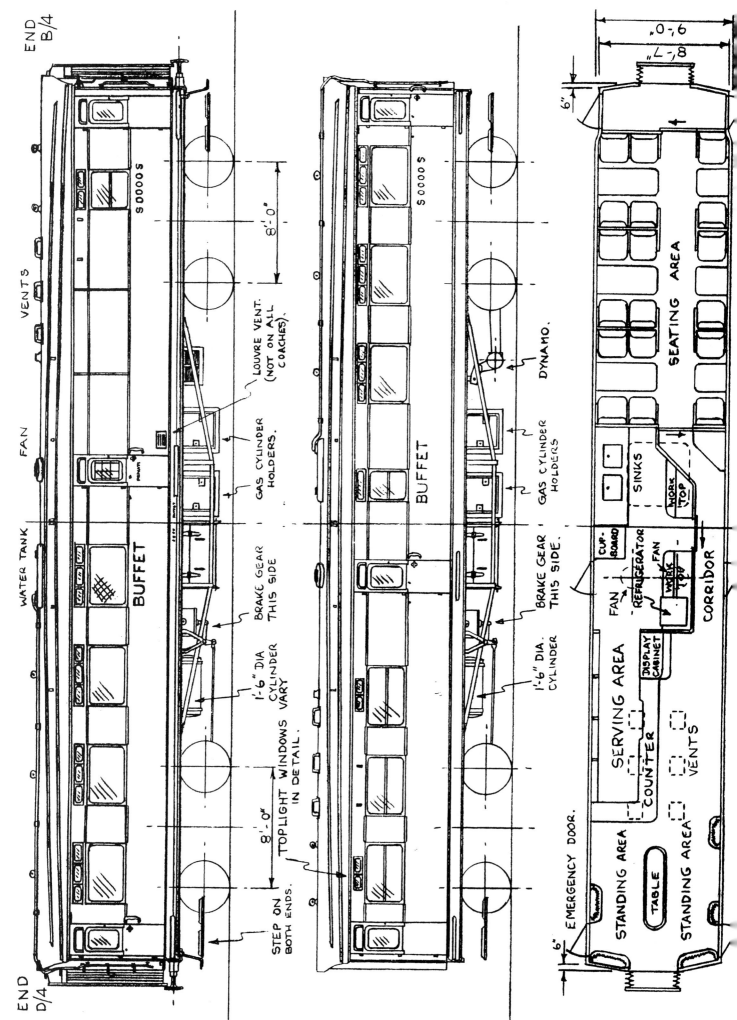

Figure 32 1953/4 Buffet car, to Diagram 2666.

Plate 106 Diagram 2661 Buffet car No 7969 at Stewarts Lane about 1961, during the period when it and the First Dining Saloon to the right were allocated to the 'Night Ferry' service. Note the electric-heating connections below the buffers. This was the last survivor of the Maunsell steam-hauled catering cars, finally being withdrawn in December 1967.
The Lens of Sutton Collection

Plate 107 One of the 1953/4 Buffet-car rebuilds to Diagram 2666, No 7945, at Seaton Junction in July 1959. These were much more extensive rebuilds than the earlier cars and involved removal of the inset double doors. *A. E. West*

Plate 108 Diagram 2675 Cafeteria car No 7939 at Exeter Central in September 1962, photographed from the corridor side. The servery was at the far end, on the other side, the seating area nearest the camera. Note the British standard (CA) gangway, non-retractable buffers and the British Railways C1 Route Restriction code. *A. E. West*

was to be made up of vehicles from other Regions is not known, but the Southern Region instead received two LNER Cafeteria cars between 1955 and 1962. Numbered S9211/3E, these were repainted in green livery soon after transfer. The two Maunsell vehicles were equipped with British Standard (CA) gangways (see **Plate 108**) and may have been used on inter-Regional services, although neither saw much use before withdrawal some 10 years later.

The Southern's allocation of Buffet cars was augmented between 1960 and 1963 by seven former Pullman cars. Nos S7872-7S were the six former Hastings-line cars, while S7879S was formerly the 'Yorkshire Pullman' car 'The Hadrian Bar'. All were repainted in green livery and could be found mostly on Waterloo-Southampton boat trains.

The 14 remaining unmodified Maunsell Restaurant cars were retained on the South Western section but by 1960 were needed only at peak periods. With the exception of car 7969 (already described), all Maunsell catering vehicles were withdrawn between 1960 and 1963 as the arrival of new BR Mk 1 catering stock allowed the 1947-9 Bulleid vehicles to be cascaded off the principal services.

The vehicle summary is shown in **Table 8**.

Table 8
Summary of Maunsell catering vehicles

Diagram No	Vehicle Type	Seats 1st	Seats 3rd	Running Nos	Built by	Remarks
2650	Kitchen/Dining First	24		7870/1, 7931/2	Eastleigh 7/32	Fletcher-Russell cooking range; Some later to Diagram 2666
2651	Kitchen/Dining First	24		7858-63 7939-42 7943-58	Eastleigh 5/27 Eastleigh 7-12/29 Eastleigh 5-9/30	Some later to Diagrams 2657/66/7/75
2652	Dining Saloon Third		64	7864-9	Eastleigh 7/27	To Open Thirds 1363-8 in 1930
2655	Kitchen/Dining First	24		7878/80, 7933/4/69/95/7/8	Eastleigh 6/34	Slater's new-type stove; Some later to Diagrams 2661/66
2656	Kitchen/Dining First	24		7864-9 (second use) 7999-8000	Eastleigh 7/32 Eastleigh 6/34	Slater's old-type stove; Some later to Diagrams 2659/66
2657	Kitchen/Dining First (with special fittings)	24 (loose chairs)		7858, 7946/9/52	Converted 1946	Ex-Diagram 2651
2658	Composite Dining Saloon	24	31	7841-4	Converted 7/47	Ex-Diagram 2652 Nos 1365-8
2659	Kitchen & Buffet car	(8 stools)		7864/5/7, 7999	Converted 1947	Ex-Diagram 2656
2661	Kitchen & Buffet car	(8 stools)		7878, 7969	Converted 1947	Ex-Diagram 2655
2662	Dining Saloon First	48		7846/7	Converted 12/47	Ex-Diagram 2652 Nos 1363/64
2666	Buffet car		18	7859/60/2/3/6/9/70/1, 7934/8/51/7/8/95	Converted 1953/4	Ex-Diagrams 2650/1/5/6; for Pullman Car Co
				7941/2/4/5/7/50/3/6	Converted 1953/4	Ex-Diagram 2651; for Hotels Executive Ltd;
2667	Kitchen/Buffet car		3	7940/55	Converted 1953	Ex-Diagram 2651 for Hotels Executive Ltd;
2675	Cafeteria car		48	7939/54 (7947/50 cancelled)	Converted 8/52	Ex-Diagram 2651; CA fitted

Notes
All coaches were Route Restriction 4.
Many of the conversions were done at Lancing.
Nos 7940/3 internally refurbished for the 'Bournemouth Limited' in July 1938; both were transferred to departmental stock in July 1948, renumbered as 98s and 99s.
Composite Saloon No 7844 withdrawn following accident damage 4/54.

Plate 109 1935-vintage open-saloon Third No 1311, as completed with simplified lining layout. The saloon was divided into three sections (two bays, three bays, two bays), but only one of the two dividing partitions had a sliding door, to segregate smokers from non-smokers. *Modern Transport*

Chapter 6.
Maunsell Stock 1935-1937

Although the overall design concept of Maunsell's carriage stock did not radically alter over the entire 1926-37 period, the vehicles completed from mid-1935 onwards exhibited a number of fundamental detail changes. Those built from July 1935 until May 1936 were very much more flush-panelled, the windows being fitted from inside the bodywork, rather than being contained within externally-beaded timber frames. On the corridor side, the 'dummy droplight' feature was at long last removed, being replaced by full-height quarterlights that matched the other large corridor-side windows, resulting in a much more modern appearance. Frameless balancing droplights were fitted to most passenger doors, with a locking lever on the inside which had to be released before raising or lowering the droplight.

Less obvious to the casual observer but immediately apparent to passengers as they entered the coach was the fact that the corridor-side doors were now positioned opposite the compartment partitions, instead of directly opposite alternate compartments. This meant that, no matter which corridor-side door was used, one always had to turn to left or right to gain access to a compartment. Viewed from inside the compartment, this gave an unimpeded view through a large corridor window, placed directly opposite the compartment. It may also have resulted in more even wear on the upholstery, since no compartment was more accessible than any other, at least from the corridor side. The compartment side was not so noticeably different from previous coaches but did not exhibit external window frames.

In terms of operation, these changes mattered little, as, dimensionally and for seating purposes, the coaches were the same as all previous Restriction 4 vehicles, but new diagrams were, of course, produced to reflect the altered details. The Southern Railway built no more Restriction 0 or 1 coaches — the next generation of narrow-width vehicles would wait until British Railways, with the Hastings- and Oxted-line diesel units.

The very last Maunsell steam-hauled stock, completed between April and August 1936, abandoned the completely flush-panelled look, perhaps due to corrosion problems and were instead provided with Alpax aluminium window frames. These allowed the corridor-side windows to be made even larger, doing away entirely with the full-height quarterlights of the 1935 designs. These final productions were probably the best of Maunsell's stock.

The 1935 vehicles, which were actually ordered between April 1933 and April 1935, were as follows:

Order 761 was authorised in April 1933, along with the last of the 1926-34 designs. Orders 798-800 were placed in March 1934 and 862 in April 1935, by which time the Drawing Office was already working on the changes that would produce the 1936 stock.

The first vehicles to appear were the Open Thirds, which had entered traffic by July 1935. At this time the usual construction procedure was for the underframes to be built at Lancing, these then being taken to Eastleigh for bodywork, finishing and painting. The Open Thirds were very similar in plan to the earlier vehicles completed between 1930 and 1933, except that luggage racks were fitted in the spaces opposite the lavatories at each end of the seven-bay saloon area. However, they had a very different window arrangement, as seen in **Plate 109**. Instead of the large droplight windows of the 1930 design, there were large fixed panes with 'MM Airstream' ventilators above. These, it was claimed in an article in *Modern Transport* for September 1935, gave ventilation without creating draughts or admitting grit into the carriage interior. (After a recent journey in coach 1309 on the Bluebell Railway, the author might be tempted to disagree with this claim!) These coaches did not have the benefit of frameless droplights — the end vestibule doors were provided with traditional timber-framed droplights, still finished in varnished teak.

Interior decoration was carried out using mahogany panelling with white celluloid stringing throughout the passenger saloon. Blue scratchproof rexine (imitation leather) was used in the end vestibules and luggage-rack areas; similar silver-grey material covered the walls of the lavatories. Ceilings were white throughout. Floors were covered with inlaid granite-coloured linoleum, with a brick-red rubber gangway runner edged in blue. Tables could be installed at all seating bays, enabling the vehicles to be used as Dining Saloons.

Externally the lining was simplified to just a single horizontal orange/black line just below the windows, with rectangular lining panels between the windows only. Class designations, using 8in-high figures, appeared in the centre of the lining panel between the vestibule and the end saloon window. This appears to have been the only use of this particular combination of lining, at least on steam-hauled stock. Roofs were stated to be white, but the photograph accompanying the article clearly shows this to be grey.

In appearance they were a considerable improvement on the earlier Open Thirds, the flush-sided look being clearly evident on coach 1304 in **Plate 110**, taken in 1962. At this time it was formed in two-set 103, one of 11 such sets made up in 1958 for West of England local services — hence their Carriage Working Notice classification of two-sets 'W'.

HOO No	Stock	Coach/set Nos
E761	30 open-saloon Thirds for general use	1282-1311
E798	50 (later 60) Corridor Thirds for general use	1841-1900
E799	25 Brake Composites for Waterloo-West of England services	6675-99
E800	25 Brake Thirds for Waterloo-West of England services	2776-92, 2831-8
E862	10 Corridor Thirds for general use,	1901-10,
	plus two replacement bodies for fire-damaged originals	802, 1834

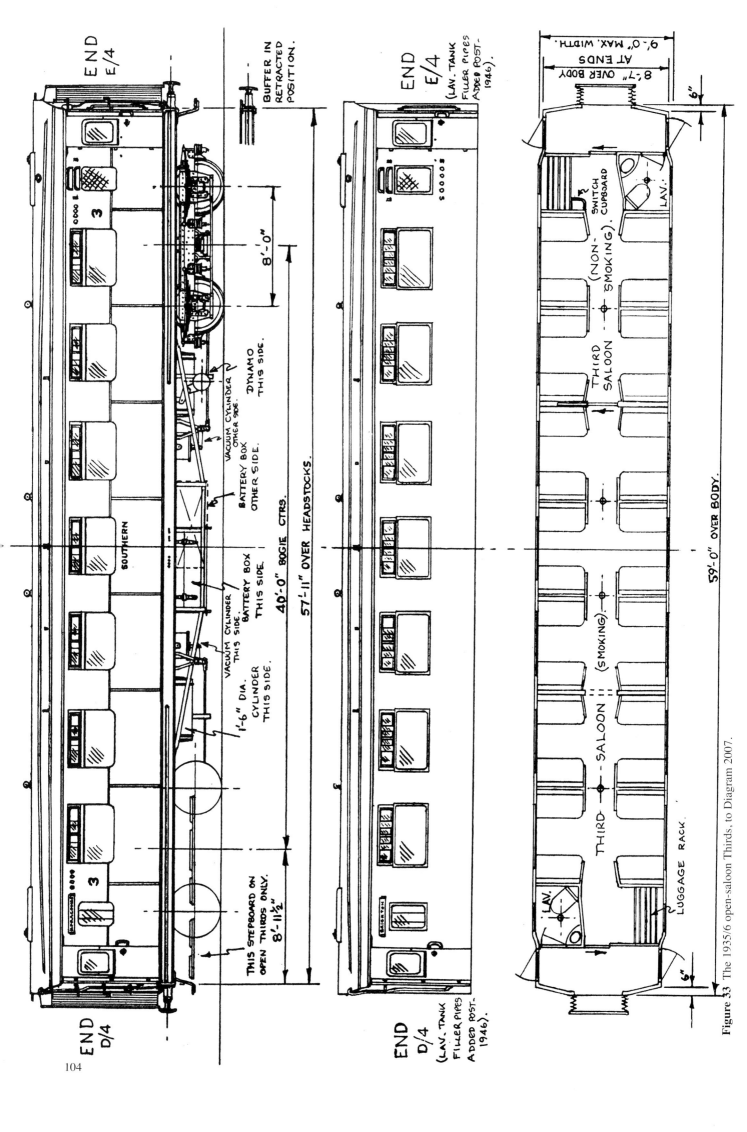

Figure 33 The 1935/6 open-saloon Thirds, to Diagram 2007.

Plate 110 Similar vehicle No 1304 at Exeter Central in September 1962, formed in two-set 'W' No 103. Lavatory-tank filler pipes are now provided, with the nozzle ends picked out in yellow.
A. E. West

Initially they were formed of a Maunsell Brake Composite and an ex-SECR 'long ten' (60ft 10-compartment Third — by then Second), but in late 1959 the non-corridor coach was replaced by Maunsell Open Thirds (now Seconds), some of which were the 1935 vehicles described here. As the lines on which these sets ran are popular with modellers, their formations are listed below:

Vehicle	Set 100	Set 101	Set 102	Set 103	Set 104	Set 105
Six-compartment Brake Composite	6599	6906	6577	6905	6589	6649
Seven-bay Open Second	1303	1300	1306	1304	1314	1327

Vehicle	Set 106	Set 107	Set 108	Set 109	Set 110
Six-compartment Brake Composite	6573	6592	6590	6594	6595
Seven-bay Open Second	1370	1399	1310	1339	1325

Plate 111 One of the two replacement Diagram 2008 bodies, on 1928 underframe of Third No 802, as completed in 1936. This shows the next livery variation, with full waistline panels only.
Southern Railway

Plate 112 The altered corridor-side window and door layout is clearly seen on Corridor Third No 1852 at Eastleigh in July 1962. Compare with the details of the 1929 coach just visible on the right. *P. H. Swift*

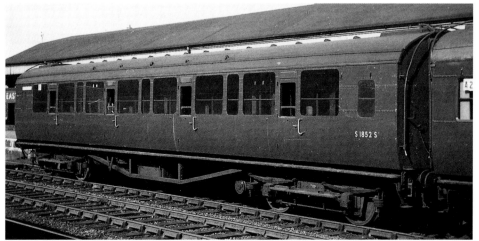

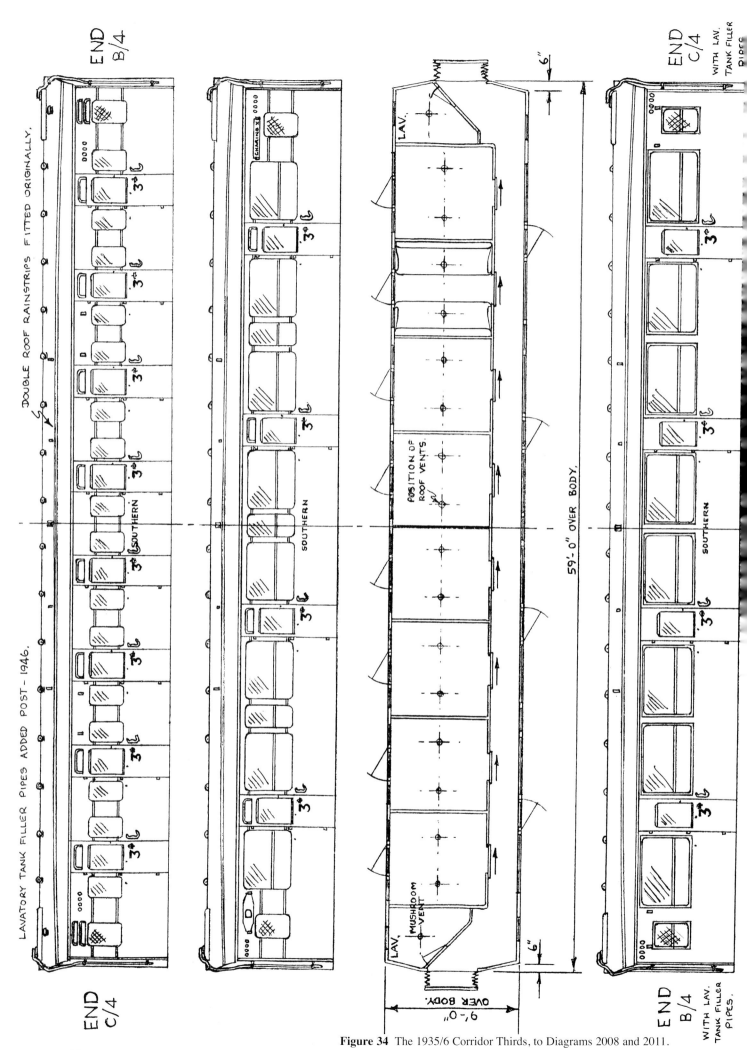

Figure 34 The 1935/6 Corridor Thirds, to Diagrams 2008 and 2011.

Some of the Open Seconds came from the 1930/3 batches, all the Brake Composites being 1926 or 1929 stock. They were supposed to be confined to services west of Axminster and could most often be found on the Lyme Regis, Sidmouth, Exmouth and Callington branches. At Lyme Regis the Brake often worked on its own, the Second standing spare for use only at busier times; coach 6595 of set 110 is seen as such in **Plate 79**. Despite the operating restriction, these sets were occasionally substituted for the more usual 2-P Maunsell or Bulleid set on a through service to Waterloo.

The above formations altered somewhat after 1962; in some instances a Bulleid coach replaced either or both vehicles, and all those remaining in service on 1 January 1963 were transferred to Western Region ownership when all former Southern lines west of Salisbury were passed to WR control.

The Corridor Thirds to Orders 798 and 862 also received the flush-panelled look, with yet another livery variation — in this case just full waistline panelling only, as seen in **Plate 111**. In total 72 were completed, the two extras being replacement bodies for vehicles 802 and 1834, their earlier-style bodies having been destroyed by fire at Dover Marine in July 1935. The revised corridor-side layout is clearly seen in **Plate 112**. None of these coaches was originally included in a set, but several were soon formed in 'Ironclad' four-coach sets 431-44 from 1937, their flush panels and high windows contrasting somewhat with the older vehicles.

Some of the Brake Thirds and Brake Composites completed between August and December 1935 were incorporated into sets immediately on completion. Several two-coach sets were formed for Waterloo-West of England and Waterloo-Lymington/Swanage through services, as follows:

Vehicle	Set 168	Set 172	Set 178	Set 196	Set 197	Set 198
Brake Third	2776	2777	2836	2778	2779	2780
Brake Composite	6695	6696	6690	6697	6698	6699

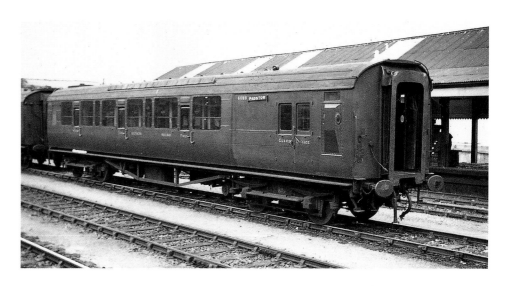

Plate 113 1935 Brake Composite No 6688 at Padstow about 1936. At this time it was a loose coach allocated to Waterloo—West of England services and would remain so until converted for push-pull service in 1960. In its later push-pull form the coach appears again in **Plate 121**. *E. L. Scaife*

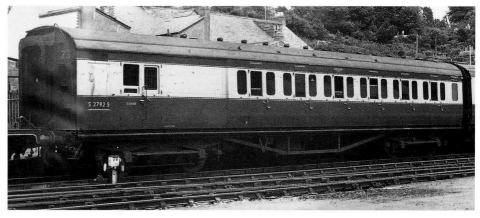

Plate 114 1935 Brake Third No 2792 at Bodmin North in June 1952, forming 2-P set 23 with Brake Composite 6575, seen on the right. Note the different styles of 'blood and custard' livery, with and without the wide crimson cantrail band. *J. H. Aston*

Set 197 did not run for many years in this form, as coach 6698 was destroyed by enemy action c1941, companion vehicle 2779 being reallocated to set 248 (about to be detailed), whose original coach 2782 was similarly destroyed at Clapham Junction in September 1940. Other sets formed using this stock were:

The original set 202, formed in 1931, was disbanded.

In these sets, the Firsts, Composite and some of the Thirds came from previous orders and therefore failed to match the new coaches in detail. All were used on Waterloo-West of England/Bournemouth services, often being made up to six vehicles by the addition of a Dining car and Open Third, or by

Vehicle	Set 202	Set 248	Set 249	Set 250	Set 400
Six-compartment Brake Third	2837	2781	2783	2785	2787
Eight-compartment Third	1827	1199	1848	1884	-
Seven-compartment First/Composite *	7672	7216	7222	7674	5654*
Six-compartment Brake Third	2838	2782	2784	2786	2788

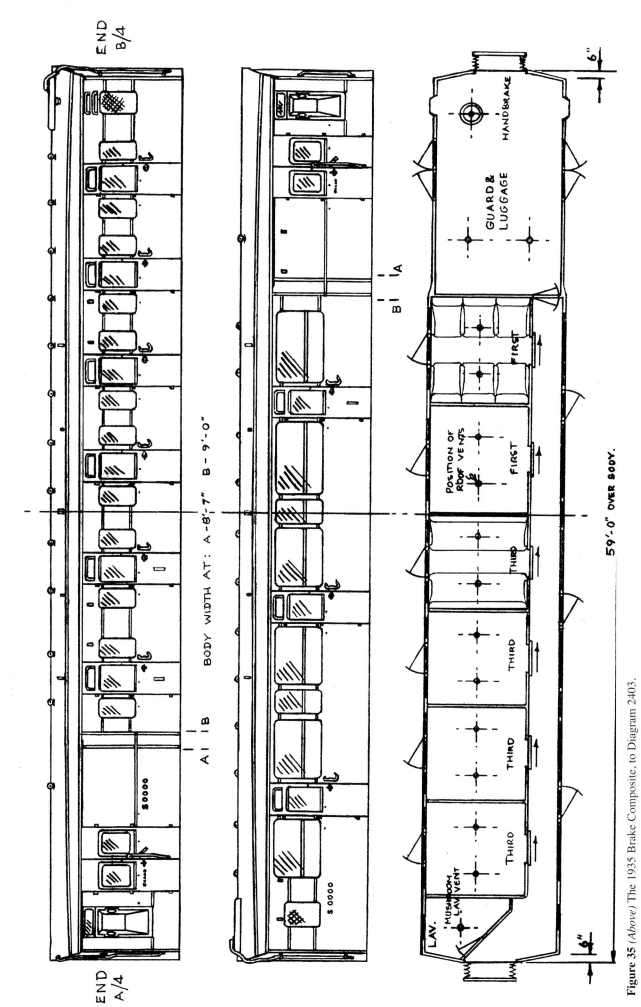

Figure 35 (*Above*) The 1935 Brake Composite, to Diagram 2403.

Figure 36 (*Below*) The 1935/6 Brake Thirds, to Diagram 2113.

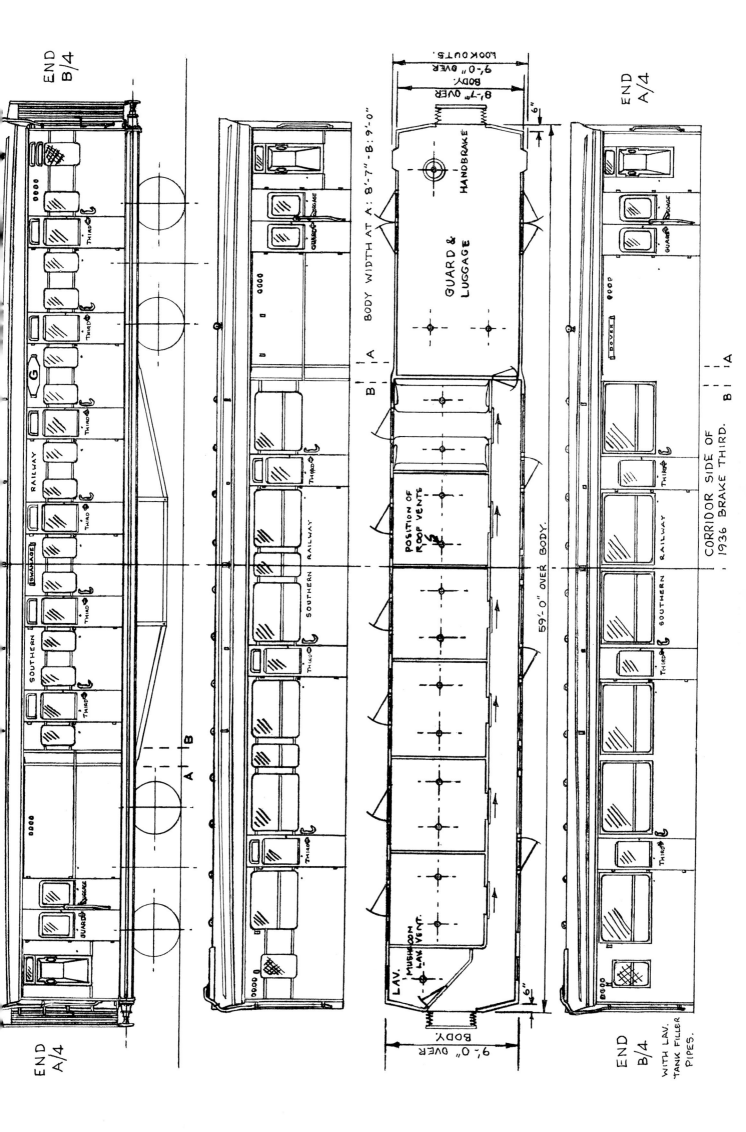

addition of a couple of Corridor Thirds. By this date there were very many of these. Most of the other 1935 coaches remained as loose stock until after World War 2, when the rapid return of holiday traffic to Devon and Cornwall required the formation of new five-coach sets 265-73, with these and some older Maunsell vehicles.

Plate 114 illustrates one of the Brake Thirds running in BR 'blood and custard' livery and formed in additional 2-P set No 23. Eight such sets — Nos 22-9 — were formed in September 1948 for West of England services. Whilst by no means all of them included 1935 vehicles, their formations are given here, as, like sets 100-10 described previously, they became a common sight on West Country branch lines until the 1960s, finally being lost to the Western Region in January 1963.

Vehicle	Set 22	Set 23	Set 24	Set 25	Set 26	Set 27	Set 28	Set 29
Six-compartment Brake Third	2790	2792	2832	3780	2831	3775	2787	2788
Six-compartment Brake Composite	6691	6575	6602	6665	6586	6603	6569	6567

Plate 115 1936 open-saloon Third No 1450, the last coach on Order E861, showing yet another lining variation, with full waistline and window panels. These were undoubtedly some of Maunsell's finest steam-hauled carriages. *Southern Railway*

Comparison of the coach numbers with the summary tables will show that every stage of evolution of Maunsell 59ft coach was represented within these eight sets! Some vehicle changes occurred from 1960 onwards as older coaches were withdrawn, while two additional sets (Nos 30/1) were added in 1962, just before Western Region takeover. Most eventually acquired 'W' prefixes to their coach numbers, becoming W2790S etc.

The fledgling Bluebell Railway would later purchase coach 6575 from set 23 in May 1960, this becoming the first Maunsell carriage to enter preservation. What is more, it may still be enjoyed today, restored to its 1930s condition.

One other odd set deserves a mention at this point, as it included a Brake Third from Order E800. This was set 760, formed in 1943 for Maidstone West-Paddock Wood-Tonbridge services, comprising Brake Third No 2833, First No 7673 and Third No 1114. Its unique make-up was similar to the previous set 760, formed of three ex-SECR vehicles that were used on the same services. This had included SECR rebuilt Composite No 5546, described at the start of Chapter 7. The Maunsell set eventually became a standard three-coach formation of two Brake Thirds and a Composite (2833+5678+2793) in 1957, joining all the other similar three-coach sets on Kent Coast services.

The last orders for Maunsell steam-hauled vehicles were placed in March and April 1935. By this time electrification of much of the Central section was nearing completion and that to Portsmouth was at the planning stage. As a result not all the coaches ordered at this time were actually built, while a total of 109 vehicles put forward for construction at this time were held in abeyance until at least 1939, without HOO numbers being issued. These were all either cancelled or incorporated in 1939 orders. Further changes to windows and corridor-side arrangements were made, as decribed at the start of this chapter. Details are shown below

The original intention for Orders E869-71 was to provide 20 four-coach sets (presumably Nos 952-71), but only the vehicles for the first 10 were completed — and even these actually ran as three-coach sets plus 10 loose Thirds. All were completed between April and August 1936, while the outstanding uncompleted vehicles were finally cancelled in June 1939.

As with the 1935 designs, construction began with the Open Thirds. Identical in plan to Nos 1282-1311 and allocated the same diagram number (2007), these were possibly the best-looking of all Maunsell's carriages, exhibiting a very handsome exterior. **Plate 115** illustrates No 1450, the last of the batch in original livery. Most ran as loose coaches or as Dining Saloon Thirds,

HOO No	Stock	Coach/set Nos
E861	41 open-saloon Thirds for general use	1410-50
E869	40 (later 20) Brake Thirds for London-Folkestone/Ramsgate services	952-61
E870	20 (later 10) Corridor Composites for London-Folkestone/Ramsgate services	952-61
E871	20 (later 10) Corridor Thirds for London-Folkestone/Ramsgate services	952-61

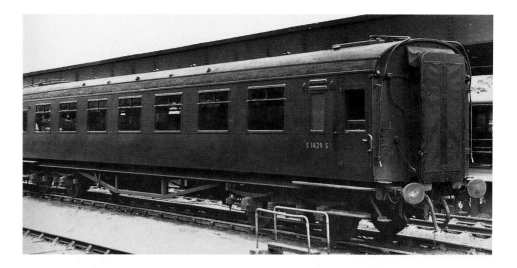

Plate 116 Similar vehicle No 1429 at Exeter Central in September 1962, in Southern Region green. *A. E. West*

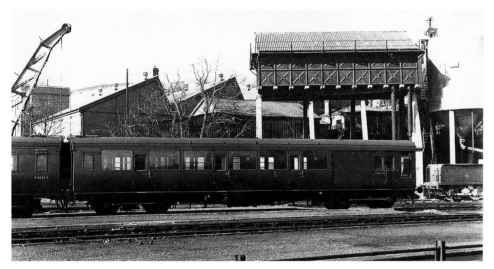

Plates 117 and 118 Brake Third 4241 and Composite 5697, from set 957, at Dover Priory in March 1953. The large corridor-side windows have now replaced any smaller intermediate corridor-side windows, resulting in another handsome design. On the compartment side only the aluminium window frames break up the flush-sided look. Note the complete lack of door ventilators. *(both) D. Cullum*

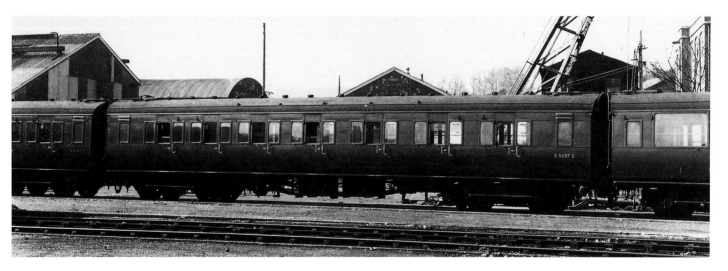

several being chosen for refurbishment by Bulleid in 1938/9 for the 'Bournemouth Limited' or as 'Improved Boat Stock', despite being only a few years old. They were among the last Maunsell Restriction 4 coaches to remain in traffic, being withdrawn between December 1962 and December 1964.

The 10 three-coach sets, Nos 952-61, entered traffic on Kent Coast services during the summer of 1936, often being referred to by the staff as the 'Folkestone' stock. These were fully lined out, unlike the Open Thirds, this just being visible in the title page picture. Formations are given below.

The Brake Thirds were actually numbered within the Second-class number block, there being few vacant runs of numbers left within the original Brake Third block by this time. The Corridor Thirds, Nos 1911-20, entered service carrying set numbers 952-61 stencilled on the solebars, but it is uncertain whether they were actually formed in the sets as originally planned. Instead the

Vehicle	Set 952	Set 953	Set 954	Set 955	Set 956	Set 957	Set 958	Set 959	Set 960	Set 961
Six-compartment Brake Third	4231	4233	4235	4237	4239	4241	4243	4245	4247	4249
Seven-compartment Composite	5692	5693	5694	5695	5696	5697	5698	5699	5700	5701
Six-compartment Brake Third	4232	4134	4236	4238	4240	4242	4244	4246	4248	4250

three-sets often ran with a Pullman car included, again seen in the title-page picture. All were 'run in' on the South Western section (most being noted at Exeter within a few days of entering service) before taking up their allocated duties. The formations remained unchanged until after Phase 2 of the Kent Coast electrification was completed, causing most sets to be reallocated to the South Western section, where several were then made up to eight vehicles in 1962/3. **Plates 117-9** illustrate these final productions of the Maunsell era.

They were joined by one more standard 1929-stock three-coach set on Kent Coast services in 1943 — No 962, formed of Brake Thirds Nos 3734/5 and Composite No 5645, all originally part of the July 1929 orders for Central- and South Western-section services. Many other sets allocated to the Central section had moved to the South Eastern section by 1936/7, while others on the mid-Sussex route to Portsmouth were transferred to the Oxted, East Grinstead and Tunbridge Wells West group of lines in 1938, giving these routes the luxury of regular corridor trains for the first time.

The completion of the 1935 orders brought the number of Maunsell 59ft vehicles built to 1,320, plus 77 'Thanets'. In addition, Maunsell had overseen the construction of all except the first 40 out of a total of 154 'Ironclads' and all 75 'Continentals'. Thus between 1921 and 1936 the Southern Railway had managed to provide for its steam-hauled services no fewer than 1,626 new modern corridor coaches. What it could not predict was that this total would have to suffice for a further nine years before construction was able to recommence after World War 2. Nevertheless, from a rather poor start, Maunsell and his team had succeeded in providing a sound (if, perhaps, not exciting) fleet of well-designed and well-constructed corridor vehicles, almost all of which would serve the railway for another 25 or more years.

Few changes were made to most Maunsell coaches, apart from that of livery. From about 1945 lavatory-tank filler pipes were provided at the non-brake ends of most vehicles, obviating the need for staff to climb the end steps when replenishing the roof-mounted water tanks, and these were a standard fitting on Bulleid vehicles. In fact sets 952-61 had these provided when built in 1936, but their fitting to earlier vehicles was a protracted process and was still incomplete in the early 1950s.

The rebuilding of the catering vehicles between 1946 and 1954 has already been covered, but three further batches of rebuildings were destined to take place in 1959/60. Four of the Nondescript Saloon Brakes were rebuilt as Ambulance Ward cars in 1959, and these are described in Chapter 14. Finally, 20 of the 1933 Open Thirds (now Open Seconds) and 20 1935 Brake Composites were converted into push-pull sets in 1959/60. At this time the Southern Region still had around 30 wooden-panelled push-pull sets in service, all being formed with pre-Grouping vehicles.

Following a rear-end collision at Barnes in December 1955, when electric arcing had set fire to the wooden bodywork of the 2-NOL electric unit involved, there had been a desire to replace any remaining wooden-panelled coaches as soon as possible. The push-pull sets were also upwards of 35 years old and were almost life-expired regardless. However, the lines on which they served were not yet being considered for closure, so replacements were needed. Orders L4634 and 4746 were issued in June 1959 and February 1960 respectively, each for the conversion of 10 push-pull sets. Set numbers allocated were 600-19, and they were formed as below:

Sets 600-9 had entered traffic by November 1959, 610-9 by June 1960. Diagram 2023 was allocated to the Open Seconds, Diagram 2407 to the Brake Composites. This, incidentally, left in traffic only three original 1935 Brake Composites — Nos 6685/6/92 — all reserved for the 'Night Ferry' service. Both conversions lost their outer end gangways (those within the set being retained) and had their lavatories sealed. The Brake Composites had two small windows fitted to the driving end and were equipped with push-pull controls for the driver, droplight windows being provided on both sides in place of the pressed-steel lookouts. The Open Second was through-piped for push-pull working, the locomotive being coupled at this end. Large buffers to electric-stock pattern were fitted at each end of the set. Although the two types did not match in style, the result was

Vehicle	Set 600	Set 601	Set 602	Set 603	Set 604	Set 605	Set 606	Set 607	Set 608	Set 609
Six-compartment Brake Composite	6693	6687	6681	6675	6676	6677	6678	6682	6689	6694
Seven-bay Open Second	1338	1351	1318	1320	1360	1349	1328	1343	1330	1353

Vehicle	Set 610	Set 611	Set 612	Set 613	Set 614	Set 615	Set 616	Set 617	Set 618	Set 619
Six-compartment Brake Composite	6679	6680	6683	6688	6690	6691	6695	6696	6697	6699
Seven-bay Open Second	1317	1323	1356	1347	1354	1341	1359	1361	1342	1331

Plate 119 At the other end of the Southern system, at Barnstaple Junction in August 1962, is Diagram 2011 Corridor Third (now Second) No 1914, forming a local service to Torrington with a Bulleid Brake Composite. The clean lines of the 1936 vehicles are obvious. *A. E. West*

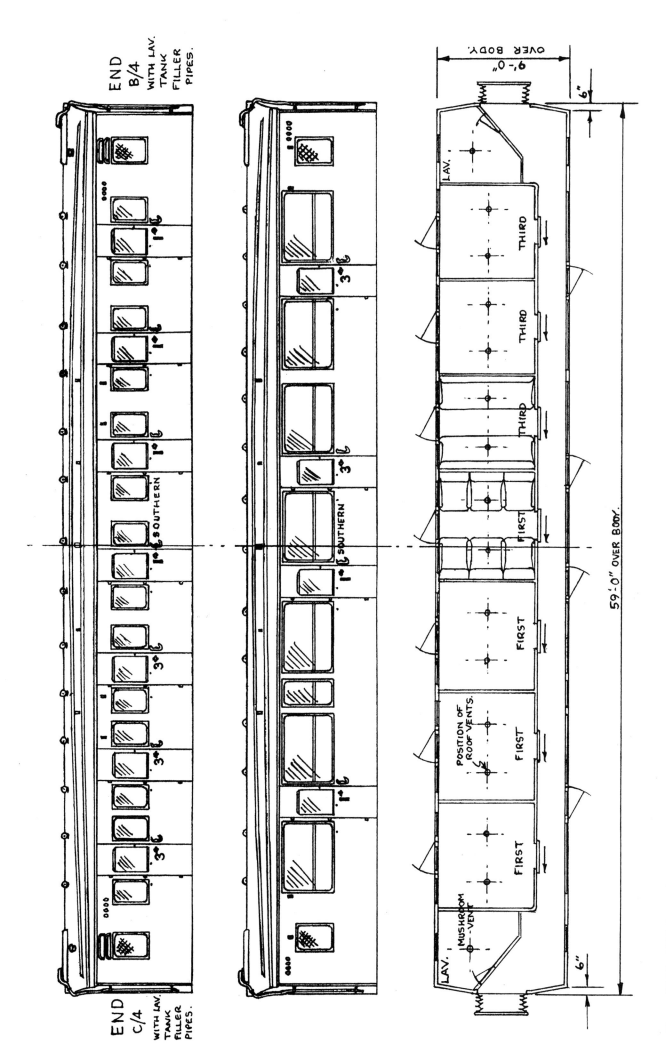

Figure 37 The 1936 Composite, to Diagram 2308.

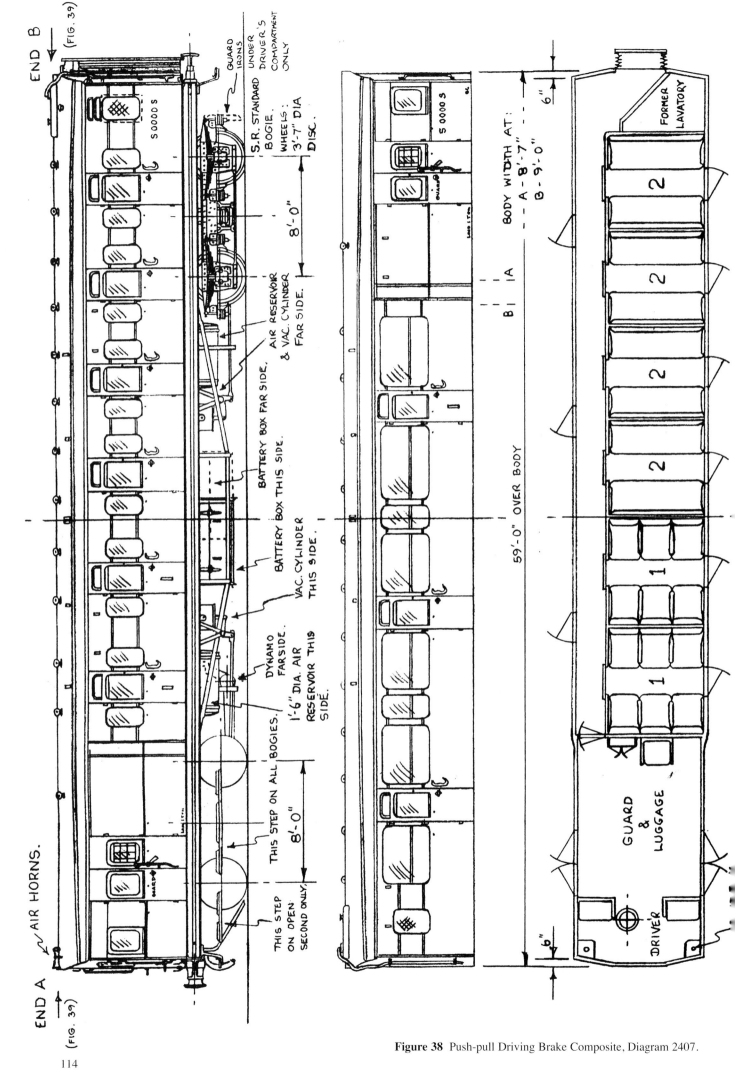

Figure 38 Push-pull Driving Brake Composite, Diagram 2407.

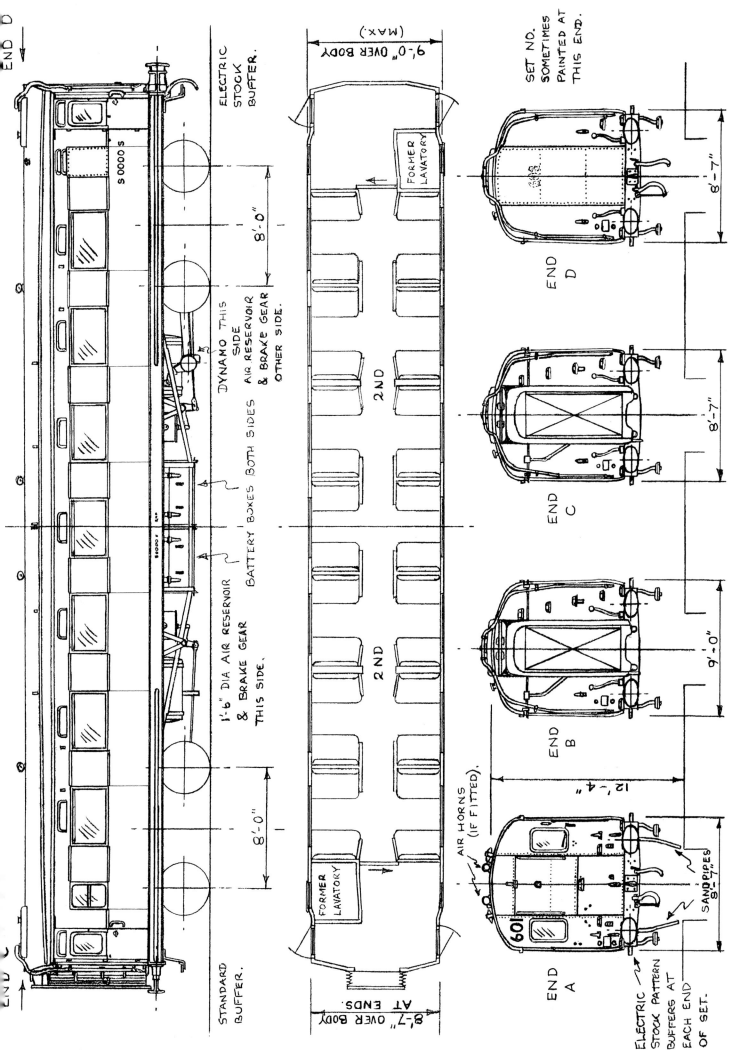

Figure 39 Push-pull Trailer Second, Diagram 2023.

certainly an improvement over the pre-Grouping push-pull sets and facilitated conductor/ guard issue of tickets if necessary. **Plates 120 and 121** and **Figures 38 and 39** illustrate these final push-pull sets.

Initially, sets 600-7/16-9 were allocated to the Central section, sets 608/9/12-5 to the South Western and 610/1 to the South Eastern. However, it was not long before many of the lines for which they were intended were being closed, and the first withdrawals took place in 1963. Sets 618/9 were disbanded, and Brake Composites 6697/9 then ran as loose coaches on the Hayling Island branch until November 1963, but not in push-pull operation. Both were later sold to Chipman Weed Killing Co of Horsham. Sets 604/6/9/13/5/7 lasted until late 1964, when operation of traditional steam-hauled push-pull services on the Southern Region came to an end.

Most other Restriction 4 Maunsell coaches were also withdrawn during the 1961-4 period, many being converted for further departmental use, leaving just a handful to survive into 1966/7. Indeed, such was the pace of withdrawals that many sidings and semi-disused branch lines were filled to capacity with stock awaiting scrapping, as BR's scrapyards simply could not cope with the volume of work. Ironically, there was sometimes a shortage of serviceable stock, since most coaches were automatically consigned to the scrapheap on reaching 30 years of age — a directive issued by the British Transport Commission in 1959. This unfortunately failed to take into account the varying ages and types of coach in each set. For example, all of a particular batch of Brake coaches might be over 30 years old, yet the companion Composites and other non-brake vehicles could be just below this threshold. However, one could not run without the other, so entire sets of coaches would be rendered useless by strict adherence to this instruction, leading to an acute shortage of stock and many changes in set formations. The directive was based to some extent on sound economic principles; at the time, the wisdom of maintaining large numbers of coaches to cater for the seasonal traveller on, perhaps, just 20 days per year was being called into question. In addition, the Summer Saturday passenger was fast deserting the railway for road transport, resulting in a rapid fall in demand — a problem that never had to be faced by the Southern Railway management in the 1930s and '40s.

A summary of 1935/6 stock appears in **Table 9**.

Table 9
Summary of Maunsell 1935/6 stock

Diagram No	Vehicle Type	Seats 1st	Seats 3rd	Running Nos	Built by	Remarks
2007	Seven-bay Open Saloon Third		56	1282-1311	Eastleigh 7/35	Flush-panelled
				1410-50	Eastleigh 4-6/36	Large windows
2008	Eight-compartment Third		64	1841-1910	Eastleigh 11/35-4/36	Flush-panelled
				802, 1834	Eastleigh 5/36 and 7/36	Replacement bodies
2011	Eight-compartment Third		64	1911-20	Eastleigh 6/36	Large corridor windows
2113	Six-compartment Brake Third		48	2776-92, 2831-8	Eastleigh 10-12/35	Flush-panelled
				4231-50	Eastleigh 6-7/36	Large corridor windows
2308	Seven-compartment Composite	24	24	5692-5701	Eastleigh 7/36	Large corridor windows
2403	Six-compartment Brake Composite	12	32	6675-99	Eastleigh 8-10/35	Flush-panelled; most to Diagram 2407 1959/60
2407	Six-compartment Brake Composite (push-pull)	12	32	6675-83/7-91/3-7/9	Rebuilt 1959/60	Ex-Diagram 2403; seats now First/Second

Notes
All vehicles were Route Restriction 4
Underframes generally ex-Lancing
Vehicles 1881, 2782, 6684/98 lost through enemy action or accident damage

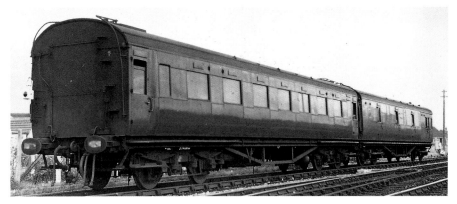

Plate 120 Maunsell push-pull set 616 at Wareham, on Swanage-branch duty, in September 1964. Open Second No 1359 is nearest the camera, Brake Composite No 6695 beyond. Notice the different bodywork styles. *A. E. West*

Plate 121 Push-pull set 613 stands in the down platform at Wareham on the same day. Brake Composite No 6688 was withdrawn in November 1964 but reinstated shortly afterwards, finally being withdrawn for the second time in September 1966. For what purpose the coach was retained is not known. The Swanage Railway Preservation Society owns both a Brake Composite and an Open Second, so, with these plus its 'M7' tank, together with plans to extend the line to Wareham, this scene might one day be re-created. *A. E. West*

Chapter 7.
Non-corridor Stock

At the start of Chapter 1 it was stated that the Southern Railway did not build any new steam-hauled non-corridor stock but that it did re-frame a number of pre-Grouping vehicles, remounting them wherever possible on standard 58ft underframes. It is now proposed to look briefly at these conversions. It should be noted that much other rebuilding of pre-Grouping vehicles also took place, such as push-pull conversions and Isle of Wight transfers, but in these instances no new underframes were required, so they remain outside the scope of this survey.

Between 1925 and 1940 over 1,300 electric-stock vehicles were rebuilt on 62ft underframes in a similar manner, so the eventual re-framing programme of some 160 steam-hauled coaches was modest in the extreme. Three additional rebuilds were later added, making use of the underframes rendered spare by the Micheldever train fire of 1936. Most of the rebuilding took the form of remounting an existing LSWR 48ft or 50ft body on a new standard underframe and splicing in a new section of bodywork to make up the additional 8ft or 10ft section. This might involve the simple addition of a guard's brake-van portion at one end or the splitting of the existing body and construction of a new compartment, plus lavatory if necessary, to fill the resulting gap. Occasionally, the work was even more involved, requiring the dismantling of an existing portion of the body before renewal could commence. To modellers, the term 'kit-bashing' certainly comes to mind! Most conversions date from the mid-1930s, although there had already been a few re-framings, involving eight ex-LBSCR coaches and one ex-SECR vehicle.

It should be made clear at this point that from time to time existing pre-Grouping coaches might also be re-framed using another second-hand underframe, also of pre-Grouping origin. This procedure was not at all unknown at Ashford, Eastleigh or Lancing Works — notably, at least 20 LBSCR coaches received this treatment between 1924 and about 1938. Not so common were LSWR or SECR re-framings, but they did occur; whether this was an indictment of LBSCR procedures, materials or workmanship is left to the reader to speculate. If two similar vehicles were in works for overhaul or scrapping at the same time, then the better bodywork from one would be united with the better underframe from the other, the discarded components being scrapped using the identity of one coach, the other re-emerging from works for a further spell of duty. Thus the accountants were satisfied, and the traffic department at least received one serviceable coach. Such re-framings were unlikely to be termed as rebuilds, as no new coach was produced and no new running or diagram number was allocated; the latter would only be considered necessary if other changes of a structural or dimensional nature were involved.

Between 1929 and 1931 eight ex-LBSCR coaches received new underframes, the existing LBSCR bogies being re-fitted. No obvious HOO number was allocated, although it may be significant that Order A103, originally authorised in 1925 for 10 bogie scenery vans, was amended in 1928 to allow for the use of reconditioned LBSCR underframes instead, so perhaps this authority was used to construct the eight new frames. Equally possible is that an existing order for electric-stock conversions may have been 'borrowed'. Officially such procedures would be frowned upon, but they did happen. As a result of these re-framings, all except one of the coaches lasted to the mid-/late 1950s — far longer than any other LBSCR 48ft or 50ft vehicles; in many instances they outlasted their contemporaries by more than 25 years. Details are as follows:

Diagram No	Vehicle Type	Running Nos	Remarks
64	48ft eight-compartment Third	1960, 2032/84/7	Two to IoW, renumbered as 2410/1 5/36
69	50ft seven-compartment Lavatory Third	2177	To M&T van 1543s 4/40 (withdrawn 5/57)
327	48ft seven-compartment Composite	5942/73	To IoW, renumbered as 6362/3 5/36
514	48ft six-compartment First	7596	Withdrawn 10/39

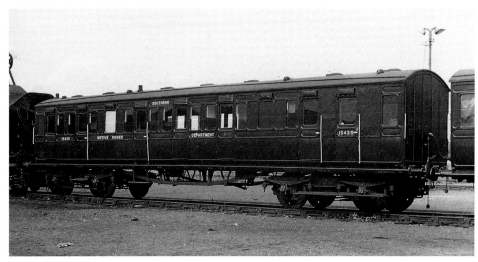

Plate 122 Re-framed ex-LBSCR 50ft Lavatory Third No 2177, running as departmental coach No 1543s and allocated to the Eastleigh breakdown train, on show at Eastleigh Works open day in August 1950. *J. H. Aston*

Thirds 1960 and 2087 ran for many years in push-pull sets 651 and 650. No new diagram numbers were allocated. Coach 2177 appears in **Plate 122** as No 1543s.

The first recorded steam-stock rebuild, in the true sense of the term, was actually the prototype for electric-stock conversion — Composite No 1440. This took the bodywork from ex-SER First No 792 (all five compartments) and Third No 568 (half of the body — three compartments only), mounting these at each end of a unique 62ft 5in underframe completed at Lancing, probably in 1924. The rebodying work was done at Ashford and involved in-filling the resulting gap with two compartments of suitable dimensions. For accounting purposes the SECR number 1440 was allocated, but it is doubtful if the coach was actually finished and lettered as such. Having proved the practicality of such a conversion, as well as highlighting any possible problems, the coach was then put aside until after completion of the 1925/6 programme of electric-stock conversions. Left with a perfectly serviceable vehicle, the Southern, in its usual thrifty manner, then made the coach ready for traffic, with four First- and six Third-class compartments, to Diagram 319 — unique in almost every respect. It entered service in April 1927 as Composite No 5546 and ran for a time in 'Birdcage' set 528. By 1935 it was formed into three-coach set 760 for Maidstone West–Paddock Wood–Tonbridge services, coupled between SECR Brake First No 7735 and Third No 1093 — yet another unique formation. In July 1943 these duties were taken over by a Maunsell set, also numbered 760 and described in Chapter 6. Composite No 5546 was then downgraded to all-Third coach No 1050, to Diagram 50, equipped with push-pull through pipework and reallocated to the South Western section. It then served as the spare coach on a number of branches, including Swanage, Lymington and Seaton, where it is seen in **Plate 123**. Withdrawal came in December 1962, by which time it was one of the last pre-Grouping non-corridor coaches in traffic outside the Isle of Wight. Then sent to the Ardingly-Horsted Keynes branch, to join 140+ other condemned coaches to await the call for scrapping at Newhaven, it was finally rescued by the Bluebell Railway, arriving there in May 1963. Painted in SECR lake livery (which, of course, it had never previously carried) but retaining its Southern Railway Third-class number, the coach was much used until the early 1970s, when it was withdrawn for complete restoration, which has yet to be implemented.

No further re-framings of steam stock were authorised until October 1933, when the former LSWR 46ft 6in 'emigrant' corridor coaches came under scrutiny. Built 1905-8, to a composite loading gauge, they were allowed to run over most lines in Britain, being shorter, narrower and slightly lower in roof profile than all other LSWR corridor stock. Of the 27 originals, two Brake Thirds (Order E216) had been modified in 1927 for Hurstbourne-Fullerton Junction services, and one other Brake Third had already been withdrawn. Order numbers L785 and L802 were then issued for modifications to 22 of the remaining vehiclesas below.

The 46ft 6in underframes were ordered from Birmingham Railway Carriage & Wagon Co in June 1934. All works were completed by March 1935. The vehicles on Order 785 were not altered beyond the fitting of the new underframes; however, in 1943 all 18 were extensively rebuilt into corridor push-pull sets 731-9, under Order L2246. Drawings and other details of these appear in *LSWR Carriages in the 20th Century* by Gordon Weddell (published by OPC, 2001).

For Order 802 the four 46ft 6in Third-class coaches were extensively altered into Brake Composites 6428-31, having a push-pull driving end and brake van incorporated in place of the former lavatory and one Third-class compartment. To run with these, four 50ft LSWR Composites were remounted on standard 58ft underframes, one additional compartment and a 1ft-wide void being incorporated into the centre of the coach. (Incidentally, this was the only occasion when a void section was included in a steam-hauled rebuild, although this feature could be found in several of the electric-stock conversions; in every case the gap was concealed behind a fully panelled exterior, so it was not obvious to anyone but the most sharp-eyed observer.) These became SR Thirds Nos 1-4. Formed in push-pull sets 652-5, they entered service in February 1935. Drawings of the Brake Composite also appear in *LSWR Carriages in the 20th Century*,

HOO No	Works	Coach Nos
L785 (10/33)	Construct 18 new steel underframes to drawing E15552/3, amended 10/34 to: Repair and fit 18 SW-section 46ft 6in corridor coaches with new underframes and bogies built by Birmingham Railway Carriage & Wagon Co.	650-61, 3081/3-5, 5073/4 (in sets 473/4)
L802 (3/34)	Eight SW-section bogie vehicles (four 46ft 6in and four 50ft) to be fitted with new underframes and bogies and altered for working push-pull services on the Allhallows branch. 50ft vehicles to be lengthened to 58ft, with underframes and bogies to be built at Lancing; 46ft 6in underframes and bogies to be ex-BRCW	1-4, 6428-31 (in sets 652-5)

Plate 123 The 'electric stock conversion prototype', SECR 62ft 6in 10-compartment Third No 1050 is seen at Seaton Junction in August 1957, in unlined crimson lake. The former First-class compartments are at the left-hand end. Note the three additional push-pull control pipes below the headstock. These were colour-coded to ensure they were connected correctly. *A. E. West*

Plate 124 Former Allhallows-branch push-pull set 655 at Hailsham c1950, with a train from Eastbourne. Brake Composite No 6431 is nearest the camera, with Third No 4 beyond. Note the slightly different proportions of the two coaches.
The Lens of Sutton Collection

but set 655 is illustrated here in **Plate 124**. Both these and 1943 corridor push-pull sets 731-9 remained in service until 1959-62, mostly on South Eastern- and Central-section duties.

By 1934 it was apparent that some attention to the ex-LSWR non-corridor stock would be necessary. Many two- and four-coach sets used on South Western-section local and branch-line services were made up using vehicles of diverse ages, combinations of 48ft, 50ft and more modern 56ft coaches often constituting a set. The 56ft vehicles would remain serviceable for some time to come, but the shorter vehicles were now reaching the end of their working lives; many ran on wooden underframes and some were gas-lit, both features now being considered undesirable. A programme of refurbishment was proposed, which included the following:

HOO No	Works
L801 (3/34)	50 48ft LSWR bogie vehicles to be fitted with new standard underframes and bogies, the bodies lengthened to 58ft and changed to electric lighting where necessary. All vehicles produced were Third-class.
L852A (3/35)	75 48ft LSWR bogie vehicles to be fitted with new standard underframes and bogies, the bodies lengthened to 58ft and changed to electric lighting where necessary. Vehicles produced were Brake Thirds, Brake Composites and Composites.
L852B	Necessary electric-lighting alterations to remaining unconverted LSWR vehicles (104 total).

Plate 125 Diagram 31 58ft rebuilt Third No 290 at Walton-on-Thames carriage sidings in 1938, carrying unlined Maunsell green — the finish probably carried by most of these rebuilds when new. The new section of bodywork consists of the lavatories and the compartment to their right. External roof-mounted water tanks were provided on vehicles built to Order L801 but not those to Order L852A. *F. Foote*

Plate 126 Diagram 32 Lavatory Third No 15 at Eastleigh in May 1949, in malachite green. Those coaches converted to Diagram 287 Composites in 1939/40 had the compartment either side of the left-hand pair of lavatories upgraded to First class. *A. E. West*

Plate 127 Diagram 97 seven-compartment Brake Third No 2609, formed in two-coach push-pull set No 3, at Bournemouth Central in 1951, wearing malachite green. The new steel-sheeted guard's van, including the pressed-steel lookout, is clearly visible. *H. F. Wheeler*

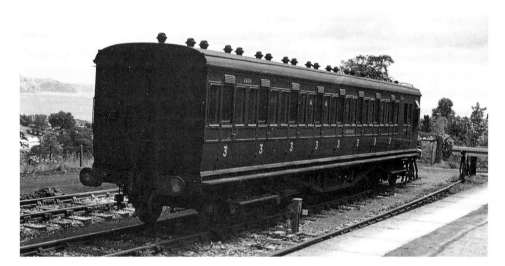

Plate 128 With Lyme Bay and Golden Cap in the background, Diagram 99 eight-compartment Brake Third No 2639 from set 45 stands at the buffer-stops at Lyme Regis in June 1948. The accompanying Brake Composite (6404) was providing the branch service single-handed. *J. H. Aston*

Plate 129 Again at Lyme Regis, but in July 1955, is Diagram 418 Brake Composite No 6401 from set 42. The livery is now unlined crimson lake. Note the position of the lookout varies from one side of the coach to the other — compare with **Plate 127**. *A. E. West*

For details of vehicles included on orders 801 and 852A, see the vehicle summary in **Table 10**.

In addition, a further 39 ex-LSWR four-coach sets (Nos 130-40/2-51, 251-63, 311-4/24) were to be reduced to three vehicles, with corresponding reductions to the number of First-class compartments in the Composite vehicles. No re-framing or other rebuilding was necessary, and the work was completed in 1939/40, under Order L990.

In total, six different types of 58ft vehicle were produced, although by fitting out the compartments in various different combinations no fewer than 12 diagrams were eventually allocated, taking into account some subsequent reclassifications and push-pull modifications. The Thirds and Composites all had their existing bodywork split into two sections and mounted at each end of the new underframes. Either one new compartment plus a pair of lavatories (side-by-side) or two new compartments were constructed to fill the remaining gap. All the Brake vehicles were rather more simply rebuilt by having a new 10ft guard's van grafted on at one end. These were steel-panelled, so did not quite match the rest of the wooden-panelled bodywork, although the final result was aesthetically quite pleasing. A characteristic feature of all these rebuilds was the triangular timber weatherboard that ran the full length of the coach at floor level, necessary because the standard Southern underframes were slightly wider than the LSWR bodywork. One odd fact is that the rebuilt Thirds were given Restriction 0 plates; the Composites were Route Restriction 1, yet they were identical in dimensions! The Brake vehicles, with their pressed-steel lookouts, were Route Restriction 3. All six basic designs are illustrated in **Plates 125-130**.

The Thirds ran originally as loose vehicles, being found anywhere on the system. Some were included in excursion and other 'long' sets from about 1938, often with ex-SECR stock. Loose Third No 360 was the first non-corridor coach seen in malachite-green livery, being recorded by observer George Woodward at Eastleigh on 16 June 1940. The Composites all ran as the centre vehicle of former four-coach (now three-coach) sets 101-16/20-6/52-67, between pairs of unmodified LSWR 56ft Brake Thirds. The Brake Thirds were placed in two-coach sets 1-21 (vehicles 2601-21) and 51-4/6 (vehicles 2625-9), but neither group was in numerical order. The other coach in the set was an unmodified LSWR 56ft Brake Composite. Sets 42-6 were the only ones wholly formed using 58ft rebuilds, comprising Brake Thirds 2636-40 and Brake Composites 6401-5, both in sequence.

In 1939/40 some further alterations were made, reducing the number of three-coach sets by six, deleting Nos 152-7. Additional two-coach sets 57-62 were formed, together with new push-pull sets 31-6, each set comprising one 56ft Brake Third and a 58ft Composite, the latter being renumbered 4744-55. Some of these were re-classed former Thirds 5-8, 12/3. The works were completed under Orders L1072 and 1095. Two-coach sets 1-6 were also converted to push-pull operation at about the same time but without any change of formation or renumbering of coaches.

Most sets remained on South Western-section local and branch-line services until withdrawn between 1956 and 1960, while the Thirds included in the 'long' sets served on the South Eastern section until 1958, latterly being joined by some of the Composites as the three-coach sets were withdrawn from traffic. Some loose coaches were allocated to specific workings during the 1950s, including the Hayling Island branch, Meldon Quarry-Okehampton workmen's services, the Bentley-Bordon branch, Torrington-Petrockstow clay workers' trains, the Somerset & Dorset line, the Exeter-Exmouth branch and Clapham Junction-Kensington Olympia services. By this time the number of loose non-corridor coaches in traffic was small, so most were listed in the Carriage Working Notices, together with their allocated duties, which tended to change from year to year. Third No 320 was purchased by the Bluebell Railway in 1960 and was then much used until the early 1970s, but has yet to be restored to Southern Railway livery.

Three additional re-framings took place in 1937, using the underframes of 'Ironclad' Firsts 7169/80 and Maunsell First 7227, burnt out at Micheldever in August 1936. Details are as shown below:

In each instance the driving Brake Composite coach was formed using the body of a 50ft LSWR Composite, mounted at one end of the underframe. One compartment was dismantled and new guard's compartments built on, being either 13ft or 14ft long, depending on the length of the original underframe (either a 57ft 'Ironclad' or a 58ft Maunsell). Unlike the 1935/6 conversions, the new sections of bodywork were fully panelled instead of being steel-sheeted. A view of set 657 appears in **Plate 131**. These sets were employed mostly on South Eastern-section branch lines until withdrawn between 1958 and 1961.

Full details of all the re-framed LSWR coaches appear in **Table 10**.

HOO No	Works	Coach Nos
L964 (4/37)	Provide three two-coach push-pull sets by lengthening bodies of three existing SW-section coaches, placing on second-hand underframes and coupling to three existing SE-section coaches (Nos 1057/77/88).	6406-8 (in sets 656-8)

Plate 130 Diagram 285 Composite No 4648 in lined crimson lake at Eastleigh in August 1949. This ran in three-coach set 113 and was reclassified as all-Third No 165 in April 1956, finally being withdrawn in May 1958. Composites altered to Diagram 286 had the far-end compartment re-graded to Third class, while the push-pull conversions to Diagram 290 had their lavatories sealed and the window plated over. *A. E. West*

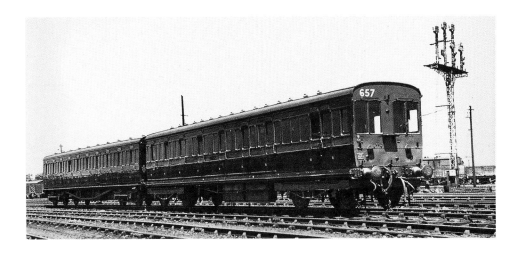

Plate 131 Push-pull set 657 at Ashford in June 1951, retaining malachite green. The Driving Brake Composite, No 6407, is mounted on a 57ft former 'Ironclad' frame, while the Third (No 1077) is an ex-SECR 60ft 1in 10-compartment vehicle, built by BRCW in October 1921. *A. E. West*

Table 10
Summary of LSWR re-framed stock 1934-7

46ft 6in vehicles

Diagram No	Vehicle Type	Running Nos	Rebuilt by	Remarks
20	Six-compartment Corridor Third (in sets 473/4)	650-61	Re-framed at Lancing 1-3/35	Rebuilt as Diagrams 101 and 288 in 1943
100	Four-compartment Corridor Brake Third (push-pull)	2646-9	Lancing 2-3/43	Ex-Diagram 128; in sets 736-9
101	Four-compartment Corridor Brake Third (push-pull)	2641-5	Lancing 1-4/43	Ex-Diagram 20; in sets 731-5
128	Four-compartment Corridor Brake Third (in sets 473/4)	3081/3-5	Re-framed at Lancing 3/35	Rebuilt as Diagram 100 in 1943
276	Six-compartment Corridor Composite (in sets 473/4)	5073/4	Reframed at Lancing 2-3/35	Rebuilt as Diagram 289 in 1943
288	Six-compartment Corridor Composite (push-pull)	4756-62	Lancing 1-4/43	Ex-Diagram 20; in sets 731-7
289	Six-compartment Corridor Composite (push-pull)	4763/4	Lancing 2-3/43	Ex-Diagram 276; in sets 738/9
417	Six-compartment Corridor Brake Composite (push-pull)	6428-31	Re-framed at Lancing 2/35	No end gangway; in sets 652-5

58ft vehicles

Diagram No	Vehicle Type	Running Nos	Rebuilt by	Remarks
30	Eight-compartment Lavatory Third	164-8	(Renumbered 1955/6)	Ex-Diagram 285 Nos 4648/71/85, 4716/39
31	Nine-compartment Lavatory Third (ex-48ft Thirds; not renumbered)	169/73/5/81/4/7/8/94, 204/8/17/9/25/31/53/67/8/80/4/90/1/9, 304/13/20/6/9/53/60/1/4/73/82/7/94, 403/76, 513	Re-framed at Lancing 1-4/35	Nos 219 and 373 push-pull fitted in 1958
32	Eight-compartment Lavatory Third (ex-48ft Composites)	5-16	Re-framed at Lancing 5-6/35	Nos 5-8, 12/3 to Diagram 287 in 1939
33	Nine-compartment Third (P-P) (ex-50ft Composites)	1-4	Re-framed at Lancing 2/35	In sets 652-5
97	Seven-compartment Lavatory Brake Third (ex-48ft Composites)	2601-21	Re-framed at Lancing 5-10/36	Nos 2604/5/9/12/20/1 P-P fitted c1939
98	Six-compartment Lavatory Brake Third (ex-48ft Composites)	2625-9	Re-framed at Lancing 10-12/36	Structurally identical to Diagram 418
99	Eight-compartment Brake Third (ex-48ft Thirds)	2636-40	Re-framed at Lancing 4/36	In two-sets 42-46
285	Eight-compartment Lavatory Composite (ex-48ft Composites; not renumbered) (three First-class compartments)	4608/11/5/7/20/5/34/5/7/40/3/7/8, 4654/9/64/8/71/2/82/5-7/96/8, 4702/10/1/3/6/20/6/7/30/8-40/2/3	Re-framed at Lancing 10/35-12/36	Some to Diagram 286 in 1939 and Diagram 30 in 1955/6. Nos 4617 and 4730 push-pull fitted in 1958; to Diagram 290
286	Eight-compartment Lavatory Composite (two First-class compartments)	4744-6 (push-pull), 4753-5	(Renumbered 6/39-3/40)	Ex-Diagram 285 Nos 4608/15/34/82, 4702/26
287	Eight-compartment Lavatory Composite	4747-9 (push-pull), 4750-2	(Renumbered 6/39-3/40)	Ex-Diagram 32 Nos 5-8, 12/3
418	Six-compartment Lavatory Brake Composite (ex-48ft Composites)	6401-5	Re-framed at Lancing 4/36	In two-sets 42-6
420	Seven-compartment Brake Composite (push-pull) (ex-50ft Composites; on 57ft 'Ironclad' frames)	6406/7	Re-framed at Lancing 11-12/37	In sets 656/7
428	Seven-compartment Brake Composite (push-pull) (ex-50ft Composite)	6408	Re-framed at Lancing 12/37	In set 658

Chapter 8.
Bulleid Stock 1938-1945

O. V. S. Bulleid joined the Southern Railway on 20 September 1937, while Maunsell formally retired on 31 October, giving the new Chief Mechanical Engineer a six-week handover period. Two more different senior men would be hard to find. Maunsell's forte was well-delegated management and efficient administration: he would give his assistants clear instructions and areas of responsibility and then leave them to get on with it — unless, of course, matters went wrong. The Maunsell carriage was therefore the product of Lynes and his Drawing Office staff, approved of and ceremonially sat in by Maunsell, according to an old Eastleigh employee.

Bulleid preferred to leave administration to others and adopted a much more 'hands on' approach, especially in design matters, and was not averse to discussing a problem directly with the man at the drawing board. By 1937 several of Maunsell's original team were also approaching retirement. His Assistant CME, G. Pearson, retired in 1938, to be replaced by E. W. Turbett, formerly Works Manager at Eastleigh, while H. Holcroft replaced J. Clayton in the Locomotive Drawing Office. Whereas some of the staff might have had difficulty in adjusting to the inevitable changes, Lionel Lynes seemingly did not, and he continued to serve the new CME until the end of his term of office, the two men contributing much to the changed designs that would appear from 1945.

To return to 1937, Bulleid found little movement on the carriage-stock front, and no outstanding orders were in place for new steam-hauled coaches, although requests for 109 passenger vehicles, plus orders for 40 more remained in abeyance. These were either all cancelled or incorporated into the 1939 orders. Electrification to Portsmouth via the mid-Sussex route was in progress, and this would complete most of the Central-section electrification, with the exception of the Oxted-East Grinstead-Tunbridge Wells West group of lines. Electrification of the lines to Maidstone would follow in 1939, with new electric rolling stock for these and for the Waterloo & City line appearing in 1940.

At first Bulleid confined his attention to improving some of his predecessor's locomotives and rolling stock. Following the interior restyling of the 'Bognor' Buffet cars (described in Chapter 1) the 'Bournemouth Limited' steam stock received similar treatment, two 11-coach trains being refurbished ready for traffic in July 1938. Externally this involved repainting locomotives and carriages in a new bright green, later known as Bulleid or malachite green. Internally, the carriages were restyled using rexine on the walls and ceilings — pale yellow in First-class compartments, a light stone colour in the Thirds. New seating was also provided — pale green for First class, pale pink (described in some accounts as lake, maybe a darker pink shade) for the Thirds. The décor was completed by new floor finishes, lighting and framed pictures, the last-named replacing the more traditional system maps and advertisements.

The Publicity Department made much of the new trains, carefully avoiding the fact that the carriages themselves were actually refurbished rather than brand-new! They entered traffic on the 7.42am Weymouth-Waterloo service, the train starting with a three-coach set, picking up eight more coaches at

Plate 132 'Schools' class 4-4-0 No 933 *King's Canterbury* heads the down 'Bournemouth Limited' under Locke King bridge (just west of Weybridge station) in May 1939. The locomotive is still in Maunsell green, with Bulleid lettering; the carriage stock, with three-set 221 leading, is in malachite. *F. Foote*

Bournemouth Central, which it departed at 8.35am. (The two-coach portion from Swanage left at 7.15am and combined with one of the six-coach sets at Bournemouth West before departing for Bournemouth Central at 8.20am.) The return working left Waterloo at 4.30pm, serving the same destinations. The other train worked a 12.30pm down service from Waterloo, returning from Weymouth at 5.37pm; however, there were some variations to the latter duty on summer Saturdays, Weymouth then being served by the six-coach set. The sets involved were as follows:

Vehicle	Set 241	Set 242
Six-compartment Brake Third	3799	3790
Seven-compartment First	7676	7675
Dining First	7940 or 7943	7940 or 7943
Open-saloon Third	1410/9	1412/3
Six-compartment Brake Third	3800	3791

Dining First 7955 was similarly refurbished in 1939, to provide a spare car.

The Weymouth portions were provided by three-coach sets 221 and 232, the Swanage through coaches by two-coach sets 180 and 199, all retaining the same formations as given in

Plate 133 Third-class compartment of 'Bournemouth Limited' Brake Third No 3791, part of set 242, as refurbished in July 1938. The scalloped top to the seat backs was a feature of these vehicles. *Southern Railway*

Plate 134 The First-class dining-saloon section of Maunsell Restaurant car 7940 or 7943, as refurbished in July 1938 for the 'Bournemouth Limited'. *Southern Railway*

Chapter 5. In addition, loose Thirds 1802/3 and Composites 5637/9 were similarly refurbished, enabling both trains to be strengthened if necessary to 13 vehicles, the maximum train length that could be accommodated at Waterloo. Several 'Schools' class 4-4-0s were repainted malachite to haul the train, although it was not unknown for a locomotive still carrying Maunsell livery to be substituted, as seen in **Plate 132**. These duties were upheld until September 1939, after which the locomotives and stock could be used on any duty. By this time a number of other locomotives and sets had also been repainted in malachite green. **Plates 14, 23, 133 and 134** illustrate some of the refurbished vehicles.

Following this, a number of other coaches were similarly refurbished for Folkestone, Dover and Newhaven boat trains, referred to as 'Improved Boat Stock'. Carriages included were:

Open-saloon Thirds	1434/9
Nondescript Brakes	4439/42
Brake Seconds	4481/2
Corridor Firsts	7232, 7410
Nondescript Saloons	4391-7 (ex-7793, 7800, 7902/4-6/11)
Brake Firsts	7750/6 ('Continental' stock)

The Nondescript Saloons and Brakes were all reclassified permanently as Second-class, hence the renumbering of the saloons into the Second-class section of the stock list. The Saloon Brakes already carried Second-class numbers, despite being nominally unclassed. These vehicles are illustrated in **Plates 35, 36, 66, 95 and 96**.

These alterations were carried out between November 1938 and April 1939 and involved the usual interior restyling and new upholstery, as well as provision of original framed drawings depicting appropriate Continental scenes. Externally, some vehicles at least were painted in the short-lived Dover green; others may have been in malachite. Again, the Publicity Department made its usual claims about 'new' boat-train stock.

The carriages would not serve for very long on their intended duties, as the onset of war in September 1939 considerably reduced Continental travel, and the coaches were no doubt soon redeployed on ordinary services.

Bulleid and his team put forward their first programme of new steam-hauled stock in the spring of 1939. Approval was given for the construction of 153 new vehicles in May 1939, as follows (most of these vehicles had been proposed for construction in March 1935, but owing to Maunsell's incapacity, had not been authorised):

HOO No	Stock
E1082	Two nine-coach trains for Victoria-Dover boat services
E1083	11 six-coach trains for Waterloo-Bournemouth services
E1084	18 Corridor Brake Composites for Waterloo-West of England services
E1085	Three open-saloon Thirds for general use (to run with E1086)
E1086	Three Buffet cars for general use (to run with E1085)
E1087	Seven two-coach trains for Waterloo-West of England services
E1088	Seven three-coach trains for Waterloo-West of England services
E1089	10 Corridor Firsts for general use

Order Nos 1090-3 were also placed for non-passenger coaching stock, and these are detailed in the appropriate chapters. In the event, not one of the above passenger coaches was completed, despite all having coach (but not set) numbers allocated. Details of these are given in Appendix 1. Perhaps as many as 66 underframes had been completed at Lancing by

November 1940, at which time all works were suspended. These were standard 58ft Maunsell products, and it is interesting to speculate as to whether any bodywork designs were produced during this period. Most of the underframes were stored until late 1944, possibly in the Portsmouth area, but a few were used during the war to transport landing craft and other equipment between Lancing Works, Eastleigh Works and Southampton Docks. At this time the workshops were engaged on many wartime productions of a non-railway nature, and it is interesting to note that the Head Office Order numbering system, which had reached 1100 in the 16 years since 1923, would now exceed 3,100 orders by March 1945, just six years later. To be fair, many of the external orders placed were small by comparison with some railway orders, but it nevertheless gives some indication of the tremendous contribution made to the war effort by the railway and its staff.

The above rolling-stock orders were finally cancelled in May 1945, but many of the subsequent postwar orders can be traced back to these, even if the carriages built were rather different from those originally envisaged back in 1939.

Towards the end of 1944 instructions were issued for the construction of 22 three-coach sets, utilising the underframes completed in 1940 against Orders 1083, 1087 and 1088. This was subsequently amended to 18 sets, the balance of four being the first of those completed to the 64ft 6in length, which would become the future standard in 1946. There appears to be some confusion over these, as two different order numbers and two different dates are quoted in the order book. Details are as follows:

Eastleigh, completion was somewhat protracted — perhaps indicative of the prevailing conditions, with shortages of manpower and other components causing many delays. Most of the 59ft Brakes were built several months before the companion Composites and had to be stored to await completion of the latter. Similar shortages were to beset the entire Bulleid construction programme over the following few years.

Constructionally, the vehicles were quite different from the Maunsell stock, but in terms of layout they were very similar, being the last multi-door steam-hauled corridor coaches built by the company. Third-class compartments were 6ft 4in between centres of partitions, Firsts were 7ft 2in (give or take the odd fraction of an inch) — dimensions which hardly varied throughout all of Maunsell's and Bulleid's steam-hauled stock. Interior finishes returned to the traditional 'stain and grain' style of the Maunsell stock, instead of the late-1930s pastel-coloured rexine schemes. However, this might have been dictated more by prevailing shortages than any other factor. The 59ft Brake Thirds had five compartments, plus a large guard's/luggage van, and in this respect were similar in plan to the Maunsell 'Thanet' Brakes, while the Composites had the usual four First- and three Third-class compartments. The 64ft 6in vehicles each included one additional Third-class compartment but otherwise followed the shorter vehicles almost exactly in their details, albeit with minor differences in dimensions of the lavatories and brake compartments. Indeed, a sharp eye was needed to spot one of these four somewhat elusive sets.

Most noticeable externally was the new Bulleid profile, introduced previously on '4-SUB' electric unit 4101 in 1941.

THOO No	Stock	Set/coach Nos
E3043 (28/9/44)	22 (later 18) three-coach trains for Waterloo-Bournemouth/West of England services	963-80
E3043A* (5/5/45)	Four three-coach trains for Waterloo-West of England services	981-4

*also listed as E3243

It is certain that sets 963-80 made use of 54 original 58ft underframes of 1940, although official records state that perhaps as many as 66 were actually completed. However, the underframes for sets 981-4 may well have been completed during 1946, once the new standard 63ft 5in length had been agreed. Possibly only some of the materials for the additional 12 frames were actually purchased, and little or no construction was undertaken back in 1940. Just how the new length was decided upon does not seem to have been recorded. Prior to 1945, main-line electric stock vehicles had been constructed on 62ft 6in-long frames (63ft 6in over body) and the only other stock to exceed this length were a number of Pullman cars, including the 'Brighton Belle' vehicles, so perhaps Bulleid took these as a yardstick. The matter is discussed further in relation to the prototype Composite coach No 5751 at the start of the next chapter. Set formations were as below:

(Bulleid — or someone — seems to have delighted in playing with figures, as the first motor coach was actually numbered 10941, the play on '41' surely being intentional!) The bodyside was formed into a continuous curve from floor level to cantrail, the steel sheets being butt-welded together and in turn bolted to 2in-square hardwood framing members and to bottom flanges that were welded to the solebar. This last feature can be seen in **Plates 135 and 136**. Roofs were formed entirely using traditional timber planking and canvas construction. To take full advantage of the maximum width, no roof gutters were fitted; at this point there was just a very narrow rain strip. Whilst this gave the carriages a very smooth profile, it proved highly ineffective in preventing rainwater from cascading down the bodysides, leading to considerable corrosion problems in later years. Aesthetically, the coaches were excellent, undoubtedly being enhanced by the malachite-green livery and 'sunshine' insignia.

Vehicle	Sets 963-80
59ft five-compartment Brake Third	2841/3/5/7/9/51/3/5/7/9/61/3/5/7/9/71/3/5
59ft seven-compartment Composite	5709-26
59ft five-compartment Brake Third	2842/4/6/8/50/2/4/6/8/60/2/4/6/8/70/2/4/6

Vehicle	Sets 981-4
64ft 6in six-compartment Brake Third	2877/9/81/3
64ft 6in eight-compartment Composite	5727-30
64ft 6in six-compartment Brake Third	2878/80/2/4

Sets 963-80 entered traffic between November 1945 and April 1946, 981-4 in June and July 1946; all were then employed on Waterloo-West of England services. Considering that instructions to recommence work had been issued in September 1944 and that underframes and some other materials were already on hand at

Suddenly the Southern Railway, with its new Pacifics and matching carriage stock, had captured the look of the moment.

Plates 137-140 illustrate all four types of coach in Southern Railway livery, while another view of the 59ft Composite appears as **Plate 16**.

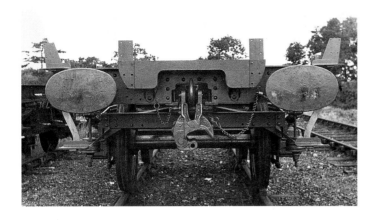
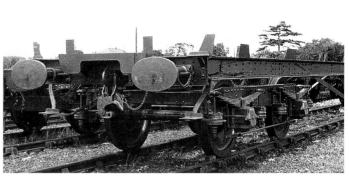

Plates 135 and 136 Two views of a Bulleid 63ft 5in coach underframe, showing the buck-eye coupling dropped down to reveal the coupling hook behind and the various steel angles welded to the frame and pre-drilled to receive the body framing. The photographs were taken at Eastleigh in August 1949, so the frame is likely to have been destined for a vehicle on Orders E3450-4. *(both) A. E. West*

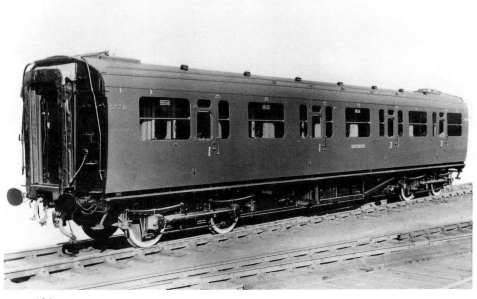

Plate 137 Diagram 2121 59ft Brake Third No 2876, as completed February 1946 and destined for three-coach set 980. The similarity with the 1941-5 electric stock vehicles is obvious. *Southern Railway*

Plate 138 Companion Diagram 2316 59ft Composite No 5726, also destined for set 980, showing the corridor side. A view of the compartment side appears in **Plate 16**. *Southern Railway*

Plate 139 The rather elusive 64ft 6in multi-door Brake Third to Diagram 2122; coach No 2882 is seen at Clapham Junction in May 1948. *D. Cullum*

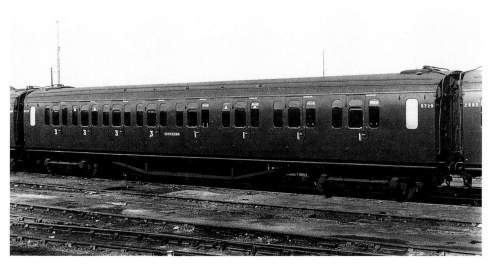

Plate 140 Companion Composite No 5729, to Diagram 2317, seen on the same occasion. Apart from the prototype Composite and the Inspection Saloon (100s), this was the least numerous design of Bulleid coach, with just four examples. *D. Cullum*

Plate 141 59ft Brake Third No 2853 of set 969, seen in Southern Region green at Eastleigh in September 1958. Note the various strengthening ribs and extra beading, applied to cover the butt joints in the side sheeting. This would become a common feature of most Bulleid coaches in their later days. *A. E. West*

The October 1945 Carriage Working Notices list sets 963-80 as about to enter traffic on West of England services, but by June 1947 they were shown as being for Waterloo-Basingstoke-Salisbury and Waterloo-Bournemouth-Weymouth trains. Sets 981-4 were by then allocated to Brighton/Portsmouth-Plymouth workings. As the later Bulleid stock was completed, these 'multi-door' sets were if possible relegated to main-line stopping services rather than the best expresses, as they compared unfavourably with vehicles built between late 1946 and 1951.

In 1959 59ft sets 963-72 were reallocated to the Somerset & Dorset Joint line, replacing Maunsell sets 390-9 on these duties. Sets 973-9 were reallocated to the Central section in 1961, usually appearing on the Oxted/Tunbridge Wells West lines and on Reading-Tonbridge and Brighton-Horsham-Guildford services. They were seldom (if ever) seen east of Tonbridge or on other lines in Kent. From 1959 to 1962 set 978 served on the Hayling Island branch, often running as a two-set plus a loose Brake Third. Sets 981-4 remained on South Western-section main-line services but were increased to eight vehicles (along with set 980) in 1962, using a mixture of Maunsell and later Bulleid vehicles. These were the first permanent changes to the set formations.

Accident victims aside, these sets comprised the first Bulleid coaches to be condemned — a process which started in December 1963. At this time all but sets 964/7/8/76/80/1/4 were deleted from stock, most coaches being condemned immediately. Those sets remaining in traffic continued to run as such until 1965, when a further round of withdrawals took place, leaving fewer than 20 loose vehicles to last into 1967. The four 64ft 6in Composites (5727-30) were re-classed as Seconds in 1964, being economically renumbered 1727-30, although no changes were made save for the painting-out of First-class insignia, and all four retained their First class trimmings until withdrawn in 1966/7.

Brake Third 2850 was sold to the Chipman Weed Killing Co of Horsham after withdrawal in 1965 and was later purchased by the Mid-Hants Railway, but the corrosion problems already mentioned, plus the five years' exposure of the frame to the elements (between 1940 and 1945) had taken their toll and resulted in the coach eventually being broken up for spares in 1991, the components going to the Swanage Railway.

The four vehicle types are drawn as **Figures 40-43**. **Table 11** gives details of these early Bulleid vehicles.

Table 11
Summary of Bulleid 1945/6 stock

Diagram No	Vehicle Type	Seats 1st	Seats 3rd	Running Nos	Built by
2121	59ft five-compartment Brake Third		40	2841-76	Eastleigh 11/45-2/46
2122	64ft 6in six-compartment Brake Third		48	2877-84	Eastleigh 6-7/46
2316	59ft seven-compartment Composite	24	24	5709-26	Eastleigh 2-4/46
2317	64ft 6in eight-compartment Composite	24	32	5727-30	Eastleigh 6-7/46

Notes
Underframes completed at Lancing, some in 1939/40.
Composites 5727-30 reclassified as Seconds 1727-30, 4-9/64. No new diagram number allocated.

Plate 142 59ft Composite No 5715, also in set 969 but now at Templecombe during its period of service on the S&DJR, photographed in August 1963. The yellow cantrail stripe indicated First-class accommodation and began to be applied earlier the same year. While most Bulleid coaches carried the marking, relatively few Maunsells ever received it. Catering vehicles had a similar red stripe. *A. E. West*

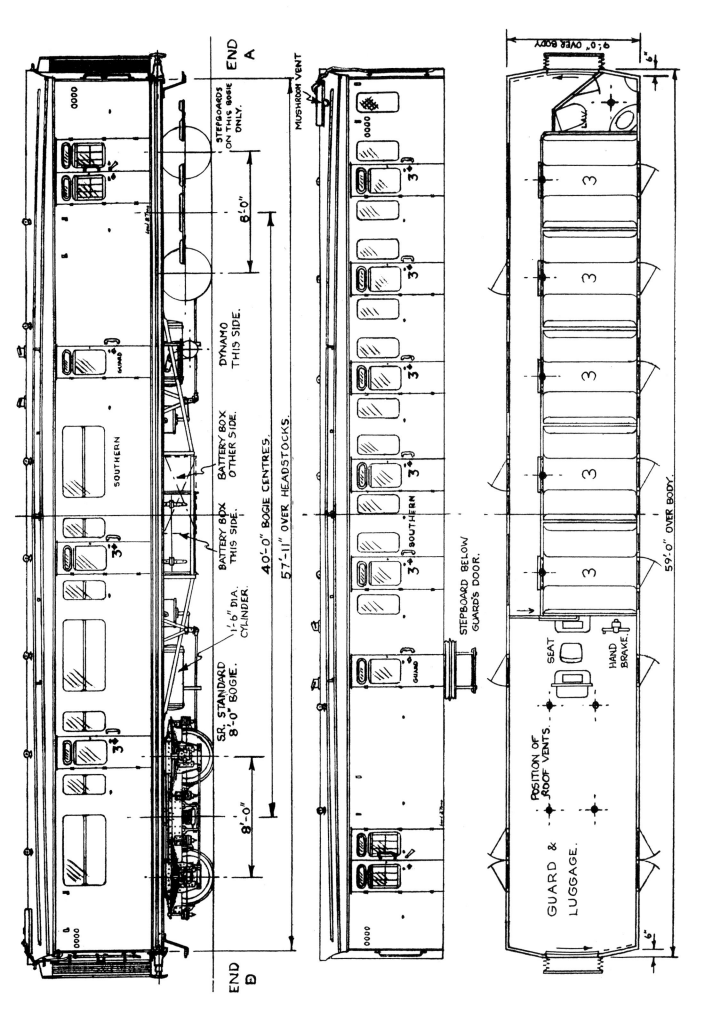

Figure 40 The 59ft Brake Third, SR Diagram 2121. For details of the coach ends refer to **Figure 46**.

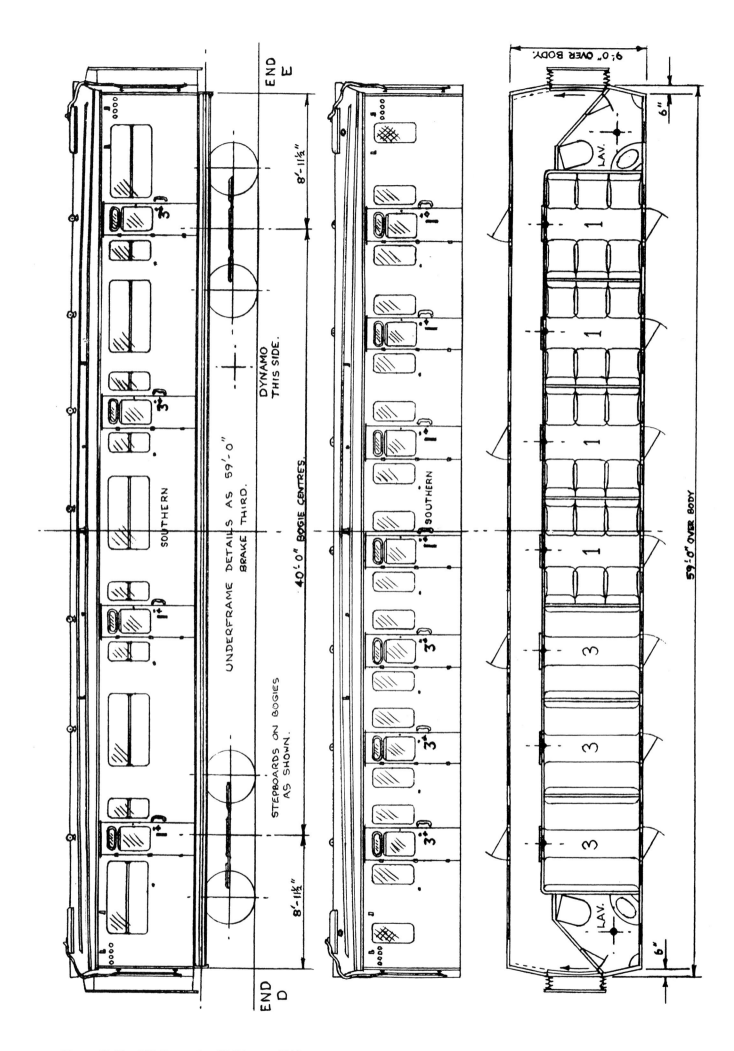

Figure 41 The 59ft Composite, SR Diagram 2316.

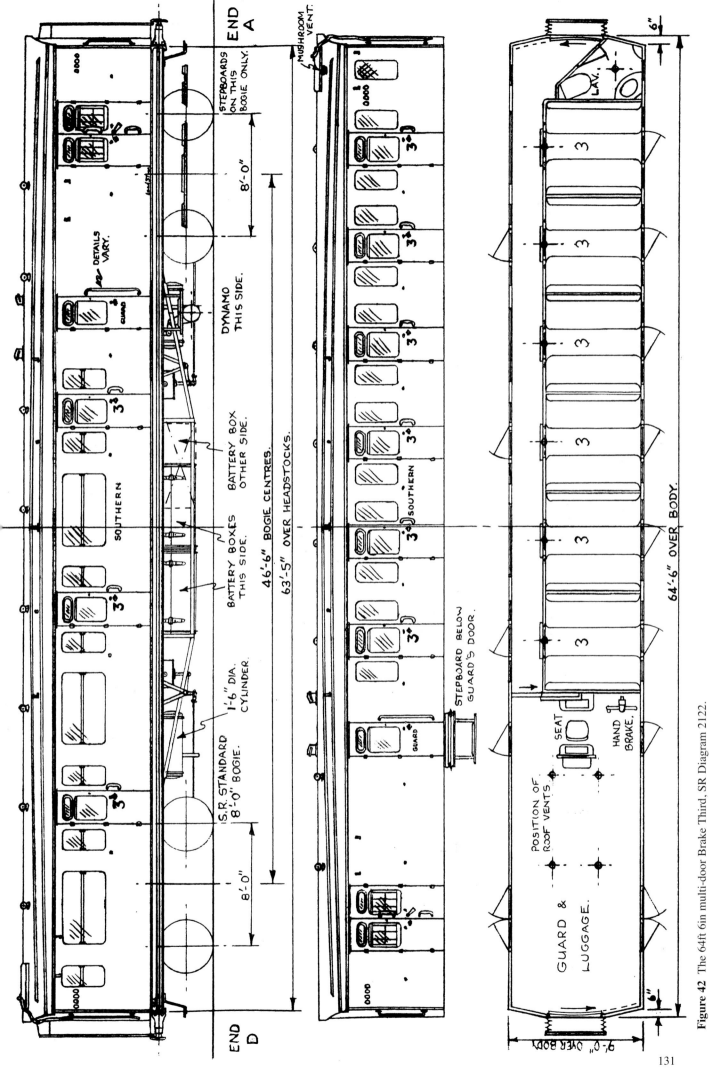

Figure 42 The 64ft 6in multi-door Brake Third, SR Diagram 2122.

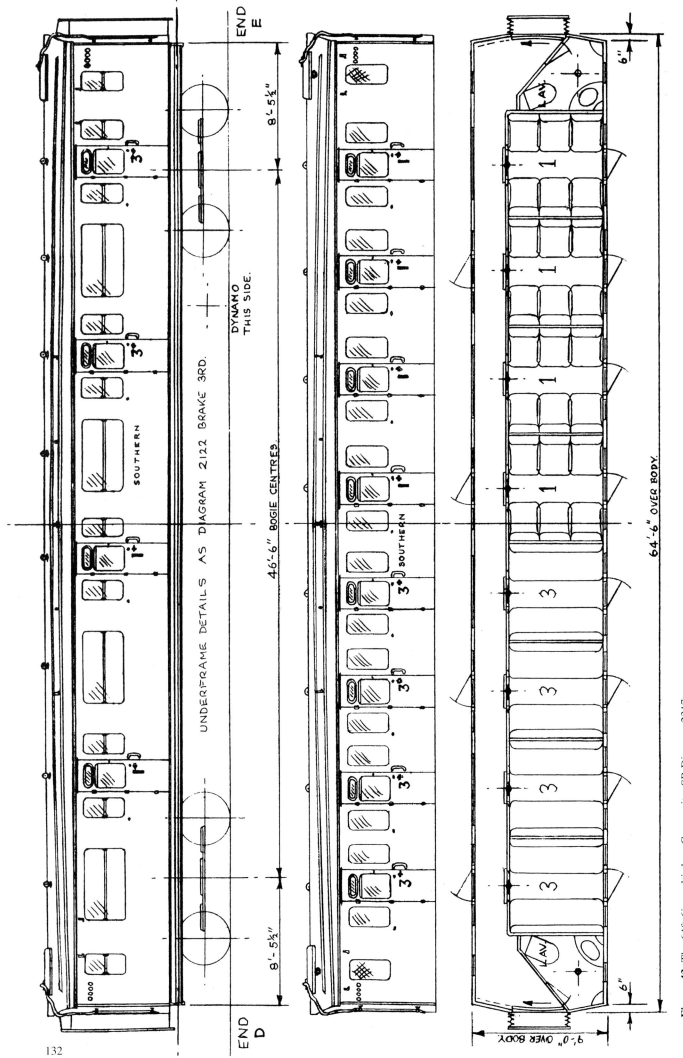

Figure 43 The 64ft 6in multi-door Composite, SR Diagram 2317.

Chapter 9.
Bulleid Eastleigh-built Stock 1946-1951

We now enter the period during which most Bulleid coaches would be completed. Since 1939, Bulleid and Lynes had worked on construction methods and welding techniques aimed at maximising the amount of available space within any new passenger coach. In particular, increasing the available body width would greatly facilitate the provision of six-a-side seating in suburban stock, even then bursting at the seams on many services. For main-line vehicles, however, improved passenger comfort and larger compartment windows were seen as more important. Weight-saving construction methods were also examined, and here welding would play an important part.

Clearly the 'multi-door' sets (963-84) were not a significant step forward — they merely made use of existing underframes (in most instances) and ensured that some new vehicles, at least, were in traffic before the start of the 1946 summer timetables. Indeed, from the compartment side they appeared little different from contemporary suburban stock.

The new ideas came to fruition in prototype Composite coach No 5751, completed and photographed on 26 September 1945 (**Plates 143-145**). This was constructed on an underframe 63ft 5in long over headstocks, having standard SR 8ft-wheelbase bogies mounted at 46ft 6in centres. Length over buffers (when extended) was 67ft 1in — some 5ft 6in longer than previous steam-hauled vehicles. The body was 63ft 6in long over corner pillars, 64ft 6in long at centre. Width was 9ft 0in, with the continuous curve from floor to cantrail that would mark out Bulleid vehicles as being so visibly different from the other 'Big Four' designs of the period. This, allied to the welded construction, increased the internal body width by 3in at waist level, compared to an equivalent Maunsell vehicle. Attention to design and construction resulted in a coach weighing no more than 34 tons — just one or two tons more than previous vehicles, despite the increased length.

The coach consisted of the usual four First- and three Third-class compartments, providing seats for 24 passengers in each class, plus a lavatory at each end. Individual compartment doors were not provided; in their place were large windows with sliding ventilators above. Those fitted on coach 5751 were unique to this vehicle, the window glazing being curved to match the bodyside profile — which gave rise to storage problems within the workshops. Characteristic Bulleid steel doors were provided, with distinctive lozenge-shaped toplight window over the droplight, the latter being of the frameless 'lazy arm' balancing variety. However, there were only three on each side, serving three cross-vestibules — one at each end of the coach and another near the centre, between the First- and Third-class compartments. This general style and layout would be followed for most subsequent Bulleid corridor coaches, although in the full

Plate 143 Prototype Composite No 5751, as completed on 26 September 1945. Note the unique square-topped aluminium sliding ventilators and the lack of vents to the lavatory windows. This coach was Bulleid's revolutionary answer to the Southern's postwar passenger-carrying problems. *Southern Railway*

Plate 144 First-class-compartment interior of coach No 5751. The seating was upholstered in green, but a rather more floral pattern was used for the production coaches. The pale-coloured veneered timber was also peculiar to this coach. *Southern Railway*

Plate 145 Third-class-compartment interior of coach No 5751. The seating was a floral brown material, later changed to a rather more maroon colour. Note the lack of communication cord and individual reading lights. *Southern Railway*

Thirds and Firsts the lavatories would be positioned opposite each other, either side of a short central corridor.

The compartment dimensions did not vary very much from those used for Maunsell stock, namely around 6ft 3in for Third class and around 7ft 2in for First. Adding approximately 3ft 9in for each lavatory, plus 2ft 9in for each cross-vestibule and fractions for coach-end/compartment partitions, resulted in a body length of 64ft 6in — and this was probably the thought process followed to arrive at the new overall length. Similar calculations for seven First- and eight Third-class compartments, with only slight adjustments to the dimensions, would show that these could be conveniently fitted within the same body envelope. Interestingly, British Railways would repeat this process in 1949/50 when designing its Mk 1 coaches, and several of these replicated almost exactly the Bulleid carriage layout and dimensions, even if constructionally they were very different.

The new coach went on public display at Waterloo and Victoria during October 1945. A memorandum dated 27 September 1945, issued by General Manager Sir Eustace Missenden, accompanied the vehicle and gave a considerable amount of information about the new carriage, inviting the public to inspect the result and give their comments in the form of a questionnaire. Particular attention was drawn to several features, these being considered the most likely to generate passenger interest, as follows.

Seating comfort
Hammock sprung seating frames have been provided to support spring insert cushions, giving maximum luggage space under seats, reducing weight and helping cleaning.

Lighting, heating and ventilation
Diffused electric lighting is fitted in compartments and there are electrically-heated foot-warming panels under the compartment floor rugs. [There followed a description of the air-extract system, the sliding top-window ventilators and the interlocking brush-type seals around the compartment sliding doors.]

Decorations and appointments
Stainless steel is generally employed for all fittings, while compartments are decorated with polished veneers of Empire-grown timbers. Mirrors in compartments have been canted out of the vertical plane to reduce reflection to the passengers when seated. Electrical indicators direct passengers to the First- and Third-class sections and to the lavatories.
The exterior of the vehicle has been painted Southern Railway green without lining and with the usual lettering.

E. J. Missenden
General Manager's Office
Waterloo
27th September 1945

Some 25,000 people viewed the carriage, of whom about 10% took the trouble to record their views. Analysis of these yielded the following results:

Subject	*Unqualified Approval*		*Criticism*	
Seating	1,278	(65%)	693	(35%)
Fittings	1,181	(64%)	659	(36%)
Lighting	1,334	(73%)	482	(27%)
Luggage space	1,010	(68%)	468	(32%)
Ventilation	992	(74%)	348	(26%)
Doors	1,231	(78%)	337	(22%)
Windows	1,340	(83%)	265	(17%)
Lavatories	1,312	(84%)	247	(16%)
Mirrors	1,169	(84%)	226	(16%)
Décor	1,266	(91%)	115	(9%)
Heating	1,105	(91%)	108	(9%)

Passenger approval levels were clearly very high and, although the many and diverse responses concerning seating and fittings proved difficult to accommodate, most other suggestions were noted and acted upon for the production vehicles completed from late 1946 onwards. Basically, the changes incorporated were:

• Provision of four individually-controlled reading lights in each compartment
• Communication cords to be provided in corridors and lavatories
• Heating to be provided in corridors and lavatories
• Ventilation to be provided in lavatory windows (none was provided in coach 5751)
• Passenger-controlled heaters under First-class seats

Additionally, passengers voted 3:1 in favour of compartments against open-saloon layouts, and this factor was also incorporated into the production vehicles, although no Open Firsts, save for some Dining Saloons, were built. Five years later BR designers must have consulted these questionnaires again, since Mk 1 prototype Composite S15000, completed at Eastleigh in 1950, included both open and compartment-type accommodation for each class, going one stage further than the Southern had done. Regrettably, this provision was not repeated in BR's production Composites, so the status quo was restored.

Coach No 5751 was then displayed at Ashford station, together with a new 'West Country' class Pacific and other exhibits, before entering traffic. From February 1946 the coach was temporarily formed in set 980, in place of 59ft Composite 5726, which was not ready until April 1946. It then ran as a loose coach until November 1947, when (along with Brake Thirds 4301/2) it was incorporated into set 770, where it remained until transfer to 59ft set 976 (augmented to eight coaches) in 1964. Dimensionally and in terms of layout, coach 5751 varied slightly from all subsequent production composites and was uniquely allocated Diagram 2315. The non-standard passenger-window ventilators and the position of lavatory access doors may have survived, but it is believed that the other non-standard features, such as the lack of individual reading lights and the omission of lavatory-window ventilators, were soon altered to conform with the later vehicles allocated to Diagram 2318. No 5751 lasted until the end of steam operation in July 1967.

Other prototype features dispensed with for later stock were the electrical indicators and the heated floor rugs, neither of which gave satisfactory operation in normal service. Another feature tried but later rejected was the incorporation of mat wells in the floor; these served only to increase the corrosion problems from which the coaches would suffer throughout their working lives.

While the design and construction work on coach 5751 was in progress, the 1945 programme of construction was put forward and approved at the May Rolling Stock Committee meeting. Proposed was an ambitious programme of no fewer than 310 main-line coaches, broken down into 24 separate orders (Nos E3234-57, detailed fully in Appendix 1); however, many of these were subsequently amalgamated, whilst a few others were revised or had their intended allocations altered, the effective result being as follows:

HOO No(s)	Stock	Set/coach Nos
E3234/40	11 six-coach trains for Waterloo-Bournemouth-Weymouth services	290-300
E3235/41/50/1	24 three-coach trains for Waterloo-Bournemouth/Weymouth and Waterloo-West of England services	770-93
E3236/42/4/52	13 two-coach trains for Waterloo-Bournemouth/Weymouth and Waterloo-West of England services	63-75
E3237/47/56	40 Corridor Brake Composites for Waterloo-West of England services	6713-52
E3238/45/53	Eight open-saloon Thirds (later Composite saloons) for Waterloo-West of England services	7833-40
E3239/48/57	Eight Restaurant cars for Waterloo-West of England services	7892-9
E3243 *	Four three-coach trains for Waterloo-West of England services	981-4
E3246/55	13 Corridor Composites for Waterloo-West of England services	5799-5811
E3254	Five Corridor Thirds for Waterloo-West of England services	1932-6
E3249	15 four-coach trains for London-Dover-Ramsgate-Margate services +	80-94

* believed added to order E3043, described in Chapter 8
+ Some sources state merely 'for Eastern section services'

Plate 146 The first three-coach set Type 'L' to enter service, No 771, photographed in December 1946. Note the temporary ventilator hoods over all windows. The exceptionally clean lines of the coaches will be noted. *Southern Railway*

Plate 147 Production interior of a Third-class compartment in set 771, now with individual reading lights and communication cord above the window. Later First-class seating was upholstered in a blue floral material. *Southern Railway*

It was fairly obvious where the greatest growth in passenger travel was expected, as large numbers of war-weary holidaymakers headed for Devon and Cornwall in the late 1940s. The prototype Composite was, for accounting purposes, included on Order E3235, while the first production coaches to appear were sets 981-4, reallocated to Order E3043A and completed in June/July 1946. These, however, owed little to the prototype coach of September 1945 and have already been described in Chapter 8.

Perhaps not surprisingly, production of the remaining 297 vehicles took some time, and the last did not enter traffic until 1949. The catering vehicles included on Orders 3238/9/45/8/53/7 would turn out to be somewhat notorious and will be described at the end of this chapter. To expedite production of further coaches during this period the Southern turned to outside contractors, in the hope that they might be able to deliver sooner than the company's own workshops could manage. In the event completion of these was equally protracted, and they were not delivered until 1947-9. These coaches are described in Chapter 10.

The first of the Eastleigh-built sets (771) appeared in December 1946, entering service on the Atlantic Coast Express on 12 December (see **Plates 146 and 147**). Accommodation for 24 First- and 120 Third-class passengers was provided, the latter including 64 seats in open-saloon sections — rather more than the 3:1 vote for compartments might have warranted, but anticipating the general trend towards open-saloon accommodation after 1950. The centre vehicle was a Composite, generally similar to the 1945 prototype, incorporating the modifications suggested by the passenger survey. However, the Brake Thirds, with their semi-open saloon layout, represented a considerable departure from previous practice. Each brake coach included a combined guard's/luggage van, entered via a pair of double doors, plus a separate single door for the guard. Next came two compartments and a lavatory, served by a side corridor, then a cross-vestibule followed by a 32-seat open saloon, with another cross-vestibule at the far end of the coach. This layout was broadly followed for all subsequent Bulleid Brake Thirds, making these easily the most numerous type of coach. Roof periscopes were provided for the guard, replacing the side lookouts fitted to 9ft-wide Maunsell brake coaches.

Some difficulty was encountered with the supply of the sliding window ventilators, and most sets entered service with temporary ventilator hoods, as seen in **Plates 146 and 147**, the permanent type being fitted during 1948 (**Plate 148**). Sets 770-93 entered service between December 1946 and November 1947, these being the first examples of what would eventually become the most numerous Bulleid set formation. Details are as follows:

Plate 148 Diagram 2123 Brake Third No 4316 at Eastleigh in June 1949, after the fitting of permanent sliding ventilators. On most vehicles these were painted body colour instead of being left in plain aluminium. *A. E. West*

Plate 149 Production Composite No 5756 to Diagram 2318, at Exeter Central in September 1958. The side panels have been re-clad, hence the various horizontal and vertical beading strips. Note the antimacassars over the First-class seats. *A. E. West*

Vehicle	Sets 770-93
Semi-open Brake Third	4301/3/5/7/9/11/3/5/7/9/21/
	3/5/7/9/31/3/5/7/9/41/3/5/7
Seven-compartment Composite	5751-74
Semi-open Brake Third	4302/4/6/8/10/2/4/6/8/20/2/
	4/6/8/30/2/4/6/8/40/2/4/6/8

On completion of Brake Thirds 4301/2 in November 1947 the prototype Composite (5751) was formed in set 770, the last set to enter traffic. All were used on Waterloo-Bournemouth-Weymouth and Waterloo-West of England services, being designated as three-coach sets Type 'L' in Carriage Working Notices. These stated that the sets should be used only on the services listed and could not work off the Southern Railway, the latter restriction remaining in force until 1954.

The original formations remained remarkably constant, although several were augmented to five coaches during the summer period only, by the addition of an extra Corridor Third either side of the Composite; in 1964 set 770 (only) was increased to eight vehicles for special traffic on the South Western section. Some Brake Thirds (Nos 4307-9/11/2/7-20/7-32/9/40, plus 4354 from Order E3234) were lost to the Western Region in 1963/4, but most other sets remained unaltered until the general abandonment of permanent set formations in March 1966, after which the vehicles ran as loose stock until final withdrawal following completion of the Bournemouth electrification in July 1967. Drawings of each type appear as **Figures 44 and 45**.

The next coaches to enter service were Bournemouth-line six-coach Dining sets 290-300, between August 1947 and March 1948. These were probably Bulleid's best carriages, this being the only time when catering facilities were conceived as an integral part of the permanent steam-hauled set formations, instead of being cut into the sets as required. Considerable care was taken over the construction, finishing and marshalling of the sets, such that the First-class compartments were placed together, with the First-class dining section adjacent to the Kitchen car, while the open-saloon Third, equipped with tables to provide extra dining capacity if necessary, was adjacent to the other end of the Restaurant/Kitchen car. Formations were as follows:

Vehicle	Sets 290-300
Semi-open Brake Third	4349/51/3/5/7/9/61/3/5/7/9
Seven-compartment Composite	5740-50
Corridor/Restaurant First	7677-87
Restaurant/Kitchen Third	7881-91
Open-saloon Third	1451-61
Semi-open Brake Third	4350/2/4/6/8/60/2/4/6/8/70

Plate 150 Bournemouth-line six-coach set 294, as completed in December 1947, with green ends. This shows the opposite end from **Plate 1**, with the Composite as the second vehicle from the camera. *Southern Railway*

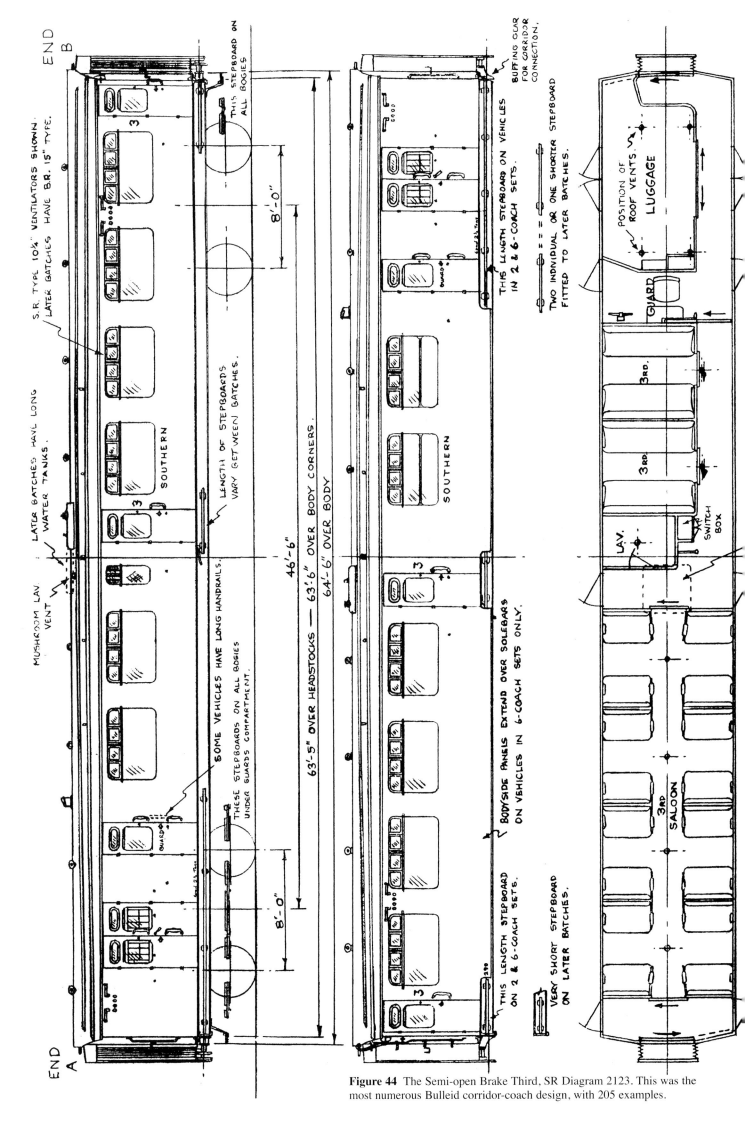

Figure 44 The Semi-open Brake Third, SR Diagram 2123. This was the most numerous Bulleid corridor-coach design, with 205 examples.

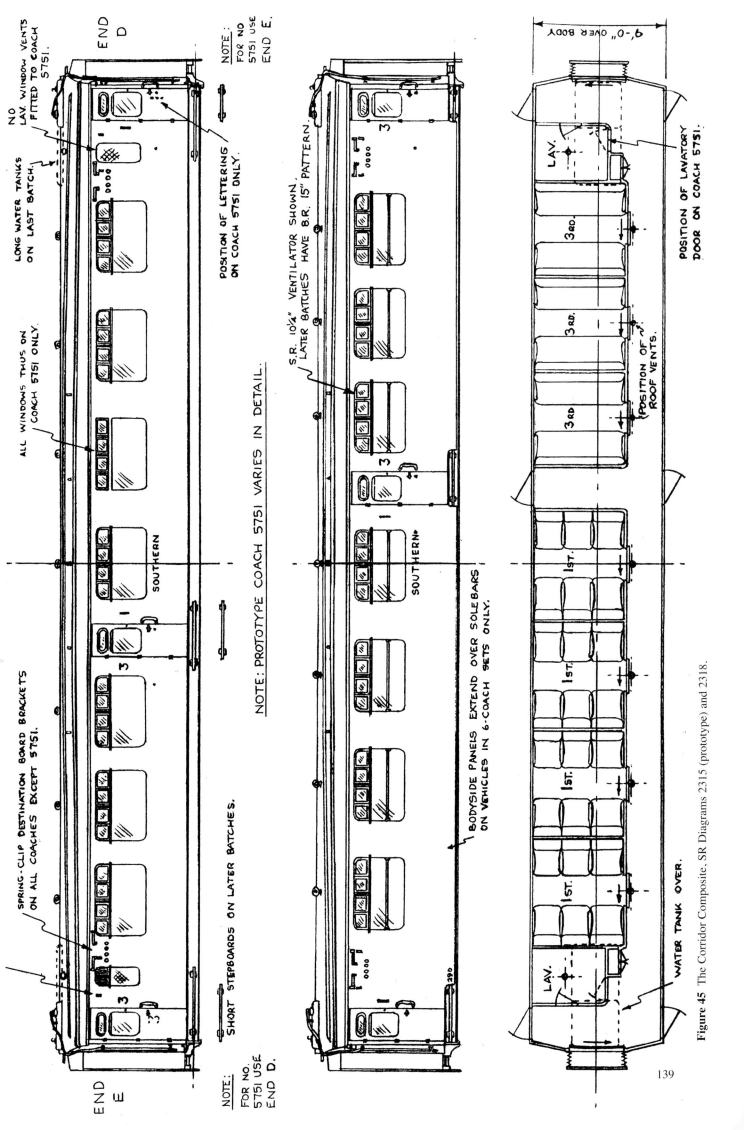

Figure 45 The Corridor Composite, SR Diagrams 2315 (prototype) and 2318.

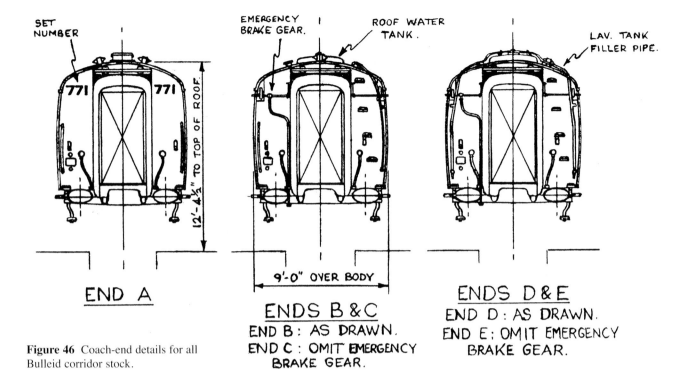

Figure 46 Coach-end details for all Bulleid corridor stock.

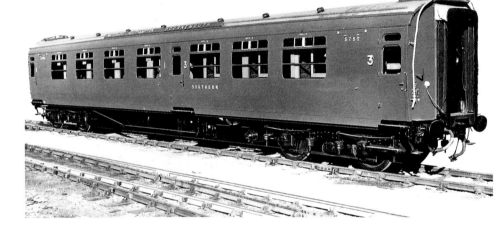

Plate 151 Corridor Composite No 5750 from set 300, as completed in March 1948 but still retaining the company title on the waistline. Note how the extended bodyside panels enhance the overall appearance.
Southern Railway

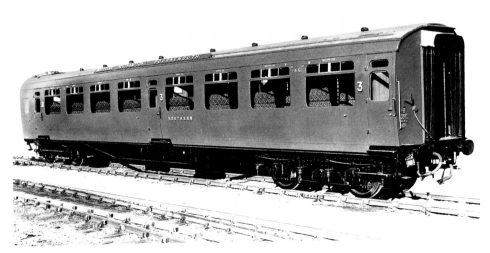

Plate 152 Open-saloon Third No 1461, also from set 300. For the drawing of this vehicle see **Figure 56**. A view of Brake Third No 4369 from the same set appears in **Plate 25**.
Southern Railway

Seating was provided for 66 First- and 216 Third-class passengers, of which 24 First and 32 Third were specifically for dining purposes. The Brake Thirds and Composites were almost identical to the vehicles in the three-coach sets, but one very distinctive external feature was the extension of the bodysides downwards to cover the solebars, this seemingly small detail undoubtedly adding much to their appearance. Apart from set 290 (seen in **Plate 1**), all had green-painted ends and chromium-plated handrails — features that once again enhanced the high-class finish (**Plate 150**); one wonders how different the end result might have been had these 11 sets had been completed as originally planned in 1939/40. The Publicity Department, of course, enthused about the sets as well as the three-coach ones completed just previously, and even the national press (not always renowned for its praise of matters railway) signalled its approval, under the headline 'The Dream Train'.

The open-saloon Third was divided into two four-bay saloons, each seating 32 passengers, separated by a transverse vestibule. There were similar vestibules at each end of the coach, plus a pair of lavatories at one end only (that coupled farthest away from the restaurant car). The Corridor First/Restaurant car (the term 'Dining Saloon' having fallen from favour) included three First-class compartments plus a lavatory, together with a 24-seat First-class dining-saloon section with loose chairs arranged 2+1 either side of the aisle. The compartments were finished similarly to other Bulleid vehicles, having East Indian satinwood panelling with Indian silver-grey wood banding. Seating was uncut green upholstery, matched by green rexine blinds. Originally each First-class compartment had a beige goat-hair rug, with a green border and featuring the letters 'SR', covering the floor. These, unfortunately, were not replaced in later years. The open dining-saloon section was, in complete contrast, finished in off-white rexine panelling, with green silk curtains, green upholstery and a maroon carpet. Lighting, in the dining section only, was provided by fluorescent tubes — the first time this had been used in a production passenger coach in Britain — together with more traditional table lamps (actually bracketed out from the coach side) with champagne-tinted scalloped-edged plastic shades. The overall effect was somewhat reminiscent of the refurbished 'Bournemouth Limited' stock of 1938 (see **Plate 155**).

The accompanying Restaurant Third/Kitchen car comprised a cross-vestibule at one end, followed by a four-bay dining saloon with 32 loose chairs upholstered in rust-brown moquette. Walls were panelled in Nigerian walnut with Indian pyinma banding. Standard tungsten ceiling lights were provided, with oval plastic shades, these being supplemented by the same style of table lamps as provided in the First-class dining saloon. The centre aisle only was covered by maroon carpet, and reddish-brown rep curtains were hung at each window (see **Plate 158**).

The design and supply of the kitchen and pantry areas was contracted out as a package to the Crittall Kitchen Equipment Co Ltd, in contrast to previous Maunsell practice, whereby the Southern's Drawing Office and workshops had been responsible for the design, purchase and installation of all necessary equipment. Crittall, in fact, sub-contracted some works to Wm. Still & Sons Ltd (for supply of tea- and coffee-making equipment) and to the Pressed Steel Co for some of the stainless-steel fittings. Cooking was by gas oil (changed to propane gas during the 1950s), and equipment included a double oven and range, griller and salamander, steamer and a thermostatically-controlled water heater for supply of washing-up water. Two gas-heated closets were provided for warming plates. The equipment was finished in cream vitreous enamel with chromium-plated fittings, with stainless-steel worktops and other surfaces. A Prestcold refrigerator was installed, accessible from both kitchen and pantry, together with an ice-cream conservator — rather novel back in 1947. Some of the equipment may be seen in **Plate 159**. To keep the kitchen clear of cooking smells and steam, a pressure-ventilation and air-extraction system was fitted. At the far end of the kitchen was a small rest compartment and lavatory, both exclusively for staff use.

The two Restaurant-car designs were not perpetuated, although further examples of the Composites, Semi-open Brake Thirds and open-saloon Thirds would appear later. Underframes were similar to previous practice, except that, in place of the usual two 22in vacuum cylinders, one 30in 'Prestall' cylinder was mounted vertically

Plate 153 Interior of a Diagram 2017 open-saloon Third from one of the Bournemouth-line six-coach sets, equipped with tables to provide additional dining capacity if needed. Note the circular mirrors on each bulkhead. *Southern Railway*

Plate 154 Restaurant First No 7687 from set 300, with the Corridor First section nearest the camera. Notice how the green livery has been taken up to the lower roof rain strip — a feature possibly unique to this set. *Southern Railway*

Plate 155 The open dining-saloon area of the Diagram 2507 Restaurant First. The tables featured glass tops with a patterned material underlay which could be changed if soiled. *Southern Railway*

amidships, reducing overall weight and also the amount of necessary brake rodding. However, they were not entirely successful, so between 1951 and 1958 the more usual arrangements were substituted, both on these and all other Bulleid corridor vehicles so fitted. Very often the original Prestall cylinder was left in place but out of use, but on the Kitchen Thirds they were removed due to weight considerations, since there was already a considerable amount of additional equipment carried on these coaches' underframes.

All 11 sets spent most of their working lives on the Bournemouth line, with occasional visits to Weymouth, and were seldom seen elsewhere. Set 299, together with three-set 788 and loose Maunsell Thirds 1200/54 and First 7224, was repainted in the experimental 'plum and spilt milk' livery in June 1948. Hauled by appropriately-liveried apple-green locomotives, the formation was then used on the 7.20am Bournemouth West–Waterloo and 3.30pm (SX) or 1.30pm (SO) return working, the three-set and some of the Maunsells providing the through Weymouth portion. After an initial burst of interest and publicity the liveries were allowed to deteriorate, although repainting in crimson lake and cream did not take place until December 1953. Between then and late 1955, sets

Plate 156 Diagram 2507 Restaurant First No 7679 of set 292 at Bournemouth Central in August 1962, awaiting the arrival of the Weymouth portion of a Waterloo express. Southern Region green livery is now carried. By this time conventional pairs of 22in vacuum cylinders were fitted, visible at the far end of the truss rodding. *A. E. West*

Plate 157 Diagram 2660 Restaurant/Kitchen Third No 7891 of set 300, showing the kitchen side. *Southern Railway*

291/3/4/7-300 were also repainted in this livery, the other four sets retaining malachite until repainted in Southern Region green from 1956 onwards.

For the summer timetables during the 1950s some sets were augmented to 10 coaches by the addition of extra vehicles adjacent to each Brake Third, the extra coaches usually being pairs of Bulleid Corridor Thirds or Open Thirds. In 1960 set 290 included one extra BR standard Open First, running as a seven-coach dining set. However, no permanent changes occurred until 1961/2, when the Restaurant Thirds (by now Seconds) were steadily replaced by new BR Mk 1 Buffet/Restaurant cars. The displaced Bulleids then appeared on other services, allowing the withdrawal of most of the remaining Maunsell catering vehicles. Coaches 7881-8 were withdrawn during 1963 (officially January 1964), but Nos 7889-91 remained in alternative employment until mid-1965. A further reorganisation of catering facilities during 1964 saw most Restaurant Firsts replaced by BR standard Open Seconds. Some of the six-coach sets were disbanded at this time, while others received BR Mk 1 Brake Composites in place of their Bulleid Semi-open Brake vehicles. Set 293 was reduced to three coaches (4355+5743+4356) and held the distinction of being the only three-coach set Type 'L' to have extended bodyside panels. By 1965 it had been cascaded to the Guildford-Horsham branch, providing somewhat more comfortable accommodation than had previously been enjoyed on that line. Save for Nos 7677/83, which lasted until 1967, the displaced Restaurant Firsts had all been withdrawn by March 1965. No 7684 had latterly run as a Composite, with the open-saloon area altered to accommodate 24 Second-class seats. No 7679 was sold to the Sadler Rail Coach Co at Droxford (on the closed Meon Valley line), where it was used occasionally for corporate hospitality; its burnt-out remains were discovered there by the author in September 1968, and regrettably no Bulleid catering vehicles survived into preservation. Drawings of both catering vehicles appear in **Figures 47 and 48**.

Next off the production line were two-coach sets 63-75, which appeared between March and June 1948 and comprised Semi-open Brake Thirds 4371-83 and Corridor Brake Composites 6700-12, formed in numerical sequence. The Brake Thirds were almost identical to those provided in sets 770-93, while the Brake Composites did not feature any open saloon but instead had four Third- and two First-class compartments, with the lavatory repositioned adjacent to the transverse vestibule at the non-brake end of the coach. These entered traffic in malachite green but without the company title, with the carriage and set

Plate 158 The Third-class dining area of a Diagram 2660 vehicle. *Southern Railway*

Plate 159 Part of the kitchen area, showing the double oven and range. It all looks pretty cramped! *Southern Railway*

Plate 160 Restaurant car 7888 at Exeter Central in August 1963, not long before withdrawal. By this time it was on West of England services, coupled to a BR standard Open Second. The last-repaint date (7.12.62), together with the code number (4041) for Lancing Works, is painted on the lower bodyside. *A. E. West*

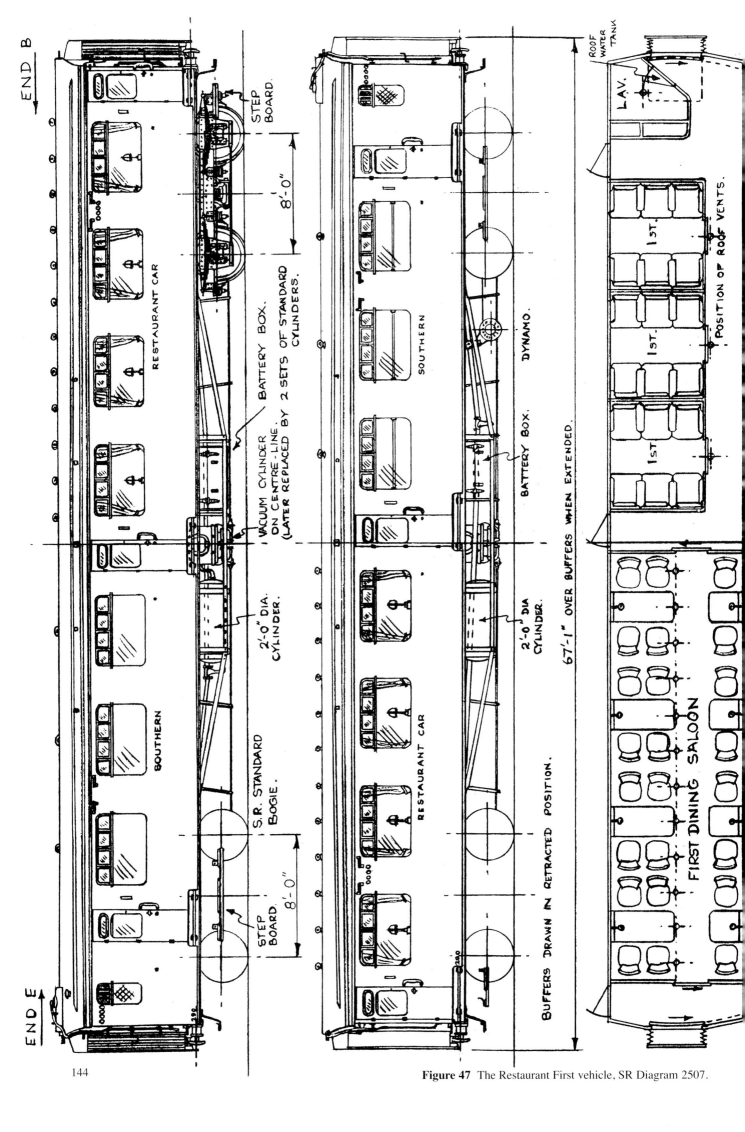

Figure 47 The Restaurant First vehicle, SR Diagram 2507.

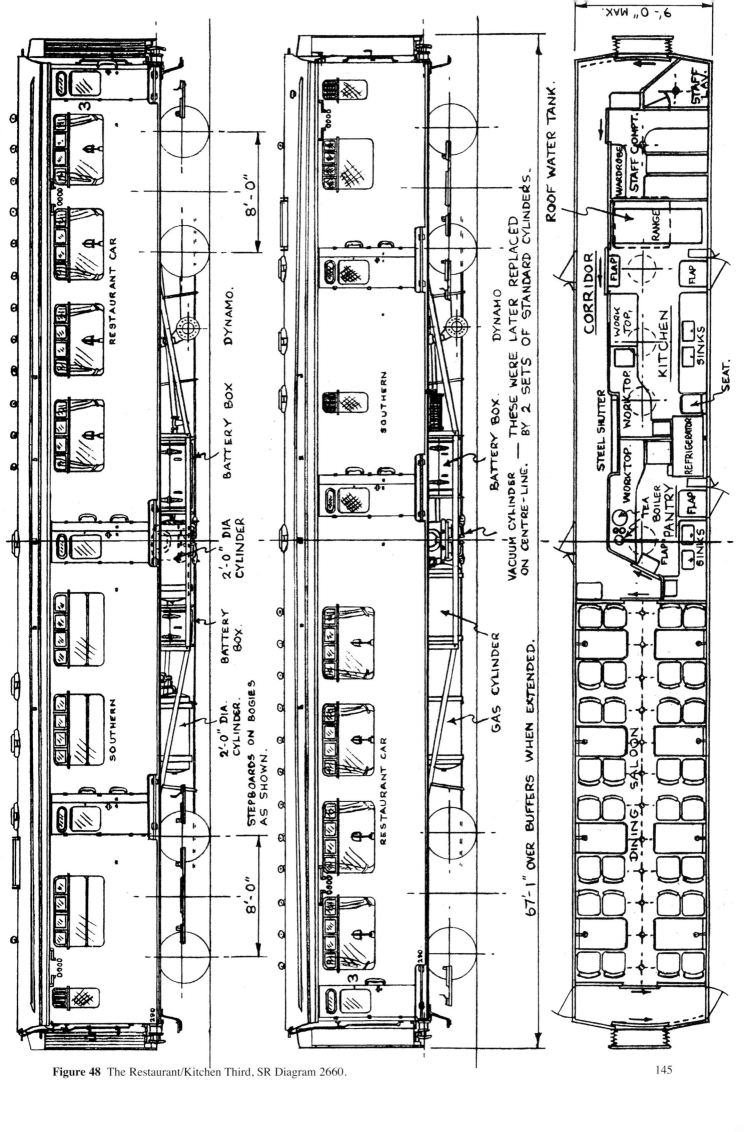

Figure 48 The Restaurant/Kitchen Third, SR Diagram 2660.

numbers prefixed 'S', as seen in **Plate 161**. When authorised they constituted no fewer than four separate orders for through Lymington, Swanage and West of England workings; however, by 1948 there were few through portions to Swanage and none at all to Lymington, so all 13 sets spent their entire lives on the West of England main line, largely ousting the 'Ironclad' and Maunsell two-coach sets from through duties to Waterloo and remaining unaltered in formation until 1964/5, when withdrawal commenced.

The next orders called for 40 Brake Composites, 13 Corridor Composites and just five Corridor Thirds, all for West of England services. The Composites were identical to those already completed for sets 770-93, while the Corridor Thirds employed the same body shell as the Open Thirds but instead had eight compartments in two groups of four, separated by a transverse vestibule. The loose Brake Composites used a layout different from that of the two-coach sets, with the lavatory near the centre of the coach rather than at the non-brake end, and were thus somewhat similar in layout to the earlier Brake Thirds. All these loose vehicles were completed during the latter half of 1948 and were the last Bulleids to feature the 10½ in-deep window ventilators. **Plates 163-165** illustrate these loose coaches.

Most Brake Composites remained on West of England services, and few were ever incorporated into sets. All the loose Thirds and Composites described above were eventually allocated to sets, albeit in some cases for relatively short periods. Two sets formed using these coaches are worth recording, both being used on Waterloo-West of England services:

Set No	Vehicles	Dates
400	6728+5803+1934+6738	1951-9
76	4282+6713	1960-4

Coach 4282 was one of those built by BRCW and is described in Chapter 10. It was originally formed in three-coach set 821, which had suffered accident damage in 1956. Brake Composites 6714-7/9/26/38/42/6 were transferred to the Western Region in 1963/4 following the boundary changes and became W6714S etc; at least two (6716/9) were repainted at Swindon in 1964, receiving lined maroon livery. They were not confined to ex-

Plate 161 West of England two-coach set Type 'R' No 74, as completed in May 1948 with 'S' prefix to both set and coach numbers. *Southern Railway*

Plate 162 Diagram 2405 Brake Composite 6702 at Exeter Central in September 1958. This shows the corridor side. *A. E. West*

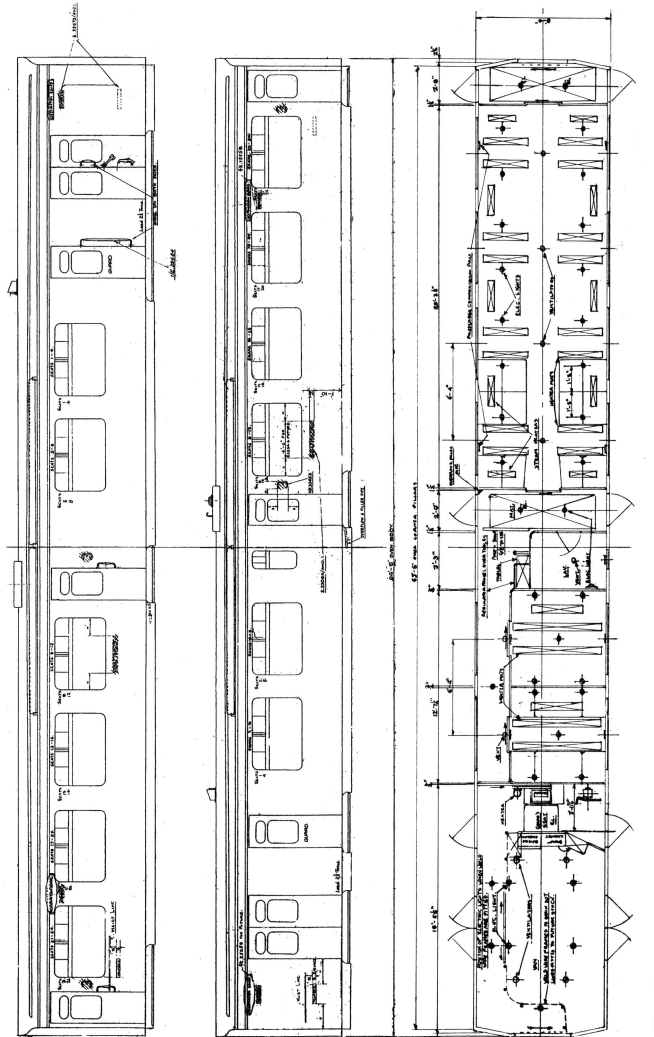

Figure 49 General Arrangement Drawing E37483, showing the Diagram 2123 Brake Third for two-coach sets 63–75. Note that the coach numbers are shown in Southern style but dropped to the waistline at each end. There is no evidence that this particular lettering layout was ever used.

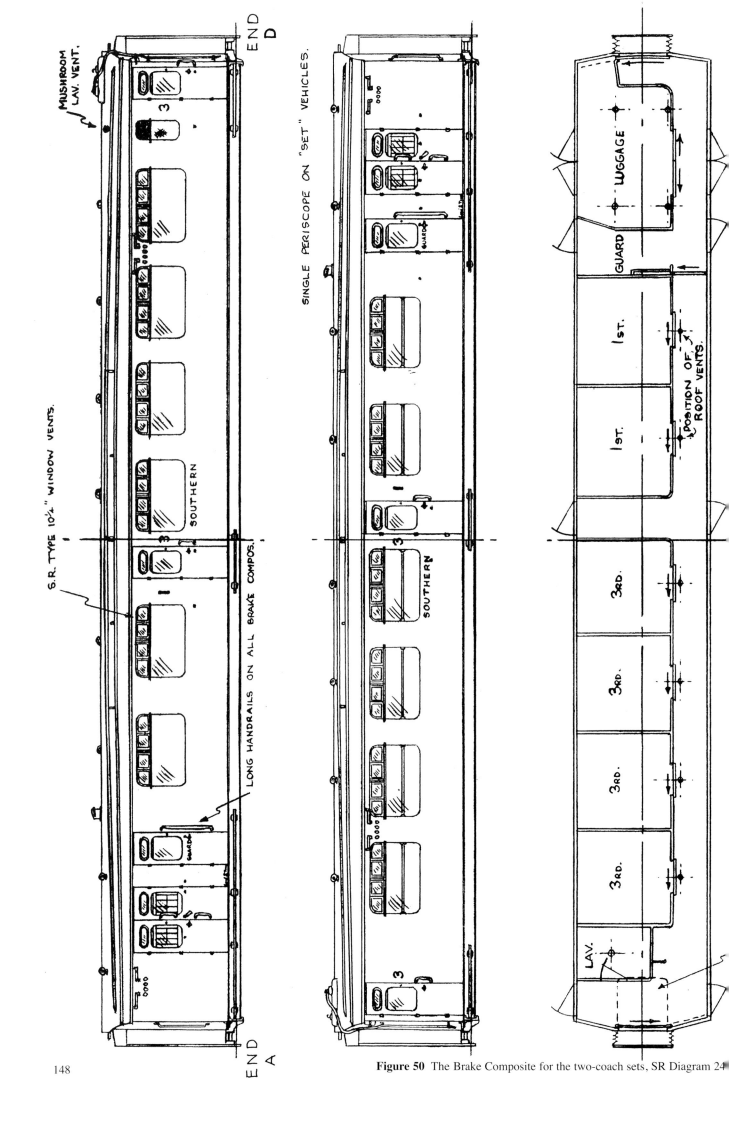

Figure 50 The Brake Composite for the two-coach sets, SR Diagram 24

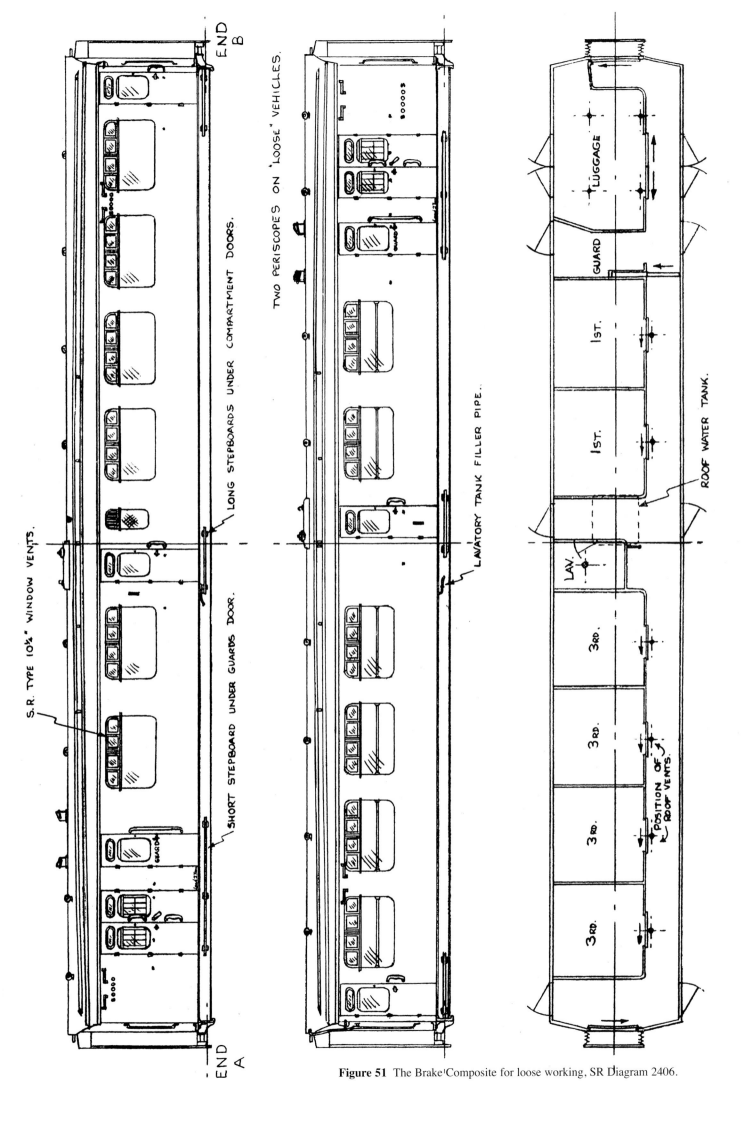

Figure 51 The Brake Composite for loose working, SR Diagram 2406.

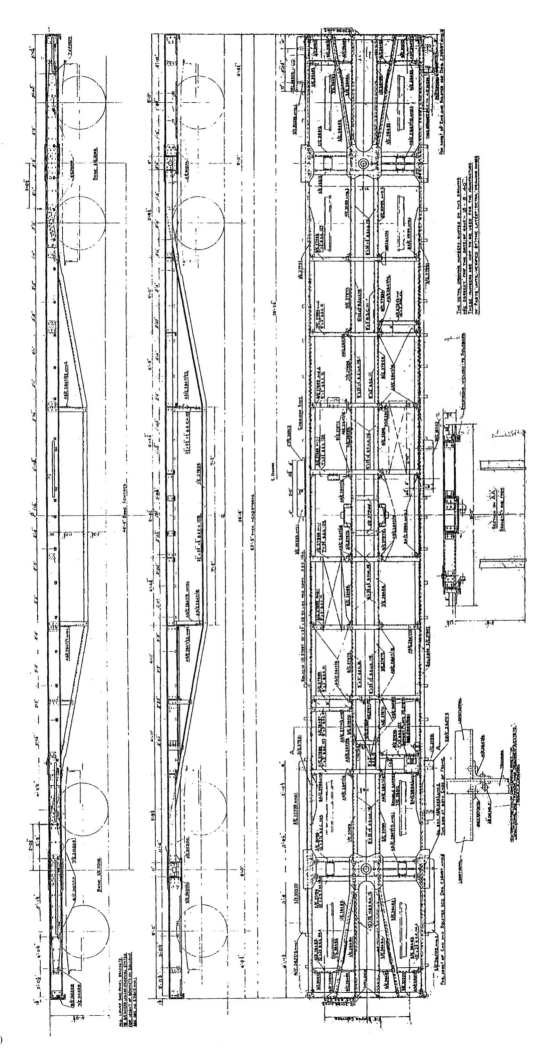

Figure 52 General Arrangement Drawing E37876, showing the Bulleid 63ft 5in underframe. Also shown is the position of the centrally mounted 'Prestall' vacuum cylinder.

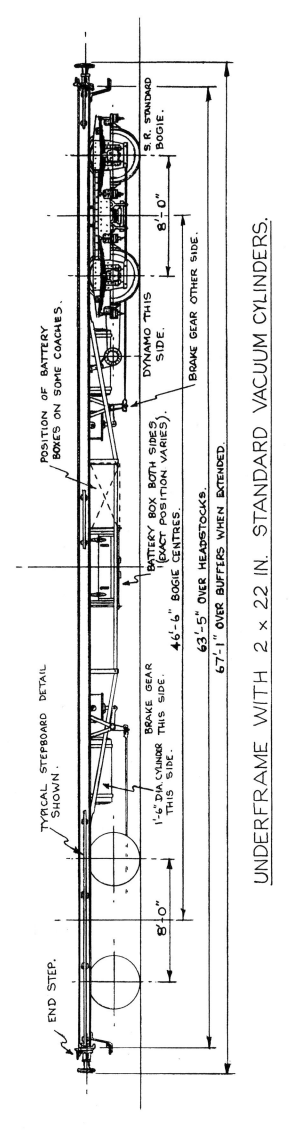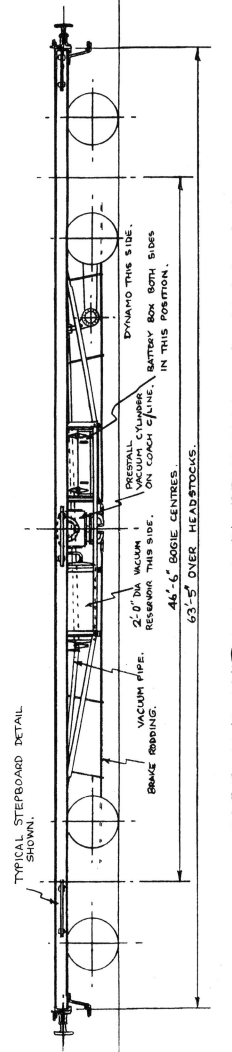

Figure 53 Elevations of both types of Bulleid underframe, showing the alternative types of brake rigging.

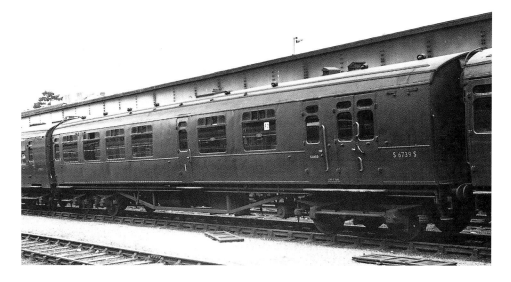

Plate 163 Loose Brake Composite 6739 standing on the up through road at Exeter Central in August 1963, about to be formed into a Waterloo express along with a rebuilt 'Tavern' car and other Bulleid vehicles. The Exeter portion of most West of England expresses usually included the 'Tavern' pair and a loose Brake Composite. *A. E. West*

Plate 164 Close-up detail of the guard's compartment and bogie of Diagram 2406 Brake Composite 6743 at Lyme Regis in June 1959, forming the through coach to Waterloo. On summer Saturdays the single coach would be increased to a three- or five-coach set and sometimes more. *A. E. West*

Plate 165 Loose Corridor Third No 1935 in malachite green at Clapham Junction in October 1949. *D. Cullum*

Plate 166 Corridor Third No 31, formerly in four-coach set 85, now running as a loose Second at Exmouth in June 1963. Note the 15in-deep window vents, as fitted from late 1948. *A. E. West*

LSWR lines during their period of WR ownership, and a few outlasted the Southern-allocated vehicles, not being withdrawn until 1968.

Prior to 1949 the only Bulleid sets running on the South Eastern section were several built by the Birmingham Railway Carriage & Wagon Co; however, from May of that year, four-coach sets Type 'N' (for new?) 80-94 entered service on London-Dover-Ramsgate-Margate services. These were the last sets to be outshopped in malachite green and the first with 15in-deep window ventilators; presumably the earlier 10½in pattern had been found inadequate, as this alteration featured on all subsequent Bulleid corridor coaches. Other details were as before, apart from very minor changes to handrails, footsteps and the position of corridor-side handrails; the last were altered to suit the shallower fixed-window glazing, this now being flat instead of curved to bodyside profile, to overcome the storage problems previously encountered. Set formations were as follows:

Vehicle	Sets 80-94
Semi-open Brake Third	4011/3/5/7/9/21/3/5/ 7/9/31/3/5/7/9
Eight-compartment Third	26-40
Seven-compartment Composite	5823-37
Semi-open Brake Third	4012/4/6/8/20/2/4/6/ 8/30/2/4/6/8/40

These immediately appeared on the most important main-line services, remaining so employed until the completion of Stage 1 of the Kent Coast electrification in June 1959, when sets 89 and 90 were transferred to the Oxted line. Sets 80 and 86 were strengthened to seven vehicles each in February 1959, being used thereafter for specific London-Dover-Margate services. Their formations were:

Set 80:   4011+26+5823+5884+1477+1479+4012
Set 86:   4023+32+5829+5886+1482+1487+4024

Further reallocation took place after the completion of Stage 2 of the Kent Coast electrification in June 1961, the above sets going to the South Western section and being further augmented to 10 vehicles. The other four-coach sets remained on South Eastern lines for a while longer, as some diesel-hauled passenger services ran until June 1962, after which most moved to the Central section, appearing on Reading-Guildford-Redhill, Guildford-Horsham-Brighton and Tunbridge Wells West-Eastbourne services as well as Oxted- and other branch-line services. Reduction to standard three-coach formations took place during 1963, the Corridor Thirds (now Seconds) being removed from the sets. Withdrawal started soon after, but sets 82/3/5/8, 90/4 were finally reallocated to the South Western section, joining sets 80 and 86, the last by then also reduced to three coaches. **Plate 166** illustrates a Corridor Third from these batches.

Plate 167 Diagram 2552 Corridor First No 7608 at Clapham Junction in September 1949, formed in a First-class Ocean Liner express for Southampton Docks along with Maunsell rebuilt Brake First No 7716 (seen previously in **Plates 20 and 61**). *D. Cullum*

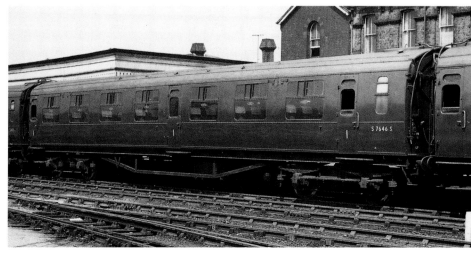

Plate 168 The compartment side of Corridor First No 7646 in Southern Region green livery at Tunbridge Wells West in June 1962, formed in Oxted-line six-coach set 897, between two BRCW-built Brakes. *J. H. Aston*

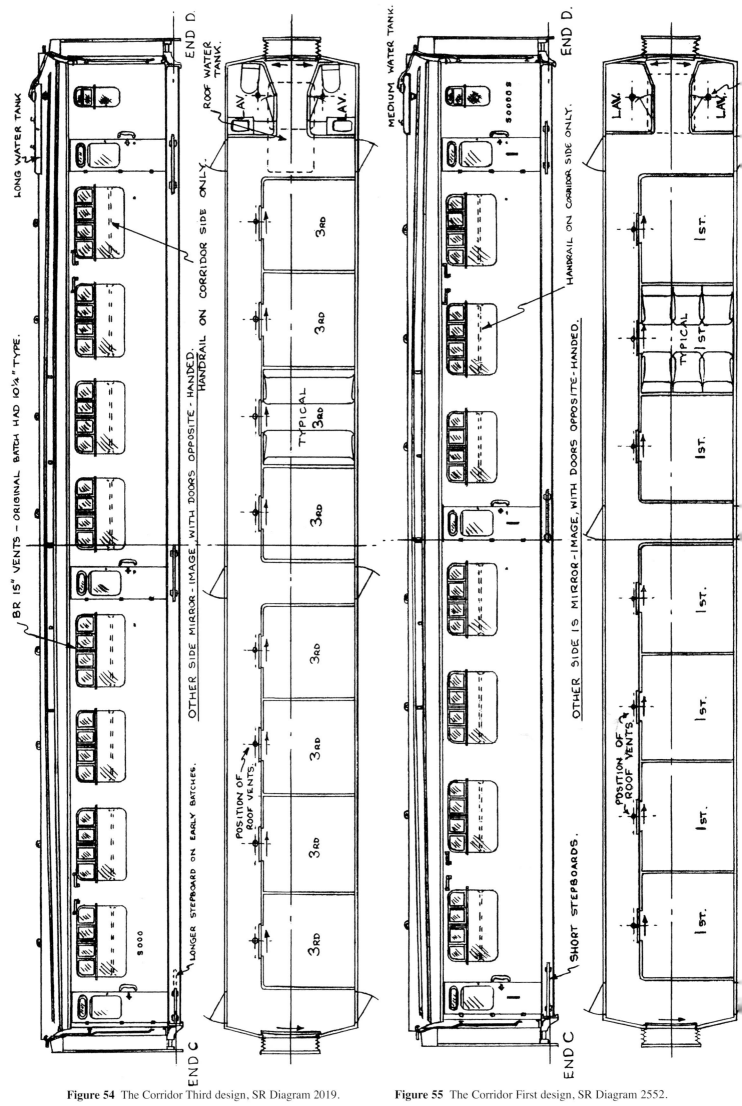

Figure 54 The Corridor Third design, SR Diagram 2019. **Figure 55** The Corridor First design, SR Diagram 2552.

Plate 169 Corridor Composite 5857, as completed in May 1950, for set 839; the set number (prefixed 'S') is just visible on the solebar. This was one of the last Bulleid corridor coaches to remain in traffic on the Southern Region, running until September 1968. *Southern Railway*

The last vehicles to appear from the May 1945 orders were the 'Tavern' cars, so, chronologically, these should be detailed next. However, they deserve rather greater attention, were most definitely non-standard and were later rebuilt, and are therefore dealt with at the end of this chapter.

Continuing with the ordinary corridor stock, the next orders were placed in August 1947, for the following vehicles:

HOO No	Stock	Set/coach Nos
E3450	40 Corridor Firsts for Dover and Southampton boat traffic	7608-47
E3451	20 Brake Thirds for South Eastern-section services	3943-62
E3452	40 Corridor Composites for South Eastern-section services	5868-5907
E3453	40 Corridor Thirds for South Eastern-section services	41-80
E3454	20 three-coach trains for Waterloo-Bournemouth-Weymouth and Waterloo-West of England services	830-49

Somewhat improved material and labour supplies meant that these 200 coaches entered traffic very shortly after the completion of the May 1945 orders, the last of which had taken no less than four years to fulfil. The first to appear were the Corridor Firsts, outshopped in June-October 1949. This was the only new design completed at this time and seated 42 passengers in seven compartments, arranged in groups of three and four, separated by a transverse vestibule. Similar vestibules were provided at each end, plus a pair of lavatories at one end only, either side of a short, central corridor. These and all subsequent Bulleid corridor vehicles carried crimson lake and cream from new, together with (in all but the final batches) left-hand-positioned numerals, as seen in **Plates 167 and 169**.

The loose Brake Thirds and Composites followed between September 1949 and January 1950 — all being similar to the vehicles in sets 80-94, save for livery — while Corridor Thirds 41-80 appeared in January-March 1950. Not all of these coaches were allocated to their intended duties. Seven sets, all for the South Eastern section, were soon made up from the nominally loose vehicles; three were three-coach sets, as follows:

Vehicle	Set 767	Set 768	Set 769
Semi-open Brake Third	3950	3952	3954
Seven-compartment Composite	5878	5880	5879
Semi-open Brake Third	3951	3953	3955

These were formed by June 1950 for London-Dover-Ramsgate-Margate services, remaining there until transferred to the Oxted line in 1955. Set 767 was then made up to eight coaches as a direct replacement for Maunsell set 194, described in Chapter 5. Like the Maunsell set, this was formed with the Brake coaches inside the end of the set:

93+94+3950+5878+7645+3951+95+96

In 1959 the formation was altered so that the Brakes were in the conventional position at each end of the set, with the result that the guard would have to leave his van and walk up the train at any station that had short platforms. After dieselisation of the route in 1962 set 767 reverted to three coaches (3950+5889+3951) and moved to the South Western section, rejoining sets 768/9, which remained as three-coach formations and had moved to the SW section three years earlier.

The other four sets were formed as shown below.

All had been formed by June 1950, for London-Ramsgate services. The Maunsell Restaurant cars were drawn from those allocated to the Pullman Car Co; after rebuilding as Buffet cars in 1953/4 they continued to run in the sets until completion of Stage 1 of the Kent Coast electrification in 1959. Sets 265/7 were then disbanded, but sets 264/6 were later transferred to the Central section and by 1963 had been reduced to three coaches only, with the usual brake, composite, brake formation.

Vehicle	Set 264	Set 265	Set 266	Set 267
Semi-open Brake Third	3946	3959	3956	3948
Eight-compartment Third(s)	55	41	46/7	43/4
Seven-compartment Composites	5881/2	5868-70	5875/6	5871-4
Restaurant car	(none)	(Maunsell)	(Maunsell)	(Maunsell)
Eight-compartment Third(s)	56	42	48-50	45
Semi-open Brake Third	3947	3960	3957	3949

Plate 170 After a gap of some 2½ years since the Bournemouth-line six-coach sets, one further batch of open-saloon Thirds was completed towards the end of 1950. These omitted the extended side sheeting and dining tables but were still allocated Diagram number 2017. Coach 1479 is seen at Exeter Central in May 1964. *A. E. West*

The 20 three-coach sets for the South Western section were not all formed as originally proposed. Sets 830-7 ran as intended, but 838-49 were all permanently increased to five coaches by the addition of loose Thirds 57-80, in pairs, in each set. Details are as follows:

Vehicle	Sets 830-7	Sets 838-49
Semi-open Brake Third	3971/3/5/7/9/81/3/5	3987/9/91/3/5/7/9, 4001/3/5/7/9
Eight-compartment Third	-	57/9, 61/3/5/7/9, 71/3/5/7/9
Seven-compartment Composite	5848-55	5856-67
Eight-compartment Third	-	58, 60/2/4/6/8, 70/2/4/6/8, 80
Semi-open Brake Third	3972/4/6/8/80/2/4/6	3988/90/2/4/6/8, 4000/2/4/6/8/10

These entered service, unusually, in reverse order between March 1950 (set 849) and July 1950 (set 830). It was not unknown for the five-coach sets to have both Thirds coupled together instead of either side of the Composite. Sets 830-7 were often made up to five coaches for the duration of the summer timetables, using Thirds drawn from the next new batch, Nos 81-130 (detailed below). Some of these were specifically allocated; sometimes they were any particular Thirds that were to hand at Clapham Yard, where most of the re-marshalling took place. Sets 834-7 were permanently made up to five coaches in June 1953, using Thirds 123-30, in pairs and in numerical order, leaving only sets 830-3 as three coaches. Finally, in July 1959, these also became five-sets, using Thirds (by now Seconds) 114-21 in pairs and in numerical order. All these three/five-coach sets spent their entire lives on South Western-section services.

In November/December 1949 came the last orders for Bulleid corridor vehicles, as follows:

The Corridor Thirds have already been described with reference to sets 830-49 (in which many of them ended up), while the other vehicles were also similar to previous orders. The six Buffet cars were to an unspecified design, but subsequently it was decided not to proceed with these vehicles. The open-saloon Thirds were identical in layout to those built for the Bournemouth-line six-coach sets in 1947/8 but omitted the extended bodyside panels, had 15in-deep window vents and were finished in crimson lake and cream, with right-hand-positioned numerals. No tables were provided, as these coaches were not intended to be used as dining saloons. One is seen in **Plate 170**. Some other small changes were made to these batches, including longer roof-mounted water tanks, and Orders E3581-3 (at least) had LMS-pattern electrical switchgear, although this would not be obvious to the casual observer; neither would the increase in size of the timber body-framing members, from 2in to 2½in square.

Several of the Open Thirds were formed in the 'Golden Arrow' service, coupled between the leading luggage van and

HOO No	Stock	Set/Coach Nos
E3580	50 Corridor Thirds for general use	81-130
E3581	45 open-saloon Thirds for Dover and Southampton boat traffic	1462-1506
E3582	One Corridor First for general use	7648
E3583	16 three-coach trains for London-Dover-Ramsgate-Margate and Waterloo-West of England services	850-65
E3584	Six Buffet cars for general use	(Cancelled 29/2/50)

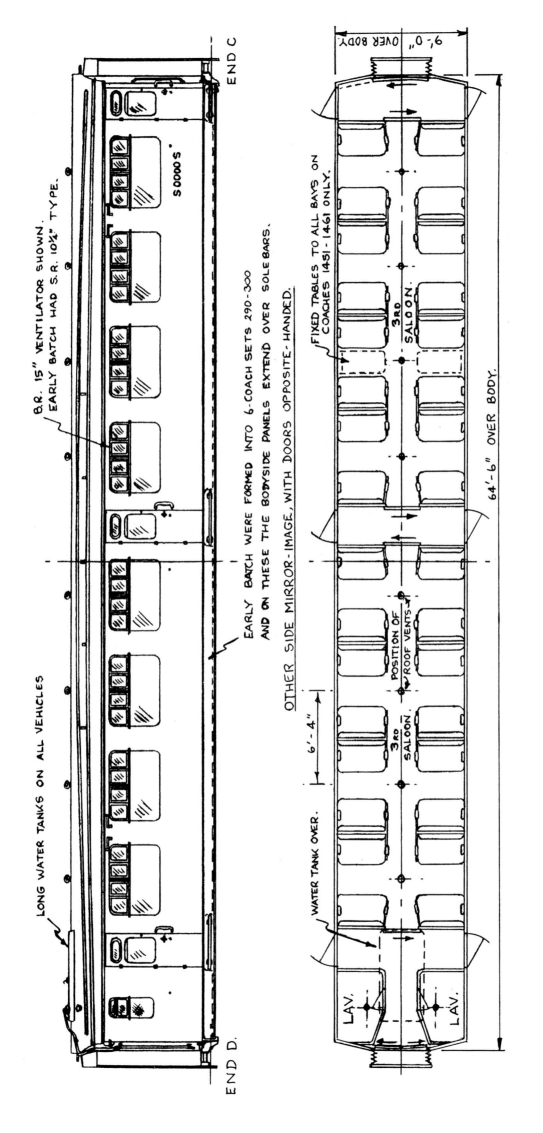

Figure 56 The open-saloon Third, SR Diagram 2017.

Plate 171 The last Bulleid three-coach sets were Nos 850-5, completed in 1951. Seen at Eastleigh in June 1962 is Brake Third No 2529 ex-set 864, complete with BR carriage-stock crest for the 'Royal Wessex' duty. *A. E. West*

the Pullman cars, while several Waterloo-Southampton Docks Ocean Liner sets were formed in 1951 with up to five of them included, plus some Corridor Firsts, coupled between Maunsell and 'Ironclad' Brakes. Details are as follows:

Vehicle	Set 350	Set 351	Set 352	Set 353	Set 354
Six-compartment Brake Composite	6649*	6662*	6650*	6570*	6644*
Open-saloon Thirds	1476/7	1467, 1502	1469, 1501	1496/86/99/81	1463/72, 1503/4
Seven-compartment Corridor First(s)	7610	7627	7609	7608/18	7620/1
Open-saloon Thirds	1478-80	1468/95/75	1498/85/91	-	-
Six-compartment Brake Composite	6601*	6587*	6669*	6651*	7711+

Vehicle	Set 355	Set 356
Six-compartment Brake First	7712+	7714+
Seven-compartment Corridor Firsts	7613/4	7615/6
Six-compartment Brake First	7713+	7716*

* Maunsell vehicle
\+ 'Ironclad' Brake First

The two First-class-only sets (355/6) found little demand, and the vehicles were all returned to loose stock early in 1952. The formations of the other five sets varied considerably over the years, most SR coaches being replaced by BR standard vehicles during the mid-/late 1950s. Set 351 appears in **Plate 78**. All the sets were maintained in crimson lake and cream, emphasising the importance of Southampton boat trains in the pre-jet age of transatlantic travel.

Sets 850-65 were the last three-coach sets Type 'L' to be completed, from February to June 1951. Formations were as follows:

Vehicle	Sets 850-65
Semi-open Brake Third	2501/3/5/7/9/11/3/5/7/9/21/3/5/7/9/31
Seven-compartment Composite	5908-23
Semi-open Brake Third	2502/4/6/8/10/2/4/6/8/20/2/4/6/8/30/2

The Composites were completed some time before the Brake Thirds and were stored, probably at Micheldever, to await completion of the latter. Both types were as previous designs but had the longer roof-mounted water tanks and LMS-design switchgear. Sets 850-7 were allocated to the South Eastern section; the rest went to the South Western, where they were immediately made up to five coaches by the addition of two Corridor Thirds for the duration of the summer timetable. All reverted to three-coach sets for the winter timetable, but some returned to five coaches during subsequent summers. Those on the SE section remained as three-coach sets, Nos 851-7 being reallocated to the SW section in 1955. Set 850 alone went to the Oxted line at this time, being used on the same duties as sets 768/9. All finally arrived on the South Western section in 1959. Few permanent set-formation changes occurred, but set 864 was reduced to two coaches only (Nos 2530 and 5922) in 1962, for the Swanage portion of the 'Royal Wessex', seen in **Plate 171**. Some coaches were not equipped with intermediate buffers, which might explain the lack of changes. Withdrawal commenced in 1964, but most coaches would survive until 1967.

The honour of being the last Bulleid steam-hauled coach to be constructed went to Corridor First No 7648, completed on 3 July 1951. Identical to the earlier Corridor Firsts, it remains a mystery just why one additional coach might have been needed. It had an order number, so its existence was perfectly legitimate, but why choose a full First? Surely one extra Corridor Third or Open Third would have been more useful? Perhaps it made use of an underframe surplus due to the completion of prototype Composite No 5751 in advance of the remainder of its order (E3235) back in 1945; Lancing may not have taken this into account when completing the rest of the order, although there had been plenty of time (and subsequent orders) to rectify the matter. There is one further confusing entry in the order book: against Order E3582 is a reference to solitary BR standard Mk 1 Corridor First S13003, completed at Swindon in 1951 for the 'Royal Wessex', against BR Lot number 30019. Did Lancing build one extra Bulleid/SR frame in error for this vehicle? We shall probably never know. Coach 7648 nevertheless entered service as a loose vehicle until 1954, whereafter it ran in set 473 until 1959 before reverting to loose stock; in 1965 it was included in the remnants of Bournemouth-line Dining set 299, remaining thus until the general disbanding of permanent sets in 1966. It was one of only two Bulleid Corridor Firsts to last until 1967 (the other being No 7616), all the rest being condemned during 1964/5.

By early 1964 most remaining locomotive-hauled services on the Southern Region were concentrated on the South Western section, with Bulleids, a few Maunsell vehicles and some BR standard coaches making up all trains. Withdrawals up to this time had been confined to three accident victims (coaches 4209, 4281 and 5898) and the first of the multi-door sets described in Chapter 8. This would soon change; dieselisation of the Waterloo-Salisbury-Exeter route and the first round of Beeching closures, followed by electrification towards Bournemouth, would soon decimate the remaining Southern Railway steam-hauled stock. From March 1966 the use of permanent sets was abandoned; withdrawals were probably taking place faster than the sets could be reformed. Most trains soon began to take on an untidy appearance, as Bulleids, BR standards and the occasional Gresley LNER buffet car were mixed in together. Some of the latter types were in maroon livery, while before long BR vehicles were being repainted in Rail blue and grey, further adding to the variety. Despite claims that Bulleid coaches carried this livery, the author has yet to confirm this fact, although a couple of departmental conversions did carry plain blue.

The Bulleids were not life-expired by 1967, but concerns had been raised over their ability to withstand accident damage if marshalled between all-steel BR vehicles; undoubtedly their composite timber-and-steel bodywork would fare badly in any collision. Additionally, BR vehicles had been designed to withstand a 200-ton end load; the equivalent figure for a Southern underframe was a mere 80 tons. It was thus decided that the Bulleid stock had to go, perhaps 10 years before their lifespan had been reached. With the completion of the Bournemouth electrification in July 1967, sidings at Clapham Junction, Barnes, Richmond, Twickenham, Walton-on-Thames, Micheldever, Eastleigh and Hamworthy Junction were soon filled with condemned coaches awaiting disposal.

By 30 December 1967 just the following 37 Bulleid vehicles remained in Southern Region stock:

Corridor Third (Second)	27, 84/8/9, 1934	(5)
Open Third (Second)	1451-4/63/4/75/81/3/8/92/6, 1504	(13)
Semi-open Brake Third (Second)	4004, 4263/71 (both BRCW vehicles)	(3)
Corridor Composite	5722 (59ft), 5740/57/61/8/9, 5857/8/60/9, 5907	(11)
Corridor First	7616	(1)
Kitchen/buffet car	7892/4/8/9	(4)

Several others, including the last seven Brake Composites (and Maunsell Buffet car 7969!) had been withdrawn earlier in the same month, but by May 1968 only the 13 Open Seconds and five composites remained. All were withdrawn before the end of the year.

Prior to this, in 1965/6, 20 Open Seconds had been transferred away, nine going to the Eastern Region and 11 to the Scottish Region, in exchange for a similar number of BR standard vehicles that were required for conversion to Bournemouth-line electric stock. Some of the Bulleids were repainted in lined maroon, with appropriate Regional prefix letters ('E' or 'SC'), before transfer. Details are:

Transferred to ER	1467/9/70/2/4/86/91/9, 1505
Transferred to ScR	1466/71/9/82/4/9/95/8, 1500/2/4

Some lasted until 1970 in Scotland, these being the final Bulleid locomotive-hauled carriages in normal traffic. The last Brake Seconds and Brake Composites, which went to the Western Region in 1963-5, were also withdrawn during 1968.

A few of these transfers and some others purchased directly from the Southern Region eventually found their way into preservation, while a mere 10 Bulleid coaches entered departmental service, in marked contrast to the 100-plus Maunsell coaches. Three were sold to the Chipman Weed Killing Co at Horsham, and two of these were subsequently sold on to preservation societies. At the time of writing (2002) only the Bluebell Railway, Swanage Railway, Mid-Hants Railway and the Keighley & Worth Valley Railway own Bulleid coaches in serviceable condition.

The 'Tavern' cars

We now turn to what must have been some of the most remarkable coaches to ever run on a British railway — certainly among the most controversial. These were Bulleid's 'Tavern' cars and their accompanying Restaurant cars, eight pairs of which were completed at Eastleigh between April and June 1949. They were the last coaches to be completed from the orders placed in May 1945, so Bulleid, together with his Drawing Office staff and the Eastleigh Works carriage builders, had plenty of time to consider the designs.

Originally conceived in the tried and trusted Maunsell catering format of pairing a Restaurant car with a Dining Saloon Third, they were ordered piecemeal on no fewer than six HOO numbers, all for Waterloo-West of England services. Bulleid, of course, remembered the effect his 1938 re-styling of the 'Bognor' Buffets had on catering revenue, and this must surely have spawned the idea of windowless dining cars, to ensure that customer turnover would be rapid. However, for most passengers the perfect railway meal is complemented by the experience of watching the scenery go by. Denied this pleasure by Bulleid, the travelling public unsurprisingly did not find this a popular feature. During 1946/7 several Maunsell catering vehicles were converted into Kitchen/Buffet cars, while two Diners were altered to Composite vehicles. These arrangements proved successful in service, so it was probably no accident that, by 1948, the original concept had changed in favour of a Kitchen/Buffet plus a Composite Diner. The Bournemouth-line six-coach Dining sets were also a success; indeed, the kitchen and pantry areas of the 'Tavern' cars were little altered from those included in sets 290-300 and thus require no further description here.

At some point during the design process — reputedly during a lunchtime conversation outside the Botleigh Grange Hotel, near Eastleigh — the suggestion of putting an 'olde worlde' pub on wheels was put forward. Bulleid was enthusiastic, and the idea took hold — indeed, some might later say took over! Having made the inside look like an old English inn, why not do the same on the outside as well? The coaches were described officially as Kitchen & Buttery cars but soon became known to all and sundry as 'Tavern' cars.

By this time the newly-formed British Railways had decreed that the new carriage-stock livery should be crimson lake and cream, so what better way of enhancing the external illusion than by painting on imitation English bond brickwork over the crimson, with fake half-timbered beams superimposed on the cream? Officialdom would thus be satisfied — until it saw what had been done to its corporate livery! Each 'Tavern' was given a name and a suitable inn sign, displayed using vitreous enamel panels on a background of duck-egg blue, affixed to each side of the vehicle. A similar sign was incorporated within the bar area. (What price at auction might these fetch today?) The names chosen were:

Coach No	Inn Sign	Paired with Composite Diner No
7892	The White Horse	7833
7893	The Jolly Tar	7834
7894	The Dolphin	7835
7895	The Bull	7836
7896	The Three Plovers	7837
7897	The Salutation	7838
7898	The Green Man	7839
7899	The Crown (later The George and Dragon)	7840

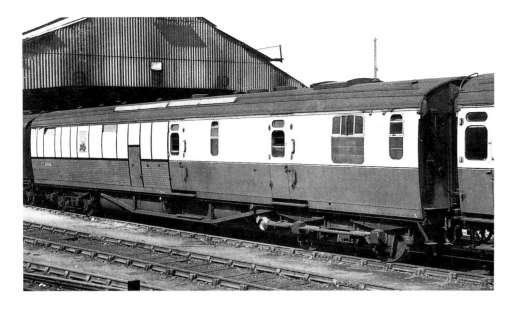

Plate 172 'Tavern' car No 7898 *At the Sign of the Green Man* at Clapham Junction in 1949, roof-boarded for the 'Atlantic Coast Express'. The brickwork and beams, plus the 'planked' service door, are clearly visible. Note also the lack of intermediate buffers between the 'Tavern' and the Composite Saloon to the right. Another view, of 'Tavern' 7894, appears as **Plate 17**.
Author's collection

All were somewhat unnecessarily prefixed by the words 'At the sign of …'
Fake leaded lights were applied to the toplight windows in the bar area — the only windows in this portion of the coach.

All this might have been acceptable until rumours started to circulate amongst railway staff that two Carriage & Wagon Department draughtsmen had been sent out on a tour of Hampshire inns to find suitable signs that could be copied; needless to say, the office 'wags' had a field day — as did the C&W draughtsmen, in all probability! Some staff cynically referred to the cars as 'doll's houses', on account of the painted decoration, while others (especially those who were teetotal) no doubt held even less favourable views.

Internally the bar area was entered through fake-leaded-light swing doors and featured dark oak settles (providing 12 seats) placed against the bodyside, together with small tables for the convenience of the drinkers. Into the ceiling were set 12-year-old oak beams with a whitewashed 'rough-cast' plaster finish; on the walls was oak panelling, and on the floor were black and red 'country style' imitation tiles. Dangling from the ceiling were miniature 'olde worlde' square metal lanterns. At the kitchen end, in complete contrast, was a modern cocktail bar/snack counter in plastic and stainless steel, the front of which was faced with polished light-oak panelling set within dark-oak framing. The whole was said to have been inspired by the décor of the Chequers Inn at Pulborough. **Plate 173** illustrates the bar-counter area.

Coupled to the kitchen end of the 'Tavern' car was the Composite Restaurant vehicle. This sat 24 First- and 40 Third-class passengers in two saloons, with a lavatory at the end farthest from the kitchen. While seating in the Third-class saloon was arranged in the customary layout of 2+2 loose chairs either

Plate 173 A posed interior shot of the bar-counter area in coach 7892 *At the Sign of the White Horse*. The caption on the reverse of the original print reads: 'Tavern cars, which combine the most modern features of both restaurant and buffet cars with the traditional style of an Old English Tavern, are being introduced on express services on the Eastern and Southern Regions of British Railways this summer [1949]'. Little did anyone realise the fuss that would be caused!
Southern Railway

Plate 174 The inn sign for coach 7892, also featuring the English bond brickwork. *Southern Railway*

Plate 175 The almost-windowless Composite Restaurant car, No 7839, photographed on the same occasion as **Plate 172**. The First-class saloon, with just three toplight windows on each side, is nearest the camera. *Author's collection*

side of a central aisle, the First-class diners faced each other, with their backs against the sides of the coach. This may have made life easy for the stewards, but it did little for the privacy or comfort of the diners. The interior was similarly appointed to the 'tavern' area; however, buff-coloured laminated plastic panelling, with light-oak framing, replaced the white plastered finish. First-class seating was upholstered in figured brocade, with a floral motif in old rose and dull turquoise; the Third-class chairs were maroon with a leaf-pattern motif. Recessed fluorescent lighting completed the décor, which, combined with the shiny plastic panels and almost windowless environment, resulted in a gloomy, school-hall-dining-room atmosphere. **Plates 176 and 177** show the uninviting saloons, guaranteed to make any diner feel claustrophobic and bolt his/her meal in double-quick time in order to return to the comfort of the rest of the train!

On 25 May 1949 one set was inspected at Waterloo by senior BR and Hotels Executive staff. Initial publicity was not always favourable, as some members of the press came away with photographs of station staff gazing in wonderment at the new creations. Despite this, it was announced that two pairs would enter service on the 'Atlantic Coast Express' between Waterloo and Exeter, while the others would be used on the Eastern and London Midland Regions for the 'Master Cutler', 'White Rose', 'Norfolkman' and 'South Yorkshireman'. Had they all remained on the Southern Region then the outcome might have been different. The patrons of the 'Master Cutler' did not take kindly to the vehicles at all, and immediately the Railway Executive began to receive a stream of complaints. First-class passengers, in particular, refused to patronise the Restaurant cars, and takings nose-dived. The local Yorkshire press, including the *Sheffield Star*, *Ollerton Echo* and *Yorkshire Post*, all started campaigns to have the cars removed from the service, claiming that the accommodation was grossly inferior to that offered previously. The then Minister of Transport, Mr James Callaghan, also received letters of protest. By the end of August 1949 the complaints had achieved their aim, and by the beginning of October all six pairs had returned to the Southern Region. By now letters of complaint were also being received from SR passengers, no doubt fuelled by the problems further north.

Such was the furore that the matter was urgently discussed at the Rolling Stock Committee meeting on 5 October 1949, which resulted in the issue of Order E3643, authorised on 31 January 1950, for the fitting of windows and traditional seating in all eight dining cars. In place of the previous Nissen-hut-like

Plate 176 Interior view of the First-class dining area. Ventilation, in the form of a fan, is provided! Note the toughened-glass luggage racks, so-designed to ensure passengers could clearly see if they had left anything behind. *Southern Railway*

Plate 177 The marginally less oppressive Third-class dining area. *Southern Railway*

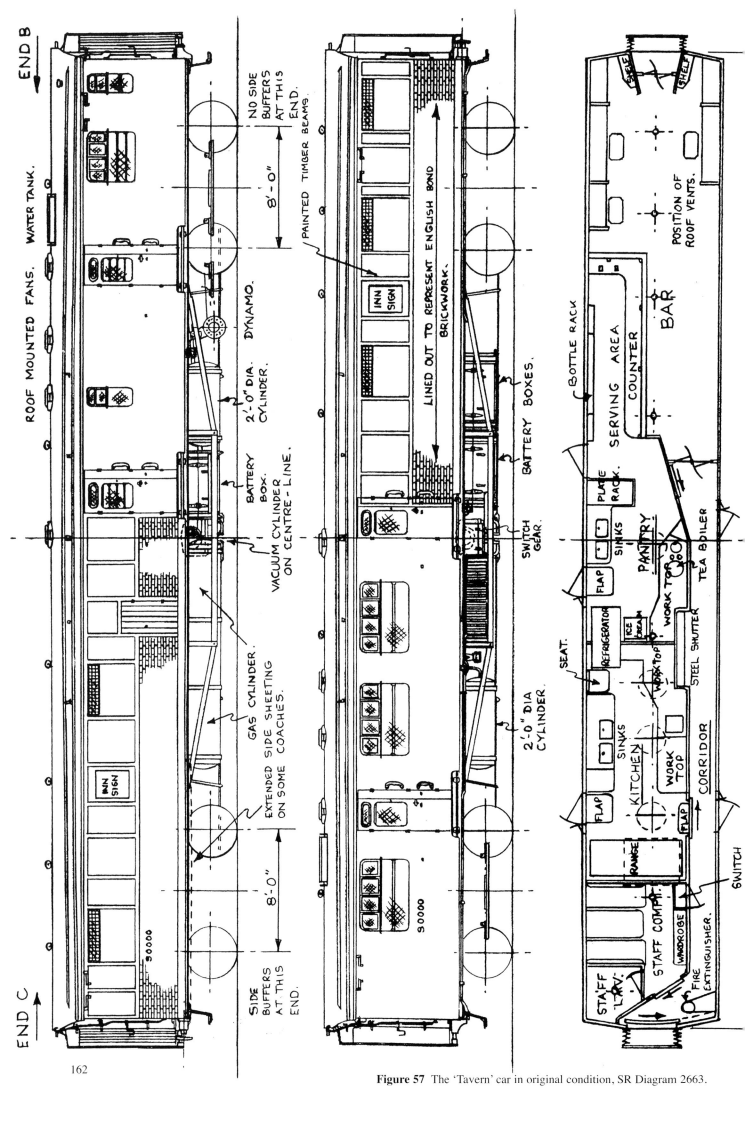

Figure 57 The 'Tavern' car in original condition, SR Diagram 2663.

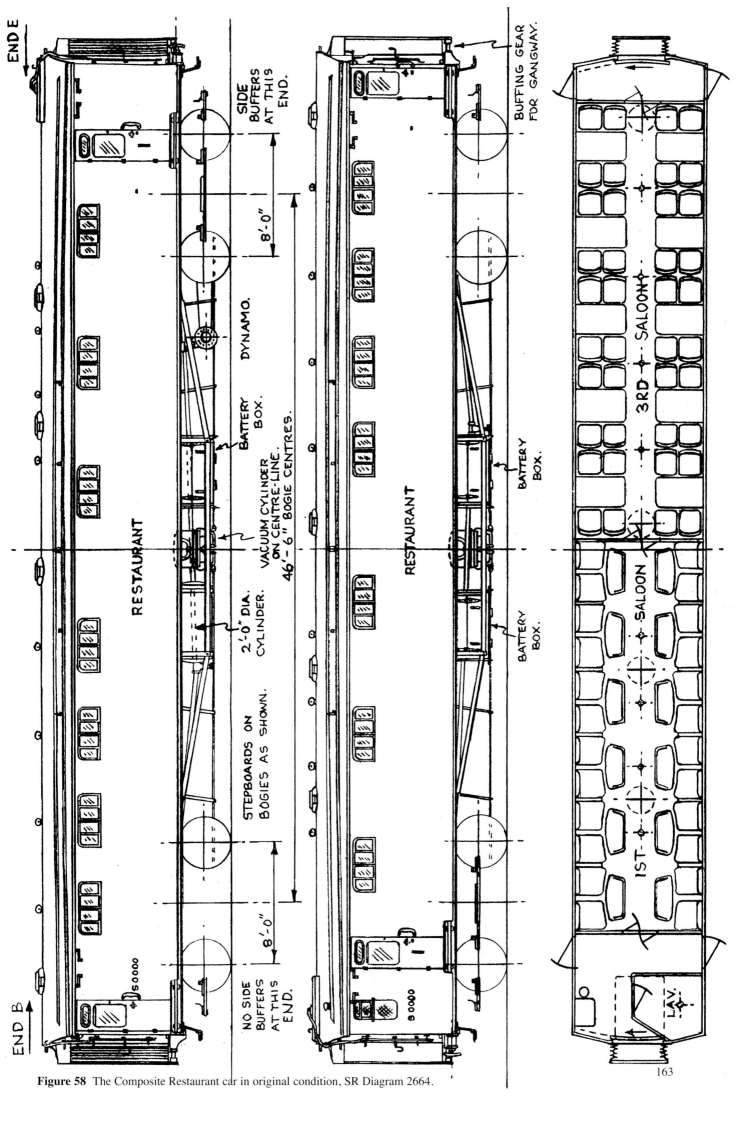

Figure 58 The Composite Restaurant car in original condition, SR Diagram 2664.

arrangements came nine sets of large windows on each side, with transverse seating for 18 First- and 36 Third-class passengers. Conversion dates are as follows:

7833	10/50	7837	7/50
7834	6/51	7838	9/50
7835	4/51	7839	2/51
7836	6/50	7840	11/50

The diagram number was amended from 2664 to 2665.

Despite the uproar, the 'Tavern' cars themselves continued to run unaltered save for the painting-out of the brickwork and beams. The complaints concerning these vehicles were by no means as vociferous; however, Order E3968 was eventually issued (in April 1953) for interior modifications, the scope of which is unknown. Time must have softened passengers' views, as this order was cancelled in August 1954, before any work had been undertaken. From about this time, one set was allocated permanently to the 'Royal Wessex' service, replacing the BR standard Mk 1 catering vehicles on this train.

Despite all the complaints the Catering Department was well pleased with the turnover, takings being higher than in any other Southern Region catering vehicle, so maybe all had not been lost. In hindsight, Bulleid's concept was probably 20 years ahead of its time, as more recent public-house conversions (albeit on *terra firma*) have proved, and publicans have seen their receipts soar. But postwar austerity Britain was not yet ready for the themed pub-cum-restaurant; this had to wait for another generation of interior designers. True, the windowless dining saloons were a bad idea — albeit conceived with the best of motives — but others would argue that they were an over-reaction to a previous good idea. Whether Bulleid was seeking to be deliberately controversial or was simply doing his job as a designer rather depends on one's viewpoint, either as a passenger or as a catering manager.

It is tempting to speculate what might have been, had Sir Herbert Walker remained in charge during Bulleid's tenure of office. Undoubtedly Walker kept a wary eye on the financial side of things, as well as the less practical ideas that were undoubtedly put before him. The later General Managers — Szlumper and Missenden — perhaps failed to exercise the same levels of control on Bulleid, and some schemes that might not have otherwise seen the light of day (or might have been sensibly toned down) became reality. It has been suggested that Sir Nigel Gresley had kept Bulleid in check on the LNER, but, on the Southern after 1937, Walker's steadying hand was missing.

The 'Tavern' cars were eventually (from 1957) repainted in Southern Region green but kept their inn signs, even when repainted. By 1954 the kitchen and pantry areas of all eight 'Taverns' and the 11 Bournemouth-line Restaurant cars were in need of some modernisation, and this work was put in hand from December of that year, although it took until 1962 for all 19 vehicles to be dealt with. In September 1956 Order L4339 was authorised for the alteration of the 'Tavern' cars into more orthodox Kitchen/Buffet cars, this work being completed between June 1959 and June 1960. During this process the cars finally lost their inn signs and were equipped with contemporary laminated-plastic interior finishes. The diagram number was amended from 2663 to 2668. By then some were in use between Waterloo and Bournemouth or Weymouth, as well as to Exeter. All previous controversy was now forgotten, and the refurbished Buffets and the Composite Restaurant cars remained in service until withdrawn between 1965 and 1968, four of the former 'Tavern' cars serving until just a few months before the demise of Bulleid locomotive-hauled stock on the Southern Region.

Table 12 summarises the Bulleid steam-hauled carriages built at Eastleigh between 1946 and 1951.

Plate 178 Rebuilt Composite Restaurant car No 7836, freshly arrived at Clapham Yard in June 1950 and not yet returned to traffic. *D. Cullum*

Plate 179 'Tavern' car 7894 *At the Sign of the Dolphin* at Clapham Junction *c*1951, with brickwork and beams painted out. It is coupled to a Maunsell open-saloon Third, suggesting the photograph was taken while the Composite Saloon was being rebuilt. *Author's collection*

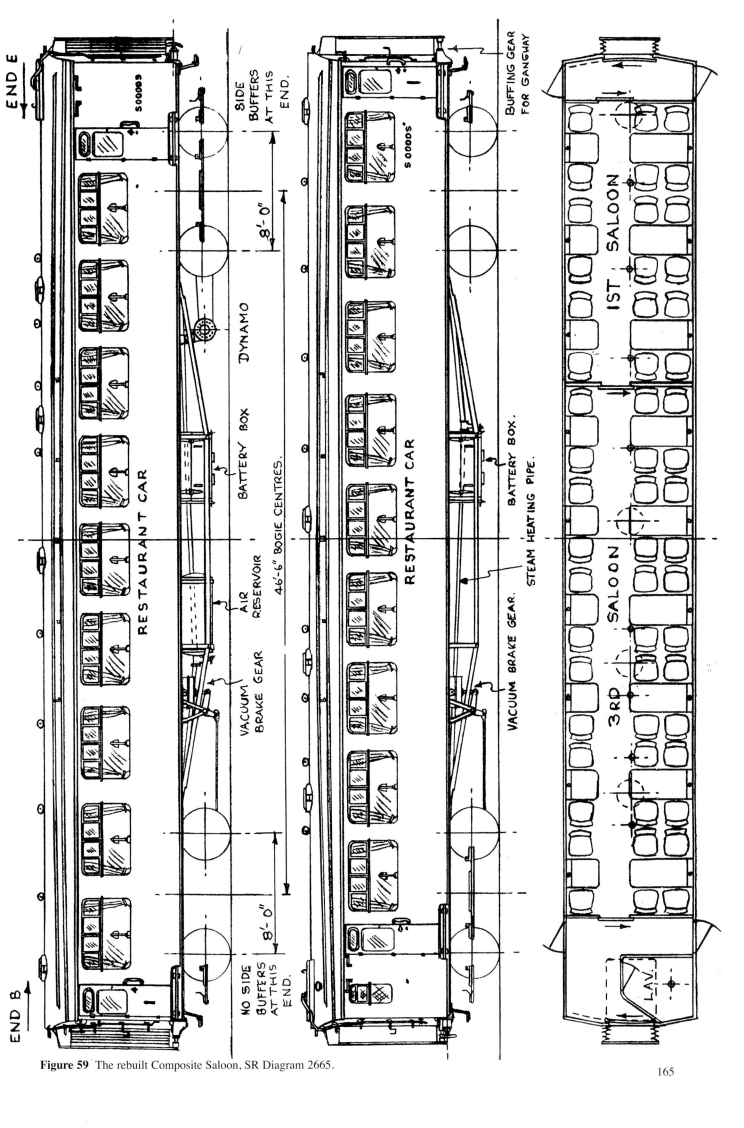
Figure 59 The rebuilt Composite Saloon, SR Diagram 2665.

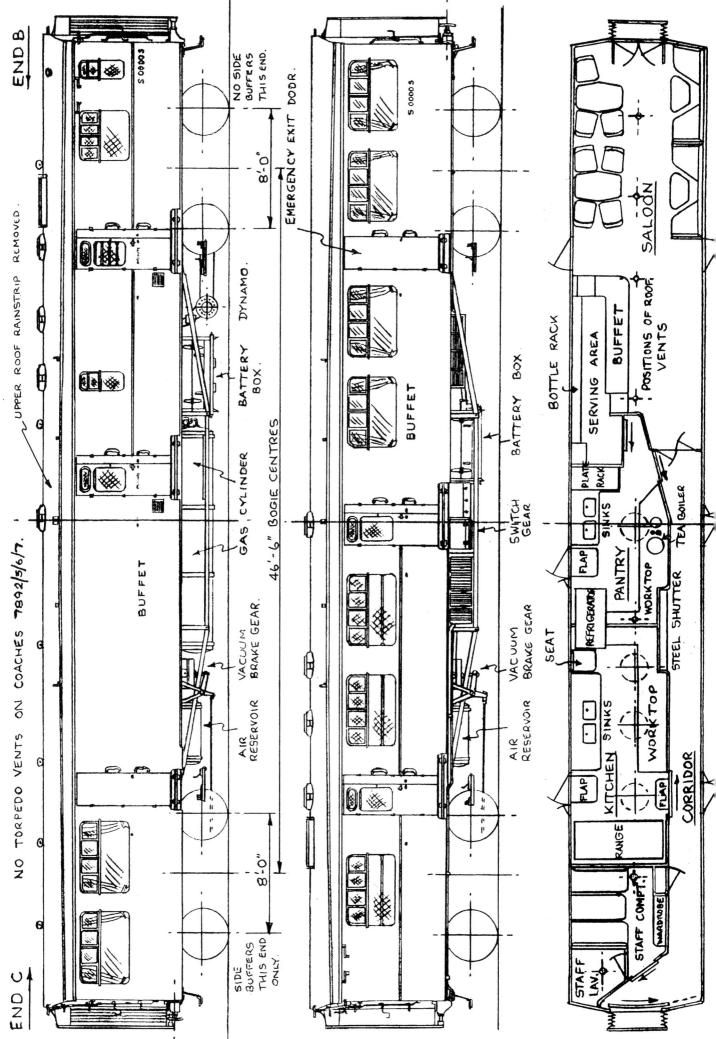

Figure 60 The rebuilt Kitchen & Buffet car, SR Diagram 2668.

Table 12
Summary of Bulleid Eastleigh-built stock 1946-51

Diagram No	Vehicle Type	Seats 1st	Seats 3rd	Running Nos	Built by	Vents	Remarks
2017	Eight-bay open-saloon Third		64	1451-61	Eastleigh 7/47-3/48	10¼in	Extended side panels
				1462-1506	Eastleigh 10-12/50	15in	
2019	Eight-compartment Third		64	26-130	Eastleigh 12/48-11/50	15in	
				1932-6	Eastleigh 9/48	10¼in	
2123	Semi-open Brake Third		48	2501-32	Eastleigh 1-6/51	15in	
	(two compartments + 32-seat open saloon)			3943-62	Eastleigh 9-11/49	15in	
				3971-4040	Eastleigh 12/48-7/50	15in	
				4301-83	Eastleigh 12/46-5/48	10¼in	Extended side panels on 4349-70
2315	Seven-compartment Composite	24	24	5751	Eastleigh 9/45	10¼in	Prototype coach
2318	Seven-compartment Composite	24	24	5740-50	Eastleigh 7/47-3/48	10¼in	Extended side panels
				5752-74/99-5811	Eastleigh 12/46-9/48	10¼in	
				5823-37/48-5923	Eastleigh 12/48-2/51	15in	
2405	Six-compartment Brake Composite	12	32	6700-12	Eastleigh 3-5/48	10¼in	For two-coach sets
2406	Six-compartment Brake Composite	12	32	6713-52	Eastleigh 6-9/48	10¼in	Loose vehicles
2507	Three-compartment Restaurant First + saloon	42		7677-87	Eastleigh 8/47-3/48	10¼in	Extended side panels. No 7684 later Composite
2552	Seven-compartment First	42		7608-48	Eastleigh 6-9/49, 7/51	15in	No 7648 built 7/51
2660	Restaurant/Kitchen Third		32	7881-91	Eastleigh 8/47-3/48	10¼in	Extended side panels
2663	Kitchen & Buttery car ('Tavern' car)		12	7892-99	Eastleigh 4-6/49	15in	Rebuilt as Diagram 2668 1959/60; extended side panels
2664	Composite Restaurant car ('Tavern' Dining car)	24	40	7833-40	Eastleigh 4-6/49	15in	Rebuilt as Diagram 2665 1950/1; extended side panels
2665	Composite Restaurant car	18	36	7833-40	Rebuilt 6/50-6/51	15in	Ex-Diagram 2664
2668	Kitchen & Buffet car		11	7892-9	Rebuilt 6/59-6/60	15in	Ex-Diagram 2663

Notes
Underframes completed at Lancing.
Composite No 5898 lost after accident damage at Vauxhall in April 1953.
Composites 5800/7/29, 5919 reclassified as Seconds in 1966, with 56 seats; 25 others scheduled but never done. No new diagram number allocated.

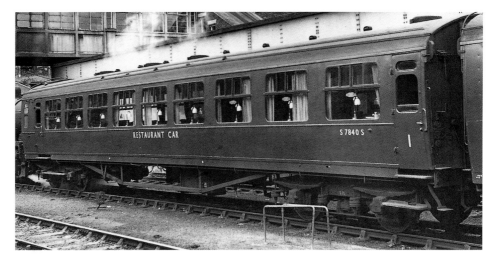

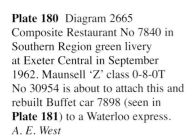

Plate 180 Diagram 2665 Composite Restaurant No 7840 in Southern Region green livery at Exeter Central in September 1962. Maunsell 'Z' class 0-8-0T No 30954 is about to attach this and rebuilt Buffet car 7898 (seen in **Plate 181**) to a Waterloo express.
A. E. West

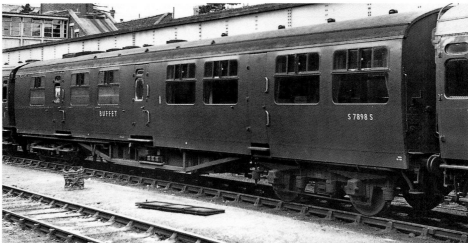

Plate 181 Diagram 2668 Kitchen & Buffet car No 7898, seen on the same occasion as **Plate 180**.
A. E. West

Plate 182 BRCW 'Cross-country' set 801, in malachite green and with coach and set numbers prefixed 'S', as ready for traffic in June 1948. The smaller coupé window is visible next to the guard's door. *Southern Railway*

Plate 183 Diagram 2124 Brake Third (now Second) No 4226, running in six-coach set 897 at Tunbridge Wells West in June 1962. Note the lack of window ventilators in the corridor. *J. H. Aston*

Chapter 10.
Bulleid BRCW-built Stock 1947-1949

Chronologically, these contractor-built vehicles were contemporary with the orders placed in 1945 for Eastleigh-built stock. At that time the country was facing a considerable shortage of manpower and materials, so it was evident from the start that there might be some delay in completing the 310 coaches ordered in May 1945. In the meantime the Southern Railway was in urgent need of as many new coaches as possible, to replace those that had been either lost to enemy action or simply become life-expired over the previous nine years, during which no new steam-hauled construction had been undertaken. Indeed, at this time the company was using a number of otherwise redundant Pullman cars on the numerous Forces' leave trains then running between Dover and Victoria or between Southampton and Waterloo.

During the immediate postwar period, external rolling-stock contractors were subject to rigorous Government controls on supplies of materials, and workshop space in these establishments was 'allocated' by the Ministry of War Transport to those railway companies wishing to order new stock by these means. In November 1945 the Southern Railway was granted workshop capacity for the construction of up to 72 new coaches, and negotiations commenced with the Birmingham Railway Carriage & Wagon Co for the construction of 24 three-coach sets, at a cost not exceeding £19,000 per set. Any costs above those which would have been incurred had the railway been able to complete the vehicles in its own workshops would be borne by the Ministry.

In February 1946 an initial order was placed for 10 sets, soon increased to 30. Finally, in July 1946, capacity for five additional sets was allocated, delivery being scheduled for 1946/7, all to be built by BRCW at a cost not exceeding £19,000 per three-coach train. In the event none was received before December 1947, and it was May 1949 before the final vehicles entered traffic, at about the same time as the last of the May 1945 Eastleigh orders. Details are shown at the foot of the page.

BRCW used its own proprietary manufacturing methods in the construction of these vehicles, resulting in carriages that were visibly different from those completed at Eastleigh, both externally and internally. Some features were not necessarily an improvement, so probably the design details were finalised before construction of the 1946 production vehicles went ahead. If the coaches had been delivered as intended they would have been in traffic long before most of the 1945 Eastleigh orders.

Externally, the most noticeable difference concerned the windows, which had externally-beaded Alpax alloy frames and were some 3in shallower than on Eastleigh stock. Corridor-side windows were devoid of sliding vents, the loss of these being balanced by provision of larger box-type roof ventilators in place of torpedo vents. The side sheeting panels were rather smaller, and their joints were lapped and screwed to the timber body framing, instead of being butt-welded. This resulted in fewer body-corrosion and re-beading problems in later years, so the coaches retained their clean bodyside lines throughout.

Internally, the seating and décor made a return to the Maunsell style of the 1930s, with reddish-brown rexine panelling below waistline and stained-timber veneers above, together with the usual white-painted ceilings. The interior was thus noticeably darker than on most other Bulleid coaches, accentuated by the smaller windows. It was this feature, plus the rather low set of the seating, that gave the least pleasing effect, the lower edge of the windows being at about chin level for the average seated passenger. However, the lighting was an improvement: in place of the bare tungsten-filament bulbs in plastic mounts were ornate glass bowls in the ceilings, covering the light bulbs.

The underframes were similar to those provided on the earlier Bulleid coaches, having the conventional two 22in vacuum cylinders instead of the single 'Prestall' variety. Otherwise, overall dimensions were the same as other 64ft 6in Bulleid vehicles, although there were some changes to the position of the lavatory in the Brake Thirds, with a luggage rack opposite, as had been fitted to most Maunsell open-saloon Thirds during the 1930s. The original 10 sets incorporated a 44-seat brake vehicle with a coupé compartment adjacent to the guard's van, resulting in a correspondingly larger luggage area. Details of these are as below:

Vehicle	Sets 795-804
Semi-open Brake Third	4209/11/3/5/7/9/21/3/5/7
Seven-compartment Composite	5775-84
Semi-open Brake Third	4210/2/4/6/8/20/2/4/6/8

These entered traffic in December 1947 (sets 795/6) and between March and May 1948 (remainder), all being run-in on the South Western section, but by September 1948 all were on their allocated South Eastern-section duties, being referred to in the Carriage Working Notices as three-corridor sets Type 'M'.

HOO No	Stock	Set/coach Nos
RSCO Minute 811 (20/2/46)	Order 10 (later 30) three-coach trains for London-Dover-Ramsgate-Margate services (later trains were for SW-section services)	795-804 (later 795-824)
RSCO Minute 867 (24/7/46)	Order five additional three-coach trains for Waterloo-Bournemouth-Weymouth and Waterloo-West of England services	825-9

(RSCO = Rolling Stock Committee Order)

The remaining 25 sets had more normal 48-seat Brake Thirds and were thus classified as three-corridor sets Type 'L', along with all the others. Details are:

Vehicle	Set 805	Sets 806-18	Sets 819-29
Semi-open Brake Third	4229	4251/3/5/7/9/61/3/5/7/9/71/3/5	4277/9/81/3/5/7/9/91/3/5/7
Seven-compartment Composite	5785	5786-98	5812-22
Semi-open Brake Third	4230	4252/4/6/8/60/2/4/6/8/70/2/4/6	4278/80/2/4/6/8/90/2/4/6/8

The various breaks in the numbering were caused by other existing orders or by older vehicles already occupying the numbers. Sets 805-29 entered traffic between August 1948 and May 1949 on South Western-section services, some sets being made up to five coaches for the summer months by the addition of the usual pairs of Corridor Thirds, this becoming a common occurrence from about 1954.

When completed, all BRCW sets carried malachite green, most with coach and set numbers prefixed 'S'. Those delivered in December 1947 omitted the prefix and carried the company title. Set 797 was specifically noted by observers as having gleaming white roofs when new, the more usual colour being grey. None seems to have been repainted in crimson lake and cream between 1949 and 1956 — which probably says something for the quality of the original paint finish — and all went straight from malachite into Southern Region green after June 1956.

No permanent set or allocation changes occurred until 1954, when 'cross-country' sets 795-802 (as those sets incorporating 44-seat Brakes were sometimes known) went to the Oxted/East Grinstead/Tunbridge Wells West group of lines and Nos 803/4 were disbanded. Incidentally, this gave these lines their first regular workings of Bulleid stock. Sets 803/4 were reformed in 1957 but with a combination of Maunsell and other Bulleid vehicles bearing no relation to the original three-coach set formations. The original coaches from these sets were used for sets 473/4 for London-Chatham-Ramsgate services, along with some other Bulleid vehicles, the formations of which were as follows:

Vehicle	Set 473	Set 474
Semi-open Brake Third	4225	4227
Eight-compartment Third(s)	81/2	85/6
Seven-compartment First/Composites	7648	5783/4
Restaurant car (Maunsell)	(often 7866)	(none)
Eight-compartment Third(s)	83	87, 90
Semi-open Brake Third	4226	4228

Upon electrification of the Chatham route in 1959 set 473 was disbanded (Brakes 4225/6 having already been replaced by BR standard vehicles) and set 474 moved to a Charing Cross-Tonbridge-Deal/Margate working and thence to the SW section in 1961. On the Oxted line sets 801/2 were increased to five coaches each and by 1956 were formed with a Bulleid First and two Thirds (soon to become Seconds) for two specific London-East Grinstead/Tunbridge Wells duties, one set being berthed overnight at the unlikely location of Forest Row. Formations were as follows:

Set 801:   4221+97+7635+98+4222
Set 802:   4223+92+7630+99*+4224
* replaced by 122 during 1957

Plate 184 Diagram 2125 Brake Third No 4255 at the rear of a Waterloo-bound train at Eastleigh in August 1962; this view shows the compartment side. Just visible beyond is the corridor side of the Composite coach, identifiable by the lack of window ventilators. Note that the three upper-end steps have been removed — a safety measure applied to all SR coaches from the mid-1950s onwards.
P. H. Swift

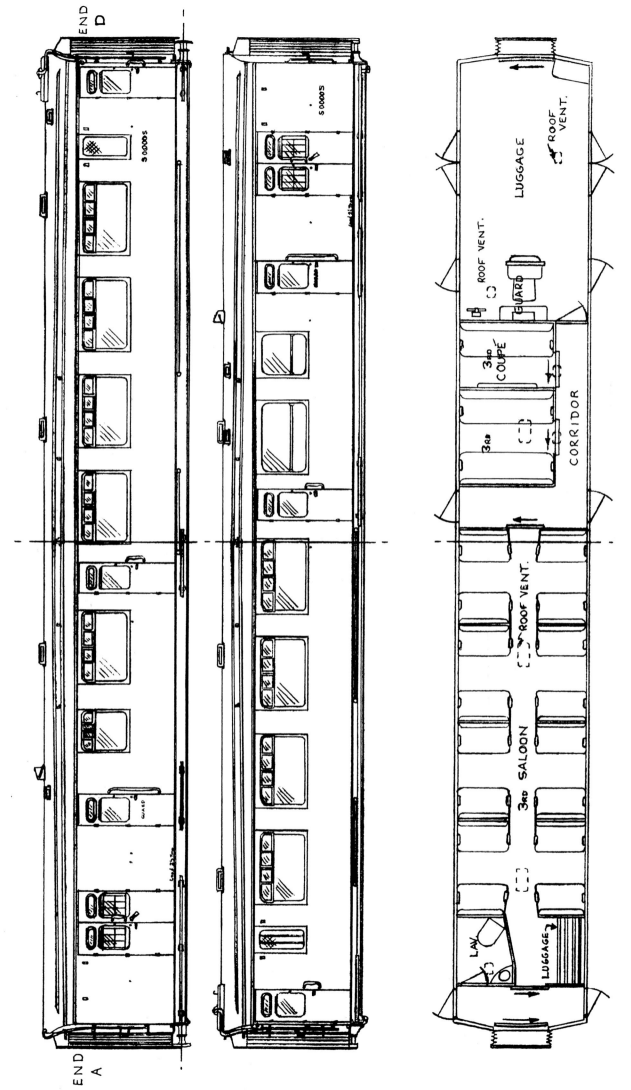

Figure 61 The 44-seat BRCW Brake Third, SR Diagram 2124.

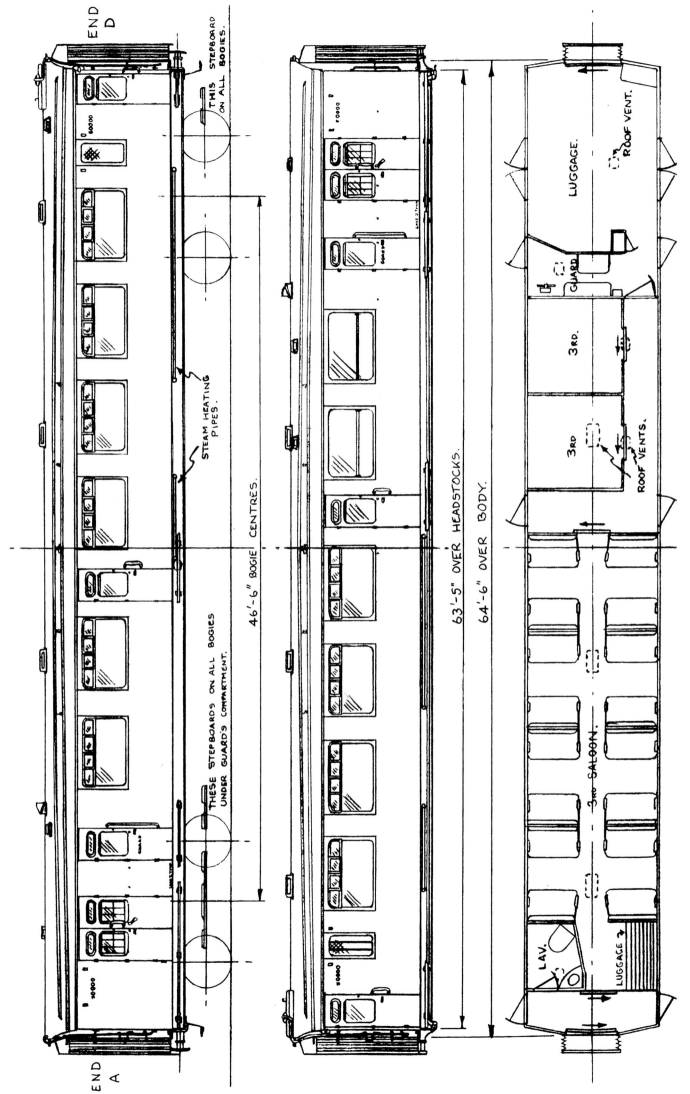

Figure 62 The 48-seat BRCW Brake Third, SR Diagram 2125.

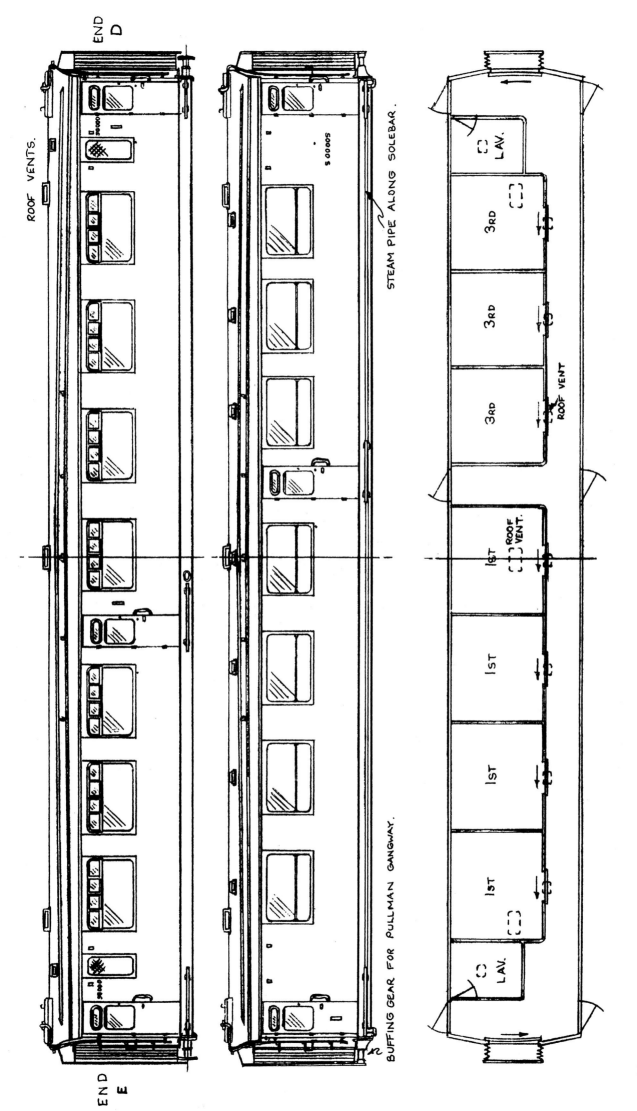

Figure 63 The BRCW Composite, SR Diagram 2320.

Both sets remained on Oxted-line workings until dieselisation in 1962. The displaced composites (5781/2) were fitted with electric heating in 1959 and were then used on the 'Night Ferry' and other electric locomotive-hauled trains on the South Eastern section, along with similarly-equipped Maunsell coaches 4435/6, 6685/6, 7846/7/69/78, 7957/69, plus a few BR standard Mk 1 coaches.

The two displaced BRCW Brakes from set 473 were meanwhile reformed into another Oxted-line set (897) with a Corridor First and three Corridor Thirds (now Seconds), formed 4225+41+7646+42+43+4226 (see **Plates 168 and 183**). The Bulleid First was replaced by a BR Mk 1 equivalent (S13143) during 1963.

Most of the remaining three-coach sets of Type 'M' were transferred to the South Western section in 1959, by which time coach 4209 of set 795 had been destroyed in the Eastbourne accident of April 1958, leading to the set being disbanded. Set 821 had been similarly damaged at Sway in December 1955, with the loss of coach 4281. Eventually coach 4210 from set 795 took the place of 4281, giving set 821 a unique formation (one 44-seat Brake, one 48-seat Brake), which caused seat-reservation problems, so this too was disbanded in 1960. Coach 4282 then went to additional two-set Type 'R' No 76, along with Brake Composite 6713, for West of England services, passing to Western Region ownership in 1964.

Set 805 became an additional six-dining set for the Bournemouth line in 1957, including a 'Tavern' pair in the formation:

4229+7622+7897+7838+S3846 (BR Mk 1 Open Second) +4230

It remained so formed until the abandonment of permanent set formations in March 1966, with the 'Tavern' coach rebuilt as a more conventional Buffet car from 1960.

Some of the three-coach sets were transferred to the Western Region with the lines west of Salisbury in 1964/5, but only the Brake Thirds (now Seconds) were actually officially reallocated. The 44-seat Brakes were preferred owing to their lower seating capacity, and Nos 4210/1/3-6/9-28/71/82 all received 'W' prefixes to their numbers. Coaches 4217/8 were similarly transferred in July 1967, while coach 4271 returned to the Southern Region late in 1966. Withdrawal of the Southern-allocated coaches began in 1964 and was completed in early 1968 on withdrawal of Nos 4263/71, the WR examples lasting only a few months longer. Examples of each type of Brake Third have survived into preservation, but no Composite vehicles remain.

Including the Inspection Saloon described in Chapter 14, Bulleid's contribution to the Southern's steam-hauled stock amounted to some 814 vehicles — approximately half the number completed during Maunsell's 15-year tenure. However, all had been built in the six years from September 1945 until July 1951, and only four failed to last until the end of 1963. Considering the difficult postwar conditions under which they had been completed, and the fact that many never cascaded off front-line duties during their 20-year lifespan, Bulleid may perhaps be forgiven the failings of his eight 'Tavern' pairs. Some of his all-steel suburban vehicles would continue to give another 25 years of service, also on the duties for which they had been designed, but that, as they say, is another story.

Table 13 details the BRCW-built vehicles.

Plate 185 The BRCW Composites were all identical, regardless of whether they ran with Diagram 2124 or 2125 Brake Thirds. Coach 5777 in set 797 is seen at Eastleigh in July 1962. *P. H. Swift*

Table 13
Summary of Bulleid BRCW stock

Diagram No	Vehicle Type	Seats 1st	3rd	Running Nos	Built by
2124	Semi-open Brake Third		44	4209-28	BRCW 12/47-5/48
2125	Semi-open Brake Third		48	4229/30/51-98	BRCW 7/48-4/49
2320	Seven-compartment Composite	24	24	5775-98, 5812-22	BRCW 12/47-4/49

Notes
Brake Thirds 4209/81 lost through accident damage in 1958/5 respectively.

Chapter 11.

Passenger Brake Vans

We must now consider the category of non-passenger coaching stock, often abbreviated to NPCS. As the term implies, these were vehicles built to run in passenger trains (or at passenger-train speeds) but did not actually carry passengers. Historically, these encompassed passenger brake (or guard's) vans, luggage, fruit, milk and insulated vans, horseboxes, special cattle vans, open and covered carriage trucks, scenery vans and Post Office vans. From 1931 the category of milk tank wagons was added. The term NPCS was hardly convenient for everyday use, so railwaymen referred to these classes of vehicle as passenger vans, as distinct from goods-rated vans, which were more correctly termed as covered goods *wagons*. Even the term 'van' has wide implications in this respect, as neither an open carriage truck nor a milk tank qualifies to be described as a van, yet it was so!

The Southern Railway prepared a separate renumbering register for these vehicles, commencing at 1 and reaching 5000, although by no means all these numbers were allocated, particularly in the higher ranges of the list. The vehicles were classified by type and origin, in exactly the same manner as the pre-Grouping carriage stock had been, with gaps left between each block of numbers to receive new post-1923 construction. This required considerable revision in later years, and many numbers were reused, particularly over the range from 1 to 2550. Indeed, such was the rate of Southern Railway construction that by 1945 virtually all the pre-Grouping brake and luggage vans had been replaced by 'utility vans', as their replacement vehicles became universally known. A summary of the numbering scheme is shown in the table below, as it stood around early 1924. Ex-S&DJR vehicles were acquired in 1930 and were then slotted into available gaps.

As will be seen from the table, the Southern Railway inherited over 3,000 of these vehicles from the pre-Grouping companies and, apart from a batch of 20 ex-LSWR vans already on order, did not need to construct any more to its own designs for some five years. Indeed, such was the stock of horseboxes that no more were ever constructed, although one batch was ordered in 1939 and later cancelled. With the exception of such obviously specialised designs as open carriage trucks, most pre-Grouping vans had traditionally resembled the carriage stock in construction and appearance. On the Great Western, LMS and LNER this situation was to continue unchanged, most NPCS matching the contemporary coaching stock with a degree of harmony. However, the Southern alone adopted a different design philosophy. Here a goods-wagon style of construction was preferred, using steel-angle body framing backed by timber-planked body sheeting, together with the semi-elliptical roof profile which was to become the trademark of almost all Maunsell/Lynes covered goods vehicles. Although this profile led to leaking roofs on covered goods wagons, the same problem did not seem to afflict the passenger vans. Perhaps the rigours of passenger usage were rather less harsh? The origin of this design may be traced back to 1918, when Lynes produced drawings for a long-wheelbase luggage van, 32ft long over headstocks — in effect almost a double-length version of his prototype covered goods wagon of three years earlier.

The prototype or 'pattern' luggage van was completed at Ashford Works early in 1919, and its first duty was to carry the body of Nurse Edith Cavell from Dover to London, on 15 May 1919. For this reason many older railwaymen would refer to any utility van as a 'Nurse Cavell van'. The design quickly proved successful, and a further 44 examples were added to SECR stock

Table 14
Renumbering of SR non-passenger coaching stock

Class of Vehicle	Number range	LSWR stock	SECR stock	LBSCR stock	S&DJR stock	Minor companies' stock
Passenger brake vans	1-1250 (later 1-1040)	1-346, 366-89*	390-685	706-929	963-78	979-94
Luggage, fruit, milk, meat vans, etc	1251-2500 (later 1041-2550)	1251-1691, 2181-2225*	1717-2022	2073-2180	1701-15	2231
Horseboxes	2501-3650 (later 2551-3650)	2501-2858, 2859*	2909-3010	3062-3317	3318-25	3368/9
Special cattle vans	3651-3900	3651-78	3731-70	3820-48	(none)	(none)
Open carriage and baggage box trucks	3901-4500 (later 3901-4400)	3901-4022, 4023*	4067-4206	4246-4327	4024	4378-90
Milk tanks	4401-4500	(none)+	(none)+	(none)+	(none)+	(none)+
Covered carriage trucks and scenery vans	4501-4900	4501-76, 4609*	4610-4705	4736-86	4734/5	(none)
Post Office vans	4901-5000	4901-18	4944-53	(none)	(none)	(none)

Notes

* These blocks were ex-LSWR duplicate stock, which had originally been allocated numbers 01-22, 0101-41, 0201, 0401/2. Vehicles could be seen still carrying pre-Grouping livery and numbering until c1930.

+ No milk tanks were inherited from constituent companies, construction commencing only in 1931.

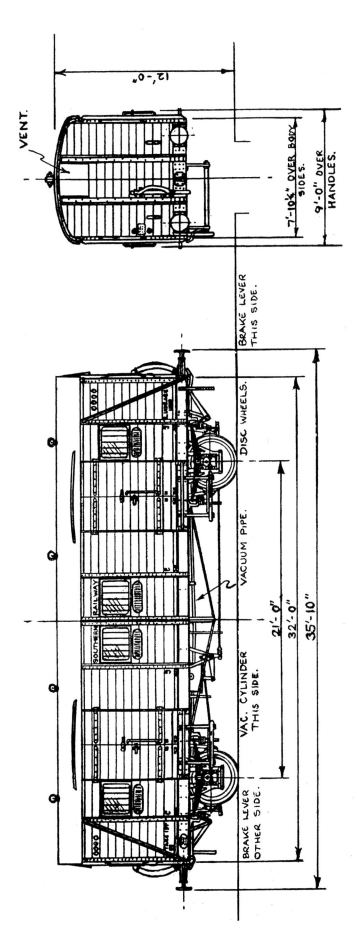

Figure 64 A drawing of the SECR utility van, allocated SR Diagram 960. SECR numbers ran from 121 to 182 but were not consecutive. The lack of ventilator bonnets below the windows was the most distinguishing feature of the SECR vans.

by 1923. **Plate 186** and **Figure 64** illustrate the original productions of 1919-22. This basic design was then multiplied, stretched and modified over the following 30 years into the 'utility van' family of vehicles, eventually numbering almost 2,000 examples. The wisdom of this design policy might be debated — it certainly did little for the æsthetic or homogenous appearance of a passenger train topped or tailed by one of these vehicles, as **Plate 187** demonstrates, but in terms of economics and longevity the Southern utility van won through, examples continuing to be built until 1955 and many remaining in BR service until the mid-1980s, often long after the demise of contemporary NPCS from the other three companies.

Apart from on one experimental batch of 10 lightweight vans, Bulleid made little alteration to the basic Maunsell/Lynes design concepts of the 1920s and 1930s, so (unlike the situation with the passenger coaches) the entire Southern Railway period may be considered as one progression and will be dealt with on a class by class basis, although this was not necessarily the order of construction. Appendix 1 on pages 218-223 lists the various order and running numbers for all vehicles. At the end of each chapter a vehicle summary will detail the differences between the various batches.

It was not until 1934 that any new passenger brake vans were required, the existing pre-Grouping stock proving adequate until then. In March of that year two rather unusual vehicles (later amended to three) were authorised for use on the 'Night Ferry' service between London and Paris, which would utilise the new Dover-Dunkirk train ferry then under construction. The design was a stretched version of the original 1919 van, 36ft long and with a wheelbase of 23ft, incorporating a centrally-positioned guard's compartment with a raised 'birdcage' roof lookout above, to conform to French operational requirements; to accommodate this the standard roof profile was lowered by 5in to 11ft 7in. Appropriately numbered 1-3 in the van list, they entered service in 1936, painted Wagons-Lits dark blue with a silver-grey roof, to match the sleeping cars forming the remainder of the through portion of the train. For this purpose they were also dual-braked, with both vacuum and Westinghouse equipment.

The ferry service commenced on 14 October 1936 and ran until the outbreak of war in September 1939. For the next eight years the vans were available for ordinary traffic and were probably repainted green at some time, although No 2 was recorded in grey livery in 1945 — one of a number of SR vans so painted during and after the war. The ferry service finally resumed in December 1947, by which time all three vans were again blue, remaining on this duty until September 1960. Although the 'Night Ferry' would continue to run for another 20 years, the ferry vans were again returned to general service, being repainted in Southern Region green in October 1960, joining the pool of ordinary non-stove-fitted passenger brake vans, then coded BY (B = brake, Y = four-wheel) under the British Railways coding system. Vans 1 and 2 were withdrawn in 1969, but No 3 remained in traffic until 1974, latterly running as a plain luggage/parcels van with all lighting stripped and the guard's compartment out of use. **Plates 188 and 189** and **Figure 65** illustrate these highly distinctive vehicles, allocated SR Diagram 3091.

The ferry vans were undoubtedly ideal for their purpose, so it was a relatively simple matter to turn the design into an ordinary passenger brake van, by substituting the standard roof profile, omitting the Westinghouse gear and replacing the 'birdcage' with two roof-mounted periscope lookouts. Coded 'Van C' by the Southern Railway, no fewer than 255 was completed between June 1937 and April 1941. A somewhat smaller compartment was provided for the guard, again in the centre of the van, flanked on either side by a luggage compartment. All except the last five were allocated to Diagram 3092.

One interesting and rather obvious constructional feature of these vehicles was the use of alternate pairs of wide and narrow

Plate 186 The prototype utility van, SECR No 132, as completed at Ashford Works early in 1919 and finished in dark-brown livery with yellow lettering. This became SR No 1972 in November 1925 and remained in ordinary traffic until August 1946, then being transferred to departmental stock as No 346s. In July 1967 it was further renumbered as internal-user stores van 082757 and thereafter confined to Guildford yard. In 1992 it was purchased by the Kent & East Sussex Railway and at the time of writing (2002) resides at Robertsbridge station, in the livery seen here. *SECR*

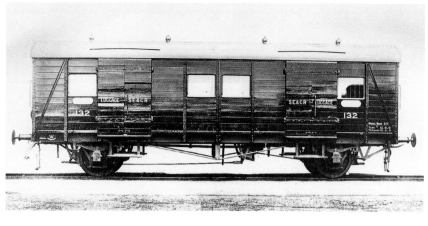

Plate 187 Aesthetically, the inclusion of a utility van did little to enhance the appearance of a Southern passenger train. Here 'Merchant Navy' Pacific No 35011 *General Steam Navigation* heads the 4.55pm Bournemouth West-Waterloo (3.50pm from Weymouth) near Shawford in August 1952, a gangwayed Bogie Luggage Van leading a Bulleid Bournemouth-line six-coach dining set. *J. Davenport/Ian Allan Library*

Plate 188 Channel Ferry van No 1, photographed at Ashford Works in June 1936 in Wagons-Lits blue livery with a silver-grey roof, together with many inscriptions in both English and French, in yellow lettering. The classification 'Baggage' was unique to these vans and the baggage box trucks. *Southern Railway*

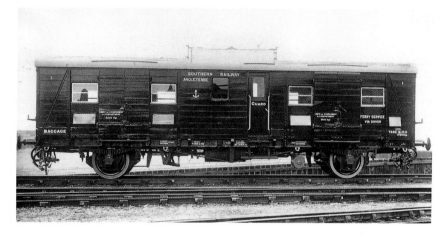

Plate 189 Ferry van No 1 again, now with British Railways lettering, at Stewarts Lane in May 1958. This shows the opposite side to that in **Plate 188**. *The Lens of Sutton Collection*

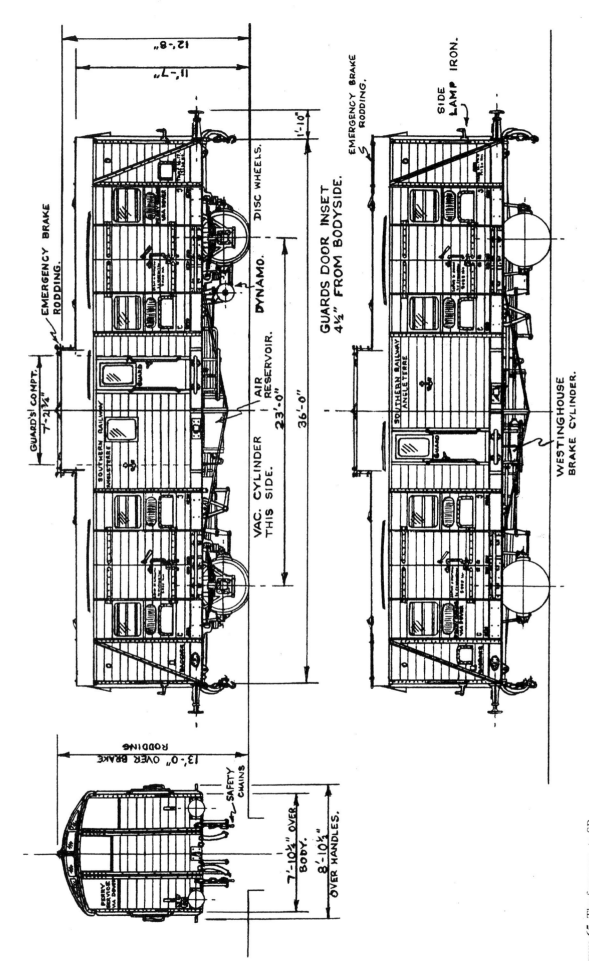

Figure 65 The ferry van, to SR Diagram 3091. Note the 'Ferry Service via Dover' lettering on the end planking.

planks for the side sheeting, instead of the more usual even planking. This was to become a common fitting on most utility vans, covered goods wagons and goods brake vans until the widespread adoption of plywood construction towards the end of World War 2. No official explanation for this form of construction has so far emerged, but it may have been an economical way of using available timber, possibly home-grown instead of imported. By 1938, with the possibility of war looming, traditional sources of timber might be threatened, and Bulleid had been asked to investigate alternative supplies and materials, so it could have been part of this process. Presumably a loss of strength may have resulted if all planking was to the narrower width, hence the compromise uneven or 2+2 arrangement. This can be clearly seen in **Plate 190**.

The first 20 'Van Cs', Nos 400-19, were stove-fitted from new, whilst Nos 420-39 received this addition at the start of World War 2, the latter vans losing them again between 1943 and 1947. To distinguish these from the rest all had orange-painted panels in the top corners of each side and a similarly-painted lower door panel, as seen in **Plate 191**. This helped to keep the vans on their booked workings as detailed in the Carriage Working Notices; moreover, they were not supposed to work off the Southern Railway. It also assisted the shunters to locate the vans in a crowded yard, perhaps under blackout conditions, etc. Additionally, vans 400/1 were fitted with side lamp irons for working as brake vans in certain West of England goods trains, mostly between Exeter Central and Plymouth Friary. Prior to their construction two ex-LSWR 44ft bogie guard's vans had been allocated to the workings. Nos 400/1 remained on these duties until at least 1964. Nos 420-30 were re-equipped with stoves during 1965/6, but general removal from all vans started in 1969 as they lost their guard's-van status and were relegated to luggage or parcels vans. From about this time many started to appear in Rail-blue livery with white lettering.

The non-stove vans (very much the majority) could work off the Southern Railway; indeed, Nos 660/1 were for many years roof-boarded 'To Work between Yeovil & Derby' with Messrs Aplin & Barrett's dairy products from Yeovil Town. This company later became part of United Dairies, but the traffic continued.

The final five vans, Nos 10-4, were equipped with safes, being replacements for six ex-SECR vans so fitted and formerly used for bullion traffic between the Channel ports and London. By the time they were completed this traffic had disappeared, so all five were placed in ex-LSWR long sets 303/4 (two vans each) and 305 (one van), to make up for a shortage of Brake Thirds — a rare use of utility vans in permanent set formations. In postwar years these five vans were not allocated any specific duties, but to emphasise their special fittings the van number was painted in large (12in) white numerals on a red background; when they were repainted in BR crimson lake this was altered to a more conspicuous blue background. The style is shown in **Plates 192 and 193**. The safe itself was hardly worthy of the name, being little more than a rectangular enclosure extending right across the vehicle, accessible only from the outside using nothing more secure than a standard carriage door key. Despite their lack of allocated duties, vans 10-3 lasted until 1976-8, No 14 being withdrawn in 1969. Diagram 3094 was allocated.

The first withdrawal was van 777, damaged beyond repair in an accident at Witham, ER, in March 1950, but no others were condemned before 1966. Eight vans (Nos 937/43/52/6/61/6/72/9) were roof-boarded specifically for newspaper traffic in 1955/6, primarily for South Western-section duties, but some ran on the South Eastern section as well. They were removed from these workings in 1964, after which only bogie vehicles were employed. In June 1965 No 938 was converted into a 'high-security van for GPO use'. Externally both guard's doors and the left-hand pair of luggage doors on each side were removed and planked up. This was done meticulously, the new planking being flush with and exactly matching the existing side sheeting. Internally the remaining pairs of double doors had steel sheeting in place of the glazing, and a lavatory was fitted, probably

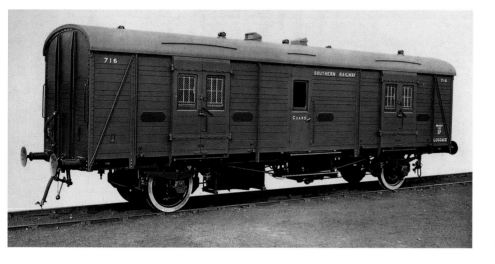

Plate 190 'Van C' No 716 when new in July 1938, having been completed at Eastleigh on an underframe supplied from Ashford one month earlier. The door droplights would be varnished teak, the lozenge-shaped chalking panels dark grey; the bodyside would be Maunsell green, the ends black. However, the tones of this photograph lead one to suspect that the van has actually been painted in photographic grey for the cameraman. *Southern Railway*

Plate 191 Stove-fitted 'Van C' No 402, complete with orange-painted door and eaves panels, at Clapham Junction in August 1952. The word 'Guard' and the door number are black, while those in the eaves panels are still in SR style, with the addition of fresh 'S' prefixes. The base livery is therefore Southern green, of whatever shade. *J. H. Aston*

Plate 192 Safe-fitted van No 11, again at Clapham Junction but in May 1951. The number, complete with 'S' prefix above, is carried on a red panel on an otherwise rather dirty SR-green finish. The safe is visible to the left of the guard's door. The increased size of the guard's compartment is evident from the position of the roof periscopes. *D. Cullum*

Plate 193 The other side of van 12, now with 'S' prefix and suffix, at Exeter Central in August 1964, carrying Southern Region green livery but still with a red background to the number. Van 10 ended its days with a standard lettering layout, without red patches. *P. H. Swift*

occupying the former guard's compartment. The van was then used on the overnight Portsmouth mail train and received electric heating in 1967. Withdrawn in 1971, it was stored at Micheldever until 1976, pending possible conversion for departmental use.

General withdrawal commenced in 1966 and was completed in August 1978, van No 713 being the last survivor in ordinary traffic. Few entered departmental use (compared with the ordinary luggage vans), but eight became Staff & Tool brake vans for the Chief Civil Engineer's Department, being renumbered into the DB975xxx series. Several are now in the hands of the preservation societies, including one of the safe-fitted vans.

In May 1936, at the same time as the first batch of four-wheeled standard passenger brake vans was authorised, a batch of 50 bogie luggage vans was also ordered. A year later this was amended to include a guard's compartment, but it was not until August 1938 that production commenced. Coded 'Van B' by both the Southern and British Railways, a total of 130 was completed in three batches, the final 30 appearing in crimson-lake livery as late as 1952/3. They shared many details with the four-wheeled design, of which they were essentially a stretched version, and were allocated Diagram 3093. **Figure 66** is a combined drawing of both types.

The 'Van Bs' were employed largely for newspaper, mail and parcels traffic, initially on the South Western section but later throughout the Southern system. Many were equipped with stoves at various times and were then allocated to specific SW- and SE-section workings. Nos 395-9 were so fitted in 1943/4, 380-94 in 1946/7 and 370-9 during 1948/9, while Nos 368/9 were added as late as 1962; all then received the orange door and eaves panels, as shown in **Plate 194**. Further stove-fitted vans were needed for Central-section duties in 1966-8, for which purpose Nos 201-3/5-31 were equipped. Some of these were outshopped in Rail blue (No 220 being the first, so painted in December 1966). Van 204 was excluded simply because at that time it was allocated to the Scottish Region, for the Kyle of Lochalsh line.

Vans 265-80 of the 1952/3 batch were roof-boarded 'Newspaper Traffic / Waterloo Padstow' (or other appropriate destination, including Ilfracombe, Torrington, Plymouth, Bude, Exeter, Yeovil or Weymouth) soon after completion and were regularly formed in the 1.15am Waterloo-West of England newspaper train, up to seven being required each night. By the 1960s the roof boards had been superseded by a 'Newspapers — Waterloo-West of England' branding on the side planking, as seen in **Plate 195**. By the 1970s only vans 272-80 were so marked, their specific duties ceasing around 1977.

Withdrawal commenced in 1966, although few had been condemned prior to 1980, when BR's parcels-collection/delivery service ceased. After 1969 most lost their guard's-van status, being reduced merely to unlit and unheated luggage vans. No 204 (still exiled in Scotland) and Nos 225-30 (on the South Eastern section) remained as guard's vans for rather longer than the others. By this time all repaints were in Rail blue, some receiving TOPS code NFV. In 1980 withdrawal commenced in earnest, and by 1982 only 30 were retained, specifically for South Eastern-section duties, principally those which might involve traversing the Tonbridge-Hastings line. Following electrification of this route in May 1986 and the singling of certain sections of line through the restricted tunnels, BR Restriction C1 stock could finally be used, and the last 'Van Bs' — Nos 236/52/4/65/76 and 399 — were taken out of use in August and September 1986; these were the last SR utility vans — indeed, the last steam/loco-hauled SR vehicles — to remain in ordinary traffic.

A small number of vans entered departmental use or have become internal-user stores vans at various locations, not necessarily within the Southern Region, while several are now in the hands of the preservation societies. **Table 15** is a summary of all vehicles.

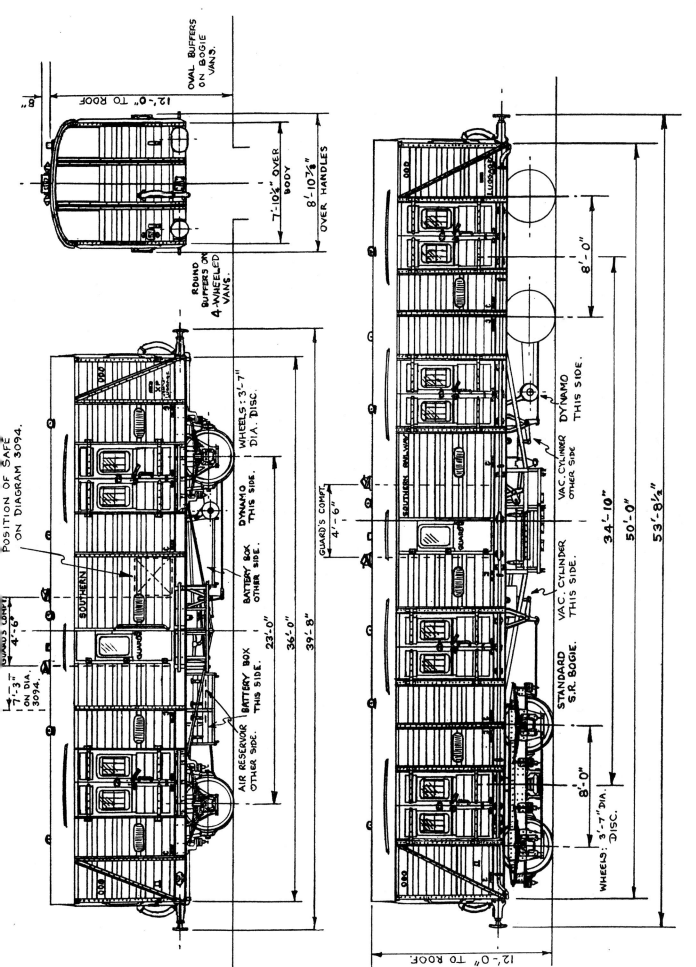

Figure 66 A drawing of both four-wheel and bogie passenger brake vans, to Diagrams 3092/3/4.

Plate 194 'Van B Stove' No 381 at Eastleigh in October 1949, in what is probably malachite green with orange panels. Apart from the deletion of the company title and addition of 'S' prefixes, the livery remains pure Southern. *A. E. West*

Plate 195 Newspaper van No 273 at Exeter Central in August 1963. This is one of the 1952/3 vans to Order L3227. The roof-board brackets have been removed and replaced by the stencilled 'NEWSPAPERS — WATERLOO—WEST OF ENGLAND' at the far end. This van is now preserved at Mangapps Farm Railway near Burnham-on-Crouch, Essex. *A. E. West*

Table 15
Summary of SR passenger brake vans

Diagram No	Vehicle type	Classification (SR/BR)	Running Nos	Built by	Remarks
3091	17-ton guard's van for Dover ferry service	Baggage/BY	1-3	Ashford 6/36	Dual-braked
3092	16-ton guard's van	Van C/BY	400-49	Ashford 6-7/37	Some stove-fitted
			651-750	Ashford/Eastleigh 3-9/38	
			751-800	Eastleigh 3-10/39	
			931-80	Eastleigh 10/40-1/41	No 938 later to Diagram 3095
3093	28-ton bogie guard's van	Van B	201-50	Eastleigh 11-12/39	Some later stove-fitted
			251-80	Lancing 11/52-2/53	
			350-99	Eastleigh 8-10/38	Some later stove-fitted
3094	15-ton guard's van (safe-fitted)	Van C/BY	10-4	Eastleigh 4/41	
3095	High-security van for GPO use	BY	938	Rebuilt Eastleigh 6/65	Ex-Diagram 3092

Notes

In some instances underframes were completed at either Ashford or Lancing, bodying and finishing taking place at Eastleigh.
All except vans 1-3 had 2+2-style body planking.

Chapter 12.

Luggage Vans and 'Covcars'

The next class of vehicle to be considered — indeed, numerically the largest class of all — is that of luggage vans. Included here are those vans equipped with end doors, coded 'Covcar' by the Southern Railway, and it is at this point that we encounter officially the term 'utility van'. Strictly speaking, and on the basis of pre-Grouping terminology, the 'Covcars' should have been regarded as covered carriage trucks and been numbered within the 4501-4900 range of the list. However, to underline their universal capabilities the Southern numbered them with the ordinary luggage vans, giving them all the operating code 'Van U'. Also included within this section are the 120 Corridor Luggage Vans built on former LSWR underframes and coded GBL (Gangwayed Bogie Luggage Vans), and these are described at the end of this chapter.

The main characteristic of a luggage van was that it had no accommodation for the guard and was usually open from end to end (although some pre-Grouping examples were divided into compartments); they were primarily used for luggage, parcels, fruit, or (in some cases) meat, fish, milk, bullion and other specialised commodities. In general the pre-Grouping vans given over to these uses had certain additional fittings, such as extra ventilation for milk, fruit and meat vans, greater security for bullion vans, etc. However, the Southern preferred to cater for almost all traffic using a standard design with only two major variants — those with large end doors (labelled 'Covcar') and those without (labelled 'Luggage'). The 45 ex-SECR 'Nurse Cavell' vans were proving extremely versatile, and in April 1925 Maunsell proposed a similar design for a general utility van based on the SECR vehicle but with the addition of large end doors plus a drop flap over the buffers. This would allow end-loading of road vehicles and would have the added advantage that they could also be used as ordinary luggage vans. Approval for the construction of 20 vans was immediately given, this being increased to 50 in March 1926.

Perhaps because of the reorganisation of the company's workshops, which was then imminent, construction of these vans was put out to tender. That from the Midland Railway Carriage & Wagon Co was acceptable, at a cost of £659 each. At the April 1925 Rolling Stock Committee meeting Maunsell had suggested a likely figure of £800; however, some savings were made by equipping the vans with reconditioned vacuum cylinders supplied by the Southern Railway. Delivery took place in March/April 1928.

The Midland RCW vehicles were probably the only ones to carry the title of 'General Utility Van' on the solebars, most later examples (built by the company's own workshops) being coded 'Covcar' at the lower right-hand end of each side. **Plate 196** illustrates one of the original batch when first delivered. Allocated numbers were 2023-72, following on from the ex-SECR luggage vans and neatly filling the gap between these and the ex-LBSCR vehicles. Carrying capacity was 10 tons, tare (unladen) weight was 14 tons, and Diagram 3101 was allocated. Internally, four wheel bars were carried, used to restrain any road vehicle while in transit. Overall dimensions were very similar to the SECR vehicles, but length over body was increased from 32ft to 32ft 4½in, due to the provision of the end doors. Four more batches were completed at Ashford Works between 1929 and 1933, adding a further 140 to the stock. Some of these are listed in the registers as being 32ft 6½in over end doors and were initially allocated to Diagram 3102 (later altered to 3101); whether there were any actual differences in dimensions or whether the length quoted was over hinges (instead of over end planking) is not clear. Some of the vans completed in 1929 were equipped with shelving to receive fruit packing cases, Nos 2251-80 being specifically noted; as conveyance of fruit was a seasonal traffic, these fittings were unlikely to have been of a permanent nature. In 1930 No 2266 of this batch was also specifically allocated for poultry traffic between Heathfield and

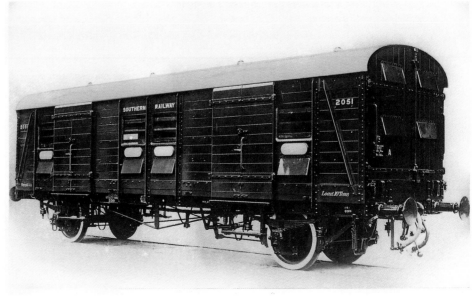

Plate 196 General Utility Van No 2051, as completed in March 1928 and showing the original style of lettering. As yet the coding 'Covcar' does not appear on the vehicle. The end doors are clearly visible. *Midland Railway Carriage & Wagon Co*

Plate 197 The more usual lettering layout is carried by van 2422, seen at Salisbury in 1935 after some three years in service. Note the pasted paper label on the window, probably giving some allocation or usage instructions. The painting diagram (Drawing E26385) shows this lettering layout exactly and states that the number and company title were in 3¼in gold letters, shaded black, while the 'Covcar' code was in 3¼in yellow letters. *J. G. Griffiths*

Plate 198 The first batch of Luggage Vans completed after the Grouping are represented by van 2217, seen at Old Oak Common in April 1951. Note that the numerals are carried on the top plank, one higher than the usual position. Most of these 1934/5 vintage vans entered departmental service during the 1950s. *A. E. West*

London, replacing several ex-LBSCR covered goods wagons previously used; this was a rare example of a luggage van or 'Covcar' being allocated to a specific working. **Plate 197** illustrates one of the 1931/2 vehicles, its livery/lettering being typical of the style used in the 1930s.

Despite the obvious virtues of the 'Covcar' design, in 1933 a return was made to the Luggage Van version, without end doors. Almost certainly, this was cheaper to build, but perhaps the end-loading facility was not being used as often as had been anticipated. Indeed, the pure Luggage Van type was eventually to become the more numerous variant, finally outnumbering the 'Covcars' almost three to one. The first batch of 50 was authorised in April 1933 and emerged from Ashford between October 1934 and March 1935. One of these is shown in **Plate 198**. Apart from minor details these were almost a carbon copy of the SECR design, the most obvious addition being the side ventilator bonnets, which had made their appearance on the 'Covcars' of 1928. Length over buffers was 35ft 8in — 2in less than that of the SECR vehicles. Diagram 3103 was allocated. In side elevation there was virtually no difference between a contemporary Luggage Van and a 'Covcar'. **Figure 67** is a combined drawing of both types, including several planking styles yet to be described.

The next batch — Order A824 — was to have been for 98 luggage vans, but this was meticulously reduced to 97 when the decision was taken to construct three ferry vans instead of the two originally proposed. The 97 entered traffic during 1935/6. Gaps in the Luggage Van numbering series had now been filled, so these took former unallocated guard's brake van numbers 1154-1250, beginning the process of filling the otherwise blank area of the list downwards as far as 1046, which continued until 1950. In 1936 van No 1215 of this batch was specifically labelled 'FOR DOVER FERRY SERVICE', presumably for the Victoria-Dover portion of the 'Night Ferry'.

One further batch of 50 'Covcars' was completed in 1938, after a break of five years since the last lot. The underframes (and presumably the steel body framing as well) were built at Ashford and then run to Eastleigh for body planking and finishing — a procedure that would become common with future orders. These vans were unique in that the side planking was in the 2+2 style, yet the side doors were even-planked, as seen in **Plate 199**. No more 'Covcars' would be completed until after Nationalisation.

Construction of luggage vans to Diagram 3103 continued unabated until 1943, by which time no fewer than 759 had been completed, including the original 45 ex-SECR vans. Although these were allocated to Diagram 960, for all purposes they were considered identical to the rest. Nos 1972-91 of the SECR batch were roof-boarded specifically for use on Continental boat expresses. The first uneven (or 2+2)-planked luggage van (No 1359) was outshopped from Ashford Works in June 1939, and this became the standard finish for most subsequent utility vans completed before Nationalisation. **Plate 200** provides an excellent illustration of this style. During 1942, however, Lancing would build just one more batch of 120 even-planked vans, somewhat different in detail from all previous (or subsequent) designs. These had body framing formed not from the usual 'L'- or 'T'-section steel angles but from 'L'- or 'U'-section pressed-steel channels. In addition, timber-reinforcing members were bolted to one side of the channels,

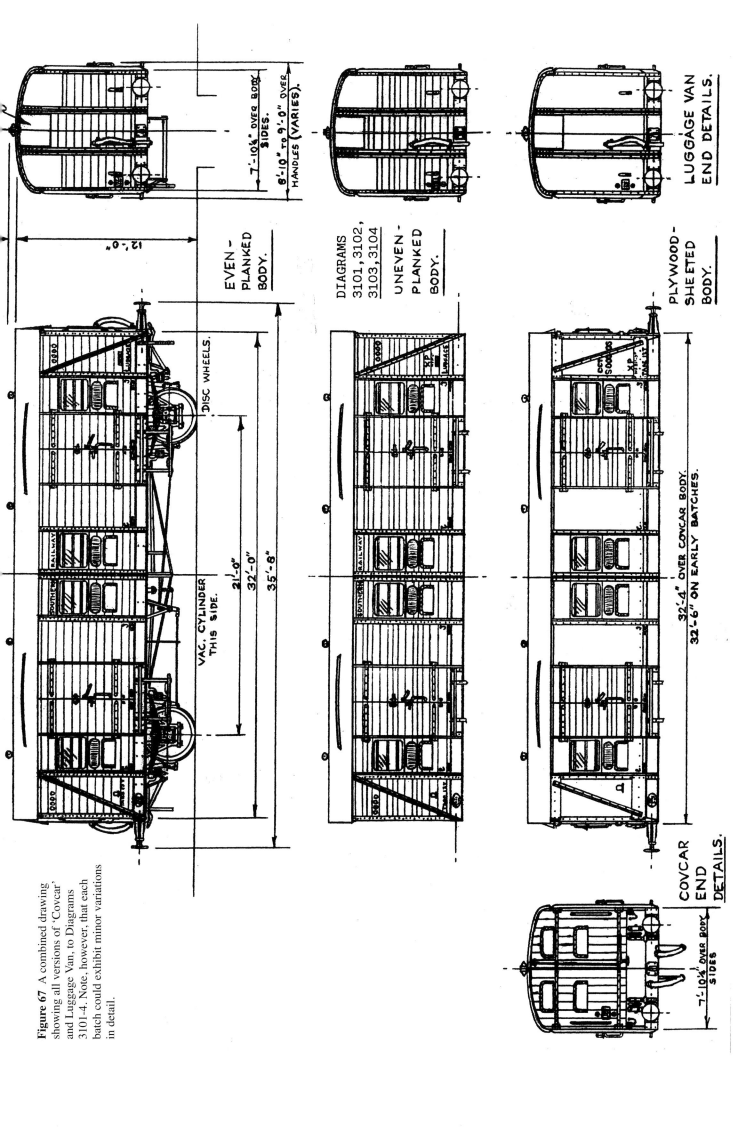

Figure 67 A combined drawing showing all versions of 'Covcar' and Luggage Van, to Diagrams 3101-4. Note, however, that each batch could exhibit minor variations in detail.

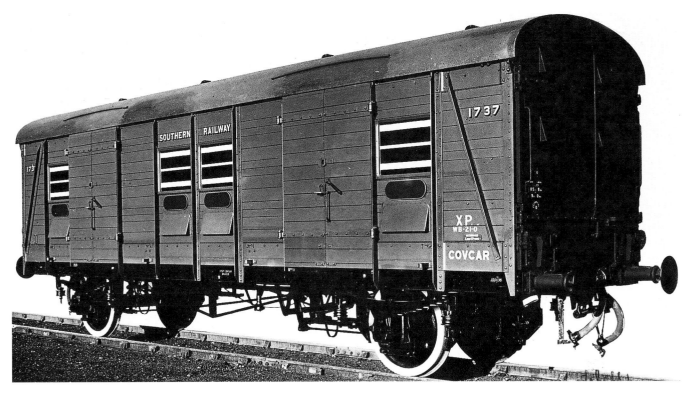

Plate 199 A 'Covcar' from the 1938 batch, unique in having 2+2 planking on the sides but even planking on the doors. No 1737 dates from November 1938 and has received the 'XP' and 'WB-21-0''' branding using 4in and 2in white letters and figures. *Southern Railway*

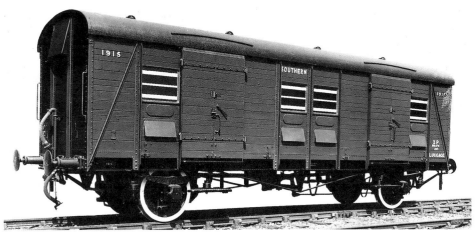

Plate 200 Luggage van No 1915, as completed in May 1940, illustrating the 2+2 planked finish. This van may be in malachite green but definitely carries the Bulleid style of company title, in gilt with 'in-line' and no shading. The other lettering/numerals are as previously. The van did not enter traffic in this livery; instead it was converted into Mobile Drawing Office stores van No 1572s, to Diagram 3104, in August 1940. It did not enter normal service until August 1945. *Southern Railway*

Plate 201 Order L1191 comprised 120 vans built wholly at Lancing during 1942, using pressed-steel body channels and planking slightly narrower than standard. Van 1813 is seen at Stewarts Lane in July 1951, in crimson lake. Note the curious appearance of the body framing, with the additional timbers bolted to one side of each channel. *A. E. West*

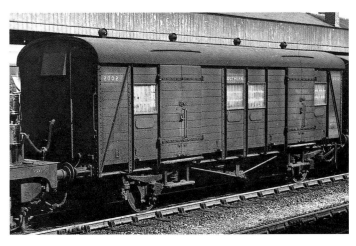

Plate 202 Ex-SECR 'air-control van' No 2002 at Tonbridge in September 1949, coupled between an 'H' class 0-4-4T and a Brighton push-pull set, on a Maidstone West service. Compared with **Plate 186** four-destination panels are now carried on each side. *K. G. Carr*

resulting in a rather curious appearance, as seen in **Plate 201**. Presumably there was some concern about the strength of the steel channels by themselves. Also, all body planking was fractionally narrower than standard, requiring the insertion of a 4in spacer plank at about waist level. Whether this form of construction was another attempt by Bulleid to make use of alternative materials — or simply a matter of expediency under wartime conditions — is not recorded.

In August 1939 five of the ex-SECR vans were fitted with through Westinghouse air pipes in order to work in push-pull services. The vans initially selected were Nos 2001-5, but No 2003 could not be traced quickly, and van 1996 was substituted. Known as 'air-control vans', they replaced a number of ex-LBSCR six-wheeled passenger brake vans; their workings were detailed in the Carriage Working Notices, their most common duties being on the Maidstone West-Paddock Wood-Tonbridge, Brighton-Horsham-Guildford and Brockenhurst-Ringwood-Wimborne-Bournemouth West lines. On the last-named they were referred to as 'pram vans', this giving a clue as to their principal use. These alone of the utility vans could be coupled between the locomotive and the push-pull set and be used in the 'push' mode, as seen in **Plate 202**. Should an ordinary van be substituted, this would have to be coupled behind the locomotive when propelling, as illustrated by **Plate 203**. These five SECR vans outlasted by many years all the other pre-Grouping examples in ordinary traffic, not being withdrawn until 1962; they were then replaced by plywood-bodied vans 1621-5, yet to be described.

An intriguing pencil entry appears in the Lancing numbering register against Nos 1041/2. This refers to HOO No 1032 for two new hearse vans for the Brookwood 'Necropolis' funeral service. Two ex-LSWR hearse vans had been used since 1899 and were now life-expired. However, before construction of their replacements took place the war intervened, and the Necropolis station at Waterloo was badly damaged by enemy action, resulting in suspension of the service. It never resumed, and the order was finally cancelled in May 1945. One is left to speculate as to what variation of utility van might have been provided for this unique service. As usual, the Southern's careful accounting methods record Order A1031 as being reduced from 150 to 148 ordinary Luggage Vans, to allow for these two special vehicles.

Between March 1940 and December 1943 23 Luggage Vans were converted into mobile workshops for War Department use, being formed into units with either two or three SR 12-ton covered goods wagons. Despite the censorship of the period, the prototype train was fully described in *The Locomotive* magazine for 15 April 1940 and has been illustrated in *Southern Wagons, Volume 4* (OPC, 2002). These conversions removed Luggage Vans 1056/73/86, 1112/27/65/88/95/6, 1200/30/9/51, 1300/12/37, 1948, 2008, 2190/2/8, 2211/21 from SR stock, and they were never returned. All except No 2008 (ex-SECR) were even-planked vans built between 1934 and 1939. Some remained at the various military railway establishments throughout the country, others travelled into Europe and the Middle East, both during 1940 and towards the end of the war. The two original units were lost very rapidly, following the fall of France in June 1940. Three other Luggage Vans were transferred to SR departmental service for the duration of hostilities, while at least three more (Nos 1106/91 and 2140) were rebodied following fire damage. In each case the even-planked bodywork was replaced by the contemporary 2+2 style.

Construction of traditionally-built vans ceased in September 1943 with Order L1659, although Sub-order E1659A, authorised in August 1943 for 10 lightweight vans, provided Bulleid with an opportunity to investigate further the various alternative materials and forms of construction then becoming available. These vehicles featured in an article published in the *Railway Gazette* for 7 April 1944, wherein it was claimed that there was an increase in capacity coupled with a saving in tare weight of 2 tons 16cwt, compared with a traditionally-constructed luggage van. They were completed between December 1943 and September 1944, running numbers 1401-10 and Diagram 3105 being allocated. **Figure 68** illustrates this unusual design.

The important design considerations were as follows:

- Reduction of weight while maintaining strength
- Avoidance of sudden shock to passengers or goods in the event of impact
- Use of new materials, such as plastics, where suitable
- Fabrication taking advantage of latest methods of same
- No increase in maintenance costs

There were several constraints placed upon the design by prevailing conditions, namely that body panels could only be produced in black and were limited in size to 6ft 6in by 3ft 3in, due to machine-press limitations, although it was hoped that under peacetime conditions these problems could be overcome. The body framing was constructed of light channel sections, 2½in by 1¼in, rolled from 12-gauge steel strip, welded together in a jig. Roof sticks were, however, made from laminated ash and

Plate 203 A Dudley–Walsall motor train leaves Great Bridge, in the Birmingham suburbs, propelled by ex-LNWR 2-4-2T No 46757 on 22 June 1949. The pristine utility van, No 1926, is not equipped with through air pipes and so is coupled at the rear of the formation.
HMRS Collection

Figure 68 The plastic-bodied Luggage Van to Diagram 3105.

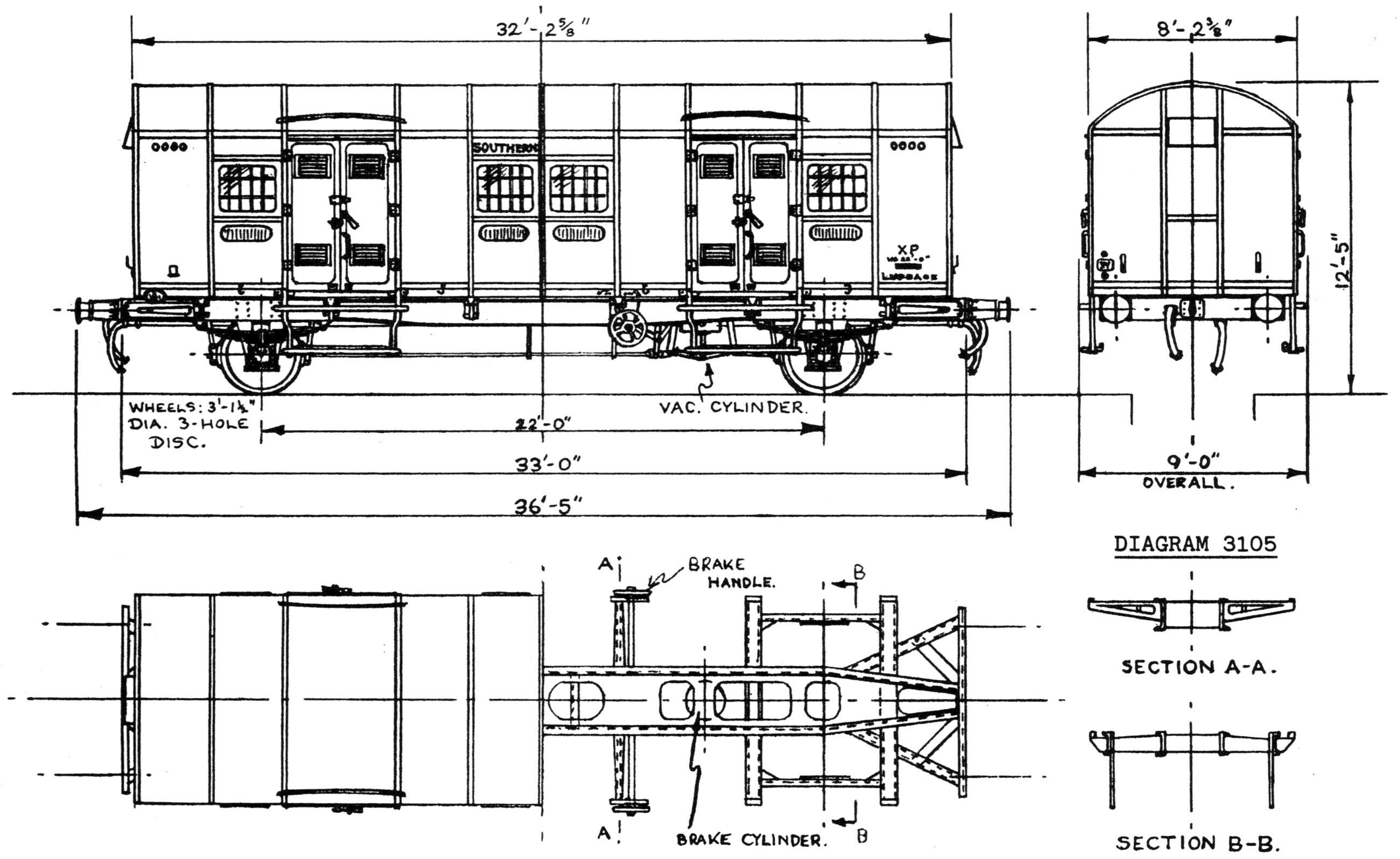

pre-formed to the correct curvature. The side, end and roof panels were constructed from reinforced plastic sheets, the reinforcement taking the form of woven high-tensile steel wire and cotton fabric, which was laminated into the plastic material. This lightweight form of body construction required some form of spring-cushioning or shock-absorbing mounting on the underframe, to prevent distortion of the bodywork under shunting impact. The doors were of light steel sheet, of 16SWG thickness, and included louvres for ventilation. The capacity of the body was 1,848cu ft — 40ft more than a standard Luggage Van.

The underframe was equally unconventional, having no external solebars. Instead there were two centre longitudinals set about 2ft 3in apart, from which the body supports, headstocks and axlebox assemblies were cantilevered. Mounted between these longitudinals were two sets of cushioning springs, which allowed the body to move up to 11in on the underframe, which was 1ft longer than the body. A centrally-positioned 'Prestall' vacuum cylinder was provided which acted directly on the brake pull rods, thereby dispensing with brake-shaft levers etc, allowing a further saving in weight. **Plate 15** shows the prototype van as it entered service in black livery, while **Plate 204** illustrates a van towards the end of its working life. No specific allocations or workings were issued for these vans; despite their being listed in the Carriage Working Appendices as 10 tons tare (instead of the more usual 13 tons) no attempt was made to restrict their use. Photographs of the 'Golden Arrow' taken in the immediate postwar period (1946-8) often show one of these vans included in the train.

Whether or not success was achieved with the lightweight vans is open to debate. They do not appear to have been failures, although no more were built, so any advantage in reduced train weight was minimal. At least four were eventually painted green, so any savings in painting costs were lost too. The original 1944 article, whilst mentioning costs, does not give any more details or comparisons with a traditional van. Despite their non-standard construction, all except the prototype lasted in normal service beyond 1960, although the rolling-stock record cards show that works visits, when they occurred, were protracted, although no reasons are given. Van 1401 was used as a store at Eastleigh Works from about 1958, while Nos 1405/6 were stored for two years prior to withdrawal in 1963. Van 1402 was the last survivor, being condemned in August 1972. The author photographed the vehicle in green livery at Micheldever soon after, when it was apparent that all the original doors had been replaced with a considerably heavier pattern.

Construction of 2+2-planked luggage vans resumed at Ashford in 1947 with Order A3229, authorised in May 1945, for vans 1501-60. These were identical to those completed four years earlier, owing nothing to the experiments carried out in the meantime. They were the last vans completed before Nationalisation and may have carried malachite green; **Plate 205** shows one running in Rail blue with white lettering, post 1970. During and after the war several vans were recorded in grey livery, whilst at Eastleigh on 2 July 1940 Nos 1075 and 2062 were both noted in malachite by Mr George Woodward, who took regular note of rolling stock at this location for many years.

Plate 204 Travel-stained plastic van No 1410, photographed at Lancing towards the end of its working life. Some panels appear to have been repainted. Note that the original rather lethal-looking brake wheel has been replaced, compared with **Plate 15**. *Author's collection*

Plate 205 One of the 1947-built vans, No 1545, at Clapham Junction in Rail blue *c*1972. Gummed paper labels have now replaced the chalked destinations.
The photographer was attempting to photograph every batch of SR utility vans — one wonders if he succeeded in recording all 37 orders. *J. H. Lewis*

Plate 206 Plywood Luggage Van No 1607, seen shortly after construction in June 1950, in crimson lake and with number and code (PMV) at the left-hand end; this was soon revised to the right-hand end, where it could conveniently be read in association with the plate detailing dimensions and tare weight. *K. G. Carr*

Plate 207 Final-batch 'Covcar' No 2513 at Lancing Works in September 1963, freshly repainted in Southern Region green livery. It has plywood sides but retains planked side and end doors. Despite the altered body sheeting, the design has changed little in 30 years. *J. H. Aston*

Van 2124 was the only other utility van so recorded, on 1 January 1944, so one must conclude that Luggage Vans in malachite green were pretty rare beasts.

General withdrawal commenced with the SECR vans during 1945, all except the 'air-control vans' (Nos 1996, 2001/2/4/5) and Nos 1976/94 entering departmental service between then and 1948. Nevertheless, many of these were to give a further 20-30 years (albeit somewhat static) service under British Railways. Seven Luggage Vans were transferred to the Isle of Wight in October 1950, these being amongst the first to be repainted in crimson lake. Upon transfer vans 1134, 1283, 1720, 1335/21/84 and 1692 were renumbered, in order, as 1046-52 and had side lamp-irons and Westinghouse brakes provided for their new duties. The Island, ever different from the mainland, classified them as PLV (Passenger Luggage Van), while the new BR code for Luggage Vans elsewhere was PMV (Parcels & Miscellaneous Van). Similarly, when BR decreed that all carriage stock of pre-Nationalisation origin should carry a Regional suffix letter as well as a prefix, these Island exiles failed to comply. In steam days they were by far the most modern items of rolling stock on the Island, and all lasted into the electrified era.

The last design change to affect the utility vans was the development of plywood as a body-sheeting material. First used by the Southern Railway for some containers in 1929 and on covered goods wagons from 1945, it was not until 1950, under British Railways, that the material was tried on Luggage Vans and 'Covcars'. In September 1949 Order A3590 was issued for 111 Luggage Vans, and these appeared variously from Ashford, Eastleigh and Lancing between April 1950 and January 1951, in crimson lake. The side doors were, however, still in the 2+2 style, perhaps for strength. **Plate 206** shows one of the vans soon after construction, with the original lettering style. One final batch of luggage vans was completed during 1951, somewhat surprisingly being built at the former LNWR works at Wolverton. These reverted to the 2+2 plank arrangement and may have been the first to have 'S' prefix and suffix letters.

After a lapse of over 12 years, construction of 'Covcars' recommenced in 1951, 150 being built between then and 1955, again with plywood body sheeting and 2+2-planked doors, but 1 ton lighter than earlier examples. The end doors remained vertically planked and were identical to those on all previous 'Covcars'. The British Railways operating code for these was CCT (Covered Carriage Truck). Numbering was somewhat fragmented, owing to the difficulty in finding sufficient vacant numbers, while the final 50 were given former horsebox numbers 2501-50, for which purpose ex-LSWR horseboxes 2530/6/8/82 were renumbered as 2703/5/6/10, already vacated by scrapping. Despite this careful planning, horsebox 2516 was not spotted, and for three months during 1955 two vehicles were in traffic with the same number! **Plate 207** illustrates the final products of the utility-van era. By 1955 no fewer than 990 Luggage Vans and 390 'Covcars' had been built, although some of the earlier Luggage Vans had been withdrawn before the last entered service.

General withdrawal of SR Luggage Vans commenced in 1949, and by 1960 most of the 1934/5 batches (Orders A762 and 824) had entered departmental service. Most were used as stores or Mess & Tool vans, many receiving minor modifications for their new roles; a few were more extensively rebuilt for other purposes. The 'Covcars' fared rather better, and, apart from almost-new van 2523, destroyed in an accident at Horsham in 1958, general withdrawal of the 1928-33 vans did not commence until 1962. Ten of these were transferred to goods stock (numbered S69000-9) in 1965 for use as barrier wagons on Fawley block oil trains, for which duties they are believed to have been repainted in the bauxite livery applied to fitted goods stock; however, their underframes did not take kindly to the buffing shocks of a train of loaded tankers, and they soon distorted badly. The five SECR 'air-control vans' were withdrawn in 1962, but push-pull operation was to continue for another two years, so

Plate 208 In the 1950s 14 vans were reserved for the use of cyclists travelling to/from the Continent. These received a white-stencilled symbol, as seen on van 1282 at Eardley Road carriage sidings in September 1956. The other vans were Nos 1055/7, 1103/13/75, 1208/93, 1305/14/7, 1454, 1728 and 1882. *H. C. Casserley*

Plate 209 Diagram 3100 Gangwayed Bogie Luggage Van No 2319, photographed after overhaul in July 1933. The steel flitching plates and their retaining bolts are visible at each end of the solebar, where extension pieces have been grafted on. These vans often ran in passenger trains, and all carried roof-board brackets; for the same reason they were often kept cleaner than other utility vans. *Southern Railway*

plywood vans 1621-5 were similarly equipped between November 1962 and March 1963. By this time most were confined to the Brockenhurst-Ringwood-Wimborne-Bournemouth West service, remaining thus until the line closed in 1964; the push-pull fittings were then removed, whereafter the vans returned to ordinary traffic.

Five more vans were converted for bullion traffic in 1963, these being Nos 1562/76 and 1613/8/28. They had their glazing replaced by steel sheeting — a modification that might escape notice, as so many vans ran with filthy windows anyway — and increased security measures incorporated in the bodywork. These involved steel sheeting behind the door and body planking, plus an additional single-leaf door inside each set of double doors and accessible only once the outer doors had been opened. Diagram 3104 was allocated (the second use of this number), and this records the tare weight of the conversions as 15 tons 16cwt — some 3½ tons greater than originally; carrying-capacity was reduced to just 5 tons to compensate. They were employed mostly between Southampton Docks and London and were seldom photographed — the services were not exactly advertised! By 1973 all five were in Rail blue, and all needed new, stronger hinges at about the same time because of their heavier doors. Withdrawal came in 1978, but all five vans were stored at Micheldever for several years pending departmental conversion.

Rail-blue livery was first applied to vans generally in 1967, although it was possible to see occasional crimson-lake examples until the early 1970s — often unnoticed beneath the grime. Whilst Southern Railway and pre-1956 British Railways liveries included black ends, post-1956 Southern Region green and Rail-blue paint finishes extended the bodyside colour to include the ends.

In the early 1960s a handful of vans received through electrical wiring for use in the few remaining locomotive-hauled passenger trains. Nos 1537/58 were done in 1961 for the 'Golden Arrow' service, while Nos 1455/76/82/95/6/9, 1626/47 were similarly equipped in 1964-6 for the Central section. All 10 received air brakes in 1967/8, being kept thereafter at New Cross Gate yard when not required. Under TOPS the vans were coded NQV (in the case of the Luggage Vans) or NOV (for the 'Covcars'). Some 'Covcars' had their end doors sealed up and were then recoded as PMV or NQV.

Withdrawals and departmental conversions continued, by the mid-1970s occurring almost anywhere in the country and not just on the Southern Region. The loss of further parcels traffic from 1980 onwards enabled British Rail to dispose of any remaining pre-Nationalisation stock; the last 'Covcars' (Nos 2239 and 2516) were condemned in February 1986, the last Luggage Van (No 1865) following in July, leaving just a handful of 'Van Bs' in ordinary service. Several still remain in departmental use at the time of writing (2002), and many are now in preservation — indeed, almost every society has at least one. Some have been purchased for their underframes only, to be reused below much older carriage bodies rescued from farms, holiday chalets and the like; as such they will give many more years of service to their new owners, albeit perhaps not quite in a manner envisaged by Maunsell and Lynes over 80 years ago.

We must now consider the 120 bogie luggage vans. In contrast to the four-wheelers their history is comparatively simple. In 1927/8 most of the remaining ex-LSWR 'bogie block' suburban four-coach sets were withdrawn and their bodies, suitably rebuilt, remounted on new 62ft underframes for electrified services. This left a considerable number of redundant underframes that were, in many instances, less than 25 years old and could usefully be redeployed. Ten ex-LBSCR underframes were about to be reused for a batch of scenery vans (see Chapter 13), so in April 1928 it was proposed that 50 bogie luggage vans be constructed using

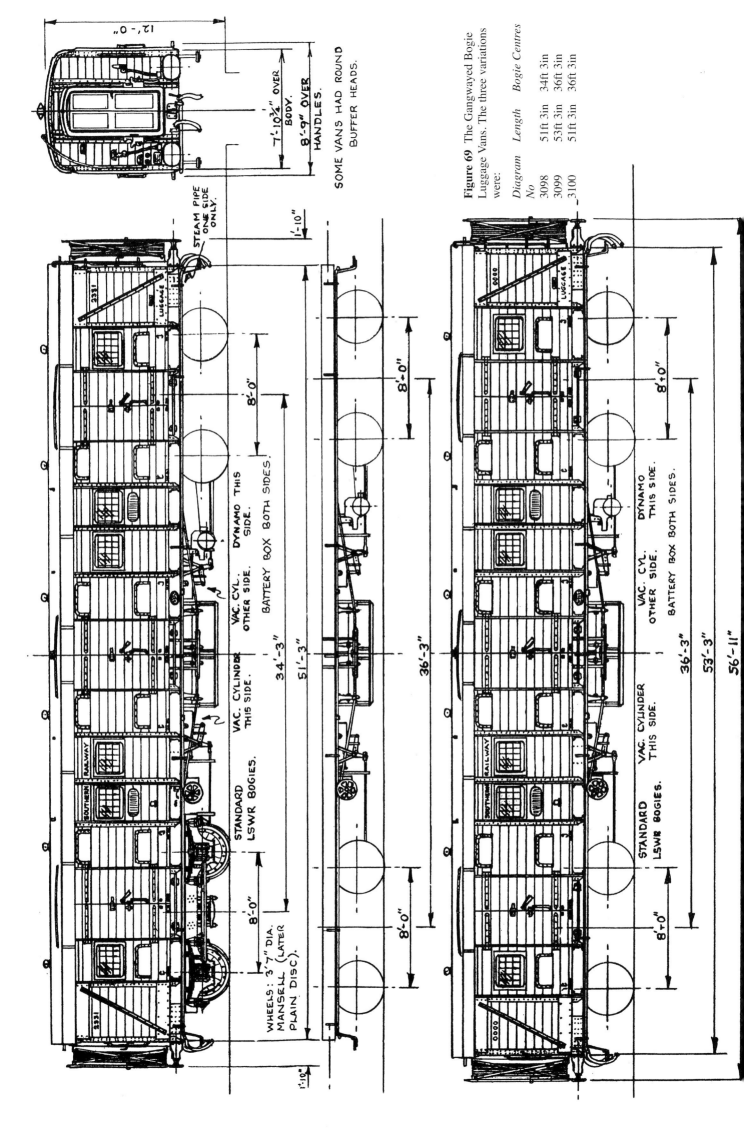

Figure 69 The Gangwayed Bogie Luggage Vans. The three variations were:

Diagram No	Length	Bogie Centres
3098	51ft 3in	34ft 3in
3099	53ft 3in	36ft 3in
3100	51ft 3in	36ft 3in

Plate 211 Van 2346, to Diagram 3096, as running in early BR crimson-lake livery and with droplights fitted to the centre pair of doors. Apart from the van number, the only bodyside lettering is the 'DISTRIBUTED LOAD 10 TONS' cast plate and code PMV, both in minute letters below the number. *Author's collection*

Plate 210 End view of van 2320 at Stewarts Lane in July 1950, showing the British standard gangway, fitted with adaptors for coupling with Pullman gangways. *A. E. West*

Plate 212 Van 2353 was damaged by fire during World War 2 and received 2+2 planking as a result, — probably the only GBL van to be so treated. It is seen in crimson lake at Exeter Central in October 1959, just six months before being transferred for internal use at Lancing Works, renumbered 081254. *A. E. West*

these LSWR frames. This was later amended to include gangways and authorised in March 1929, followed soon after by two more batches, bringing the total to 120 vehicles (HOO Nos 443, 467 and 573). These were completed at Ashford between March 1930 and September 1931 on underframes reconditioned at Lancing.

The existing underframes were unsuitable without modification, as not all had conventional buffing gear at each end. To accommodate this, all frames were lengthened by varying amounts at each end, prominent steel flitching plates covering the solebars where old and new sections were spliced together. There were also two lengths — 49ft and 51ft. The first batch used only the longer frames, but the two later batches used a mixture of the two, resulting in three slightly differing versions of GBL — the operating code allocated to these vans, an abbreviation for Gangwayed Bogie Luggage Van. The three diagrams are illustrated in **Figure 69**, while numbering details appear in Table 16 at the end of this chapter. **Plate 209** shows one of the vehicles to Diagram 3100. All had British standard gangways fitted and so required adaptors to enable them to couple with vehicles equipped with Pullman-type gangways, as seen in **Plate 210**.

The vans were much used for Southampton Docks and other South Western-section services, being rather less common in other areas of the Southern Railway until later years. They allowed through access by passengers from within the train and so were used on the various overnight newspaper and mail trains from Waterloo, although whether it was always possible for a passenger to negotiate the piles of papers, mail, etc to reach the rest of the train is another matter! Some were also used for milk traffic; for many years vans 2341/2 were reserved for Messrs Aplin & Barrett's dairy products from Yeovil Town, being stencilled 'TO WORK BETWEEN YEOVIL & LONDON ONLY'. Nos 2300/15/22/6 and 2470 were also labelled 'TO BE RETURNED TO CHARD JUNCTION', specifically for Wilts United Dairies milk traffic in churns; this took the vans as far afield as Bristol, Crewe, York and Glasgow, running via Taunton and the GWR main line. Another special use involved van 2351, which during the 1930s was reserved for Royal duties and often ran coupled to the ex-SECR Royal Train or Pullman specials.

Just before World War 2 the Southern Railway was requested to make up three casualty-evacuation trains, Nos 32-4. Each included 10 stretcher vans, and these were provided by converting 30 Gangwayed Bogie Luggage Vans, under Order E1107. These were removed from SR stock until 1945, while several others became Ambulance cars, being used as such between 1943 and 1947. When returned, many of these had received droplights in the centre pair of doors, as seen in **Plate 211**. This resulted in the allocation of two extra diagrams

— Nos 3096/7 — details being recorded in Table 16. The first to be permanently taken out of ordinary traffic was No 2297, transferred to departmental stock as No 300s as early as March 1946. However, no other departmental transfers took place until 1958. Most vans required extensive underframe repairs between 1945 and 1948, during which time the Mansell wheels were replaced by those of steel-disc pattern.

British Railways crimson-lake livery began to appear in 1949, van 2463 being the first repaint in this colour, as part of the 'Newhaven Continental' set, in April of that year. Despite being corridor vehicles, they did not receive 'blood and custard' livery — indeed, just how this might have been interpreted is best left to the imagination! The BR operating code was also altered to 'COR PMV'. During the 1950s one van was allocated to the 'Golden Arrow' service, its smart red finish being obvious in colour photographs of the period. By 1959 a green van was in use, still on this prestige duty despite the age of the underframe. On the South Western section, vans 2296 and 2480 had been roof-boarded 'NEWSPAPER TRAFFIC' in 1953, for use between Waterloo and Bournemouth, so were still also in front-line service at this date.

Withdrawal came rapidly between 1958 and 1960, once the Southern Region received 130 BR standard bogie GUVs, and only vans 2290, 2331/3/44/7/9/56/68, 2464/76/87/8 were retained, for pigeon traffic, until November 1961; two of these are just visible in **Plate 68**. The body of No 2291 was reconstructed for motor-car van 4501, described in the next chapter, while former pigeon van 2464 was repainted in the Pullman livery of umber and cream in July 1962 in readiness for a more sombre duty. This it fulfilled on 30 January 1965, when it was used as the hearse van to convey the body of Sir Winston Churchill from Waterloo to Hanborough (Oxfordshire) following his State funeral at St Paul's Cathedral. The van was later sold to the 'City of Industry', Los Angeles, California, for £350 and left this country on 28 October 1965 — and was returned to Britain for restoration in 2007. A few others were relegated to internal-user stores vans at various locations, including Newhaven Harbour, Weymouth, West Moors station and Orpington, while in the period 1959-62 six entered departmental service, of which two have subsequently been preserved. Several of the departmental conversions had their doors enlarged to assist in the loading and unloading of bulky items of Civil Engineer's Department plant.

Table 16
Summary of SR Luggage Vans

Diagram No	Vehicle type (SR/BR)	Classification	Running Nos	Planking	Built by	Remarks
3096	25/26-ton Gangwayed Bogie Luggage Van 51ft 3in long	GBL/COR PMV	2333/5/7/9/43/4/6-9/52, 2482-4/6/7/90	Even	Modified 1945	Ex-Diagram 3098 with droplights
3097	27-ton Gangwayed Bogie Luggage Van 53ft 3in long	GBL/COR PMV	2355/6/62/5/7/9, 2464/7-9/72/4/5/7-9	Even	Modified 1945	Ex-Diagram 3099 with droplights
3098	25/26-ton Gangwayed Bogie Luggage Van 51ft 3in long	GBL/COR PMV	2331-54	Even	Ashford 11/30-4/31	Some later to Diagram 3096
			2482-90	Even	Ashford 8-9/31	
3099	27-ton Gangwayed Bogie Luggage Van 53ft 3in long	GBL/COR PMV	2355-70	Even	Ashford 1-4/31	Some later to Diagram 3097
			2461-81	Even	Ashford 7-8/31	
3100	25-ton Gangwayed Bogie Luggage Van 51ft 3in long	GBL/COR PMV	2281-2330	Even	Ashford 3-10/30	None fitted with droplights
3101	13/14-ton covered carriage truck (some Diagram 3102)	Covcar/CCT	1411-50	Plywood	Ashford 10-12/51	13 tons tare
			1731-80	2+2	Ashford/Eastleigh 11-12/38	Doors even-planked
			1977-91, 2006-20	Plywood	Ashford 10-12/51	13 tons tare
			2023-72	Even	Midland RCW 3-5/28	Original batch
			2073-82, 2171-80, 2231-40	Plywood	Ashford 10-12/51	13 tons tare
			2241-50, 2491-2500	Even	Ashford 2-4/33	Originally to Diagram 3102
			2251-80	Even	Ashford 4-7/29	
			2371-2460	Even	Ashford 4/31-2/32	Originally to Diagram 3102
			2501-50	Plywood	Lancing 6-12/55	13 tons tare
960	13-ton Luggage Van (No 1972 12-ton)	Luggage/PMV	1972-2016	Even	Bristol W&C Co/ Ashford 1919-22	Ex-SECR vehicles with detail differences
3103	12/13-ton Luggage Van	PLV	1046-52 (ex-1134, 1283, 1720, 1335/21/84, 1692)	Various	(various)	To Isle of Wight and renumbered 10/50
		Luggage/PMV	1054-1250	Even	Ashford 4/35-4/37	
			1251-1358	Even	Ashford 2-7/39	
			1359-98	2+2	Ashford 7-12/39	
			1451-1500	2+2	Wolverton 1-8/51	12 tons tare
			1501-60	2+2	Ashford 6-8/47	
			1561-1671	Plywood	Ashford/Eastleigh/ Lancing 4/50-1/51	12 tons tare; some later to Diagram 3104
			1053, 1692-1730, 2083-90	2+2	Lancing 5-9/43	
			1781-1820, 2091-2170	Even	Lancing 8-12/42	Pressed-steel sections
			1821-1920	2+2	Lancing/Eastleigh 2-8/40	No 1915 to Diagram 3104
			1921-70	Even	Ashford 10-12/38	
			2181-2230	Even	Ashford 10/34-3/35	
3104	Mobile Drawing Office store	(not classified)	1572s (departmental stock number)	2+2	Ashford/Eastleigh 8/40	Ex-No 1915 8/40-8/45
3104	16-ton Luggage Van (security)	PMV	1562/76, 1613/8/28	Plywood	Converted 9/63	Ex-Diagram 3103
3105	10-ton Luggage Van	Luggage/PMV	1401-10	Plastic	Eastleigh 12/43-9/44	Bulleid design

Notes
Underframes for all Gangwayed Bogie Luggage Vans reconditioned at Lancing Works
Distributed load for all Luggage Vans was 10 tons (5 tons for security vans to Diagram 3104).
Some batches were not completed in strict numerical order.

Chapter 13.

Livestock Vans, Milk Tanks, Carriage Trucks, Scenery Vans and Post Office Vans

The only remaining non-passenger coaching stock left to be dealt with are the 176 vehicles covered by the above descriptions. All were somewhat specialised, and none was particularly numerous; indeed, two of the categories include just single-figure totals. Despite this, no fewer than 19 different diagrams are involved.

Livestock vans
The most numerous single design was the special cattle van, with 60 examples. These were employed for the conveyance of prize stock and from 1923 onwards were classified as passenger vans. This was not always the case, however, and opinion differed between railway companies. The LBSCR, for example, judged its 'cattle boxes' to be goods vehicles prior to 1921 but in that year renumbered them into the passenger-carriage series. The LSWR could not make up its mind either — its were passenger stock between 1906 and 1912 but goods stock both before and after that period; ordinary cattle wagons, in contrast, were universally classed as goods stock. Horseboxes, by contrast, have always been regarded as passenger-rated vehicles. This might seem an odd distinction until it is remembered that, in the earlier days of railways, the wealthy would hire a saloon coach in which to travel and would take their horse and carriage along with them, so the necessary horsebox and open carriage truck would need to be passenger-rated. Clearly, no cattle would ever travel in this manner, and it was only later, when a requirement to carry prize or pedigree animals was identified, that the 'special cattle van' classification came into being.

This requirement was never extensive — certainly not when compared to horse traffic, the Southern Railway inheriting just 96 special cattle vans compared with 720 horseboxes. Only one batch of 25 horseboxes was ever authorised for construction post-Grouping — Order E1093 in May 1939 — and these were never built, owing to wartime restrictions, despite the fact that most inherited horseboxes were pretty small and ancient-looking vehicles. Three more batches (each of 25) were proposed for construction in 1940/1/2 but were never even authorised. Whereas all horseboxes included a groom's compartment, not all the special cattle vans did so. All but five of the LBSCR vehicles, plus most SER and some LSWR vans, were in need of early replacement, and in April 1929 authorisation was given for 20 replacements, increased to 50 the following November. Order A529 was issued for their construction at Ashford, but all were eventually completed by the Birmingham Railway Carriage & Wagon Co, being delivered in mid-1930. Some official records state that the underframes were actually built at Lancing, only the bodywork being undertaken by BRCW.

A special cattle van could certainly be mistaken for a horsebox, having a centrally-placed groom's compartment with a cattle compartment at each end, and it is certain that these vehicles were used for horses when necessary. Steam heating and vacuum and Westinghouse brakes were provided, although removal of the last commenced in 1937. Numbered 3679-3728, they were 26ft long

Plate 213 Special cattle van No 3683 when new in June 1930. The vertical sliding shutters at the left-hand end are in the raised (closed) position; those at the right-hand end are in the lowered (open) position. The door droplight and the quarterlight window-frame are varnished teak, the rest of the bodyside being in Maunsell green.
Birmingham Railway Carriage & Wagon Co

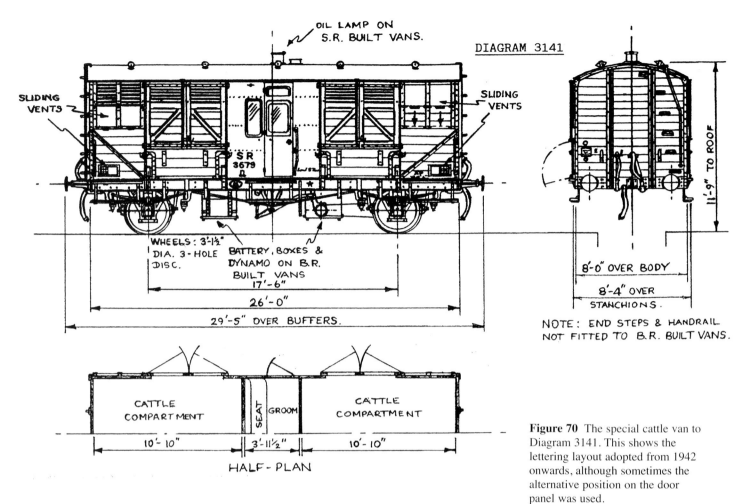

Figure 70 The special cattle van to Diagram 3141. This shows the lettering layout adopted from 1942 onwards, although sometimes the alternative position on the door panel was used.

Plate 214 One of the 1952 vans with electric lighting, No 3729, seen at Sturminster Newton (ex-S&DJR) in September 1965. Several of the vans were stored here between 1965 and 1968, even after the closure of the line to passenger traffic. Livery is Southern Region green, including the ends. *A. E. West*

and were rated at 8 tons' capacity. Diagram 3251 was initially allocated, revised almost immediately to 3141. Perhaps because they might find themselves included in a goods train, lighting was provided by just a single oil-lamp, accessible by means of end steps and handrails. The Southern's operating code was CATOX, possibly an abbreviation of the LBSCR term 'cattle box'. **Plate 213** and **Figure 70** illustrate the design.

The special cattle vans would be seen primarily at locations where agricultural shows and markets were held, such as Ashford, Guildford and Salisbury. Sometimes they were used to carry the animals from travelling circuses, in which case the occupants might be rather more exotic than cattle! Maunsell green, with 12in company initials, remained the standard livery until changed to grey (with 4in initials) *c*1942, as detailed in **Figure 3**. Only van 3697 has been noted in malachite, being recorded in July 1941 and again in November 1944. Interior finish was stone buff, with a black floor and red fabric to the groom's seating. From 1949 British Railways crimson lake, together with the BR code (SCV), was applied, most vans having received this colour by 1956.

By Nationalisation just 10 pre-Grouping special cattle vans remained in traffic (one LSWR, two LBSCR and seven SECR), and the decision was taken in September 1950 to replace these with 10 further examples to Diagram 3141, to Order L3706. There seems to have been no urgency, as vans 3729-38 did not appear from Lancing until late 1952. Apart from the provision of electric lighting, for which a dynamo and battery box were carried on the underframe, they were practically identical to the original vans of 1930. As access to the roof would not be required, the end steps and handrails were omitted.

Only a few years after their completion, the traffic in prize cattle started to dwindle, and all the original 1930 vehicles were withdrawn from service in 1961-3. Several bodies were sold to farmers for use (rather appropriately) as cattle sheds, mostly in Scotland. Several took some time to be cut up, No 3706 being noted intact at Eastleigh in September 1964, almost two years after withdrawal, still in crimson lake. Two were extensively rebuilt as train-heating boiler vans Nos DS70190/1 and were used at Bournemouth West and Weymouth (and later at Oxford). The 1952 vans lasted a little longer, being withdrawn between 1966 and 1971, although some spent time in store at Sturminster Newton (see **Plate 214**), Salisbury and Micheldever before final scrapping. No 3733 was then retained for preservation by the National Railway Museum and is still, at the time of writing, in its reserve collection.

Milk-tank wagons
Far greater in terms of type of vehicle, if not in actual numbers, were milk tanks. The conveyance of milk by rail is a fascinating and complicated subject and one worthy of a book in itself.

The passage through Surbiton of the 3.54pm Clapham Junction-Exeter Central milk empties was the highlight of the author's mis-spent schooldays, bringing as it did the sight of an Exmouth Junction Light Pacific — hopefully a rare one at that!

Milk-tank wagons constituted the one class of vehicle that did not feature in the 1923 stock-renumbering scheme. Historically, milk was carried in churns, loaded into luggage or purpose-built milk vans. For such traffic the South Western had a number of special ventilated vans which had been painted in all-salmon livery instead of the more usual salmon and brown, in an attempt to reduce the heat absorbed by the bodywork on hot days. The LBSCR had several slatted-sided milk vans, the construction of which ensured that the contents were kept cool on their journey from countryside to city. All these vehicles were renumbered into the Luggage Van series on passing to the Southern Railway in 1923. The clatter of milk churns being rolled along a station platform was then a familiar sound and one which took many years to disappear, as churns remained a (slowly-diminishing) feature of milk traffic until the 1960s. Vauxhall station, where most of the South Western section's milk traffic was destined, once echoed to this sound for most of the day and night.

Milk was a heavy commodity as well as an extremely perishable one, and, as the traffic increased, bulk transportation was seen as the only way to handle it efficiently. One milk-tank wagon could carry 3,000 gallons — the equivalent of three vans of churns — so in 1927 the GWR and the LMS, in association with United Dairies Ltd, introduced some short-wheelbase four-wheeled tank wagons. The LNER followed suit a year later, but it was not until 1931 that the Southern, rather belatedly, entered the field. Interestingly, in all instances the underframe was constructed and owned by the railway company, yet the tanks themselves (which were aluminium, stainless steel or glass-lined) were owned by the dairy companies and carried their own series of numbers.

According to the *Southern Railway Magazine*, in the 12 months ending June 1931 the company carried 27,684,202 gallons of milk in 1,977,443 churns to London, mostly from Sherborne, Gillingham (Dorset), Templecombe, Semley and Salisbury on the South Western main line from the west, but this total also included 71,000 churns from Sussex, loaded at stations such as Horam, Midhurst, Petworth and Billingshurst. A typical milk train leaving Salisbury might consist of 30 vehicles and weigh upwards of 800 tons — a formidable load and one that would often require double-heading.

The matter was discussed at several Traffic Committee meetings between 1927 and 1930, and agreement was eventually reached for the construction of three mobile milk-tank trucks for conveyance of CWS road trailers and six fixed milk-tank trucks to receive United Dairies 3,000gal tanks, construction of these being undertaken at Lancing from September to November 1931. Confusingly, both were designated 'Type 1' — mobile milk-tank carriage truck Type 1 and fixed milk-tank wagon Type 1. All nine vehicles were four-wheelers — the only such Southern milk-tank wagons. Diagram and running numbers are given in Table 17 at the end of this chapter.

The mobile milk-tank trucks were a new idea, in effect being dedicated open carriage trucks equipped with floor runways, guides and pulleys that enabled the road tankers to be hauled onto the truck using steel ropes. Hinged end flaps were provided so that the trailer could be run onto the vehicle from any end-loading dock. By this method, dairies with no direct rail access could be served.

R. A. Dyson of Liverpool provided two road tankers (later increased to three) for Co-operative Wholesale Ltd, and these carried the standard CWS livery of dark-green tank with white lettering, edged in black. Each road tanker had six wheels with solid rubber tyres, the front pair of which were equipped with Ackerman steering operated through a tiller bar to which the draw gear was attached. Motive power to/from the dairy could be provided by motor lorry or tractor. The tankers entered service on 10 October 1931, as recorded in **Plate 215**, running daily between Cole (S&DJR) and Clapham Junction, via Templecombe. Two tankers and trucks were thus needed for the service, the third being spare for use as required. On arrival at Clapham Junction the tanker, still in place on the truck, would be shunted adjacent to the CWS depot, where the milk would be unloaded and the tank cleaned and sterilised, ready for the return journey to Cole the next day. Weight and height restrictions limited the capacity of these road tankers to 2,000 gallons — two-thirds the capacity of a fixed tank but still equivalent to 200 churns.

The six fixed-tank wagons entered service in November 1931, carrying United Dairies 3,000gal glass-lined tanks finished in white (or possibly silver), with a combination of black and vermilion lettering, as seen in **Plate 216**. Rough riding had already been encountered with the short-wheelbase GWR and LMS tanks, so these were mounted on standard RCH underframes, 21ft 6in long and with a wheelbase of 12ft, in the hope that this problem would be overcome. The tanks ran between Sherborne and Vauxhall or Sherborne and Stewarts Lane via Victoria, so were regularly formed as 'tail' traffic in passenger trains.

Despite the longer wheelbase, rough riding soon became apparent again, so the Southern was forced to restrict the operation of the four-wheeled vehicles, as outlined in the Appendices to the Working Timetables:

- If run in passenger trains they must not be formed between vehicles conveying passengers.
- If formed in trains which exceed a speed of 40 miles per hour at any point, they must not be attached to the rear without a six- or eight-wheeled vehicle, or a four-wheeled vehicle having a wheelbase of not less than 15ft, being attached immediately behind.
- Four-wheeled milk tanks and mobile milk-tank trucks loaded on four-wheeled trucks may be formed in any position in non-passenger trains which do not exceed a speed of 40 miles per hour.

Even before these vehicles entered service the Board of Trade had recommended that the minimum wheelbase for vehicles to run without speed restriction be 15ft, unless six-wheeled. The railway companies had argued this last concession, pointing out that most locomotive tenders were six-wheeled and often had a wheelbase of less than 15ft yet ran perfectly satisfactorily. The end result was that all later SR tank wagons and trucks were

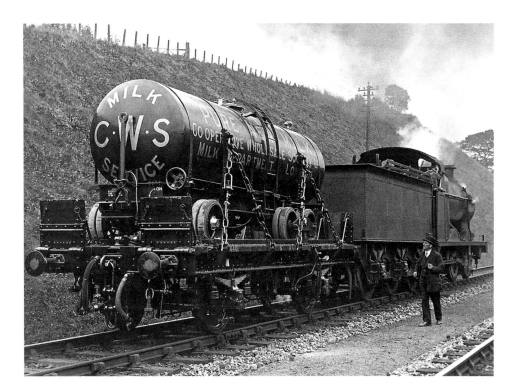

Plate 215 The inaugural run of the CWS milk tankers, 10 October 1931. An LMS '4F' 0-6-0 picks up milk truck 4401 at Cole, S&DJR, prior to setting back onto the early-afternoon stopping passenger train for Templecombe. Note the runway flaps in the raised position at each end of the truck and the rail clamps below the buffers; these were provided to ensure that the truck did not 'up-end' during the loading process. *Modern Transport*

Plate 216 Diagram 3152 four-wheeled milk tank No 4408 at Lancing in November 1931. The tank itself may be white or silver, 'SR' and 'United Dairies' are vermilion, while 'Glass Lined Milk Tank' is black; lettering on the underframe is white, except for the 'WB 12ft 0in' inscription, which is in 1¼in yellow characters. These were the only United Dairies tanks to carry full-height ladders — a feature they retained on re-framing in 1937/8. *Modern Transport*

Plate 217 Express Dairy aluminium tank No 9, mounted on an underframe carrying (incorrectly) the number 4401 — it should be 4410. The tank is white, but close examination of the lettering will reveal that the company title and tank number are in a lighter tone than the words 'Milk for London / Insulated Tank'. The latter are presumably black; the former may be vermilion or (more likely) pale blue. The later 1930s livery for these tanks would be as shown in **Plate 222**. *Southern Railway*

Plate 218 During and after World War 2 most milk tanks carried a simplified livery. Here is No 4410 again, in grey livery with minimal lettering, at Seaton Junction in 1945. The three 'fast traffic' stars indicate the highly-perishable nature of the cargo and were introduced c1942.
R. S. Carpenter collection

Plate 219 A mobile milk-tank truck Type 2 at Forest Hill station in 1933, for the loading demonstrations, of which a number of official photographs were taken. A Dyson four-wheeled trailer, in 'Azo' orange livery with golden-yellow letters edged in black, is shackled onto the truck, ready to travel. By the late 1930s (or, more probably, during the early war years) some of these trailers carried the same lettering but on a grey tank. *Modern Transport*

equipped with 20ft 6in-long six-wheeled underframes of 13ft wheelbase. All rough-riding problems were overcome, and in due course the four-wheelers were proposed for re-framing.

Express Dairy now entered the bulk-transportation market, with four vehicles equipped with aluminium tanks that were anchor-mounted to the underframe, so these vehicles did not have the distinctive end stanchions and crossheads so typical of all other SR tank wagons. Described as fixed milk-tank wagon Type 2, these were white with either vermilion or blue lettering, as seen in **Plate 217**. These also had a canopy over the top half of the tank, with air scoops at each end, to help keep the tank itself cool in hot weather. They later carried the more familiar Express Dairy cobalt-blue livery with bold cream (later white) lettering, this being replaced by dark grey during and after World War 2 (**Plate 218**).

United Dairies now commenced a road/rail service, for which purpose seven six-wheeled trucks were completed in 1932/3, for use between Gillingham (Dorset), Salisbury and Forest Hill in South East London. A demonstration of loading took place at Forest Hill station in 1933, as shown in **Plate 219**. The vehicles were described as mobile milk-tank carriage trucks Type 2. To run with these, R. A. Dyson completed at least 10 2,000gal road trailers with stainless-steel tanks carried on four wheels with Dunlop low-pressure pneumatic tyres mounted on Dyson's patent drum-wheel system. The drum wheels engaged in the runway on the truck, guiding the vehicle onto it and taking the weight off the road tyres for the duration of the rail journey. Drawgear was also provided at both ends, to assist loading and unloading. At least two liveries were carried by these tankers during the 1930s, **Plate 220** illustrating very different colours from those shown in Plate 219. **Figure 71** gives details of these trucks, allocated SR Diagram 3154.

From this point, all subsequent milk-tank wagons were very similar in appearance, the main differences concerning access arrangements to the filling points: United Dairies preferred short ladders with a catwalk on each side of the tank, while Express Dairy opted for longer ladders reaching to the top of the tank. The next order was for six United Dairies tanks, for services from depots in Wiltshire and Somerset to Vauxhall. These are illustrated in **Plate 221** and carried silver livery, with a similar lettering layout to the original four-wheelers. **Figure 72** illustrates two types of United Dairies fixed milk-tank wagon. Next came two tanks for Express Dairy, completed in May 1933 and finished in cobalt blue, as seen in **Plate 222** and **Figure 73**. Four more followed in September 1933, for United Dairies Wholesale Ltd, and these were lettered 'UDW' in dark green on a silver tank. Until now all frames had been built at Lancing, but the next pair were completed at Ashford. These were ordered in the name of West Park Dairy, but by the time they were completed in April 1935 West Park had been taken over by Express Dairy, so the intended colourful livery of chocolate-brown tank with yellow lettering was never carried. All these

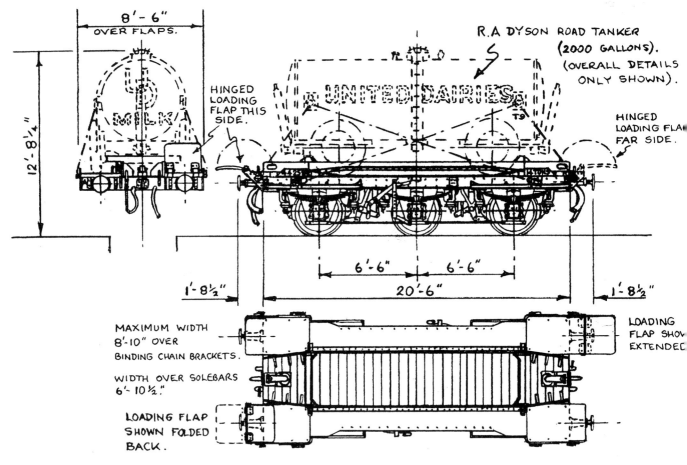

Figure 71 Mobile milk-tank carriage truck Type 2, to Diagram 3154. This shows the original design for Nos 4414-8; Nos 4425/6 had full-width runways over the entire length of the truck.

Plate 220 Dyson United Dairies trailers being loaded at Salisbury in 1934. Truck No 4417 is on the right, while slightly different vehicle 4426 is farthest from the camera. Milk tankers T7 and T9 are in place on the trucks, wearing silver with black lettering; their interlaced 'UD' letters on the ends are outlined in golden yellow. Note that an access ladder is provided on one side only. After World War 2 the tankers carried overall dark grey, relieved only by the tank number in white figures. *HMRS Collection*

Plate 221 Six-wheeled United Dairies tanks 4423/4, as completed at Lancing in October 1932, wearing silver livery. The lettering colours are as given for **Plate 216**. *Modern Transport*

Figure 72 Two types of United Dairies tank wagon, showing original lettering layouts.

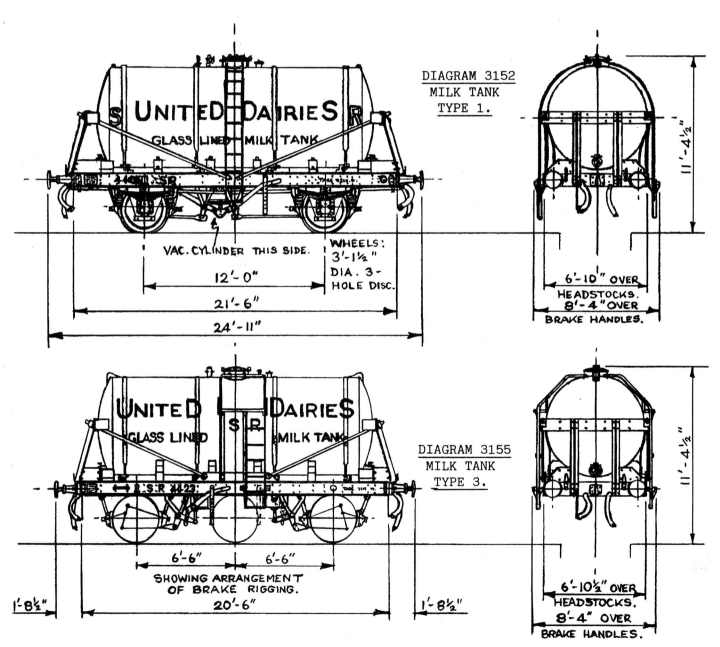

Plate 222 Express Dairy tank No 4427 at Lancing Works in May 1933 in cobalt-blue livery with pale-cream (later white) lettering. Nos 4435-8 were similarly finished but were lettered 'STAYBRITE STAINLESS TANK NO [XX] / MILK FOR LONDON ' below the waistline. Tank numbers noted include 66 and 67. *G. Bixley collection*

Figure 73 Two types of Express Dairy tank wagon, showing original lettering layouts.

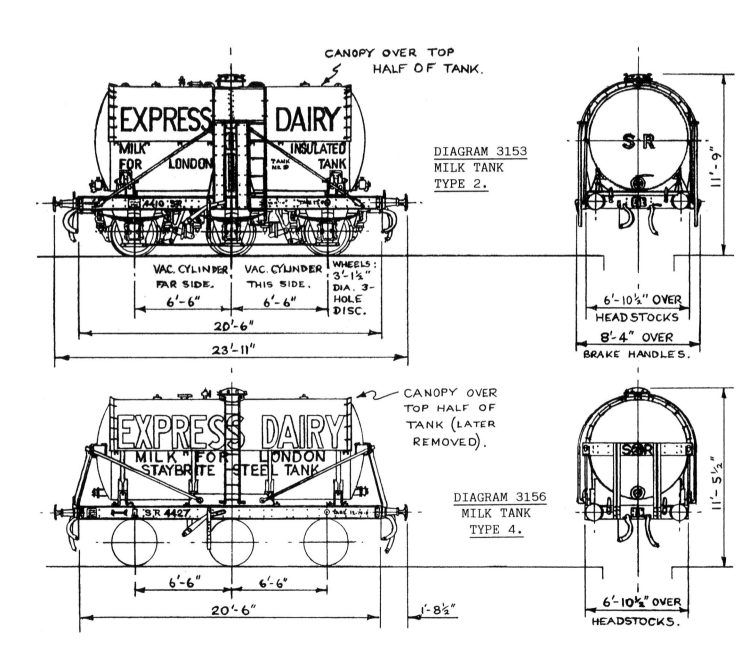

Plate 223 An up milk train passing Woking yard in the spring of 1938. A 'T14' 4-6-0 heads a train that includes three utility vans, a re-framed United Dairies Diagram 3159 tank (lettered 'UDW' in black on silver) and two Diagram 3154 trucks loaded with Dyson trailers. The guard is travelling in the ex-SECR double-ducketed brake van. *F. Foote*

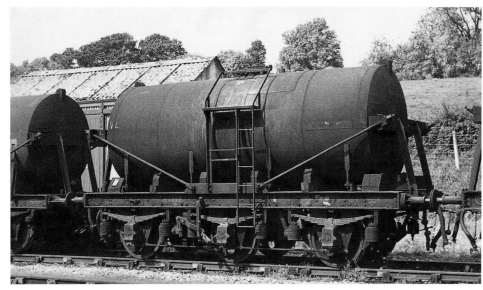

Plate 224 Diagram 3155 United Dairies tank wagon No 4422 at Hemyock (Western Region) in August 1963, showing the typical appearance by that date. Only the plate affixed to the tank side indicates its ownership. *P. H. Swift*

Plate 225 Diagram 3161 Express Dairy tank No 4444 at Eastleigh in July 1950. The photographer recorded the livery as 'aluminium blue', recalled as a somewhat pale shade of turquoise. *A. E. West*

different batches received individual type and diagram numbers, as recorded in **Table 17**.

The running restrictions of the four-wheeled vehicles continued to be a cause for concern, so in June 1936 authorisation was given for the construction of nine new six-wheeled underframes to replace the originals; the recovered frames were to be used to construct nine additional 20-ton mineral wagons to Diagram 1386. The six United Dairies fixed-tank wagons (Nos 4404-9) were re-framed between August 1937 and April 1938, retaining the same running numbers, but the three CWS replacements were instead built by the GWR, as the CWS contract with the Southern Railway terminated in December 1938. CWS road tankers continued to reach the Southern but were carried on GWR 'ro-rail' trucks. One of the re-framed United Dairies vehicles, lettered 'UDW' in black on a silver tank, can be seen in **Plate 223**.

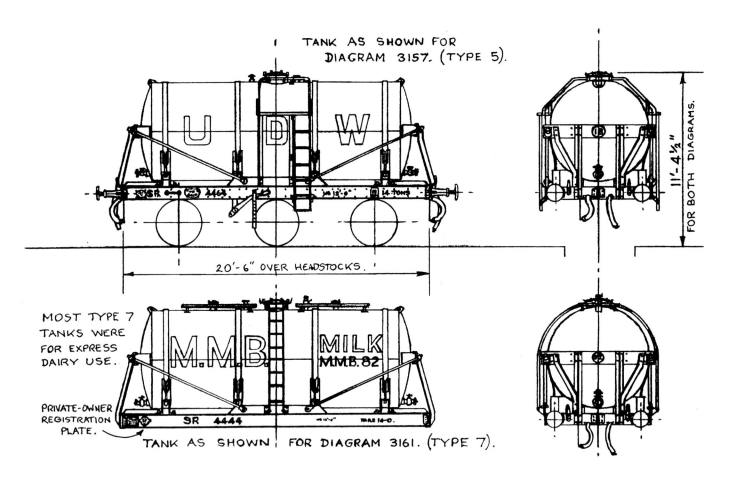

Figure 74 The later tank wagons, including both types ordered by the Ministry of War Transport. The lettering layouts are noted from photographs and so may not be correct for the MWT vehicles.

Four more Express Dairy tanks were completed at Ashford in 1937/8, becoming Type 7 in the classification — the last new type to appear — bringing to 38 the number of tanks in the SR fleet. These were again cobalt blue, with a lettering layout slightly different from that shown in **Plate 222**.

With the onset of war the Ministry of War Transport took responsibility for ordering the remaining 28 additions to the Southern fleet, and these appeared in a very much plainer grey livery than previously. The first four were part of an order for 12 tanks for Express Dairy (the others being built by the GWR and LMS) and became SR Nos 4439-42, having been completed in 1942. Finally, in 1943/4, 24 more were completed at Eastleigh and Lancing, 12 each being for Express Dairy and United Dairies. Although these last batches were allocated SR running numbers 4443-66, they were in fact registered as Ministry of War Transport property and classed as private-owner wagons, receiving entries in the SR private-owner wagon register. Never actually Southern Railway property, they were finally taken into British Railways stock in January 1952. **Figure 74** illustrates these, including possible lettering layouts which include the Milk Marketing Board livery of white letters on a grey tank, known to have been seen on services to Vauxhall from 1943 onwards. After World War 2 only Express revived its colourful blue livery (and this was not applied to all tanks), so by the early 1950s ownership was indicated merely by small plates riveted to the tank sides, as depicted by **Plates 224 and 225**. The total stock of Southern Region tank wagons now stood at 63, with a combined capacity of no less than 182,000 gallons.

By 1936 tank-wagon workings were almost wholly confined to the South Western section, running daily from Torrington, Lapford, Crediton, Seaton Junction, Chard Junction, Yeovil, Gillingham, Sherborne, Semley and Salisbury, plus Bason Bridge (Highbridge), Cole, Wincanton, Sturminster Newton and Bailey Gate on the S&DJR (connecting with the West of England traffic at Templecombe), and from Cricklade on the M&SWJR (via Andover Junction), to London. Clapham Junction, Vauxhall, Stewarts Lane, Wood Lane and Forest Hill were the main receiving stations, but churn traffic was also worked to Tonbridge, being detached from up West of England trains at Woking and running via Guildford and Redhill; after 1948 this working was extended to Gravesend via Tonbridge and Maidstone West. The Portsmouth Direct line also generated some milk tank traffic from Petersfield, but the former LBSCR traffic in churns from Sussex had already been lost to road transport. Other milk depots existed throughout South London, including Wimbledon, East Croydon, Mottingham and Morden South, the last opening as recently as 1954; however, not all were served by SR services, some being supplied by GWR/WR tanks that had travelled up their own main line from Penzance and thence over the West London Line to Clapham Junction.

With the ASLEF locomen's strike of May/June 1955, some users were forced to switch to road transport and found this to be a perfectly satisfactory alternative. By 1960 the road/rail traffic was also failing, and all the mobile tank trucks were condemned in June 1961, having seen little or no use over the preceding 12 months. Withdrawal of the fixed tanks soon gained momentum, while the rationalisation by the Western Region of the ex-SR Salisbury-Exeter route in September 1964 saw all milk traffic concentrated on the WR main line. By now ex-GWR, ex-SR and BR tanks were being mixed indiscriminately, and in January 1970 the remaining tank wagons were all transferred from passenger-van to goods stock, this reclassification affecting

Plate 226 Baggage truck No 4207 at Stewarts Lane during the 1950s, loaded with four SNCF boxes. The British Railways operating code of CTO (carriage truck — open) is just visible at the far end, below the tare-weight inscription.
The Lens of Sutton Collection

40 ex-SR tanks (4404-9/19-24/7-37/9-42/51/5-66) which were still extant at that time. While some of these remained with Express Dairy, others were now serving Unigate Creameries and still others St Ivel, the last-named employing a rather eye-catching livery — of orange and white with blue company logo — which contrasted with the dirty grey finish that identified the other two companies.

Milk traffic finally ceased in 1980, by which time just a handful of ex-SR tanks remained. Some of these were stored at Swindon for a time, as there were hopes of a revival of milk traffic. A few became departmental water tanks (some as early as 1960), while Nos 4409/30 have been preserved. The split ownership remained to the end, as the tank of No 4430 was donated to the Bluebell Railway by St Ivel, yet the underframe had to be purchased from British Rail.

Carriage trucks and scenery vans

The next type of vehicle to be considered is the true carriage truck (as opposed to the 'Covcar'), which was a combined luggage van/covered carriage truck. In fact, the Southern built no vehicle that it described purely as a carriage truck, of either the open or covered variety. The scenery vans, although technically covered carriage trucks, were always classified as being for scenery traffic and described as such.

As far as open carriage trucks were concerned, their duties were already declining in 1923, and that year's total stock of 350-plus vehicles was to dwindle to below 30 by 1937. A dozen of these were ex-SECR six-wheeled baggage box trucks used on Continental boat-train services, and these alone survived into World War 2, when the changed circumstances of war rendered them redundant. Alternative departmental duties were found for them, and none remained serviceable by 1946, when boat-train services were resumed. The Southern resorted to the simple expedient of using goods-stock 'Conflat D' wagons to Diagram 1383, but in April 1950 it was considered necessary to dedicate just two of these wagons to the 'Golden Arrow' service. Goods wagons Nos 39582 and 39614 were duly transferred to the passenger-van stock list and renumbered 4207/8, following on from ex-SECR aeroplane trucks; they were also repainted in passenger-stock crimson lake (notwithstanding the fact that this involved only the side rails), changed to green from June 1956 — until February 1961, when the use of baggage boxes ceased and the vehicles resumed their former goods-stock numbers and livery. **Plate 226** shows one in 'Golden Arrow' service. Diagram 1106 was allocated. A drawing appears as Figure 22 in *An Illustrated History of Southern Wagons, Volume 4* (OPC, 2002).

Turning now to covered carriage trucks, most pre-Grouping examples featured a high-pitched roof, and this, plus the large end doors, made them suitable for carrying (amongst other bulky items) theatrical scenery. In the 1920s and '30s there were many travelling repertory companies that would tour the country visiting provincial theatres, and many made use of the railway to transport themselves and their props. Such traffic was thus not to be ignored, and the Southern Railway ordered three batches, each of 10 such vehicles, to cater for it. The vans might be seen singly,

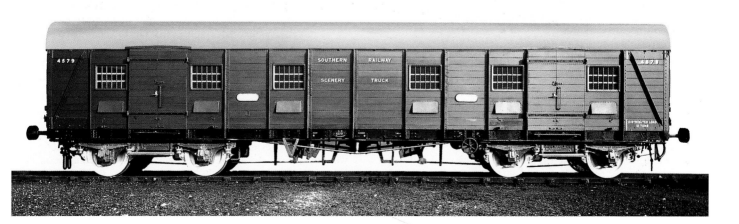

Plate 227 Scenery truck No 4579 as outshopped at Eastleigh in December 1928. This retains LBSCR bogies and Westinghouse brakes, which may have been a reason to utilise reconditioned LBSCR underframes. Within 10 years ex-LSWR bogies had been fitted and the Westinghouse equipment stripped out. The lettering style was peculiar to the original 10 vans. *Southern Railway*

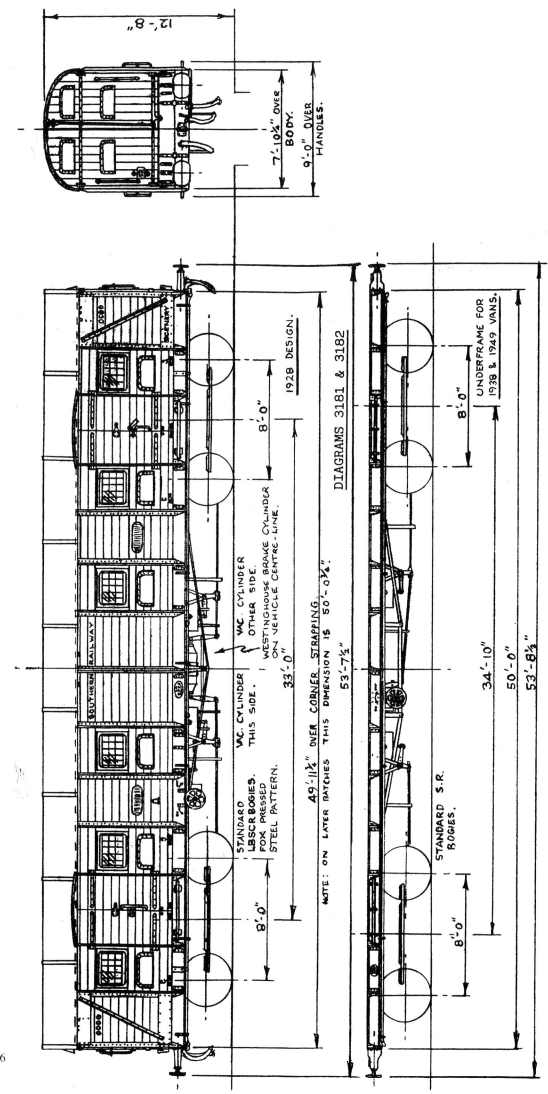

Figure 75 Both versions of the scenery van, to Diagrams 3181 and 3182.

Plate 228 Later van No 4587 at Clapham Junction in July 1947, with the more usual lettering layout. *D. Cullum*

added to the rear of a passenger train, or run as a complete train of vehicles for the theatre company, with passenger accommodation included for the players. Any station with a theatre nearby might be host to the vans, including locations as diverse as Brighton, Chichester, Farnham, Leatherhead, Ilfracombe and Victoria. The original 10 were ordered as early as May 1925 (HOO 103 — the SR's first order for passenger-van stock) but because of more urgent work were not completed until 1928/9. By this time the order had been amended to utilise recovered LBSCR coach underframes, possibly releasing any already-completed new frames for use under eight ex-LBSCR passenger carriages, described at the start of Chapter 7. The bodywork, however, was new, in typical utility-van style, as seen in **Plate 227**.

During the 1930s a new traffic presented itself for these vans — elephants. Several travelling circuses were then touring the country and required a van with large doors and good headroom for the animals, the scenery vans being ideal. Over the years Nos 4584/98 and 4601 were equipped with steel floor plates, tethering rings and stronger springs to cater for the additional weight. This traffic was not without incident, especially when 5 tons of elephant became temperamental! Bertram Mills Circus was the last user, continuing to tour the country from its base at Ascot West until 1965. By this time the vans were all in Southern Region green livery and were coded either CCT or GUV (General Utility Van), although most still carried the word 'Scenery' in SR transfers on an otherwise BR paint finish.

The original 1928 scenery vans were withdrawn between 1958 and 1962, but most of the later vehicles continued to run until 1976-81, several acquiring Rail-blue livery. Van 4601 was the final survivor in ordinary traffic, lasting until March 1981. However, all scenery traffic had ceased by the early 1970s, after which the vans were used for the carriage of ordinary parcels and might be seen anywhere in the country. Most later entered departmental service, and at least six have been purchased for preservation.

Rather surprisingly — and, indeed, very late in the development of the utility-van family — there came just one more covered carriage truck. In September 1960 Eastleigh Works mounted the body of Gangwayed Bogie Luggage Van 2291 onto the underframe of former Maunsell Hastings-line coach 6897, to produce motor-car van No 4501. Almost certainly an experiment, this made use of an underframe which had seen only 26 years' service and a body only four years older. End doors were provided, as well as a short piece of bodywork acting as a spacer at one end. Four sets of wheelbars were carried, allowing up to four small cars to be loaded. Uniquely for a Southern van, buckeye couplings and retractable buffers were retained. Diagram 3183 was allocated, and this one-off vehicle is illustrated in **Plate 229** and **Figure 76**. At the time there was a regular traffic in Volkswagen vans between Ramsgate and Sidmouth, for Devon Conversions Ltd to rebuild into caravanettes, and the van was tried on this service. However, by 1964 it was regarded as just another CCT and, being non-standard, was condemned in March 1966 after a working life of less than six years.

Post Office vans

Built to the requirements of the Royal Mail, all Post Office vans exhibit certain similarities, regardless of the company of origin, their most distinctive feature being the offset British standard gangways. The Southern had just eight examples, constructed between 1936 and 1939, partly to replace and partly to augment the inherited stock of LSWR and SECR Post Office vans used on overnight mail trains from Waterloo to Bournemouth, Waterloo to Dorchester, Holborn Viaduct to Newhaven Harbour and London Bridge to Dover. However, they did not entirely replace the pre-Grouping vehicles: this did not happen until 1960, when the Southern Region received some ex-GWR and ex-LMS vans.

Two basic types of vehicle were involved — a sorting van with pigeonholes along one side (that farthest away from the gangways), used by GPO staff to sort the mail *en route*, and stowage vans which were open from end to end (save for a staff locker), used for storage of mailbags until they could be sorted in the adjacent sorting van. All eight vehicles conformed to Maunsell's usual Restriction 4 profile and dimensions, despite the fact that all bar one were completed after his retirement. They did, however, have flat ends, screw couplings and non-retractable buffers to suit the British standard gangways; the later sorting vans (but not the original 1936 vehicle) also included a staff lavatory. None of the SR vehicles had nets for picking up and setting down mailbags on the move. British Railways operating codes were POS (for the sorting vans) and POT (for the stowage vans).

The first vehicle, sorting van No 4919, was completed in December 1936 for the Waterloo-Dorchester run, replacing an obsolete LSWR vehicle. The GPO contributed £575 towards its construction, possibly to ensure that it had greater input into the design process. On the corridor side the vehicle had two sliding

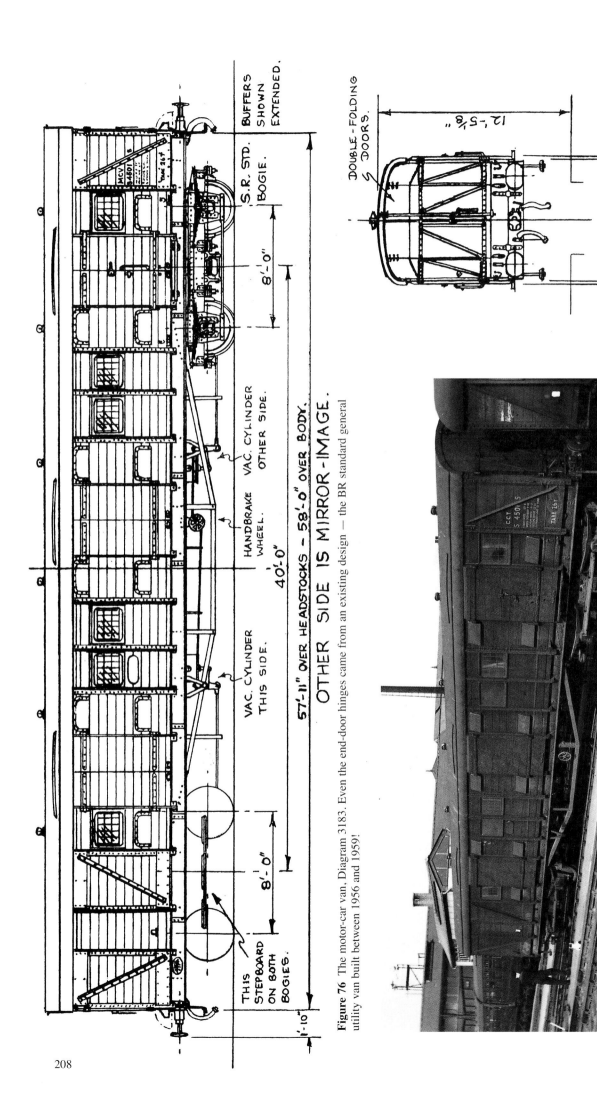

Figure 76 The motor-car van, Diagram 3183. Even the end-door hinges came from an existing design — the BR standard general utility van built between 1956 and 1959!

Plate 229 Unique motor-car van No 4501, already reclassified CCT, at Clapham Junction in May 1961. The new section of bodywork is at the far end. *D. Cullum*

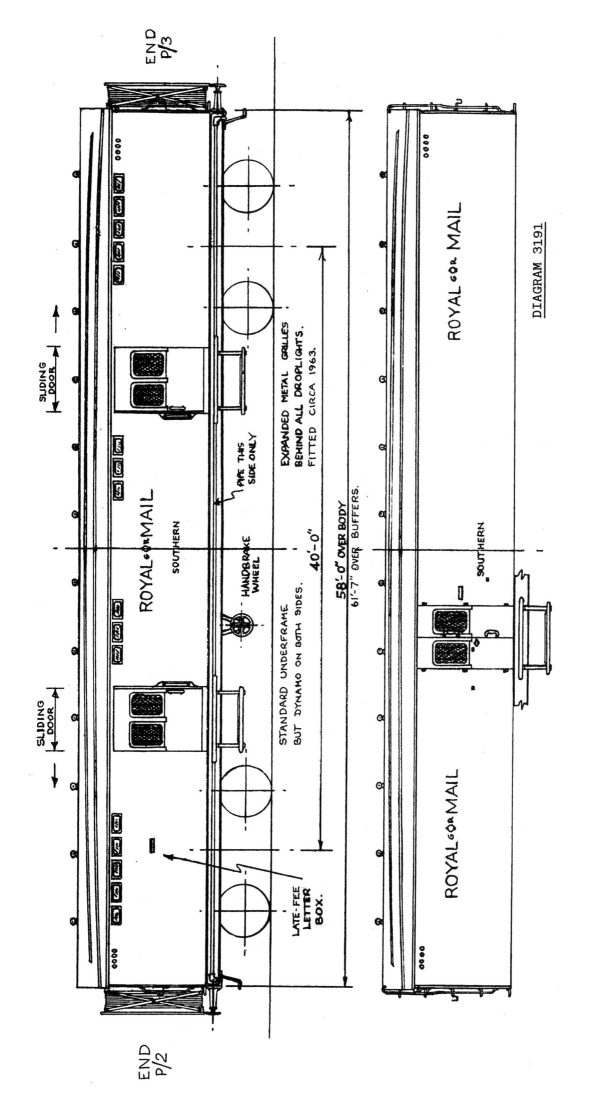

Figure 77 Diagram 3191 sorting van. For end views see **Figure 78**.

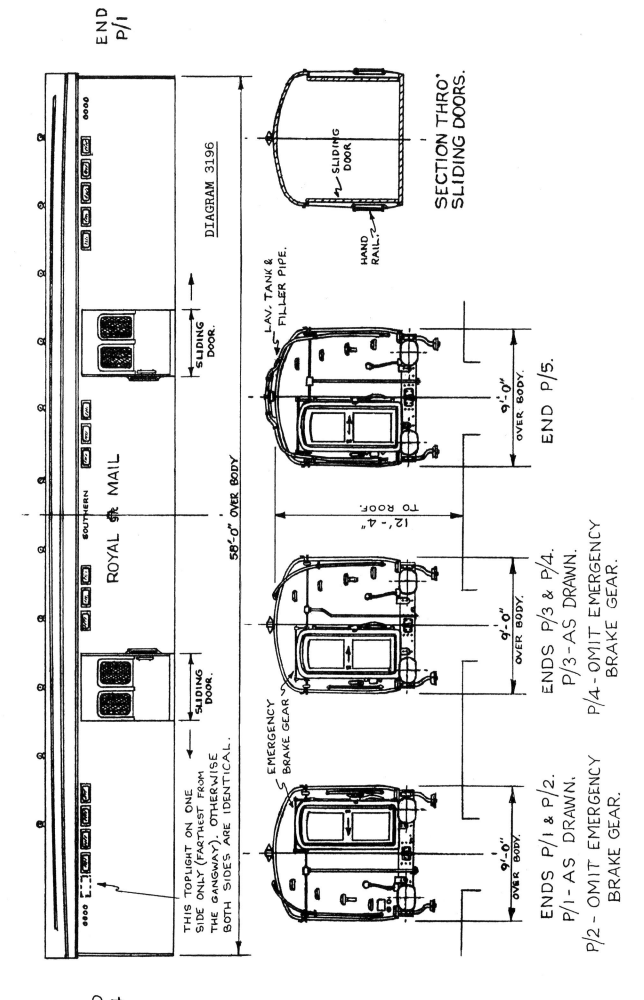

Figure 78 Diagram 3196 stowage van, plus end views for all three vehicles.

Plate 230 The 1936 sorting van, No 4919, at Clapham Junction (where else to see SR vans?) in September 1960, showing the non-corridor side and wearing Southern Region green livery. None of these GPO vans appears to have carried either crimson lake or Post Office red while on the Southern Region. Just visible to the right is a lavatory-fitted sorting van to Diagram 3192. *J. H. Aston*

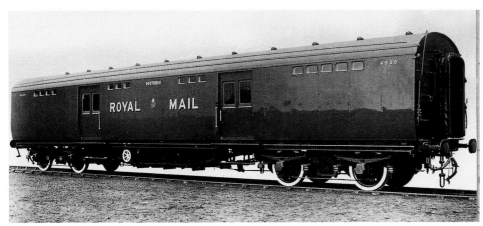

Plate 231 Stowage van No 4959, as completed in 1939 and probably finished in varnished malachite green. This shows the non-corridor side; the position of the staff locker is indicated by the four (as opposed to five) toplights at the far end. *Southern Railway*

doors and a row of toplights only; on the non-corridor side there was just a pair of ordinary double doors for entry into the van, as seen in **Plate 230**. Diagram 3191 was allocated and details may be found in **Figure 77**. Alone of the Maunsell GPO vans, No 4919 entered service bearing the insignia of King Edward VIII, all the later ones carrying that of King George VI.

To run with the sorting vans, four stowage vans were completed in early 1939 at Eastleigh on frames from Lancing. Diagram 3196 and running numbers 4957-60 were allocated, these being the highest numbers allocated to any Southern passenger van. **Figure 78** and **Plate 231** give details. The sides of these were almost identical, being very similar to the corridor side of the sorting vans; indeed, from this side it would be almost impossible to tell the vehicles apart. Only three stowage vans were needed for the Dorchester run, so van 4957 was used between London Bridge and Dover. The service between Waterloo and Dorchester usually comprised two sorting vans and a stowage van in each direction, plus other parcels vans and one or two passenger coaches.

In June/July 1939 three more sorting vans were built, these being Nos 4920-2, to Diagram 3192. They were very similar to van 4919 but included a lavatory, the position of which could be identified by a frosted window on the non-corridor side. As a result, the double doors on this side were about 2ft closer to the centre-line of the vehicle. Their completion allowed the withdrawal of several older LSWR vehicles, although, with no spares available, at least three LSWR vans were retained to cover overhauls and other maintenance requirements. **Figure 79** and **Plate 232** illustrate these last GPO vans.

All the sorting vans included a late-fee letterbox, where members of the public could post a letter provided it carried (in 1939) an extra halfpenny stamp. In the 1970s this surcharge stood at one new penny.

The duties of these vans varied little over the years. The Dorchester service left Waterloo at 10.30pm each night, with the return working starting from Dorchester at 9.55pm, both trains running into and out of Southampton Terminus. On the South Eastern, the Dover mail ran (via East Croydon and Redhill) at 11.50pm (down) and 10.40pm (up). Rather surprisingly, van 4957 was usually kept in reserve as the spare vehicle, the ex-SECR vans being preferred whenever possible. War brought the suspension of the Dover run and removal of the sorting vans from the Dorchester service, the displaced vehicles being appropriated for storage and distribution of ARP equipment, for which their pigeonholes proved ideal.

All vans returned to Post Office use after the war, resuming their former allocations. In 1960 Weymouth was substituted for Dorchester, to replace a withdrawn Western Region service to/from Paddington, while the closure of Southampton Terminus in 1965 resulted in the direct route being taken; minor alterations to departure times were also made. Van 4957 was released from the Dover run in 1960, when the Southern Region received several electrically-heated ex-GWR vans, and this vehicle was reallocated in April 1962 to the London Midland Region (where it would serve for a further 10 years), as seen in **Plate 233**.

The Great Train Robbery of 8 August 1963 resulted in greater emphasis being placed on security, and all vans were modified at Swindon Works during May/June 1964. Van 4919 received two 'humps' in the roof (one at each end), which are believed to have housed radio transmitters and receivers. All lavatory windows were sheeted over and other security measures taken. With the Bournemouth-line electrification, electric heating was provided in 1967, at which time all seven remaining SR-allocated vans received Rail blue and grey; apart from two Ambulance cars (described in Chapter 14) they were the only Southern locomotive-hauled vehicles to carry this livery.

Van 4919 was withdrawn in July 1973, but Nos 4920-2/58-60 remained on the Waterloo-Weymouth service until 1974, when they were replaced by converted British Railways Mk 1 stock. This was not quite the end, however, as the former London Bridge-Dover service, now running into Victoria, still required one sorting and one stowage van to make a circuit each night, so these six elderly vehicles provided the service until late 1976, as seen in **Plate 234**. Final withdrawal came in March 1977, three vans surviving into preservation.

Table 17 lists all vehicles described within this chapter.

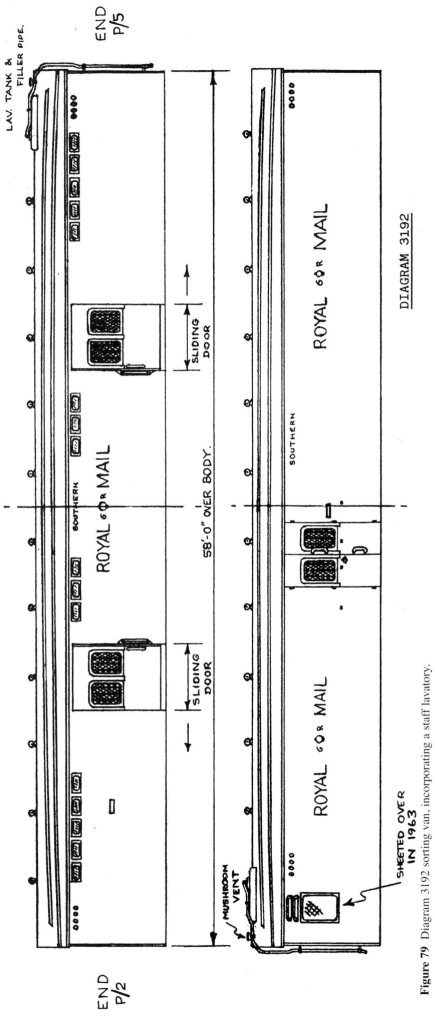

Figure 79 Diagram 3192 sorting van, incorporating a staff lavatory.

Plate 232 The 1939 sorting vans are represented by No 4922 in unvarnished green, presumably malachite. This shows the corridor side and the late-fee letterbox with surrounding Post Office-red panel. *Southern Railway*

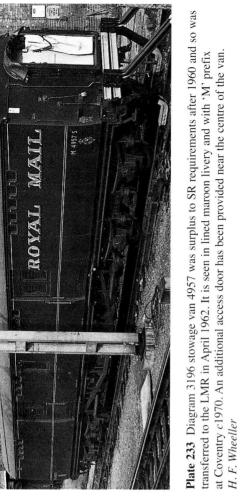

Plate 233 Diagram 3196 stowage van 4957 was surplus to SR requirements after 1960 and so was transferred to the LMR in April 1962. It is seen in lined maroon livery and with 'M' prefix at Coventry c1970. An additional access door has been provided near the centre of the van. *H. F. Wheeller*

Plate 234 Sorting van 4920, together with stowage van 4960 (at the right), seen on the Dover mail train at Ashford on 5 June 1975 — the most recent photograph in the book. Electric-heating connections are visible below the buffers, while the lavatory window has been sheeted over. Livery is Rail blue and grey, with full blue ends. *D. Gould*

Table 17
Summary of SR livestock vans, milk tanks, carriage trucks, scenery vans and Post Office vans

Diagram No	Vehicle type	Classification (SR/BR)	Running Nos	Built by	Remarks
3141 (orig 3251)	12-ton special cattle van (8 tons capacity)	CATOX/SCV	3679-3728 3729-38	BRCW 6-7/30 Lancing 9-10/52	Oil lighting Electric lighting
3151	Four-wheel mobile milk-tank carriage truck for CWS trailers	Truck Type 1	4401-3	Lancing 9/31	Proposed for re-framing in 1936
3152	Four-wheel fixed milk-tank wagon for United Dairies tanks	Tank Type 1	4404-9	Lancing 10-11/31	Glass-lined tanks; to Diagram 3159 in 1937/8
3153	Six-wheel fixed milk-tank wagon for Express Dairy APV tanks	Tank Type 2	4410-3	Lancing 5-6/32	Anchor-mounted aluminium tanks
3154	Six-wheel mobile milk-tank carriage truck for United Dairies trailers	Truck Type 2	4414-8 4425/6	Lancing 6/32, 8/32 Lancing 2/33	Detail differences between batches
3155	Six-wheel fixed milk-tank wagon for United Dairies tanks	Tank Type 3	4419-24	Lancing 10/32	Glass-lined tanks
3156	Six-wheel fixed milk-tank wagon for Express Dairy tanks	Tank Type 4	4427/8	Lancing 5/33	Stainless-steel tanks
3157	Six-wheel fixed milk-tank wagon for United Dairies tanks	Tank Type 5	4429-32 4455-66	Lancing 9/33 Lancing/Eastleigh 1943/4*	Glass-lined tanks Built to MWT order
3158	Six-wheel fixed milk-tank wagon for West Park / Express Dairy tanks	Tank Type 6	4433/4	Ashford 4/35	Glass-lined tanks
3159	Six-wheel fixed milk-tank wagon for United Dairies tanks	Tank Type 1 (converted)	4404-9	Re-framed at Ashford 8/37-4/38	Glass-lined tanks Ex-Diagram 3152
3160	Six-wheel mobile milk-tank carriage truck for CWS trailers	Truck Type 1 (converted)	4401-3	(Order cancelled 8/37 — built by GWR)	Ex-Diagram 3151; design was prepared
3161	Six-wheel fixed milk-tank wagon for Express Dairy tanks	Tank Type 7	4435-8 4439-42 4443-54	Ashford 12/37-3/38 Ashford 1942 Eastleigh 1943/4*	Stainless-steel tanks Built to MWT order Built to MWT order
1106	14-ton baggage box truck (ex-'Conflat D')	CTO	4207/8	Ashford 1933	Ex-goods stock from 4/50 until 2/61
3181 (orig 3102)	22-ton covered scenery truck	Scenery/CCT	4577-86	Eastleigh 11/28-1/29	On ex-LBSCR underframes
3182	24-ton scenery van 25-ton scenery van	Scenery/CCT or GUV	4587-96 4597-4606	Ashford/Eastleigh 10-11/38 Lancing c12/49	Detail differences between batches
3183	26-ton motor-car van	MCV or CCT	4501	Rebuilt Eastleigh 9/60	GBL body on Maunsell coach underframe
3191	Post Office sorting van	POS	4919	Eastleigh 12/36	No lavatory provided
3192	Post Office sorting van	POS	4920-2	Eastleigh 6-7/39	Lavatory provided
3196	Post Office stowage van	POT	4957-60	Lancing/Eastleigh 2-3/39	No 4957 transferred to LMR 4/62

* Ministry of War Transport orders, taken into British Railways stock January 1952

Notes
Tare weights of milk-tank wagons and trucks varied between 10 and 14 tons, distributed load 14 tons.
Distributed load for all scenery vans was 10 tons; that for the motor-car van was 12 tons.
All vehicles were to Route Restriction 0 except Diagrams 3183, 3191, 3192 and 3196, which were Route Restriction 4.

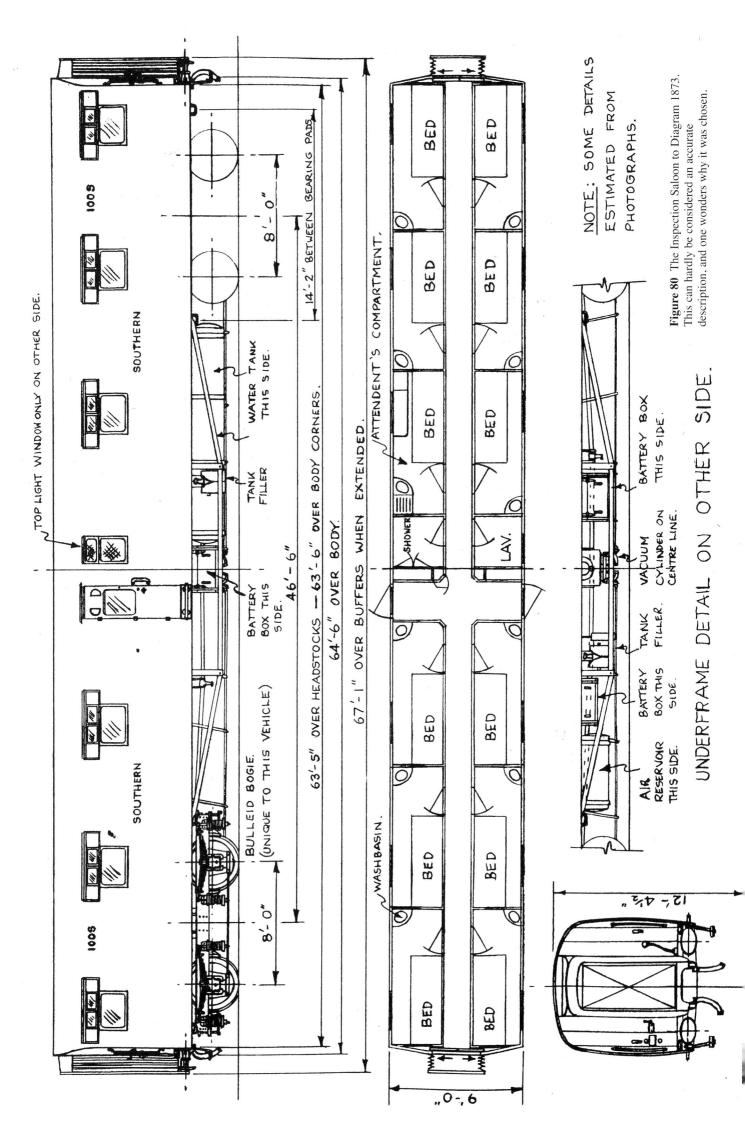

Figure 80 The Inspection Saloon to Diagram 1873. This can hardly be considered an accurate description, and one wonders why it was chosen.

Chapter 14.
Inspection Saloons and Ambulance Cars

In this chapter we shall look briefly at four types of special vehicle used mostly by the railway's own staff and not the general public, and thus numbered in the departmental stock list rather than in the general series. The exceptions were the four Ambulance Ward cars, which were intended for Lourdes pilgrimage traffic and were numbered as general saloons.

In Chapter 4 it was noted that 'Thanet' Composite No 5537 was damaged by fire at Swanley in March 1938. Its underframe was salvageable, and in the same month Order E1020 was authorised for its conversion into a cinema coach capable of seating 60 persons, for staff instruction use. It was divided into a small projecting room at one end, accessible by a single door, and a large auditorium with 15 bench seats (each taking four persons) and a screen across the end of the coach; access to the auditorium was by pairs of double doors on each side. Numbered 1308s, the vehicle was ready in November 1939, together with a generator van, No 1309s, converted from a former LSWR 24ft passenger luggage van. **Plate 235** shows them when new, probably in malachite. When first converted, the two vehicles were used mainly for screening wartime instructional films (notably on air-raid precautions), and they doubtless travelled widely around the system during this period. They had long lives in this form, both being repainted in blue and white (not quite Rail blue and grey) early in 1964 and continuing to tour the Southern Region until c1973. The generator van, by then numbered DS1309, was later purchased by the Bluebell Railway.

Plate 235 Cinema coach 1308s, together with generator van 1309s, at Nine Elms in August 1940. Livery is presumably malachite green, with the company title having Bulleid's green 'in-line' (compare with the black-shaded words 'CINEMA COACH'). The screen was placed across the right-hand end of the coach. *Southern Railway*

Plate 236 Bulleid Inspection Saloon 100s in malachite green, seen c1950 inside one of the former LCDR buildings at Longhedge (Stewarts Lane), with generator van 97s visible behind. Part of the radial-bearing-pad assembly is just discernible below the buffers at this end. *The Lens of Sutton Collection*

In April 1946 Bulleid was given authority to construct one saloon for inspection purposes, under Order L3359. Construction proceeded rapidly, giving yet another opportunity for Bulleid to design something different. Numbered 100s, the vehicle was actually a sleeping car, having 11 beds placed longitudinally in individual compartments served by a central corridor, plus an attendant's compartment, a lavatory and a shower room. Each compartment was equipped with a washbasin and a trouser-press, to ensure that the staff were always immaculately presented! However, although produced to standard Bulleid dimensions and profile — 64ft 6in by 9ft 0in over body — that was where any similarity with his other coaches ceased.

Body construction was entirely of plywood. This had been used extensively by the Southern during World War 2 (mostly for non-railway orders), and the new coach clearly provided the opportunity for an extension of these techniques; Bulleid was interested in promoting this form of construction and would use it again for carriages during his days at Inchicore. The coach was constructed somewhat in the form of an inverted ship's hull, the keep plate or ridge rail running along the centre of the roof, above the corridor, rather like a keel. To this rail and to the underframe were bolted pre-formed bodyside sections 9ft 5in wide (corresponding to the width of each sleeping compartment), of ⁹⁄₁₆in-thick nine-ply birch that was resin-bonded to the saloon framework, which was constructed of similar material. The ply itself was supplied by the SARO Plywood Co Ltd and was prepared on the Isle of Wight. Similar pre-formed sections were used for body ends and floors; to ensure that the joints were waterproof, these were covered with self-adhesive tape before final finishing and painting.

The underframe itself was a standard 63ft 5in product — indeed, judging from the date of construction it was amongst the earliest completed to this length and was probably the first to have the centrally mounted Prestall 30in vacuum cylinder. The bogies, however, were unique to this vehicle, each having two radial bearing pads, about 4ft 6in long, set 14ft 2in apart, at either end of the bogies, instead of the more usual central spherical bolsters. These pads were sprung, effectively acting like small transverse bolsters. The bogie was thus very restricted in its vertical movement, so each bottom radial pad was attached to the bogie via a coil-sprung subframe, resulting in a very smooth ride. Additional lubrication was given by an oil bath (yes, Bulleid managed to incorporate this on a coach too!), although this was provided rather more simply, by including a 2in-high lip around the bottom radial pad, which was filled with oil; within this was placed a phosphor bronze bearing plate, both fittings ensuring that there would be no sluggishness in the rotation of the bogie when entering a curve. **Plate 236** and **Figure 80** illustrate this most unusual coach.

On the relatively few occasions when the coach was given a fast demonstration run, all went well and those present were most impressed by the ride. However, the reliability of the design was never tested under general service conditions, so on ordinary stock Bulleid was probably wise to stick to the tried-and-trusted Maunsell/Lynes standard bogie.

While Bulleid remained CME the vehicle saw a reasonable degree of use, often running in a special train, along with generator van 97s (converted from ex-SECR utility van 1987), Maunsell Dining Firsts Nos 98s and 99s (ex-Diagram 2651 vehicles 7940/3) and unclassed Saloon Brake No 4444, the latter renumbered as departmental coach 444s for the purpose. By mid-1951 only the generator van and 99s remained in the set, which was usually stabled at Stewarts Lane when not required. It was officially condemned in December 1953, but could still be seen at Lancing as late as June 1955, by then painted all-over dark grey and clearly not in use. The record card gives the last repair date as August 1954 and final dismantling as taking place during 1956. Also of interest is that the card is rather misleading about the actual date of completion, both July and November 1946 being quoted; if the former is correct, then the coach must have been built almost before authority was granted for its construction — perhaps explaining why the CME's staff sometimes denied its existence!

The only coaches described in this chapter to be used by members of the public were the four Ambulance Ward cars, Nos 7920-3. Converted in April/May 1959 from unclassed open-saloon Brakes, under Order L4559 dated November 1958, they were allocated Diagram 2699 in the general-saloon series. They retained the lavatory and first two bays of seats at the non-brake end of the coach, but the remainder of the passenger saloon was converted into an ambulance ward, having three tiers of bunks down each side, giving accommodation for 11 seated passengers and 24 more severely disabled travellers in cots. The guard's compartment was converted into a kitchen area. Intended for Lourdes pilgrimage traffic between Victoria and Dover, all four were stabled at Stewarts Lane depot when not in use. They were painted in standard Southern Region green livery, as seen in **Plate 237**. Nos 7921/2 were withdrawn in 1968, but Nos 7920/3 were repainted in Rail blue and grey — the only Maunsell passenger vehicles to ever carry this livery — and retained in occasional use until 1973/4. Both were then used in departmental service until sold into preservation in the late 1970s, although No 7920 has since been broken up.

Plate 237 Ambulance car No 7920 standing in Victoria station in April 1959. The kitchen occupies the former brake-van section, while only the two bays of seats farthest from the camera remain unaltered from the original saloon configuration. *British Railways Southern Region*

Plate 238 Engineer's Inspection Saloon DS70155 in Southern Region green livery at Weymouth loco shed in July 1966, during an inspection tour. Motive power was provided by BR Standard Class 4 4-6-0 No 75075. The train made a very hurried and unscheduled stop at Surbiton on the return journey, to allow two members of staff to be quite literally thrown out! *J. Scrace*

For most of the Southern Railway/Region period, two Inspection Saloons were available for staff use — Nos 1s and 291s. The former was an extremely ancient LSWR vehicle; the latter came from the LBSCR but was to Route Restriction 1 and so could not traverse the Tonbridge-Hastings line. In August 1961 Order L5045 was issued for conversion of Hastings-line Corridor Composite No 5600 into an Inspection Saloon to replace DS1 (as No 1s had become). The order was later transferred to Eastleigh, whence coach 5600 emerged, suitably transformed into Inspection Saloon DS70155, in November 1962. Described on Diagram 1958 as an Engineer's Inspection Saloon, this took over the duties formerly carried out by DS1, including route-learning training for drivers. It included an 18-seat saloon at one end and a nine-seat saloon at the other, with a lavatory, kitchen and brake compartment served by a side corridor in the centre. The vehicle was therefore a self-contained train in itself and usually ran just with a locomotive — sometimes being propelled — for official inspections. It is illustrated in **Plate 238** on one such trip. Repainted in Rail blue with full yellow ends, it remained in stock until 1990, by which time it was one of the last Maunsell coaches to serve in the Southern Region departmental fleet; it was then sold to a group of enthusiasts on the Kent & East Sussex Railway.

Table 18
Summary of SR Inspection Saloons and Ambulance Ward cars

Diagram No	Vehicle type	Route Restriction	Running No(s)	Built by	Remarks
1873	Inspection Saloon	4	100s	Lancing 7/46 or 11/46	Plywood body
1911	Cinema Coach	1	1308s	Rebuilt Eastleigh 11/39	Ex-Composite 5537
1958	Engineer's Inspection Saloon	0	DS70155	Rebuilt Eastleigh 11/62	Ex-Composite 5600
2699	Ambulance Ward car	1	7920-3	Rebuilt Eastleigh 4-5/59	Ex-Saloon Brakes 4438/44/5/9

Appendix 1
Orders for Southern Railway passenger rolling stock (excluding electric stock)

HOO No Remarks	Date Completed authorised	Details#	Running Nos	by*	Page ref
E4	7/6/23	41 x CK	5505-45	'Thanet' stock	5/25	49-51, 54
E5	"	18 x TK	977-94	'Thanet' stock	5/25	49-51, 53
E6	"	18 x BTK	3562-77	'Thanet' stock	5/25	49-52
(None)	/10/23	41 x Dover boat-train vehicles (12 x BTK, 12 x SK, 8 x FK, 9 x BFK)	3548-59, 4168-79, 7376-83, 7748-56	'Continental' stock; built by Metropolitan and BRCW	8/24	30-38
E16	30/4/24	6 x Dining cars	7852-57	'Ironclad' stock	7/25	40, 44, 48
E17	"	4 x FK	7202-5	'Ironclad' stock	9/25	42, 44, 48
E18	"	7 x FK	7652-8	'Ironclad' stock	12/25	42, 45, 48
E19	"	1 x CK	6287	'Ironclad' stock	5/25	45, 48
E20	"	5 x BCK	6560-4	'Ironclad' stock	10/25	43, 44, 48
E21	"	8 x TK	755-62	'Ironclad' stock	9/25	42, 44, 48
L22	"	1 x TK	2341	'Ironclad' stock	12/25	45, 48
E23	"	8 x BTK	3203-10	'Ironclad' stock	9/25	41, 44, 48
E24	17/10/24	5 x BTK	3211-3, 4052/3	'Ironclad' stock	10/25	43, 44, 48
L24	"	2 x BTK	4043/4	'Ironclad' stock	10/25	45, 48

(Note: From this point on, most orders were subdivided into individual vehicle types — A, B, C etc)

HOO No Remarks	Date Completed	Details#	Running Nos		by*	Page ref
E85	22/4/25	11-coach set 472	4046/7 2346-8, 7659-64	'Ironclad' stock (Order E85A, B, etc)	1/26	45, 48
E94	13/5/25	10 x three-coach sets (390-9)	3214-33, 5137-46	See Orders L113 and E336	11/26	56-59, 68
E95	6/8/25	1 x eight-coach set (470)	4050/1, 2354/5, 7671-4		12/26	56, 59, 68
E96	"	1 x eight-coach set (469)	4048/9, 2349-51, 7665-7		2/27	56, 59, 68
A97	"	11-coach set (unnumbered)	4481/2, 2352/3, 4483-6, 7668-70	Newhaven boat stock, including Second class	5/27	56, 59, 68
E98	6/8/25	6 x Dining cars	7858-63	With kitchen	7/27	56, 63, 68
E99	"	6 x Diner Thirds	7864-9	Without kitchen	5/27	56, 63, 68
E100	"	1 x 10-coach set (unnumbered)	7715/6, 7208-15	Southampton boat stock, First-class	6/28	56, 60, 68
E101	6/8/25	10 x BCK	6565-74		9/26	56, 59, 68
E102	"	10 x General Saloons (8ft 6in wide)	7974-83	Underframes ex-Midland RCW	1/28	56, 68, 89
E103	11/5/25	10 x scenery vans (deferred until 1928)	4577-86	On ex-LBSCR underframes	1/29	205-7, 213
A104	11/5/25	20 (later amended to 50) x GUV (General utility vans)	2023-72	Midland RCW; see Orders E279 and E292	5/28	183-5, 194
L113	13/5/25	10 x BTK		Part of Order E94	(cancelled)	56-59, 68
E160	5/11/26	2 x eight-coach sets (467/8)	4063-6,765-8,5151-8	8ft 6in wide	11/28	64, 66-68
E162	"	10 x Dover boat vehicles (4 x TK, 6 x FK)	779-82, 7384-9	'Continental' stock, ex-Metropolitan/BRCW	10/27	31, 33-37
E163	5/11/26	10 x General Saloons (8ft 6in wide)	7984-93	Possibly built by Midland RCW	2/28	64-68, 89
E208	20/9/26	Enlarge pantry in 4 x Pantry Thirds	713-6	'Ironclad' stock	5/28	39, 46, 48
E241	26/2/27	10 x TK	769-78	Southampton boat stock	8/27	64, 65, 68
E242	"	12 x FK	7216-27	Southampton boat stock	11/27	64, 65, 68
E250	"	4 x three-coach sets (445-8)	4055-62, 5147-50	Possibly built by Metropolitan	9/28	64, 65, 68
E268	29/7/27	50 x TK	783-832	Underframes (at least) ex-Metropolitan/BRCW	7/28	64, 65, 68
L277	2/9/27	30 x GUV	2251-80	Bodies (at least) built Ashford	7/29	183-5, 194
E279	18/8/27	Recondition 50 second-hand 18in vacuum cylinders		For vans 2023-72 (see Order A104)	9/27	183-5, 194
E286	22/12/27	2 x eight-coach sets (465/6)	7390-7, 833-6, 4079-82	8ft 6in wide	4/29	64, 67, 68
E288	"	6 x four-coach sets (449-54)	4067-78, 5159-70	8ft 6in wide	1/29	64, 67, 68
E292	25/1/28	Complete 50 x GUV (ex-Midland RCW Co)	2023-72	See Orders A104 and E279	5/28	183-5, 194

HOO No	Date authorised	Details#	Running Nos	Remarks	Completed by*	Page ref
E336	2/6/28	Remove intermediate buffers on 10 x three-coach sets (Order E94)		Sets 390-9	11/28	56-59, 68
E340	4/6/28	Equip 20 (possibly 50) GUV with fruit trays		Nos 2023-72	7/28	183-5, 194
E354	13/7/28	50 x passenger luggage vans on existing underframes		Replaced by Order A443 (with gangways)	Cancelled	191-3
E361	9/8/28	1 x six-coach set (456) + 1 x three-coach set (387)	7398/9, 5171/2, 837, 4083-6		12/29	69, 92
E362	9/8/28	4 x four-coach sets (181-4)	5173-7, 5582-4, 4087-94	8ft 6in wide	11/29	69, 92
E363	"	1 x nine-coach train	7939, 5585/6, 6575/6, 838/9, 3664/5	Included in set 458; for through services	7/29	69, 70, 92
E364	9/8/28	1 x 10-coach train	7940, 5587-9, 840/1, 3666-9	Included in sets 427/59; for through services	7/29	69, 70, 92
E365	9/8/28	1 x 11-coach train	7941, 6577-80, 842-4, 4095-7	For through services	8/29	69, 70, 92
E366	"	1 x 11-coach train	7942, 5590/1, 6581-4, 1113/4, 3670/1	Included in set 428; for through services	12/29	69, 70, 92
E376	25/8/28	2 x eight-coach trains	7400-3, 5592-5, 3672-9	8ft 0¾in wide; included in sets 475-8	9/29	69-71, 92
E377	"	1 x eight-coach train	1115/6, 5596/7, 3680-3	8ft 0¾in wide; included in sets 479/80	10/29	69-71, 92
A443	29/3/28	50 x Bogie Luggage Vans on existing underframes	2281-2330	With gangways	10/30	191-4
E444	20/3/29	Equip 30 x GUV with fruit trays	2251-80		(not stated)	183-5, 194
E461	17/5/29	20 x Open Thirds	1369-88		12/30	71-73, 92
E462	"	50 x BCK	6585-6604/43-72		4/30	71, 74, 92
E463	"	20 x General Saloons	7781-7800	8ft 6in wide	7/31	71, 89, 92
E464	"	10 x Dining cars	7943-52	With kitchen	6/30	71, 93-102
A467	"	40 x Bogie Luggage Vans on existing underframes	2331-70	With gangways	6/31	191-4
A468	17/5/29	40 x GUV	2371-2410	U/frames possibly built at Lancing	6/31	183-5, 194
E476 (+ others)	27/5/29	Fit 360 vehicles with BS gangways with adaptors		First of several orders for this work	3/31	55
E487	4/7/29	1 x 10-coach train	3724-7/32, 1397, 7675, 5634, 7957, 6673	Included in sets 179, 202/7	9/30	73-83, 92
E488	4/7/29	1 x 12-coach train	3728-31/33, 1398-1400, 7676, 7958, 5635, 6674	Included in sets 180, 201/6	9/30	73-83, 92
E489	4/7/29	2 x 10-coach trains	7228-31, 7953/4, 1121-30, 3716-9	Included in sets 204/5	7/30	73-83, 92
E490	4/7/29	2 x 11-coach trains	7232, 7406-12, 7955/6, 1389-96, 3720-3	Included in sets 208/9	8/30	73-83, 92
E491	4/7/29	2 x eight-coach trains	5636-43, 3734-41	Included in sets 193/4/9, 200/3	7/30	73-83, 92
E492	"	2 x eight-coach trains	5644-51, 3742-9	Included in sets 195, 426/9/64	11/30	73-83, 92
E493	"	2 x eight-coach trains	5602-9, 3692-9	8ft 6in wide; included in sets 185-8	2/31	73, 84, 92
E494	"	2 x eight-coach sets (217/8)	5610-7, 2356-9, 3700-3	8ft 6in wide	2/31	73, 84, 92
E495	"	2 x eight-coach trains	5618-25, 3704-11	8ft 6in wide; included in sets 189-92	3/31	73, 84, 92
E496	"	2 x eight-coach sets (219/20)	5626-33, 2360-3, 3712-5	8ft 6in wide	4/31	73, 84, 92
E497	"	22 x General Saloons	7901-11/59-68/94	8ft 6in wide	5/31	73, 89, 92
E498	"	2 x nine-coach trains	7404/5/15/6, 5598-5601, 1117/8, 3684-91	included in sets 213-6	1/31	73, 85, 92
A/E502/3	20/7/29	Recondition 100 vacuum cylinders		For GBL vans	(by 3/29)	191-4
A529	9/11/29	20 x (later 50) special cattle vans (amended 26/3/30)	3679-3728	Built by BRCW	7/30	195-7, 213
A572	16/5/30	10 x scenery vans		Deferred to Order A975	Cancelled	205-7
A573	"	30 x Bogie Luggage Vans on existing underframes	2461-90	With gangways	9/31	191-4, 223
A574	16/5/30	50 x GUV	2411-60		2/32	183-5, 194
E633	14/4/31	20 x four-coach sets (221-40)	3750-8, 2754-71/93-2805, 5652-91	Some ran as three-coach sets	4/32	86, 87, 92
E634	14/4/31	1 x 10-coach train	3234-7, 7414/8, 5578/9, 1119/20	8ft 0¾in wide; formed as seven-coach set 939 and three-coach set 940	4/32	86, 87, 92
E635	14/4/31	10 x Dining cars	7864-71, 7931/2	With kitchen	7/32	86, 93-102
A636	"	20 x GUV	2241-50, 2491-2500	Underframes ex-Lancing	4/33	183-5, 194
L661	9/6/31	3 x four-wheel trucks for conveyance of CWS milk trailers	4401-3	Truck Type 1; Dyson trailers	9/31	197-8, 213
L673	31/7/31	6 x four-wheel underframes for United Dairies milk tanks	4404-9	Tank Type 1	11/31	197-201, 213
E686	17/11/31	25 x TK	1131-55		6/32	86, 87, 92
A687	"	25 x TK	1156-80	Built at Eastleigh	9/32	86, 87, 92
L697	15/2/32	4 x six-wheel underframes for Express Dairy APV milk tanks	4410-3	Tank Type 2	6/32	197-202, 213
L698	26/2/32	5 x six-wheel trucks for conveyance of United Dairies milk trailers	4414-8	Truck Type 2; Dyson trailers	8/32	197-200, 213

HOO No	Date authorised	Details#	Running Nos	Remarks	Completed by*	Page ref
E705	21/3/32	50 x TK	1181-1230		12/33	87, 88, 92
E706	"	50 x Open Thirds	1312-61		5/33	88, 92
E707	"	30 x BTK	3771-3800		9/33	87, 88, 92
E708	"	20 x General Saloons for boat traffic	4431-50	With brake compartment; 8ft 6in wide	7/33	88, 90-92
E709	21/3/32	10 (later 22) x TK (amended 21/12/32)	1019-40	8ft 03/4in wide; included in sets 476, 941-51	3/34	88, 91, 92
E710	21/3/32	24 x BTK (amended 21/12/32 to 24 x BCK)	6881-6904	8ft 03/4in wide; included in sets 476, 941-51	4/34	88, 91, 92
E711	21/3/32	12 x CK		Amended 21/12/32	Cancelled	88
E712	"	4 x FK	7419-22	8ft 03/4in wide; included in set 951	5/34	88, 91, 92
E713	21/3/32	10 x Dining cars	7878/80, 7933/4/69/95/7-8000	With kitchen	6/34	88, 93-102
L721	18/6/32	6 x six-wheel underframes for United Dairies milk tanks	4419-24	Tank Type 3	10/32	199-203, 213
L739	28/10/32	2 x six-wheel trucks for conveyance of United Dairies milk trailers	4425/6	Truck Type 2	2/33	197-200, 213
L747	3/1/33	2 x six-wheel underframes for Express Dairy milk tanks	4427/8	Tank Type 4	5/33	199-203, 213
E760	21/4/33	100 (later 90) x TK	1231-80, 1801-40	Amended 28/3/34; balance on Order E798	11/34	88, 92
E761	21/4/33	30 x Open Thirds	1282-1311		8/35	102-5, 116
A762	"	50 x PLV (Passenger luggage vans)	2181-2230	Without end doors or wheelbars	3/35	184, 185, 194
L768	31/5/33	4 x six-wheel underframes for UDW milk tanks	4429-32	Tank Type 5	9/33	199, 213
L785	22/2/34 (amd 10/34)	Repair 18 x LSWR 46ft 6in Corridors and fit with new underframes	650-61, 3081/3-5, 5073/4	Underframes ex-BRCW (ordered 6/34)	3/35	118, 122
E798	23/3/34	50 (later 60) x TK	1841-1900	Amended 28/3/34	3/36	103-6, 116
E799	"	25 x BCK	6675-99	Some in two-coach sets	10/35	103, 107-10, 116
E800	"	25 x BTK	2776-92, 2831-8	Some in two- or four-coach sets	12/35	103, 107-10, 116
E801	"	Fit 50 x 48ft LSWR bogie vehicles with new underframes	5-16, 169/73/5/81/4/7/8/94, 204/8/17/9/25/31/53/67/8, 280/4/90/1/9, 304/13/20/6/9, 353/60/1/4/73/82/7/94, 403/76, 513		7/35	119, 122
E/L802	23/3/34	Fit 4 x 46ft 6in and 4 x 50ft LSWR bogie vehicles with new underframes	1-4, 6428-31	46ft 6in underframes ex-BRCW (ordered 6/34)	2/35	118, 119, 122
A824	21/3/34	98 (later 97) x PLV	1154-1250	Amended 3/8/34	2/36	184, 185, 194
A825	"	2 (later 3) x Train Ferry vans	1-3	Amended 3/8/34	6/36	176-8, 182
A828	27/9/34	2 x six-wheel underframes for West Park Dairy milk tanks	4433/4	Tank Type 6; later Express Dairy	4/35	199-203, 213
E/L852	29/3/35	Fit 75 x LSWR coaches with new 58ft underframes	(see Chapter 7)		12/36	119-122
A855	3/4/35	100 x PLV	1054-1153		4/37	184, 185, 194
(None)	3/35	14 x four-coach sets	(numbers not allocated)	Most of these vehicles were reordered in May 1939 under Orders E1082-9	Authority refused	-
		9 (later 11) x Dining cars	"		"	96
		4 x Buffet cars	"		"	96
		94 further Corridor vehicles			"	110
E861	16/4/35	41 x Open Thirds	1410-50		7/36	104, 110, 111, 116
E862	"	10 x TK + 2 x new bodies for Nos 802, 1834	1901-10		6/36	103-6, 116
E869	24/3/35	40 (later 20) x BTK (sets 952-61)	4231-70 (later 4231-50)	Final 20 cancelled 2/6/39	8/36	109-112, 116
E870	"	20 (later 10) x CK (sets 952-61)	5692-5711 (later 5692-5701)	Final 10 cancelled 2/6/39	8/36	110-116
E871	"	20 (later 10) x TK (sets 952-61)	1911-30 (later 1911-20)	Final 10 cancelled 2/6/39	8/36	110-116
E879	26/8/35	1 x Post Office sorting van for Waterloo–Dorchester	4919	Partly paid for by GPO	12/36	207-211, 213
E891/2	9/12/35	Fit 33 vehicles with BS gangways with adaptors		Done at New Cross Gate	6/37	55
E904	31/1/36	Convert 4 x Pantry Thirds to TKs	713-6	'Ironclad' stock	7/36	39, 46, 48
A927	28/5/36	50 x Bogie Luggage Vans (later passenger guard's vans)	350-99	Amended 3/11/37; underframes Ashford, bodies Eastleigh	10/38	180-182
A928	28/5/36	50 x four-wheel passenger guard's vans with stove aperture	400-49	Underframes Ashford, bodies Eastleigh	7/37	179-182
A938	3/7/36	9 x six-wheel underframes to be fitted to milk tanks 4401-9		Amended 3/8/37 to six only, for Nos 4404-9	4/38	203, 213
L964	16/4/37	Convert 3 x LSWR bodies and mount on second-hand underframes	6406-8	Underframes from fire-damaged vehicles	12/37	121, 122
A972	6/5/37	50 x GUV	1731-80	Underframes Ashford, bodies Eastleigh	12/38	184, 185, 194

HOO No	Date authorised	Details#	Running Nos	Remarks	Completed by*	Page ref
A973	6/5/37	50 x PLV	1921-70		12/38	184-7, 194
A/E974	"	100 (later 50, later 80, finally 100) x four-wheel passenger guard's vans	651-750	Some built Ashford, others Ashford/Eastleigh	9/38	179-182
E975	6/5/37	10 x scenery vans	4587-96	Deferred from A572	11/38	205-7, 213
A986	8/6/37	4 x six-wheel underframes for Express Dairy milk tanks	4435-8	Tank Type 7	3/38	204, 213
E999	3/11/37	4 x Post Office stowage vans	4957-60	Underframes ex-Lancing	3/39	207, 210-3
E1020	3/3/38	New body for Cinema Coach and convert ex-LSWR PLV	1308s 1309s	Underframe ex-Composite 5537	11/39 11/39	215, 217
A1029	14/6/38	50 x bogie guard's vans	201-50	Underframes Ashford, bodies Eastleigh	12/39	180-182
A1030	"	50 x four-wheel passenger guard's vans	751-800	Underframes Ashford, bodies Eastleigh	10/39	179-182
A1031	14/6/38	150 (later 148) x PLV	1251-1398		12/39	184-7, 194
A1032	"	2 x four-wheel hearse vans	1041/2	'Necropolis' service	Cancelled 5/5/45	187
E1043	29/7/38	3 x Post Office sorting vans for Waterloo–Dorchester	4920-2	With lavatory	7/39	207, 211-3
E1082	4/5/39	2 x nine-coach sets for Dover boat train (BFK+FK+SK+SO+SO+TO+ TO+SK+BSK)	7757/8, 7423/4, 4487-90, 4398-4401, 1451-4, 4479/80		Cancelled 5/5/45	124
E1083	15/5/39	11 x six-coach sets for Waterloo–Bournemouth (BTK+FK+TK+TO+RES+BTK)	4195-4216, 7677-87, 1921-31, 1455-65, 7881-91	Some underframes built 7-11/40	Cancelled 5/5/45	124
E1084	15/5/39	18 x BCK	6707-24		Cancelled 5/5/45	124
E1085	"	3 x Open Thirds	1466-8	Run with E1086	"	124
E1086	"	3 x Buffet cars	7970-2	Run with E1085	"	124
E1087	"	7 x two-coach sets (BTK+BCK)	4251-7, 6700-6	Some underframes built 7-11/40	"	124
E1088	"	7 x three-coach sets (BTK+CK+BTK)	4217-30, 5702-8	Some underframes built 7-11/40	"	124
E1089	"	10 x FK	7688-97		"	124
A1090	16/5/39	50 x four-wheel passenger guard's vans	931-80	Underframes ex-Lancing; amended to Eastleigh 18/10/39	1/41	179-182
A1091	16/5/39	5 x four-wheel passenger guard's vans (safe-fitted)	10-4	Underframes ex-Lancing; amended to Eastleigh 18/10/39	5/41	179-182
E1092	18/10/39	80 (later 100) x PLV	1821-1920	Underframes ex-Lancing	7/40	184-7, 194
E1093	16/5/39	25 x four-wheel horseboxes	2861-85		Cancelled 5/5/45	195
E1107	27/6/39	Convert 30 x GBL for casualty-evacuation purposes	2355-61/3-70, 2461-9/71-3/5/7/80		10/39	193

(Note: From this point onwards, many orders were issued for war work, often of a non-railway nature.)

HOO No	Date authorised	Details#	Running Nos	Remarks	Completed by*	Page ref
L1191	1/4/40	120 x PLV	1781-1820, 2091-2170	Pressed-steel-section body framing	12/42	184-7, 194
(None)	4/40	25 x four-wheel horseboxes	(Nos not allocated)	Cancelled	-	195
	"	150 x passenger coaches	"	"	-	124
L1584	29/5/41	Convert 6 vehicles to mobile offices for Southern Divisional Superintendent	801, 4449, 7781/91, 7963, 2285 (GBL)		9/41	-
(None)	4/41	25 x four-wheel horseboxes	(Nos not allocated)	Cancelled — *possibly repeat of 4/40 order*	-	195
	"	150 x passenger coaches	"	"	-	124
L1659	19/7/41	58 (later 50, later 48) x PLV	1053, 1692-1730, 2083-90	Amended 2/42	9/43	184-7, 194
(None)	4/42	25 x four-wheel horseboxes	(Nos not allocated)	Cancelled — *possibly repeat of 4/40 order*	-	195
	"	150 x passenger coaches	"	"	-	124
E1659A	12/8/43	10 x lightweight PLV	1401-10	Plastic body	9/44	187-9, 194
A1750 (MWT)	14/10/41	4 x six-wheel underframes for Express Dairy milk tanks	4439-42	Tank Type 7	12/42	204, 213
E2600 (MWT)	10/7/43	12 x six-wheel underframes for Express Dairy milk tanks	4443-54	Tank Type 7; registered as private-owner wagons	4/44	204, 213
HOO2602	13/7/43	Fit 5 x bogie guard's vans with stoves	395-9	Stoves ex-four-wheel PBVs	11/43	180
L2630 (MWT)	19/8/43	6 x six-wheel underframes for United Dairies milk tanks	4455-60	Tank Type 5; registered as private-owner wagons	1/44	204, 213
E3040 (MWT)	27/9/44	6 x six-wheel underframes for United Dairies milk tanks	4461-6	Tank Type 5; registered as private-owner wagons	4/45	204, 213
E3043	28/9/44	22 (later 18) x three-coach sets (963-80)	2841-76, 5709-26	Underframes ex-Orders 1083/7/8	5/46	125-130
E3043A	5/5/45?	4 x three-coach sets (981-4)	2877-84, 5727-30	See also Order E3243	7/46	125-132
L3227	5/5/45	10 (later 30) x bogie guard's vans	251-80	Deferred to 1951	2/53	180-2
L3228	"	10 x scenery vans	4597-4606	Deferred to 1948	12/49	205-7, 213
L3229	"	60 x PLV	1501-60	Built at Ashford	9/47	185-9, 194
E3234	"	4 x six-coach sets (290-3)	4349-56, 5740-3, 7677-80, 7881-4, 1451-4	Dining sets	10/47	135-145, 167
E3235	5/5/45	4 x three-coach sets (770-3)	4301-8, 5751-4	5751 was prototype 64ft 6in coach	11/47	133-9, 167
E3236	"	4 x two-coach sets (63-6)	4371-4, 6700-3		4/48	135, 146, 167
E3237	"	18 x BCK	6713-30		8/48	135, 146, 167
E3238	"	2 x Open Thirds (later Composite Saloons)	7833/4	'Tavern' Dining Saloons	4/49	135, 159-167
E3239	"	2 x Restaurant cars	7892/3	'Tavern' cars	4/49	135, 159-167
E3240	"	7 x six-coach sets (294-300)	4357-70, 5744-50, 7681-7, 7885-91, 1455-61	Dining sets	3/48	135-145, 167
E3241	5/5/45	3 x three-coach sets (774-6)	4309-14, 5755-7		11/47	135-9, 167
E3242	"	3 x two-coach sets (67-9)	4375-7, 6704-6		4/48	135, 146, 167

The Rolling Stock Committee recorded in 1943 that non-passenger carrying vehicles would be built according to availability of materials and labour, but the outstanding passenger vehicles were to remain in abeyance.

HOO No	Date authorised	Details#	Running Nos	Remarks	Completed by*	Page ref
E3243	5/5/45	4 x three-coach sets (981-4)	2877-84, 5727-30	Believed added to Order E3043	11/47	125-132
E3244	"	2 x two-coach sets (70/1)	4378/9, 6707/8		5/48	135, 146, 167
E3245	"	2 x Open Thirds (later Composite Saloons)	7835/6	'Tavern' Dining Saloons	5/49	135, 159-167
E3246	"	4 x CK	5799-5802		9/48	135, 146, 167
E3247	"	2 x BCK	6731/2		8/48	135, 146, 167
E3248	"	2 x Restaurant cars	7894/5	'Tavern' cars	5/49	135, 159-167
E3249	"	15 x four-coach sets (80-94)	4011-40, 5823-37, 26-40		5/49	135, 152, 167
E3250	"	2 x three-coach sets (777/8)	4315-8, 5758/9		11/47	135-9, 167
E3251	"	15 x three-coach sets (779-93)	4319-48, 5760-74		11/47	135-9-167
E3252	"	4 x two-coach sets (72-5)	4380-3, 6709-12		6/48	135, 146, 167
E3253	"	2 (later 4) x Open Thirds (later Composite Saloons)	7837-40	'Tavern' Dining Saloons	6/49	135, 159-167
E3254	5/5/45	5 x TK	1932-6		10/48	135, 146, 167
E3255	"	9 x CK	5803-11		10/48	135, 146, 167
E3256	"	20 x BCK	6733-52		9/48	135, 146, 167
E3257	"	2 (later 4) x Restaurant cars	7896-9	'Tavern' cars	6/49	135, 159-167
RSCO Min 811	20/2/46	Order 10 (later 30) x three-coach sets (795-824)	4209-30/51-88, 5775-98, 5812-7	Built by BRCW	2/49	168-174
L3359	27/4/46	One saloon for inspection purposes	100s	Build date recorded as both 7/46 and 11/46	11/46	214, 216, 217
HOO 3361	13/6/46	Fit 15 x bogie guard's vans with stoves	380-94	Stoves ex-four-wheel PBVs	NX Gate 3/47	180
E3387	25/11/46	Convert PLV 1987 to generator van (to run with 100s)	97s	Ex-SECR PLV	Not stated	216
L3434	27/6/47	Convert 8 x LSWR coaches to push-pull sets (381-4)	4052/3, 3211/2, 6560-3	'Ironclad' stock	9/49	44, 47, 48
RSCO Min 867	27/4/46	Order 5 x additional three-coach sets (825-9)	4289-98, 5818-22	Built by BRCW	5/49	168-174
E3450	5/8/47	40 x FK	7608-47		11/49	153-5, 167
E3451	"	20 x BTK	3943-62	Some in sets (264-7, 767-9)	11/49	155, 167
E3452	"	40 x CK	5868-5907	Some in sets (264-7, 767-9)	1/50	155, 167
E3453	"	40 x TK	41-80	Some in sets 838-49	4/50	154, 167
E3454	"	20 x three-coach sets (830-49)	3971-4040, 5848-67	Some ran as five-coach sets	7/50	155, 167
L3518	11/10/48	Fit 10 x bogie guard's vans with stoves	370-9		2/49	180
E3580	30/11/49	50 x TK	81-130	Some in sets (830-7)	11/50	156, 167
E3581	1/12/49	45 x Open Thirds	1462-1506		1/51	156, 167
E3582	"	1 x FK	7648		7/51	156, 167
E3583	"	16 x three-coach sets (850-65)	2501-32, 5908-23		6/51	156, 167
E3584	"	6 x Buffet cars	(unspecified)		Cancelled 29/2/50	156
A3590	13/9/49	111 x PLV (includes war loss replacements)	1561-1671	Some at Eastleigh and Ashford	1/51	185, 190, 194
E3590/1	13/7/50	Fit bodywork to 15 x PLV on underframes ex-Ashford	1570/1/3/81-3, 1609-11/20-2/4/5/53	See Order A3590	12/50	185, 190, 194
E3643	31/1/50	Convert 8 x Composite Restaurant cars as per Minute ref 5/10/49	7833-40	'Tavern' Dining Saloons	4/51	164, 165, 167
L3645	21/2/50	Fit 2 x PLV to accommodate 21 (No 1103) or 34 (No 1208) cycles		Others done later; see also Order L3803	4/50	192
L3659	22/6/50	Convert 7 x PLV to Westinghouse Brake for Isle of Wight	1046-52	Ex-1134, 1283, 1720, 1335/21/84 and 1692	10/50	190
(LMS)	(not known)	50 x PLV	1451-1500	Built at Wolverton	8/51	185, 190, 194
A3702	8/9/50	100 x GUV	1411-50, 1977-91, 2006-20/73-82, 2171-80, 2231-40	Some numbers previously allocated to SECR vans	12/51	185, 190, 194
L3706	12/9/50	10 x special cattle vans	3729-38	As 1930 vans	10/52	195-7, 213
L3735	2/11/50	Convert 8 x coaches for push-pull (included ex-LSWR set 385)	3213, 6564	'Ironclad' stock and others	3/52	44, 47, 48
L3764	5/2/51	50 x GUV	2501-50	Deferred to 1955	12/55	185, 190, 194
L3803	(not known)	Fit 52 x cycle hooks to PLV No 1317		See Order L3645	9/51	192
L3827	11/10/51	Substitute standard 22in vacuum cylinders for 30in 'Prestall' type		572 Bulleid vehicles	2/58	141, 142
L3871	30/4/52	Fit non-return air valves to 19 Dining cars	7881-99	Bulleid vehicles	3/54	164
E3889	11/6/52	Convert 5 (later 15) x Restaurant cars to cafeteria/party cars	7939/47/50/4 + one other	Only Nos 7939/54 done; 7947/50 later cancelled	7/53	99, 101, 102
E/L3941	10/12/52	Special renovation of 101 coaches for Hastings services		All Restriction 0 Maunsells	3/54	71, 91
L3966	30/3/53	Convert 14 x Restaurant cars to Buffet cars	7859/60/2/3/6/9-71, 7934/48/51/7/8/95	For Pullman Car Co	2/55	99-102
L3968	10/4/53	Interior alterations to 'Tavern' Restaurant cars	7892-9		Cancelled 11/8/54	164
E3971	14/4/53	Convert 2 x Restaurant cars to Buffet cars	7940/55	For Hotels Executive Ltd	12/53	99-102
E/L3972	14/4/53	Convert 8 x Restaurant cars to Buffet cars	7941/2/4/5/7/50/3/6	For Hotels Executive Ltd	3/54	99-102
L/E4043	25/9/53	Convert 62 x Restaurant cars from oil gas to propane gas		Only 61 done	11/59	99, 141

HOO No	Date authorised	Details#	Running Nos	Remarks	Completed by*	Page ref
E4096	30/3/54	4 x FK for Hastings service (sets 934-7)	7423-6	4 x eight-coach sets	Cancelled 16/5/55	91
E4097	30/3/54	20 x Open Thirds for Hastings service (sets 934-7)	1507-26	4 x eight-coach sets	Cancelled 16/5/55	91
E4098	30/3/54	8 x Open Brake Thirds for Hastings service (sets 934-7)	3238-45	4 x eight-coach sets	Cancelled 16/5/55	91
E4103	1/4/54	Convert saloon 99s to Restaurant car		Reverted to 7943	3/54	99, 102
L4126	11/8/54	Rearrange pantry and kitchens in 8 x 'Tavern' and 11 x Dining cars		Bulleid vehicles; started 12/54	11/62	164
L4137	21/9/54	Alter 2 x Kitchen/Buffet cars	7878, 7969	Previously rebuilt in 1947	5/55	99, 102
L4138	"	Re-line ceilings and walls in 2 x Dining Saloons	7846/7	Previously rebuilt in 1947	5/55	99, 102
E4333	30/8/56	Fit 20 x Open Brake Seconds with standard periscopes	4431-50	Only Nos 4431-7/9-41 done	12/56	90
L4339	24/9/56	Modify 'Tavern' section of 8 x 'Tavern' cars	7892-9	Buffet cars	6/60	164, 166, 167
L4559	10/11/58	Convert 4 x Open Brake Seconds to ward/invalid cars	7920-3	Maunsell Restriction 1 vehicles	5/59	216, 217
L4634	10/6/59	Convert 20 coaches for push-pull working (sets 600-9)	(see Chapter 6)		1/60	112-6
L4746	16/2/60	Convert 20 coaches for push-pull working (sets 610-9)	(see Chapter 6)		2/61	112-6
E4926	16/1/61	Convert BCK No 6897 to motor-car van	4501	Diagram 3183; body ex-GBL No 2291	9/60	207, 208, 213
L5045	11/8/61	Convert CK No 5600 to Inspection Saloon	DS70155	To replace DS1; transferred to Eastleigh	11/62	217
L5046	11/8/61	Fit 2 x bogie guard's vans with stoves	368/9		2/62	180
E5270	11/9/63	Modify 5 x PLV for security traffic	1562/76, 1613/8/28	Diagram 3104	10/63	192
HOO 5451	30/3/63	Convert 10 x GUV for Fawley block oil trains	69000-9	Done by Outdoor Machinery Dept	8/65	190
E5462	4/5/65	Modify BY 938 for security of GPO mails		Diagram 3095	6/65	179, 182
HOO 5466	26/5/65	Strengthen 3 x scenery vans for conveying elephants	4589/98, 4601	Done by Outdoor Machinery Dept	5/65	207
E5485	10/9/65	Fit 39 x guard's vans with stoves	201-28, 420-30	Started 12/65; No 204 not done	6/68	179, 180

Order numbers checked as far as HOO 5778, dated 29/5/68.

\# In general, coaches have been described here using the British Railways coding system, e.g. CK (Corridor Composite), TK (Corridor Third), FK (Corridor First), TO (Open Third) etc.

* This is date order closed, which may be slightly after works were completed.

Plate 239
Gangwayed bogie luggage van No 2464 as repainted in the Pullman Car colours of umber and cream in July 1962, in readiness for use as the hearse van for Sir Winston Churchill's funeral train, which took place on 30th January 1965. This picture was taken in July 1963, during one of the van's rare appearances outside Stewarts Lane carriage sheds.
Author's collection

Appendix 2
Restricted working of coaching stock

Southern Railway steam train coaching stock which must not work over certain portions of the Southern Railway is indicated by a Route Restriction plate fixed on the end of each vehicle, *viz*:

RESTRICTION 1
          Vehicles so marked may pass over all portions of the line except between:
- a   Grove Junction (Tunbridge Wells) and Battle
- b   Hastings and Winchelsea

RESTRICTION 2
          Vehicles so marked may pass over all portions of the line except between:
- a   Grove Junction (Tunbridge Wells) and Battle
- b   Hastings and Winchelsea
- c   Tonbridge and Grove Junction (Tunbridge Wells)
- d   Gipsy Hill and Crystal Palace Low Level

RESTRICTION 3
          Vehicles so marked may pass over all portions of the line except between:
- a   Grove Junction (Tunbridge Wells) and Battle
- b   Hastings and Winchelsea
- c   Tonbridge and Grove Junction (Tunbridge Wells)
- d   Gipsy Hill and Crystal Palace Low Level
- e   Cooksbridge and Lewes

RESTRICTION 4
          Vehicles so marked may pass over all portions of the line except between:
- a   Grove Junction (Tunbridge Wells) and Battle
- b   Hastings and Winchelsea
- c   Tonbridge and Grove Junction (Tunbridge Wells)
- d   Gipsy Hill and Crystal Palace Low Level
- e   Cooksbridge and Lewes *
- f   Charlton and Plumstead
- g   Dartford and Strood
- h   Hawkesbury St. Junction and Archcliffe Junction (Dover) +

* May work between Cooksbridge and Lewes providing no other train is allowed on the adjacent line in Lewes Tunnel at the same time.
+ May work between Hawkesbury Street Junction and Archcliffe Junction providing no other train is allowed on the adjacent line between those points at the same time.

RESTRICTION 5
Vehicles so marked must be confined to the section of line which originally constituted the London, Brighton & South Coast Railway. They may not work between Gipsy Hill and Crystal Palace Low Level. They may not work on the Eastern and Western sections of the line [SR].
Coaches Nos 6926, 7638, 7639, 7640, 7642, 7643 and 7775 may not work between Gipsy Hill and Crystal Palace Low Level or between Cooksbridge and Lewes.

RESTRICTION 6
Vehicles so marked must be confined to the section of line which originally constituted the London & South Western and London, Brighton & South Coast Railway. They may not work between Gipsy Hill and Crystal Palace Low Level.

Note:
No coaching stock, except open carriage trucks, may be allowed over the Canterbury West & Whitstable Harbour goods line.

The above is taken from the Appendices to the Working Timetables dated 26 March 1934 until further notice; added subsequently was Restriction 2A, which applied only to certain Pullman cars. Restrictions 1-5 were physical, dictated by stock dimensions, whereas Restriction 6 was operational and applied only to ex-LSWR 'gate' stock.